The Best of Nash Buckingham

The Best of Nash Buckingham

edited by George Bird Evans

Winchester Press

Copyright © 1973 by George Bird Evans and Irma Buckingham Witt
All rights reserved

Library of Congress Catalog Card Number 72-96093
ISBN 0-87691-103-3

3 4 5 6 7 8 9 0 — 84 83 82 81 80

WINCHESTER PRESS
1421 South Sheridan
Tulsa, Oklahoma 74114

Printed in the United States of America

Acknowledgments

I am most grateful to the following friends of Nash Buckingham for the help they have given me: Robert S. Anderson, William F. Andrews, John P. Bailey, Berry B. Brooks, Hugh E. Buckingham, Mrs. Henry P. Davis, Clifford Green, Werner O. Nagel, John M. Olin, Mildred and Robert G. Stoner, Charles J. Wicks; and especially to Nash's daughter Irma and his son-in-law Roy Witt.

—G.B.E.

To Nash and his Irma

Contents

Foreword

It gives me special pleasure to introduce this collection of stories and articles by the late Nash Buckingham, for my long association with their author both in and out of the hunting field was one of my most treasured relationships. I knew "Mister Nash" for almost half a century, and it was a friendship that wore well.

Nash and I went back a long way together. I met him at the Grand American Trapshooting Handicap in Chicago in 1919. In the early 1920's, while I was developing the Super-X shotshell and the principle of long-range, short-shotstring loads, Nash field-tested Super-X in its experimental stages. I had read some of his articles in the magazine *Sporting Goods Dealer* suggesting that the ammunition industry had better begin giving thought to the propagation and preservation of game bird populations, for, even then, they were under too heavy an attack.

In June of 1925, at my invitation, Nash Buckingham became our Director of Game Restoration for Western Cartridge Company—the first such expert ever employed by an American industry. It was then that he coined the term "game restoration" and worked to increase game through habitat improvement—a giant step beyond the common practice of restocking game range that did not meet wildlife's needs.

As Nash said, that word "restoration" has covered a lot of mileage, and it still has a long track ahead of it. But in his work at Western, it became associated with the word "biology," and as a result some good things have happened.

As one of America's first writer-conservationists, Nash spanned four great periods of conservation history: the limitless hunting of the late nineteenth century, the low ebb of game supplies following World War I, the 1930's when he fought for struggling new conservation programs, and the past two decades in which he worked tirelessly to guard and consolidate the gains that had been made.

If ever a man had found the fountain of youth, it was Nash Buckingham. I remember how he looked that night of January 18, 1963, at the Lockhaven Country Club at Alton, Illinois, when at eighty-two, he accepted the Winchester-Western Award of Outdoorsman of the Year for 1962. He had been selected by nomination and vote of the nation's 4,000 outdoor writers. Nash made an address that subdued and inspired one of the most knowledgeable groups of gun editors ever assembled. It was, in Nash's colorful manner, a sermon and a virtuoso performance that brought everyone present to his feet to applaud the message and the man.

If, as Nash said that night, he had "grown up with Winchester," Winchester-Western and the rest of the industry has grown up as the result of Nash Buckingham's efforts. He was a superb gunner, but to his shooting he also brought a deep understanding of the game that he hunted, and an unyielding set of ethics that guided him afield and in his conservation struggles.

If there is one word that best describes Nash Buckingham, his life and work, it is "loyalty." He was loyal to his friends and his principles, of course, as a gentleman must be. But he was also loyal to the land, and to the wild creatures that were such a vital part of his life. He defended those with courage and strength all through his long life, and I never knew him to back down from a good fight.

That loyalty, and his deep love of quality outdoors, shines through his writing like an autumn sun rising over the frosty quail coverts of Tennessee. It was this quality that made him a valued friend, and the premier outdoor writer of the century.

—JOHN M. OLIN
At Nilo, October 1972

PORTRAIT OF NASH

I HAVE IN MY hand one of the rarest of out-of-print sporting books—Nash Buckingham's copy of the Derrydale edition of his *De Shootinest Gent'man,* number 576. Bound in simulated blue morocco with a fine gold border and a full-color medallion of a brace of canvasbacks, it is not, with its brown-edged fragile pages, in mint condition, for Nash used his possessions the way he used his days—for living. I turn the pages with a reverence I do not consider exaggerated, for this is not only Nash Buckingham's first but, in my opinion, his best book, with *Mark Right!* a close second, both written with his flow of narrative in full flavor.

Winchester Press asked me to put together what I consider the best of Nash's works and tell of him as I knew him, an invitation to make a writer drool. I read, and listened as Kay read aloud to me (a test as exacting as proving a pair of barrels), one hundred and eleven Buckingham stories and articles, covering eight books and most of his magazine pieces. In addition, we read the seventy-nine chapters and profiles of *National Field Trial Champions,* a collaboration with William F. Brown. I have chosen thirty works, some famous, a few nearly unknown—an assortment of Buckingham vintages, none less than nice little wines, certain ones great.

The Best of Nash Buckingham is Nash Buckingham himself, for when he writes of his feeling for a dog, his response to mallards caught by shafts of early morning sunlight, he is living it again. He had a flair for titles, although it would seem that Ho'ace gave him two of his finest—"De Shootinest Gent'man" and "A Shootin' Po' Soul." His writing has guts, and it put him above most sporting writers of his period. Except for "the Judge" in a couple of the stories, Nash was too good to resort to the stereotyped character, and if he used the hackneyed "wiped his eye," it got past me. His characters were not cutouts but people in almost always actual situations. His fiction works were, in my opinion, his less distinguished efforts.

Nash wrote with a sense of image because he was there to see it—lines like: "The Big Hatchie... fans into a sheet of greenish black enamel... switching to lumpy amber when heavy thunderstorms scour the seamed faces of the basin's red headlands"; and describing a pointer striking scent, "... when he went particularly 'fragrant' as Horace used to put it"; and "Down from the northwest with the wind on its tail, swept a lone black duck, like a gale-pushed ace of spades on its way to somewhere."

His descriptions of predawn the countless times he witnessed it, of "shavings of snow" beginning to fall, of a "saw-edged north wind [that] fragiled our ears," put the reader there. Each of us with years on his gun has been in these places, each knows he can't go back except in the way Nash takes him back. Even in writing technical detail, Nash makes you participate through his quality of experience. Whether he writes about the courageous performance of a dog in a field trial, of thousands of ducks and geese he saw and shot, of countless covey rises in old sedge fields, part of his genius lies in making his reader believe that it was so. These pieces are so much a part of the man who wrote them it is difficult to decide whether he was more a shooting man or a writer. For me, he was both, and at top pitch. Legendary in his skill with a shotgun (only once did Nash mention a rifle to me), he was innately a raconteur, and what came out was shooting literature.

I don't intend this "Portrait of Nash" to be biography, but rather to present Nash Buckingham as I knew him and know of him—things his readers, and I, have aways wanted to know. Nash's daughter, Irma Buckingham Witt, "baptized first in the faith, and second from a duck boat" according to his dedication in *Blood Lines,* and her husband Roy Witt, together with Nash's shooting companions, with whom I have been in close touch, have achieved for me the nearly insurmountable in spanning distance and years. Portions of my first concept of "Portrait" became parts of introductions to the stories—it is impossible to separate the man from what he wrote—and so the entire book ends up being Nash.

I never shot with him, but I know exactly how he swung past a duck or waited out a covey rise; that on the rare occasion he missed an easy shot he uttered a disgusted *Oooo.* My first contact with him was in January of 1944 when he was sixty-three and I was thirty-seven, but through his books I saw him as a boy give himself to shooting with a fervor that remained a grand obsession to the aging man. My admiration for him grew during our correspondence, and through his writings. I cherish the label from a riding coat he wore at trials, I have one of his ties (a pheasant design), and a treasure of old photographs he sent to me in October 1970, sensing, I almost believe, that I would someday do this book. A disappointment was that neither his family nor his friends know of any gun diary, although in "Great Day in the Morning" he mentions his "private shooting diary of decade's standing," and speaks of a diary in several other stories. I know of each of his guns, although I never balanced the ten pounds of Becker magic, and I can feel the worn leather of his saddle scabbard as surely as if I had put my fingers on its initials I.L.J. (his wife Irma's). I know Tom Cotton and Don and Kate as though I had run my hand over their sleek pointer heads and lumpy ribs; I have been privileged to read letters to him from his friends and readers, literary agent and editors, and more importantly to read Nash's letters to them. After absorbing and living with these things for nearly a year, I at times have the curious impression that I am recently dead at nearly ninety-one. Knowing Nash Buckingham in this manner, I evaluate his writing differently from the men who shared Buckingham country.

They saw him as a hero. If I may oversimplify, I see him as a man suffering from a hero syndrome, not always an unpleasant state. He captioned photos "The *great* springer spaniel Chubby," "The *famous* Burt Becker Magnum" (even "magnum" was capitalized). All who knew him made up a Most Worshipful Society of Friends of Nash Buckingham. Tributes such as the following did little to dispel the image:

From Colonel H. P. Sheldon, August 17, 1937, concerning a manuscript: "Nash, this is absolutely gorgeous. You are building a monument to yourself and your friends in these books of yours."

Copy to Nash from Horace Lytle of reply to *The Sporting Goods Journal,* August 22, 1929: "Answering your telegram just received, I regard Nash Buckingham as the best all around marksman in America. I think that Mark Arie would possibly beat Nash on clay birds but no man can beat Nash Buckingham in the field, whether it be on wildfowl or upland game."

Heady stuff to live up to. This enthusiasm wasn't confined to the past. My recent queries to his friends invariably brought responses such as these:

Dr. William Andrews: "I can say that my experiences with Nash Buckingham were some of the highlights of my life."

John Bailey: "I am happy you are going to write a book about Nash. He was the most interesting character I ever spent a day with, whether in a duck boat, on a horse or around a fireside."

Clifford Green: "Nash was constantly thinking of others. On our duck hunts at Peckerwood and Section 16 we stayed at the old hotel at Clarendon, Ark. There were wood-burning stoves in the rooms, and the whole thing was held together by two old ladies who eked a limited existence therefrom. Nash went out of his way making things a little easier for these two."

A number of Nash's friends, varying widely in age, have lent me letters he wrote them, and responded patiently but eagerly to my almost endless questions. For them he is so recently alive it has been the next thing to asking these questions of Nash himself. When I inquired as to his physical appearance at different ages, they provided detail. Later, among Nash's papers, I found a studio photograph, taken in Knoxville in the spring of 1902, of Nash at twenty-two in the glory of weightlifter's sandals and jockstrap—a powerful young bull with impressive shoulders. (Charles Wicks, now retired from the gun room at Abercrombie & Fitch, wrote me: "I knew Nash Buckingham, who dropped in whenever he was in the City. One thing that always amazed me was the tremendous pair of shoulders he had.") On the reverse of the photo are Nash's measurements, and his friends had them to within a millimeter: Height 5′ 10½″, weight 190 lbs., chest (normal) 45″ (expanded) 49″, waist 34½″, neck 16½″, arm 16½″, calf 16″, thigh 25½″— not so tall, but like his duck guns, magnum. He retained this general physique into his seventies.

Mr. Buck and his friends in his stories caught nine-pound trout, found enormous numbers of birds, shot over dogs perfect in manners and nose. To Nash, shots were hits, all women were beautiful (though his loyalty to his Irma never faltered), even his companions were heroic. To the ordinary mortal who sees faults in his dogs and to whom there are unproductive hunting days, Nash's personal Camelot may appear a shade unbelievable. But perhaps this state of perfection came from Nash's way of looking at life in superlatives. This might be a pretty nice way to see it, and the thought occurs that by emulating Nash, the rest of us could become the fabulous sort of person he was. Or believe we were.

Nash's father, Miles Buckingham, blooded his son early and well, if a bit too enthusiastically, instilling in the eight-year-old the idea that game was to be shot in large quantity so long as it was done with as few misses as possible. It was some years before the attitude changed appreciably. In his onslaught on game—almost any game—young Nash followed this indoctrination fanatically, even to sluicing ducks on the water. I find no evidence that Buckingham *père* objected.

It is logical that his father should have had the greatest influence on Nash, for Nash adored him. He describes him as he saw him when about nine years old, in a kind of Currier & Ives view:

> A treasured memory is of my father as I saw him shooting bobwhites on the Le Master farm southeast of the original Greenlaw field trial grounds. I rode muleback behind Dan Bostwick, Dad's colored coachman, who led Dad's shooting pony while he followed some scattered single birds. Brilliant sunlight of midafternoon, bathing embrowning fields and russet foliage, flushed my parent's velveteen hunting coat with a warmer patina of gloss. He wore a flat-brimmed hat of the same material, and his corduroy breeches were tucked into knee-high gaitered laced boots. His coat had semi-tail-pockets and when he tossed up his gun to fire I could see the bulge of his cigar case or flat flask against his hip. Two coal-black setters stood ahead of him on point. From where Dan Bostwick and I sat astride our mule, I thrilled at the dogs' pop-eyed tenseness and quivering flanks.
>
> Three birds whirred from the low cover and Father bowled over two of them with his light twelve-gauge hammer fowling piece. On anything like an even try he rarely missed a quail. Chick and Dee, the Gordons, stood like graven images until clucked to the retrieve. In a jiffy both returned and nosed the birds into their master's hand, and he knelt and caressed both animals. Then, slipping his English gun into its saddle scabbard and the bobwhites into his pouch, he remounted briskly and blew his dogs on with two jerky blasts from a buckhorn whistle.

A fine view for any son to have of his father.

In addition, Nash's character was molded early by his father's fellow members at Wapanoca and Beaver Dam duck clubs. All, especially Arthur Wheatley, humored the boy. In an introduction to Colonel H. P. Sheldon's *Tranquillity* (A. S. Barnes & Co., 1945), Nash wrote:

In my youth a very dear old gentleman presented to me a shooting diary hand-penned through many decades. Child that I was, I sensed when he put it in my hands that somehow its giving was linked mysteriously to tears that shone in his eyes. I asked, wonderingly, "For me?" And he whispered—"Yes, Boy, I give you back my years!"

This handing down of shooting traditions and ritual in a sort of apostolic succession from Wapanoca and Beaver Dam members to Nash, and from Nash to younger men such as John Bailey and William Andrews, and more widely to the readers of Buckingham stories, cannot be measured in ordinary value. I have had it bestowed on me by older sportsmen, and like to think I am passing on the touch of hand to discerning shooters younger than I—and from them to those that follow.

Nash writes in "Blood Lines" of his grandfather Henry Buckingham with warmth but perhaps with the license of memory:

I adored my Grandfather and missed him terribly, especially for those evenings when I'd climb into his lap and listen to tales of bear and deer hunting. Sometimes Grandfather would put me down and cross to a tall cabinet of dull mahogany. He'd take down a carved hunting horn and raise it to his puckered lips and puff out his chest and blow such high, ringing toots that old Roy, the lop-chopped hound, would struggle up onto his backsides and mingle music with the ruckus. Then Grandfather would pick out first one gun and then another from a long rack. "Here," he'd say, "is the double rifle that killed the biggest bear we ever took in the Chulahoma Bottoms," looking the piece over from butt plate to front sight while he spoke and holding its locks close to his ear as hammers were drawn. *C-l-i-a-c-k c-l-i-a-c-k* they'd go! And he'd smile and pat the gun before putting it back in the rack. Or he'd say, "Here's my Manton partridge gun, Buster." I was getting on toward being able to heft that one because of its lightness, and I thought the gold-inlaid carvings of dogs and birds about the locks so beautiful.

There were other memories of Grandfather and the plantation with its half mile of cedars lining a driveway through giant oaks, beeches and ash. And the springhouse and mint beds. And the morning I was playing with Unc' Willis. Mother and Father and I had been driven hurriedly to the plantation and my not seeing Grandfather since arriving had worried me. There was a screen in front of his downstairs room in the east wing of the house, and Dr. Robert Maury's phaeton came and went. There was an awed silence over everything and the house Negroes walked on tiptoe and spoke in whispers. Finally, Father emerged from the front door and walked slowly toward us across the piazza. Unc' Willis was very old and when he looked up and saw Father, his wrinkled black face became troubled and he got up very shakily. Father nodded to him gently and the old slave, leaning against a vast white column, began to whimper softly. "How is Grandfather?" I asked, and Daddy turned swiftly, and that was the first time I ever knew the dreadful agony of seeing tears in a strong man's eyes.

Not all of Nash's identification with the past came from men:

> Writing this, I look up at an old engraving of an oil by J. M. Tracy—
> Field Trial Champion Gladstone in a pose of classic pointing integrity.
> Head aloft and swung to the left, his tail at two o'clock, he has fastened
> his quarry. Backing him with gorgeous intensity is another winner of
> that day, Mr. Bryson's great setter bitch Peep o' Day. In the background
> two gunners are advancing toward Gladstone's bevy.
>
> Gladstone, winner on the bench and field trial circuits, was a particu-
> lar buddy of mine. I used to scale our board fence and drop into our
> neighbors', the Brysons', kennel to romp with and feed the old champ
> cookies slipped me by our cook, Aun' Lucretia Moody. Many a Sunday
> afternoon I watched Gladstone and other field trial aspirants of the
> middle and late eighties run impromptu heats across upland that is
> today near Memphis's center. Father, Mr. Wheatley, Mr. Jack Hays,
> both the Brysons, and Judge Sam P. Walker drove out in their buck-
> boards and buggies to exercise their dogs. In those days, competition
> included single runners or brace *vs.* brace. Mr. Jack Hays kept and
> hunted the "native" Joe Jr. for his owner Mr. Campbell, and I heard
> him say that a Joe Jr./Gladstone bird hunt was usually decided by the
> "breaks."

Nash was born nearly twenty years before the turn of the century on May 31,
1880, received his first shotgun on Christmas 1888, and married Irma Lee Jones
on June 1, 1910.

Like obituaries while he was still alive, news clippings on the occasion of each
award or participation in a conservation struggle or the publication of one of
his books recounted Nash's every achievement to date. Almost anyone who has
read his name on jacket blurbs or in forewords to his books knows his athletic
record: baseball, Memphis Chickasaw team 1899; four-letter man, University of
Tennessee (football, baseball, track, boxing); captain Tennessee Vols 1902;
weight lifter in vaudeville; Southern AAU of America heavyweight boxing champion 1910. Nash attended Harvard from 1898 to 1900 and University of Tennessee 1901 to 1903; he was in the insurance business and concurrently wrote a
sports column for the Memphis *Commercial Appeal* from 1903 to 1910.

Nash wrote me, September 28, 1970: "The first story I ever tried to write (a
Negro dialect tale of the Civil War) was published in the February 1900 *Harvard
Monthly,* the amazing thing being my nerve as a starry-eyed Rebel outlander
daring to submit such a story to a bunch of abolitionists, and surprise that they
were gracious enough to publish it. Shades of today! My first real outdoor yarn
went to *Recreation,* Casper Whitney, in 1909." The setting of the 1909 story
was his father's Big Beaver Ranch in Colorado, where Nash lived at times between
1904 and 1913 and where he and Irma spent their honeymoon.

Nash wrote the famous "De Shootinest Gent'man" in 1916. While a partner
in the sporting goods firm of Buckingham, Ensley, Carrigan & Company from

1917 to 1925, he wrote some for *Field & Stream* and *Outdoor Life*—mostly verse, though one of his finest stories, "Thou and Thy Gun Bearer," was published in *Field & Stream* in March 1922. And, more than anything, he shot.

Nash led an urban existence—atypical of a man whose life was built around guns and dogs. Unlike me, whose old country house has harbored a bloodline of setters stretched out on sofas or hearths, Nash, who did not own land, lived for years in an apartment. One Mississippian wrote of seeing him in the old days in Memphis "at lunch at the Arlington Hotel. Again, my cousin pointed him out at the Peabody Coffee Shop. I began to expect to see him whenever I went downtown. Sometimes he sat in the captain's chairs that circled the Hotel Peabody's entrance on the Main Street sidewalk. Just anywhere you went in downtown Memphis that athletic, sartorially replendent Nash Buckingham was there, never alone, always the center of a group."

Nash even had a desk in the cotton district until about 1955, where he put in an appearance on days he wasn't shooting. He apparently never drove a car but traveled from his apartment by bus. Berry Brooks, to whom Nash dedicated *Hallowed Years,* calling him "World Big Game Hunter" and "Sportsman in the Highest Sense of the Word," wrote me:

> He first had a desk in the office of his cousin, Lemmon Buckingham, on Front Street (Memphis is the largest cotton market in the world and cotton offices line the street). He later had desk space with another cousin, Hugh Evelyn Buckingham, on the same street and when Ev closed his business, Nash moved to the office of Kirby Saben. Nash and I regularly had breakfast together in the Cotton Exchange Cafe during the cotton season. One morning I told Nash a story I'd heard my father tell many times. He and my uncle, Tom Salmon—my mother's brother—were principal characters. It happened in Tunica, Mississippi, about ten miles from Beaver Dam Club. All the men mentioned were big cotton planters from nearby. While I told the story, about twelve breakfasters pulled three tables together and listened, while Doug Stamper replenished our platter of sausage and biscuit. That story became "The Gallows Bear" in *Game Bag,* with the name of the town changed to Landon, not to offend anyone.

John Olin, with whom Nash had a long friendship—they first met in 1919 in Chicago at the Grand American Trapshooting Handicap—tells in his foreword of their relation at Western Cartridge Company at East Alton, Illinois, where Nash was Director of Game Restoration from 1925 until 1928. In 1928 he went to Washington and was Executive Secretary of American Wildfowlers (later More Game Birds, then Ducks Unlimited) until 1932. He stayed on in Washington until 1936 and was associated with Wildlife Institute. As always, nothing interfered with his shooting.

During these years Nash was writing some of his best stories, mostly for *Field & Stream,* owned and published by his friend Eltinge Warner. Nash told me:

"I knew 'em all at *Field & Stream*—Warren H. Miller, my dear old friend Ed Cave, Hi Watson, Ray Holland, Dave Newell, Hugh Grey. Elt Warner—we were almost the identical age—and I made three great movies for *F&S* film library— a dux pix at Wapanoca, the best goose pix of Mississippi sport below Lake Providence, La., and then Mississippi bobwhites near where I shoot today west of Coffeeville. For years I was an associate editor of *Field & Stream* but when Elt sold out I quit."

Nash's immense energy and outgoing temperament drew people to and around him, not only as friends but in relationships that would not ordinarily have occurred, such as the group of people interested in Harold Money of "De Shootinest Gent'man." Nash had a quality of making each person who met him or to whom he wrote feel that he was Nash's special friend and Nash his. There was more to it than admiration for his shooting or his wit or the rugged masculinity of him. It was, I think, because he genuinely liked people—people at a honky-tonk lunch counter the night before opening day of duck season, in an elite club, at a sportsmen's banquet. Perhaps it was because no one could resist listening to him. And while Nash may not have appeared to do much of the listening, there had to be times he listened also, for there was no other way he could have so perfectly caught the sound of the characters he used in his writing.

John Bailey tells the following:

"Hilliard Griffin and I had lunch with Nash at a Holiday Inn just across the street from his apartment his last fall in Memphis. When we were seated, Nash started telling some old duck hunting story. The waitress came over and Nash ordered, I ordered, and Nash continued his story to me while Hilliard ordered. When Hilliard finished giving his order and noticed that the waitress did not take his menu, he looked up. The waitress, startled and embarrassed, said, 'I'm sorry, I didn't hear a word you said. I was listening to him,' and pointed to Nash. Imagine, a twenty-year-old waitress forgetting to take a customer's order to listen to an eighty-nine-year-old man tell a seventy-year-old duck story."

There were his wonderful letters—part love for people, part compulsion to put words on paper—typed with an outrageously dim ribbon on both sides of odd scraps of stationery, poured out to the edge of the paper where a word like "put" might be divided, or perhaps a period carried to the beginning of the line below. The dashes would reach from here to Memphis. John Bailey has three hundred and fifty letters; I treasure every one Nash wrote me.

One of Nash's closest friends—if it is possible to reduce the mass of his close friends to "closest"—was Henry P. Davis, of whom Nash wrote me in June 1970:

> You'll find "A la Belle Etoile" in the Derrydale *Blood Lines*. It's addressed to my old friend Henry P. Davis, whose fame as a field trial judge is nationwide and with whom I've shared the salt since the day in 1926 when I discovered Henry, then a reporter for the Memphis *Commercial Appeal,* with a vast yen for closer relationship with field trials

and the conservation world. I put him in touch with L. T. Waller, Director of Game with Du Pont. Henry eventually ended with retirement as Public Relations head of Remington Arms, and is still writing the *Sports Afield* column on "dawgs." We've judged National Field Trial Championships and other top trials together (retrievers included). We've hunted and fished o'er Land's Breadth.

In 1944 Henry and I were judging the Free-for-All at Shuqualak, Mississippi, pronounced "Sugarlock," and noted for gourmet lunches and the Indian names along the once-upon-a-time railroad. Saturn was a Derby that year and Ariel won. In the Derby race we were along a road past a high stone bluff and Saturn pointed on a bit of levee right ahead. The gallery halted and Clyde Morton hastened up with his gun (the season was open and you could shoot). Henry and I were about 15 feet apart and 30 yards back. A single bird flushed and whisked back past Clyde and flew straight at Henry and me. Clyde whirled and swung onto the quail headed directly between me and Henry. Henry went over one side of his horse, I slid off mine as Clyde fired. By some miracle we escaped. Henry bawled poor Clyde out and I have never seen a chap so broken up as Clyde. He was always keyed up but a fine and Godly lad. I'm sending you this photo Henry took that year of Clyde and A. G. C. Sage and Saturn, Ariel, and Luminary.

Mrs. Henry P. Davis wrote me on September 8, 1972:

> I believe Mr. Bob Stoner, Henry Bartholomew and Henry Davis could be counted among Mr. Nash's very best friends. I quote these inscriptions to let you know the great devotion Henry and Mr. Nash had for each other. The Derrydale *Mark Right!* copy number 6, a gift from Mr. Nash, was inscribed: "Dear Henry—Here is the second barrel; the greatest problem is some more hunts together. Nash Buckingham April 1935." *Blood Lines,* also a gift, was autographed: "Dear Henry—Hol' yo hat on boy—he'ah us goes again! Best to Mack and Sue. Buck At Home, Memphis, Tenn., November 1938."

Among Nash's acquaintances, there would appear to have been a proliferation of captains and an exaltation of colonels. This was not confined to Southerners. Colonel Hal Sheldon and Captain Paul Curtis were rarely referred to without address of rank. With his enthusiasm for the setting, it is almost incomprehensible that Nash should have missed a military career.

One of the warmest and longest relationships of Nash's life was with Horace Miller—"Ho'ace" of the stories. Strangely, in Nash's writings I can find no mention of Horace's age or when he died. My queries to Nash's friends bring: "before my time." An entry in the old Beaver Dam Club minute book written on May 5, 1902, by the Secretary, J. G. Handwerker, reveals the following:

> The object of this meeting was to consider a new keeper in place of R. E. Curtis; to wit, Horace Miller, one of Dr. Owen's trusted Negro tenants who has paddled for the club. That is, if he is permitted to accept the place by the Doctor. After deliberation the committee came to the

conclusion that Horace Miller is a good man with a better record and we could get no one to serve the club better if Horace's services in the past are taken into consideration. The Secretary was instructed to offer him $15 a month the year round and a home, garden, cow, mule, etc., at Beaver Dam.

Horace and Molly (frequently spoken of as Molly Merritt) presided at Beaver Dam as club keeper and cook from 1902 to 1920, as the following letter from Horace to Nash, January 1920 indicates:

I writes to consolate you and Miss Erma on the death of yore fine father an mother an I hears you are going to leave Beaver Dam an shoot at som club in Arkensaw. If so, I hopes, Mr. Nash you will git me a job over there an I will be in town befo long an see you in regards to same.
Always a servant,
HORACE MILLER

In 1923 Nash had moved again and Horace indicated a desire to follow:

September 1923
Mr. Nash I wold not like to stay at the Arkensaw club to paddle sense you an Maj. Insley has opened the new club down the river. I will jes go down there an take charge of same for you all as I knows that is the way you an the maj. wants it.
Always a servant,
HORACE MILLER

This is the last date I can attach to Horace's existence, though he will live on as long as Nash's stories are read. John Bailey said Horace was dead when he first knew Nash in 1933. There are three photographs of Horace in the Derrydale *De Shootinest Gent'man*, revealing a wonderfully appealing person, the one facing page 228 being the photo Nash described to me as captioned: "White man's dawg, don' lie t' me!"—a title that appears to have been altered.

The Putnam *Mark Right!* carries a repeat of one of the photos, and one of Horace and Tom Cotton and Girl. Among old photographs of Nash's I discovered a great picture of Horace in 1916 on the goose camp houseboat at Ship Island Bar, with the pointers Girl and Don, and looking blissfully happy and exactly right, holding a cluster of bobwhites and a big old swamp rabbit straight out of an A. B. Frost drawing.

It is difficult to estimate by his appearance, but my guess is that Horace was very near Nash's age. It is redundant to say that Nash and Horace were close friends; their devotion to each other is present in everything they shared. In his poem "Me an' Cap'n," Nash opens with:

Ho'ace, whut yu' studyin' 'bout,
Settin' up 'longside dat fi'ah,

and ends with:

Ole Ho'ace's Gawd d' same as Cap'n's,
I tells HIM—'thank yu', SUH, f' dis my fren',
Please mek YO' LIGHT t' shine us to YO' CAMP,
An' le'me serve my Marsters dere, Amen!'

If this sort of thing bothers you, skip it. To me it rings true.

As regards his shooting, there was no false modesty about Nash Buckingham. He was a good shot and knew it—an important part of being one. It was at the two early duck clubs—Beaver Dam, organized in 1882, and Wapanoca, founded in 1887—that Nash learned to shoot. He described Wapanoca's 5,500 acres in Arkansas, about thirty miles northwest of Memphis, as normally carrying "a quarter of a million ducks and 6,000 geese." Exposure to that quantity of water-fowl and what now seems an incredible number of bobwhites made a shot out of almost any man who could lift a gun. The brilliant shots like Nash were the naturals, with the additional blessing of an opportunity to develop in such a setting.

According to Horace's letter, Nash left Beaver Dam soon after his father's death in 1920, for what apparently was Lakeside Club in Arkansas. Bob Anderson wrote:

> To the best of my memory, Nash left Wapanoca by 1925 when he went with Western Cartridge Co. In 1941 he asked me and some of his friends to join Peckerwood. It was primarily an irrigation company in Arkansas. Edgar Queenie was the big backer. There were 3,500 acres of water, all in the trees. The first year the shooting was wonderful, the second year a lot of trees had fallen but the shooting was still good. I soon found that the hotel in Stuttgart was too noisy and moved over to Clarendon where Nash was. One day three of us were sitting in the drug store expressing some dissatisfaction about the shooting when the drug-ist, C. H. Pennington, got me off to the side and told me he knew of a place if we would include him. We talked it over and agreed. That was the start of Section 16 Club. We leased the section from the owner, hired a surveyor, a bull dozer and a dragline, and put a good dam in—it is still there. We started shooting the fall of '44. As work progressed, we found that three people was too few, so enlarged the club to 16, all Memphis people. Shooting was excellent as long as we had water, which we got down Big Lagrue and Lost Island creeks.

Clifford Green wrote me:

> Our opening day hunt the first season that Peckerwood was open to shooting has always been outstanding in my mind. Peckerwood was a vast area of flooded pin-oak flats, with boat roads and blinds, and it seemed to me that there could not possibly be any mallard ducks any-where else. On this morning we paddled down a boat road and stopped at the first blind. (There were no other hunters on the place.) We were hardly established when two mallards appeared in the distance headed toward us. I had a Winchester Model 12 loaded with heavy 4's

sitting in one corner of the blind. When Nash suggested that I take a shot, the ducks appeared so high to me I thought he was kidding, and did not pick up my gun. When he realized I did not intend to shoot, he let fly with his magnum. He ejected the shells and reloaded his gun before the first duck hit the water. They were both very dead ducks. This was the beginning of the finest duck shooting I have ever seen. Nash was without doubt the top shot. He constantly killed ducks that other hunters considered out of range. He did not cripple them down, but *killed* them. His double gun was a Burt Becker magnum on a Fox action, and on the rib was engraved, "Made for Nash Buckingham by Burt Becker." His favorite duck shell was not too heavy, but extremely fast—3″ shells with 1⅜ ounces of #4 Lubaloy shot made by Winchester and sent to Nash by Mr. Olin. They had to be the finest shells manufactured. I saw Nash kill ten high ducks, with ten shots, the closest duck hitting the water at least 40 yards from where we were standing. At times he used a Model 21 Winchester gun, which he liked a great deal, and I would very much like to have this gun hanging on my wall right now.

As part of his appeal to people, Nash came naturally to be an organizer. He was a founder of the Outdoor Writers Association of America in 1927 and as chairman of their Waterfowl Committee received their top award in 1960. As Director of Game Restoration at Western Cartridge and during his later period in Washington, he was active in game conservation legislation. Nash's concern was not with protecting game from shooting (as long as the shooting was controlled) but with restoration of game populations to provide shooting. The conservation idealist who stresses no shooting tends to lose the important support of millions of pragmatist shooters who strive for an abundance of game for sport, even to raising it on game farms. Nash felt that practical cooperation between the two types can realize and maintain game populations that the too literal conservationist group cannot achieve.

In 1947 Nash received the first *Field & Stream* Trophy for Outstanding Service to Conservation ever given an individual; was given the 1962 Winchester Outdoorsman of the Year Award; was elected to the Field Trial Hall of Fame in 1963.

For generations, the goal of some dog breeders has been to produce the "compleat byrde dogge"—one capable of winning top field trial competition and handling perfectly for shooting. Nash proved more nearly "compleat" than most such dogs, in that he was a superb field trial man—judging the Nationals from 1934 to 1951—and simultaneously a shooter's shooter. Importantly, Mr. Buck was a brilliant writer of stories of the old South and the fabulous hunting he knew there, but it would not be honest appraisal to suggest that everything he wrote was equally good. Living up to his reputation detracted nothing from his shooting but contributed little toward literary self-criticism—perhaps a pleasant way to write but not an analytical one. As he was heroic to his friends, he was equally a hero to his editors. Eltinge Warner of *Field & Stream* and Eugene Connett, publisher of the Derrydales, bought his things as they flowed from his typewriter and asked only for more. Nash wrote as he lived, in superlatives. The dogs' faults were turned into virtues—as with Jack, a covey dog who would point singles only when he felt inclined, a miss or two and he went on out for coveys; he would look to see if he was watched when a rabbit jumped (Nash said he waited for permission), then would run it.

As Nash rarely missed a quail, according to his stories he never missed a meal—to eat it or to tell about it—dividing his interest in game birds equally as targets and as delectable food. In the title story in *Tattered Coat,* he reveals a passion for food, even as a twelve-year-old, in a wonderful scene at old Beaver Dam:

> Watching Mr. Tel carve and then ladle giblet gravy onto the savory stuffing he spooned from the gobbler's smoking interior, I'd picture that monster bird roaming canebrakes and open forest before falling victim to Jackson's ten-bore and incredible skill with a wing-bone turkey call. The slightly darker shade of its flesh brought visions of the stately fowl feeding off carpets of woods mast and strewings of frosted wild grapes and berries. The amount of succulent gobbler breast or second joint a small boy could consume was prodigious. One just kept packing in turkey and baked tomatoes regardless of knowing that Victoria had some sort of pie or pudding in reserve. But what was a hungry and growing lad to do?
>
> When we went on gunning trips, Mother invariably cautioned me against overeating at night. The practice always produced nightmare, but I worked on the principle that stowing too much good grub might not be good for me, but it was good to me, and let it go at that. I got so I even knew what food combinations produced which nightmare. An excessive voltage of pork, for instance, produced the incubus of Jack and the Beanstalk. The only difference between the pork nightmare and the fairy book was that instead of sliding down the beanstalk ahead of the giant, I fell through the opening and missed the stalk.
>
> Too much shrimp gumbo mixed with overindulgence in suet pudding and hard sauce saw me perish miserably and by inches. Stalking a flock of enormous wild turkeys, my double-barreled gun slowly centered the outstretched necks and clustering heads of those huge birds. They seemed to stare right at me, incredulity and scorn mantling their quivering red and purple wattles. God of my ancestors, how hard I'd yank at those triggers and they wouldn't budge. Only when I wrapped two fingers around them and strained gruntingly would the hammers begin slow-motion, nerve-wracking descent. By the time they struck the firing pins I'd be sweating but to my horror no explosion ensued. The enraged gobblers, grimacing, flew straight into my face. I tried to dodge—and yelled.

How many times how many shooting men have dreamed such a dream.

Nash's stories are punctuated by meals—every breakfast is described, hunting lunches relived, the suppers are chefs-d'oeuvre. In spite of this cholesterol-heavy diet, something saved him for a grand old age—perhaps 10-gauge arteries, or it may have been the vigorous life he lived. For entertain no notion that hunting with Mr. Buck was a soft sport. He slept in uncomfortable tents and shacks, got up at three a.m. in miserable cold, pushed a boat through ice to a distant blind, rode long days on horseback in big quail country. Judging the Nationals was no simple canter, being as hard riding as the individual chose to make it, and Nash didn't spare himself.

Nash expressed particular feeling for the beneficence of a drink after a long, cold day outdoors. In "A la Belle Etoile" after taking the big smallmouth he wrote: "Aye lad . . . that called for a Tom Collins doubled and redoubled." I first suspected a bit of leg-pulling on Nash's part when I asked Irma and Roy Witt to tell me the name of Nash's favorite bourbon (what else for a Southern gentleman?) and was told he cared very little for whiskey. Berry Brooks gave a similar response to my question:

> Nash's favorite drink was water. I never saw him take an alcoholic drink. I have just talked with Joe Mercer, who fished and hunted with Nash occasionally during the past 30 years. Joe said that Nash once told him that he had on some rare occasions sipped a tablespoonful of brandy before retiring but during his entire life he had not drunk a quart of brandy all together. As for food, Nash always ate a big breakfast and a big lunch. Hardly ever did he eat an evening meal—sometimes crackers and sweet milk. He was early to bed, often at 7:30 if possible, and up 30 minutes to an hour before daylight.

This about no sumptuous suppers came as a disillusion to me. Irma Witt says: "True, when he was very late getting in from a hunting trip, he'd eat light— soup, sandwiches, dessert—didn't like going to bed on a full stomach—and in the very late years, he didn't eat as much, but only the late illness dimmed his appetite and he never lost his love and interest in good food."

A fascinating aspect of gathering impressions and memories of a man from his friends is the variation in recollections. This is not discrepancy so much as difference of viewpoints and contacts with Nash at different periods of his life. Speaking of Nash and food, John Bailey recalls:

"Nash always enjoyed very much the suppers we had together. Although easy to please, he appreciated good food and talked about it. It was probably in his last few years when Nash was preparing his own meals at home that he ate no supper. Whiskey was never important to Nash but he enjoyed a drink. We would usually have a drink on the way back after a hunt and maybe another after we got home. I liked to see him around a fire with a drink in his hand. The first sip or two always made him sneeze."

In 1944 Nash wrote me: "It's mighty thoughtful of you to write an aging guy such a nice letter," revealing an awareness at sixty-four that time was slipping away, not knowing he had so many years to enjoy—years he relished to full measure as he expressed beautifully in his stories. But like their bird dogs, all shooters eventually acquire limitations, the first usually being impairment of hearing. Most of his friends think Nash's deafness was aggravated by the thousands of heavy duck loads he shot.

Bob Anderson said: "Nash's deafness started to get bad in the 40's but being deaf never bothered him too much in shooting; sometimes he couldn't hear a bird get up behind him or hear ducks overhead. What did bother him was having a cataract removed from his right eye in 1963. It was particularly bad in estimating range. I watched and puzzled about this for some time. Many times he would jump up long before a dove came in range and I would have to hold his sleeve. Then he could shoot quite well. I think it was magnification in the one lens that made things look too close."

John Bailey describes this: "Nash kept the lens over his left eye blacked out most of the time after the cataract operation. He said his left eye was stronger and as he shot from the right shoulder he didn't want the left eye taking over."

Berry Brooks recalled: "I last shot with Nash during the dove season before he moved to Knoxville. His eyesight was very poor but I would spot the doves and say, 'A dove is coming from the right, just over the tree tops right in line with that big oak tree, about a hundred yards out, about two o'clock.' Nash would pick him up and bust him. He bagged his limit that last day."

Any wing shot knows what shooting with one eye means, yet Nash took it merely as a handicap to overcome. In September 1970 at past ninety he wrote me: "I had the cataract job in '63, and for a season or so you have to readjust as to magnifications—but you get the hang of it."

Readers and even some acquaintances thought of Nash living as he wrote and shot—on a heroic scale. Few knew that during his last years he was confronted with realities far from grandiose. The heroic thing was the manner in which he fought these problems.

As far back as 1934 on the last page of the Derrydale *De Shootinest Gent'man,* Nash wrote with strange premonition: "For there was Irma, patting my hand and smiling the dear old message up at me through wet, joyous eyes." On June 18, 1970, he wrote me from Knoxville, where Irma was in a nursing home: "My Irma had me read your letter to her, and when I'd finished she said, with brimming eyes, 'We have been happy, haven't we, Big Boy? And I wish we were younger and able to enjoy friendship with Mr. and Mrs. Evans.' And then, after an exchange of kisses she added, 'Do thank them both.'"

While still at home in Memphis, Nash came to know that bitterest anguish—to see the woman he loved progressively deteriorate in health. In letters to me and I suspect to almost everyone, he gave no hint of what he was going through, courageously maintaining an attitude of hope that Irma's condition might improve. Only in his letters in '68 and '69 from Memphis to Dr. William Andrews, then in East Africa, do I find the situation revealed—an eighty-eight-year-old man shopping, preparing meals, keeping house and attending devotedly to a very ill wife, and still endeavoring to write. In these letters to Dr. Andrews, there were happy thoughts of dogs and duck prospects, reports of quail from John Bailey— and football. Even here, the sad state of wildfowl conservation worried Nash, but a lack of elasticity was beginning to show: "In the next Life, I just don't think I'll try Conservation, which today is 90% waste."

Writing to me during this period, Nash was gloriously game, with comments like "I've never been sick a day in my life" and "It's a great life." When I later saw photographs of him taken at that time, I was shocked. The great shoulders and frame were still there, but the stooped posture and loss of weight made me know I was looking at an old man. To be surprised at this in a man of eighty-eight or -nine seems ludicrous, but not in the case of Nash Buckingham. In some photographs he looks years younger, perhaps because he was on a shooting trip. One, taken at his typewriter at past ninety a few days before his serious illness, shows a keenness that is ageless, with eyes that still appear to look down the barrels of the Becker with the old glint.

Because Nash consecrated his life to sport and because of the men he associated with, many think of him as a man of considerable wealth. He was a successful writer, but publishers reserve their fabulous advances for ex-Presidents and such, few, if any, of whom write their own books. Nash's books sold well, but the Derrydales were in editions limited to 950 or 1250 copies, and none of the others were runaway bestsellers. Nash was never a businessman and didn't let anything like making money interfere with enjoying dogs and shooting, which can involve considerable cost in money expended as well as money not pursued.

Under oppressive medical expense and the greatest burden, worry, Nash tried to write at an age when no writer should do so other than for the pleasure of creative work. Writing under pressure to earn money already spent before the idea for an article is conceived causes stress no sensitive man can endure. On November 6, 1968, he wrote to Dr. Andrews:

> I sold one story, which they changed around a bit, but it's all right with me just so they bought it. It's like my old nurse Aunt Lucy Lee, who used to say—"You sho' can't take 'much obliged' to the grocery."

At this time he was trying to organize a collection of his pieces and stories for a last book but with small hope of managing it. To his old friend Major Carlos Lowrance in Catawba, North Carolina, he wrote:

> I'm trying to write a few stories, but whether in this strange new world there'll be a place for sentiment of outdoor yarns, I dunno. My Irma sends you her best wishes, and we'll try to hold on and talk Father Time into a bit of indulgence.

In one of his letters to Dr. Andrews he wrote:

> Larry Pryor sent his copy of the quarterly *American Sportsman* for me to autograph my story therein about great dogs I've shot over. The magazine is $7.00 the copy. I wouldn't spend $7 to see David fight Goliath. If two more stories go, I can beat the rap yet. I sort of live with crisis.

Any man can be a fighter when he has his opponent on the ropes; proof of what he is comes when he is on the ropes, himself, being unmercifully mauled, and Nash proved his gameness throughout the decline in Irma's condition, thoughtlessness of hospital and clinic accounting departments, even to being forced to try to sell an Inness painting and his gun.

Nash's last time shooting with Dr. Andrews had been dove shooting on Hugh Buckingham's place near Memphis before Dr. and Mrs. Andrews left for Africa in the fall of 1968. I saw movies of this day and again was touched by the change in Nash's appearance. In November 1968 he was planning a hunt at Beaver Dam with Dr. Andrews's sons Rad and Bill:

> Bob Stoner is going to take me to Beaver Dam and I'll get P.W. to give us a look at things. As soon as possible I'll get with Rad and we'll plot against the mallards and gadwalls. I'd like, and so would Irma, to spend a weekend with you. Your family's befriending of us has touched us deeply and will rest with us forever.

On December 18, 1968, after more excited letters about the proposed hunt, Nash wrote:

> Dear Chub:
> Bill got home and in touch immediately. He and Roy Witt, who came down with Irma for a visit, and I went to Beaver Dam morning of 16th to size up matters. Water over the platform and out into some of the lower lying fields. P.W. had to raise blinds nearly 30 inches; it is about 4 inches in the old blind at Round Pond. We pushed up to Handwerker stand and jumped considerable flights, mostly blackjacks.
> Bill was right back next a.m. at 4. We were early in the Handwerker blind, Bill went across on the other blind and we put out decoys in between. Day was quiet and cloudy. We bagged 10—2 small ducks, 2 drake spoonbills, 2 gadwalls, the rest blackjacks. I shot the new 1400 Winchester and did fine after getting the hard trigger pull reduced— bagged 2 blackjacks and 2 others.
> This morning we were back on the job; heavy south wind. I sent Bill and Roy to Round Pond. Three can't shoot out of that blind and anyway I wanted them to have the shooting. I didn't see half a dozen ducks. In the Ark.-Tenn.-Miss. areas there is a skimpy supply.

This was Nash Buckingham's last duck shooting, after all those years since his first day in 1890 at old Wapanoca.

Toward the end of 1969, Nash faced the impossibility of carrying on alone with Irma, and on December 8, Irma and Roy Witt took them to their home in Knoxville. On December 13, 1969, Nash wrote to Dr. Andrews:

> Irma is so happy with the children. . . . From here out, it's me and the typewriter. I'm in three Halls of Fame, which are collateral for memory only. At terminal I get enough to fetch me home. . . . Irma sleeps a lot but eats well and likes her nurse. I stay close and Irma and Roy have been wonderful.

In March of 1970, Irma had to be taken to a nursing home, where Nash spent as much time with her as he could, still courageously pretending to himself that she was improving. Through all of this, his letters revealed his same empathy for others. Writing about the death of an old friend, Richard Owens, he remarked, "And I'm sorry, too, for Richard's little fat dog, the poor little creature will grieve."

Nash Buckingham's final day with his gun was the opening of the 1970 dove season. He mentioned shooting a 20-gauge Model 21. His daughter Irma wrote me:

> September 1st never rolls around that we don't get that faraway look in the eye and point imaginary wingings! And it will seem so strange not to have TNB with us—that was really always his day, and he loved to hunt up here in East Tennessee. I remember that last opening day so well. We had wondered whether he would be able to go, but go he did— at 90. All the "boys" he loved so well—Charlie Wayland, Hugh Van DeVenter, Paul Elder and the late Howard Van Gilder—were along, their destination the fine Hodges farm up in Sevier County, a splendid river bottom where they had had many a fine hunt. Roy and Daddy were not aware that the others had decided to make a real party of it. Realizing it would be Daddy's last time with them, Charlie had had quail saved up and cooked to perfection, fried chicken, salad, ham and beaten biscuit, lemonade by the gallon, iced tea, cake cookies—a real feast. Roy said that about midafternoon, Daddy squared off on one bird a mile high and down it came, but they couldn't find it. Hot as it was, Daddy set out and tramped and tramped through all the high grass and corn rows and finally came staggering back, holding the bird high, grinning, and said, "I may not be able to see 'em or hear 'em so good any more but by golly I've still got a good nose!" He had really bird-dogged that critter and "fetched." It was a great day for Daddy.

In October, Nash was full of plans for a visit to Memphis and duck shooting with Dr. Andrews at old Beaver Dam. But Anno Domini always wins.

The first stroke occurred on October 26, 1970. I have in front of me the scrap of paper on which Nash endeavored to write, unable to express himself by speech. At first glance, it is the illegible writing of someone making notations in the dark, but on closer examination the letters appear almost perfectly formed. There is repetition in the manner the brain recycles a thought—a sort of mental mumbling in darkness. There is clearly an attempt to write *Irma,* although the *m* is missing each time. The word *other* appears several times, and one phrase: *But the ther are the other—for the other for the of ideas—for—* For Nash, it was always Irma, and after that, ideas for one more story, one more book.

After seven days in the hospital, Nash awoke, astounding the doctors by speaking normally. While there were residual effects, such as anxiety, he wrote coherently to some of us in the next few months. His last letter to me was on January 22, and the last letter he wrote, to John Bailey, was on February 13. But he had become progressively weaker after Christmas Day, and on March 10, 1971, at nearly ninety-one, he died in his sleep.

Roy Witt tells a touching story of Nash's dedication to his readers. Two days before he died, a reader sent some of Nash's books to be autographed. Nash inscribed them with difficulty, for he could scarcely see. Going over the desk after Nash's death, Roy found several dollar bills beside Nash's wallet—carefully autographed along with the books.

When I set out to do this book, I began with Nash's stories. But in the letters and old photographs, and in the thoughts of this man, I have discovered what was the best of Nash Buckingham. It was his gameness and his wonderful approach to life. Nash is a legend, a big man who could express contempt for a despicable type of shooter or shifty character but without hating anyone. In one of his favorite phrases, "me and him had it," he shows deference for any adversary worthy of a fight. It is no surprise that Nash has been confused with the character in his most famous story. Nash was one of the shootingest gentlemen I have known, but I think he might well be called one of the most gentlemanly of shooters. His last period was like one of his days at evening—cold pink sunset on an ice-covered world, a biting wind, but beautiful for the fullness of the day. Like one of his big Chesapeakes, he fought his way through the roughest of conditions because he was bred and trained to do it thus.

In giving you the picture of Nash Buckingham to the end, I don't intend leaving an image of a man in his decline. This is a happy book, not to be saddened but enriched by his aging. In his stories he is an ageless, virile Nash. Left behind, with his gun, are his books, which like the famous hat bear the badge of honor.

Nash expressed belief in a hereafter so implicit as to have me pretty well convinced there is such a place where he and Irma will take the big ones in some white-water river, where he and Horace and Hal and all those others will be shooting ducks again. Heaven knows, Nash sent enough ducks there to last him an eternity. This signifies something. A man who hopes that heaven will be exactly what he has experienced here on earth must certainly be among the most fortunate of mortals.

I have my own concept of immortality—that a man lives for as long and as frequently as he is remembered. Writers, especially, achieve a continuing existence through their books, far better than an extended identity via a tombstone. Nash's immortality lies between the blue or red bindings of the Derrydales, the Putnam editions' familiar jackets. The thirty stories and pieces in this last collection breathe and taste and feel those things Nash lived. If each time we remember a person who is gone, that person lives again—seeing a fiery sunrise over marshland, a string of geese against dawn, watching mallards cup wings and slant toward decoys, thinking that this was how Nash saw them feeling the same sweet thrill—then Nash Buckingham will not be dead. The old hero will be reincarnated with the smell of powder yet unburned when these stories of bob-whites and ducks and doves are read by someone very young who has never heard the name Nash Buckingham. Nor will he be dead for as long as one yellowed letter written by a reader in the early part of this century lies folded among brittle photographs—a letter that tells, "I have just read, and re-read to my wife, one of your stories . . ."

To read again these stories I have selected has been an experience for me like listening to the firm soft voice of the man who gunned these magic marshes and sedgelands, who tells about famous dogs, having been there when the things that made them famous happened. If you will only search, you will surely sense the touch of hand, and hear him say:

"Here—for you. This is what I lived for. I give you back my years."

Old Hemlock   —GEORGE BIRD EVANS
Bruceton Mills, West Virginia
October 1972

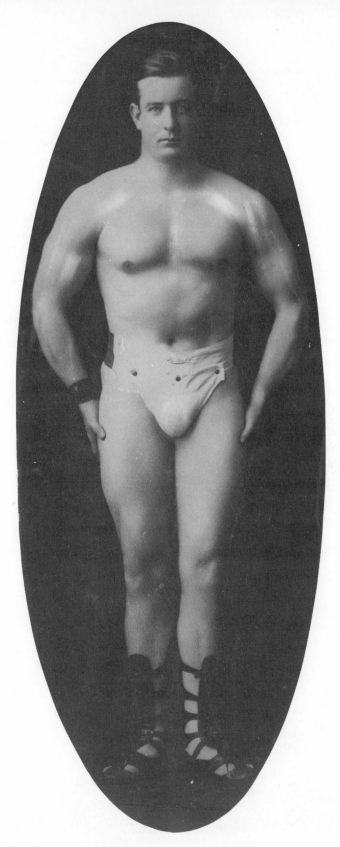

Nash Buckingham at twenty-two as a member of "The Milo Trio" weight-lifting act. He proudly inscribed his dimensions (chest normal 45", expanded 49"; waist 34½") on the reverse of this picture. In the fall of the same year, 1902, Nash captained the University of Tennessee football team.

Nash at twenty-five with Tom Cotton and a bag of bobwhites. The gun is his old Winchester Model 1893, later handed on to his nephew James Ware, who still has it.

Nash with setter Jimmy at Hal Howard's home in Aberdeen, Mississippi, in 1908.

Nash shooting Harold Money's famous 1897 Winchester pump gun in a live-pigeon shoot at Rogers Springs, Tennessee, in 1910. Nash noted on the picture, "I won $350 on that last shot."

Nash at thirty-two, quail shooting with Don and Kate near the Ames Plantation. The picture reveals what happened to his nose the time he "forgot to duck" in a boxing match.

Irma Jones Buckingham, whom Nash married in 1910, was his idea of a top woman shot. He inscribed this picture of her and a bag of greenheads at Beaver Dam in 1913 with the remark, "a wildfowler in her own right and with a high trap and quail shooting average, to boot."

Irma shooting at Lakeside Club, Arkansas. In the stern is Perry Hooker, "Master of the Art" of duck calling. Nash stated that he never heard a caller "remotely in the same class."

Protagonists in "De Shootinest Gent'man": Horace Miller, shown cooking catfish at O.K. Camp around 1914, and Capt. Harold Money, "champion gunner and ace sniper in WW-1, home on a brief vacation."

At left, Nash and Horace coming in from a morning's shoot at Beaver Dam about 1916, the year the story was written; right, Nash with Berry Brooks in the Handwerker blind where it all took place, some four decades later.

Horace Miller, with Girl, Don, and quail and rabbit shot at Ship Island Bar, surveying the world from the deck of the goose camp houseboat.

Another view of the houseboat base for goose shooting at Ship Island Bar.

Nash accepting a bird from Bob Carrier's pointer Barnacre Curt Swango about 1933. The little double is his Burt Becker quail gun, which he obtained just about this time.

Thirteen years later, in the quail field at Benning with Flash. Nash was still in his prime physically and as a wing shot at the age of sixty-six.

Pat of "The Family Honor" and her litter mate Fritz, Chesapeakes belonging to Marse Henry Bartholomew, bring in a double on canvasbacks on the Potomac.

The greatest dogs in America Fritz + Pat—a double.

Grouse of Arden, Edgar Queeny's great Lab, on a stump in the flooded Arkansas duck cover where Nash described him in "Not Unsung."

Photograph taken by Henry P. Davis in 1944 of A.G.C. Sage and his handler, Clyde Morton, with three famous Sage pointers, Saturn, Ariel, and Luminary. Nash wrote on the reverse, "Notice that Saturn looks a derby beside two veteran national champs. I judged all but one of the Sage-Morton wins." Ariel won the National championship in '41, '43 and '45, Luminary in '42, and Saturn in '47.

Nash as a field-trial judge, a role he loved, judging the Florida-Georgia Shooting Dog Stake on Walter Teagle's Norias Plantation near Thomasville in 1958.

Three early favorites, photographed by Nash in the early twenties, identified on the back as a heavy Parker 12, .410 Merkel over-and-under, and a Super Fox 12—"all purveyors of 'short shot-strings to tall marks.'"

Nash in 1934 with his favorite gun, the first Burt Becker magnum "Bo Whoop," and the springer spaniel Chubby, probably the favorite of all his dogs.

"Ropes and Tools": Left, three duck calls of the type described in "The Ne-glected Duck Call," fashioned with the care and finish of a fine gunstock; right, the saddle scabbard Nash had made to his specifications in 1910, still in use in the quail field by John Bailey.

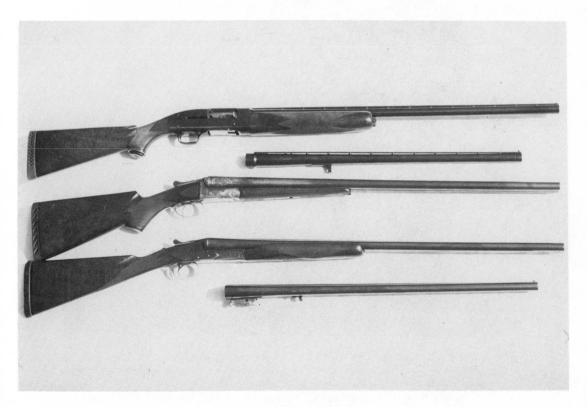

Three favorite guns, all custom-built for Nash: top, his M50 Winchester autoloader; middle, the second Burt Becker magnum, and bottom, his Winchester 21 with two sets of barrels. (The first Burt Becker was lost in 1948 and never recovered.)

The lodge on John Bailey's Quail Hills Plantation, where Nash stayed in "Pipeline Pott'iges." Left rear: Catherine Bailey with Ruthie (who cooked the dinner) and Ludie Welch; seated left, John with his setters Rex and Billy (the gun dogs in the story), Jerry Webber, and Johnny Farris.

Lovely old "Brick House," dreaming away the years in the dignity of memories.

Beaver Dam as it looks today, a private preserve of the Owens family.

Nash at sixty-eight at Tom Bash's "Lost Quarter" near Swan Lake Refuge, Missouri. The gun seems to be the first Becker magnum, to be lost within a month, though the leather stock boot appears in no other picture.

Bob Anderson, Nash, and Werner Nagel shooting in "the best pits I ever used" near the Swan Lake Refuge. This was the scene of "Duke," the story of Tom and Doris Bash's "crisscross water spaniel." Note that Bob and Nash preferred gloveless trigger fingers, and that Nash has chosen the high bird.

Nash at Quail Hills in 1969, shooting the Winchester Model 21 made to his specifications in 1933. The photo was taken near the "trampoline" described in "Pipeline Pott'iges."

Nash at eighty-seven, with Dr. William Andrews at Beaver Dam. The gun is the second "10-pound Becker Magnum, 3-inch Western cases and copper-coated 4's" as Nash noted on the back of the picture.

Nash's last duck hunt, at age eighty-eight, December 1968 at Beaver Dam. The blacked-out left lens was needed to ensure right-eye dominance after his 1963 cataract operation.

Friends for more than fifty years: Nash receives Winchester's first "Outdoorsman of the Year" award from John Olin, whom he had first met at the 1919 Grand American Handicap.

Part One:
WILDFOWL

Minutes and Years

Few things can turn the clock back more irresistibly for shooting men than entries in an old gun diary or a logbook. When the giant pecan tree that stood at Beaver Dam Duck Club was blown over in a tornado in the early twenties, destroying the "moss-shingled" clubhouse, Nash salvaged several sporting prints, a primitive drawing of Arthur Wheatley's setters—Joe III and Morgan, sons of "native" Joe Jr.—and the club logbook, a precious distillate of years.

Excerpts from this logbook and club records make up "Minutes and Years" in Blood Lines, *and I have selected some of these to open this section on wildfowl. The original report, dated December 3, 1880, was written by Arthur Wheatley when Nash was six months old. "A. F." in the memo refers to* The American Field, *which at that time had been published for six years. Judge James M. Greer, named as a member in the 1882 entry, is "The Judge" in "De Shootinest Gent'man," according to Horace Lytle, who knew Judge Greer's grandson, Rowan Greer, Jr.*

The unnamed Northern member of the December 9, 1901, incident (who resigned) not only inspired the name for the "Hog Stand" blind, but, by negative example, planted the idea that a "limit" of fifty ducks per day might be a shade beyond sportsmanship. Considering that at Wapanoca in the late nineties, twenty-two guns had logged fifty-duck limits (eleven hundred ducks in one day), some sort of increased restraint seemed in order.

Eugene Palmer, of the group mentioned in the December 20, 1915, entry, was with Winchester and shot with Nash. The four girls were the same guests in the holiday hunt in "After All These Years," which took place five years earlier. Sam Walker was a Memphis lawyer.

While Nash was a superlative shot on quail, there were other bobwhite shots as good—some dedicated more exclusively to bird shooting. But there is small doubt that, in his time, Nash was "Mr. Wildfowl," goose and duck, both as to knowledge of the birds and as to shooting—especially on high or long shots. Harold Money might have been good that day at the Handwerker blind and perhaps, as Horace put it, left question as to whether he "EVAH missed er duck." Others have also said that Harold "De Shootinest Gent'man" Money was a brilliant shot on ducks. The difference between the two was that Nash lasted. Age and eyesight

—and hearing—exacted their price, but that came only after thousands of shells (and wildfowl), and hundreds of days in the blinds had fed the gunner's soul of Nash Buckingham. Both at Beaver Dam and Wapanoca the young Nash got duck feathers in his eyes, setting off a fever that burned in him till he was ninety.

IN A TIME-EMBROWNED envelope found beneath the false cover of an old minute book, along with sundry communications relating to the possibility of planting wild rice successfully in flowless waters of the deep South, I discovered notes covering a period in the existence of the Beaver Dam Ducking Club prior to its organization in 1882. As the club—miraculously —is still in active existence, it seems of interest to preserve here certain high lights in its past that should be inspirational in today's struggle for existence by wild-life resources.

December 3, 1880

Last week made interesting visit to large lake called Beaver Dam, situated some nine miles inland from Austin, county seat, our party of four arriving by Lee Line steamboat with some equipment. Our plunder hauled to cabin of man named Knight living on lake bank as tenant of Dr. Owen. Lake is completely edged with yellow "saw grass," making fine cover for boat stands. Our party composed of M. L. Selden, J. G. Handwerker, Tom O'Sullivan, and myself. We slept in our tent on comfortable corn shuckings, and Knight's wife fed us good meals, particularly venison rib roast. Weather pretty cold. Lake horseshoe-shaped and said to be about eight miles from end to end. Main body probably two and half miles open water, balance cypress forests and water-covered flats of button willows and stumpage. Lake simply covered with ducks, geese, and swans that kept us awake nights. Knight rustled up two or three colored men to help paddle the heavy bateaux. Total bag for three days before having to leave and catch the up-boat home, 480 ducks, 5 swans, and 22 geese. Country sparsely settled and no market hunters about. Rather singular. Shot completely out of shells and brought along no extras, powder, shot, or loading tools. But just as well. Knight wants us to return for bear and deer hunt in heavy forest east of here; said he can get some fair hounds. Left our tent and bedding at Dr. Owen's plantation against a hoped-for return.

W. A. WHEATLEY

Memo. Compile details and write story for A. F., using pen name my dog Guido.

W. A. W.

December 2, 1882

Beaver Dam Ducking Club formally organized after return from our hunt last week. The cabin built for our use under lease from Dr. Owen has double bunks sleeping ten men, and space left for living quarters. We will feed in the Knight kitchen as formerly; it is amply large. Officers elected: Dr. Robert Mitchell, president; Miles S. Buckingham, vice-president; W. A. Wheatley, secretary and treasurer; George Handwerker, Metellus Selden, and Tom O'Sullivan, members of Executive Committee. Privates in the ranks: A. C. Treadwell, Sam P. Walker, Bun F. Price, and Judge James M. Greer. Greer is counsel. Ducks and geese about same as last year, although some of the boys think fewer swans seen. Dr. Owen stopped in and had two meals with us. He owns a tremendous lot of land hereabouts. No further business.

W. A. WHEATLEY

December 16, 1883

(Notice sent to all members.)

A log book has been purchased and left at Beaver Dam Club and each hunter is specifically requested not to forget to duly enter therein what he bags during his stay and particularly the kinds of ducks taken. Also note where ducks are feeding and flight best, stage of water, and other addenda possibly helpful to the shooting. The Executive Committee considers record keeping of all game killed including deer, bear, wild turkey, and even squirrels, quail, and rabbits as highly important. For the reason that this country will not remain for long as wild as it is now and we must take steps to keep natural conditions as nearly so as possible. Our annual meetings have been set for the first Monday in each October.

W. A. WHEATLEY, Secretary

January 9, 1884

At a special meeting of the Beaver Dam Club held at the State National Bank, M. S. Buckingham submitted an offer from three landowners to sell Beaver Dam Club the lake and surrounding acreage up to 10,000 acres for $2.50 an acre or $22,500.00. It would be a direct deal and no com-missions. Half cash, balance one, two, and three years with interest. After considerable heated discussion a motion by Judge James M. Greer to pur-chase the land and seconded by Mr. Miles Buckingham was put to vote and lost six to four; your secretary wishing to be recorded as in favor of buying. Adjournment.

W. A. WHEATLEY, Secretary

(Note by author: As it turned out, in a few years a hundred acres of that timber would have paid for the entire property.)

November 3, 1892

(Note from logbook. In handwriting of author's older brother.)

As guests of Messrs. Miles S. Buckingham and Mr. Arthur Wheatley and Judge Jim Greer, Miles and Nash Buckingham and their friend Howard Risley from South Carolina came here last night and hunted today. Total bag eighty-six ducks, mostly mallards. Weather fair and cold. Large flocks of geese settled in south end of lake about sundown. We are going coon hunting tonight with Jackson Bounds as Howard Risley has never been. Then home on the morning train. P.S. We caught three coons.

MILES GIFFORD BUCKINGHAM

May 18, 1901

(Note from minute book.)

The object of this special meeting is to elect a secretary in place of W. A. Wheatley, deceased, who has been secretary of the Beaver Dam Ducking Club since its organization in 1882. He also hunted three years before that date. Honorable James M. Greer offered the following:

"To every man is granted opportunity for some particular expression in life of some peculiar virtue. To a few men is given the opportunity to, at times, live and express all the virtues. He who has given more of good than of evil to the life he has lived, and carries out of life more of love than of hatred, has, we can truly say, rounded out his career. But, when there falls by the wayside one who has never received the hatred of his fellow man; one who has held, for always, the love and admiration of his intimates, there, indeed, is vacancy which mantles his companions in a pall of sorrow. When Arthur Wheatley died, he carried to his grave the heart of every man and

woman who knew him well. And we, particularly those who were his followers beneath the Stars and Bars as well as at old Beaver Dam, do but feebly
express the truth of sentiment in highly resolving that no braver, more
wholly genial, generous, loyal, and beloved citizen or father ever passed to
divine realms."

PERCY GALBREATH, Recording Secretary

Appended

To the Members of the Beaver Dam Ducking Club.

I thank you here and now for past courtesies as a fellow member and
chairman of the Executive Committee, also for your compliment in electing
me secretary to succeed my noble friend and comrade Arthur Wheatley.
For your information headquarters of Beaver Dam will remain at Mr.
Wheatley's office, 287 Main Street, as his son, Mr. Pinckney Wheatley,
wishes to continue it that way so news of the lake will come as usual during
his father's lifetime. He invites us all to come up and make ourselves at
home just as in days gone by.

J. G. HANDWERKER, Secretary

(Note by the author. On his birthday, May 31, 1938.)

Come thus far, it is well to pause for daydreaming. I see again that home-
like, old-fashioned office of Mr. Arthur's with its oils of field-trial champions
(the great Gladstone and his red conqueror, native Joe, Jr.) ; foxhound
data, favorite retrievers, and photographs of gunning cronies. There are
comfortable, leather-lined chairs for all, and firearms are stacked in practically every corner. My mentor's inkstand is fashioned from a rosewood
case containing two exquisitely inlaid flintlock dueling pistols, and hunting
horns, powder flasks, and shot pouches dangle from pegs in a towering
mahogany desk. Correspondence—more of dogs and guns than of business,
I fancy—litters a table at his elbow.

A chubby youngster of twelve, I stand before him that long-agone afternoon in 1892. Shotgun in one hand and a package of shells in the other,
I listen attentively. Young for a lad to be afield alone? Not for youngsters
of that day and time! We had no tennis courts, country clubs, public
golf courses, automobiles to dash about in, or camps and dude ranches to
be chucked into by parents bound elsewhere. We taught ourselves to swim;

we played sand-lot baseball and football; and for the rest we began going hunting and fishing with our parents when we could toddle.

But Mr. Arthur was saying, "So you're off for a Saturday at Beaver Dam, eh, Buster? Well, here's the key to that old trunk of mine—use what you've a mind to, and if your shells don't seem to have any shot in them, why, dig out some of those long green ones in my cartridge case. They may kick you out from under your hat, but hold on tight. Have Jackson Bounds take you into that big timber back of the Evans place for a turkey hunt." I thank him kindly, and, with an arm about my shoulder, he goes with me to the door.

December 9, 1901

(Note from logbook.)

Came down night before last for my first visit to Beaver Dam Club since acquiring a membership. Shot from what is known as the outer Teal Hole stand. Began at sunrise and by nightfall had 139 ducks, mostly mallards and gadwalls. Decided to try again early this morning before traintime. The flight continued heavy—weather thickening. Bagged 18 ducks and two Canadian geese—making total of 157 ducks. My visit has been delightful in every respect and I anticipate others.

W— B—

December 14, 1901

(From the minute book.)

A special meeting was held this day with the following members present: R. W. Mitchell in the chair; H. R. Miller, James M. Greer, M. L. Selden, P. Galbreath, M. S. Buckingham, J. G. Handwerker, Tom O'Sullivan, and George I. Neptune. The President stated that the recent killing of 157 ducks in one shoot at Beaver Dam had been noised about and the County Board of Supervisors (rightly) expressed indignation and threatened regulations against nonresidents shooting in the county. In fact, a petition to such effect is in circulation. Mr. Buckingham moved that a committee be appointed at once to appear before the Board of Supervisors and explain that the member who did this was newly elected and a nonresident from New York who ignored the club limit. Also that said nonresident member be notified of a fine of $100 which he could pay or sell his certificate. Mr. Galbreath moved that in future the limit be made thirty-five ducks a day instead of fifty. Mr. O'Sullivan moved that the stand from which the member shot be called in future the "Hog Stand." No further business—adjournment.

J. G. HANDWERKER, Secretary

(Note by author: It is still known as the "Hog Stand," to this day.)

December 20, 1915

(Note from logbook.)

House party consisting of Sam P. Walker and Anne Carter; Eugene Palmer and Mary Robinson; Hal Howard and Mary Traylor; Nash and Irma Buckingham came down Sunday night. Weather warm and rainy but that night turned bitter cold. Monday lake beginning to freeze—shooting fine. All men killed legal federal limit of twenty-five ducks. Tuesday, Walker, Buckingham, and Howard and Irma B. killed limits—Palmer and Miss R. having returned to city. Walker and Miss C. left Tuesday night. Lake frozen solid. Wednesday Nash and Irma B., with Mary Traylor and Hal Howard, walked to south end of lake on ice, with Horace and Ed sledding boats. Thousands of ducks in cypress brakes and trails kept open. Killed four limits by noon—home on fast train.

Great Day in the Morning!

In a letter to me in June of 1970, Nash implied that "Great Day in the Morning!" was one of his favorite stories. It was published first in Field & Stream, *April 1941, in the collection* Tattered Coat *in 1944, and reprinted in* Field & Stream, *November 1955.*

I select this story not only because Nash liked it but because it gives a vivid impression of what shooting at Beaver Dam was like in those days. It was part of the sport, using a 10-gauge gun, to try with one shell for multiple kills at bunched flying birds—massed wildfowl in such numbers made it difficult at times to avoid hitting more than one. Ducks and geese in thousands seemed to present a challenge most sportsmen would today find puzzling, but the urge exists as a residual heritage in some, and it is just as well for them to get it out of their systems by reading about it.

Concern, when it at last showed itself among the duck club members, was with the idea of overkill not as immoral but as a threat to future wildfowl populations —fewer birds to shoot. Oddly, the huge kills, by any method, being perpetrated by market hunters appeared to cause no misgivings, but rather held a fascination, perhaps because of the deadly efficiency of the men who did it. Duck club members were first stirred by outside activity when the common man began shooting large quantities of ducks and geese, and "commercial" shooting became something to combat. In the last portion of the original version of this story (deleted here), Nash discusses changing conditions in the Mississippi flyway, the effects of droughts and over-shooting, and efforts to overcome the drop in wildfowl populations.

In this story, the almost fierce pursuit of three species of game to the fullest bag allowable, or agreed upon, seems to strike a false note in a man thousands admired as a sportsman. Obviously, purveying game to the Old Men's Home and St. Agnes Hospital was not the raison d'etre *for sport shooting. The desire, approaching a need, to shoot large limits was present nearly all of Nash's life and is evident in his stories—a sort of athlete's striving for excellence by the highest score, and I suspect it might have been rooted in early experience on the playing field.*

In his last years he lost the urge—and the opportunity—to kill in those numbers without losing any of his wonderful enthusiasm for the sport. On September 28, 1970, at past ninety, he wrote me:

> About 60% of the duck stamp buyers are fairminded decents, but the minority 40% kill five times too much. Fortunately, I am thru with the so-called "club" duck shooting life, and do mine at old Beaver Dam, which is privately owned by one family—12,000 acres of plantation and 8 miles around the lake. I like to go along these days, take a shot now and then and keep in shape as to paddling and walking a bit. With only four ducks to bag, Dr. Andrews and I get a thrill from just poking around. I've known "Chubby" Andrews since his childhood at Beaver Dam.

Dr. William "Chubby" Andrews shot with Nash from December 1958 until 1968. Their last hunt together at Beaver Dam was, according to Dr. Andrews's logbook, on January 2, 1968, after which Nash contracted a severe case of flu that, as Dr. Andrews noted, "nearly did him in." Studying this logbook, with a few gray duck feathers pressed between the pages, I was struck with the attitude expressed in notations of "good shooting" or "a fine day" after kills of three or four ducks each. Dr. Andrews lent me his movies of shooting at Beaver Dam with "Mr. Buck." The low-eye-level perspective from the boat, rafts of ducks boiling up and resettling far out on the water, others flashing white underparts against distant shoreline timber, glimpses of Cross Arms, Round Pond, the Teal Hole, the Grass Blind, and Nash enthroned on a wooden Canada Dry box in the bow like an old honker surveying home waters put me back in the late '90s and early 1900s with skies full of milling wildfowl, and I could hear Horace's soft voice calling limit after careful count on birds down. Horace's Molly and her "receipt" for smothered mallards, the "Limb Dodger" rattling down the track from Evansville—all are there.

Hal Howard was in more of Nash's stories than any other character, and logically, for he shared more of Nash's shooting days, from their boyhood until his death about 1933. John Bailey said, "His longtime friend Hal Howard, who probably saw him shoot more shells than anyone, told me that Nash's all around shooting skill was what made him greatest." Nash's gun performance in this story gave Hal no reason to change his mind. And so I give you one of Nash Buckingham's great days in the morning.

ACROSS DIMMING COTTON fields I saw lights springing up in tenant cabins and winking through low-hanging wood smoke from fall burnings. Eastward, I could just make out the black rampart of the vast Owen cypress brake—thousands of forest monarchs towering just as God grew 'em.

Beyond and without blemish of ax or saw lay the Dooley and Savage woods with Walnut Lake winding through them. Ample stocks of deer, wild turkey, and bear harbored there. South of us lay clearings crosscut by a wide bayou winding luxuriantly through second growth. Westward, stars brimmed above sundown's afterglow. A jagged sky line of timber stood sharp against a belt of dull, smoldering amber.

Just then the rattley "Limb Dodger," evening accommodation train from Memphis, whistled sharply for Beaver Dam's lonesome, uncovered stop sign amid the tall trees. Hal, I told myself, would be getting off it, with Horace on hand to assist him in unloading the pointers Ticket and Flash from the baggage car.

As usual, any number of delightful presupper chores confronted us. The pointers were allowed to ramble before feeding time. This included a visit to the boat dock to observe the water stage and listen to roosting geese in the saw grass sloughs of the far South End. For early December the water was still pretty low and the moss heavy. Those honking geese were music to our ears, for we planned a long hunt at the goose camp over on the river. Our tent there was on an Indian mound just off Ship Island sand bar, and we itched to get in that game pocket.

We retraced our steps to the clubhouse for those puttings away and settings about that are ritual with any long-organized and convivial wild-fowling outfit. Ticket and Flash made themselves at home. When Hal and I go shooting, those bullies never step out of character as home folks. This includes bunking on our beds if they so elect. As Hal used to say, "What are a few fleas among pals?"

The club ledger revealed that only two members had hunted at Beaver Dam during the week previous. This was rather surprising in view of Horace's report that there was a "worl' o' ducks."

Came supper, and what a meal! Smothered mallard, rice and giblet gravy, grilled tomatoes and savory bacon for snack garnishment with the hot biscuits.

Aunt Molly, expecting us, had quite thrown herself away in getting those ducks to just that right stage of juicy succulence no other cook in my lifetime has ever even tied. And I've done trencherman's fatigue behind some of the allegedly top-flight saucepan and spider artists—from cajun concoctions to *salle à mangers* where the help wear fancy pants and bumblebee weskits, and the carpets are so thick that you need snowshoes to stay on top. Let me give you Aunt Molly's recipe for smothered mallard just as she told it to me that evening in her own kitchen.

"Whin I heahs you an' Mist' Hal is comin', I teks 'bout fo' mallets whut's bin hangin' out in de col' fo' two-three days, an' dresses dem ve'y keerful. I don' nevah put no watah on my ducks. No, suh! I jes' wipes 'em dry wid er rag an' lets 'em set awhile. Den I gits me er stew pot an' puts in some red pippers, vinegar, an' fine yarbs outa de gyarden, an' den I adds er li'l watah an' lays in de mallets.

"I brings all dis to er slow bile fo' 'bout tin minutes. Den I teks out de mallets an' dries 'em off an' sets 'em out in de col' air fo' 'bout er hour. But I saves de watah dey done bin biled in. Nex', I gits my ol' deep skillet hotter 'n de hinges o' hades an' swinges off de mallets quick on bofe sides. O' cose, dey done bin split wide open up dey backs.

"Atta dat, I sets de skillet onto de back side o' de stove an' po's in some melted butter an' some o' de bile watah. I puts de ducks back into de skillet wid dey breastes dow'ud, an' covers 'em wid er flat top an' lays er smoothin' iron on top o' dat. Ev'y now an' den I adds er sluicin' o' elderberry cordial an' er li'l mo' bile watah. Den I draps in er few bay leaves an' er mite o' Tabasco. O' cose, I keeps de baste po'hd ovah de mallets all de meanstwhile.

"Whin I heahs de Limb Dodger blow fo' de flatform, I sets dem mallets in de oven to jes' sorter brown 'em er li'l bit mo'. I meks my gravy an' stirs de hot bile watah an' some mo' elderberry wine into hit. Den, whin I sees you-all is really heah, I finishes wid de tomatoes, rice an' biscuit. Dat's de way I cooks dem mallets, suh!"

Ah, me! Aunt Molly of marvelous culinary attainments! Cooks have gone to Heaven for far less than those "mallets."

After supper we sat around in the snug clubroom with its prints and antlers looking down on us from walls and rafters that began accumulating grime in the late seventies.

An English friend had just presented me with a trim, handsomely engraved sixteen-gauge autoloading shotgun with two sets of tubes: improved cylinder for upland birds, and a full-choked one for wildfowling. I decided, however, to use it only on quail next day, for I was headed for some tall timber gunning and never believed in sending a boy on a man's errand.

Hal and I never shake the dice box or draw for stands and paddlers when no other members are at Beaver Dam. Horace just naturally takes charge of my boat, and burly Jesse Taylor looks after Hal's interests. Hal likes to jump-shoot ducks in the North End trails, for big Jesse is particularly adept at squirming the sneak float noiselessly through button willows and elbow brush. But of course we have an understanding that if the shooting turns out poor for either of us, the other fellow comes at once where the sport sounds good.

When bedtime came, Hal took the walnut couch in the northwest corner by his locker, and I always favored the feather bed in my southwest niche. Horace left the clubhouse door wide open; and when frost cooled the stove, the dogs each crawled aboard a bed. Breakfast was, as usual, informal; we never bothered going to Aunt Molly's dining room unless a crowd was down.

Stirrings-about in Horace's quarters, and wood chopping, generally awakened us. Then Horace entered, got the stove going, and lit the center lamp. Returning with the white china coffee dripper, he tinkled on a cup with a spoon. That meant the end of extra snoozing and to come alive. And by the time that eye-opener and ablutions were over, Horace was back with eggs and battercakes.

That particular morning, the five-thirty Y & M V express had just rumbled northward when we parted at the dock. The last thing Hal said to me was: "If I'm not in by nine o'clock, don't wait for me. Take the dogs and kill a mess of quail— Irma and Marion want them for their dinner party."

Then he and Jesse disappeared in the swallow-ups of misty predawn.

Horace yanked our little duckboat's nose southward and paused to take bearings off a big white star. I knew that by holding it true aft we would hit the trail opening into the South End right on the nose. But before hitting that mark, we had to pole across a quarter mile of willow stumpage.

Masses of mallard, gadwall, and widgeon thundered into flight, and we could hear them resettling nearer the woods. The geese we had heard the evening before had moved westward during the night; I could hear them cackling and grunting over in the Teal Pond. Horace and I decided to wade and sled the boat rather than push through the top moss. We entered an aisle through the forest and, though walking as noiselessly as possible, raised clouds of birds ahead.

It was breaking day when we rounded the bole of a huge stunted cypress with our destination—the Clover Leaf Hole—in front of us. Hundreds of mallards roared out of it. Their strident alarm set the whole marsh swarming with ducks. Through lacelike boughs the heavens were a-twinkle with milling *Anatidæ*.

Suddenly a bunch of perhaps fifty widgeon lowered delicately into the pool just across the buckbrush from us. Quietly they settled to feed and preen. They were perfectly safe, too, for what Horace and I had in mind was a shot at those geese in the Teal Pond. He knew without my telling him that his next job was to wade a circle around those honkers and, if possible, send them over the woods my way. Leaving me seated on the end of the duckboat, he picked up his gun and faded from sight up the trail.

Distant goose agitation soon told a story of suspicion. Rasping cackles and guttural conversation became more and more confused. Then a muffled beating of wings told me that the flotilla of *Branta canadensis* was getting under way. In stalking game, Horace had a sixth sense. I heard him shouting, and knew that he was on the outside of the gaggle and trying to shoo them against the bank timber and more nearly over me. By then I saw them too, gaining altitude over the willows and headed my way in a swinging loop. I sat perfectly still; that was no time to flush the unsuspecting widgeon and have them flaring skyward in alarm.

Then the geese were over me. I turned the heavy ten-bore ahead of their veering mass formation and scored a double kill with its first tube. At the report the widgeon leaped and almost obscured my second blast, which downed another bird. I heard Horace's yell of congratulation. There were ducks every way I looked.

By the time Horace rejoined me, he had quite some retrieving to do. But I delayed this and stationed him across from me about fifty yards. The ducks were crossing heavily, and our combined calls lowered them to just above the treetops. The ten-gauge cracked regularly and successfully. It was one of those mornings when a fellow doesn't let many get away. So heavy was the flight that I shot only greenheads. It was just eight o'clock when Horace, sloshing through the woods, called out: "Dat's d' las' un, Cap'n. You got d' limit."

Laying aside my gun, I helped him pick up, and we waded up the now sunlit trail. Out across Stumpy Opening and into paddling water, and the lake became a picture. Its deep, unmolested coves, rimmed with yellow saw grass, were packed with ducks. Its broad bosom flashed with color off the white and black of concentrated scaups. Great patches of greenish moss seed swung with the wind drift, and I thought of summer and fall days when a bass fly tossed to the edges of such scum fetched heavy strikes and battles royal.

At the club I cleaned up a bit, changed to field boots, unleashed Flash and Ticket, and shoved the sixteen-gauge autoloader into my gun scabbard. By then Horace had the mules saddled. We heard Hal's gun working in the North End; so I knew it was all right for me to begin accumulating those bobwhites for the girls.

Hardly had we crossed the railroad and skirted new ground east of the club before Flash found, and rugged Ticket honored the point. When the bevy flushed, I repressed the inclination to empty the piece, and downed two birds with three shots. The gift gun handled superbly.

Horace marked the escaping singles beyond some mutton cane and briers separating the new ground from a cornfield. Emerging there, I dismounted hurriedly, for, almost side by side, Ticket and Flash were pointing stanchly in opposite directions. Off to the right a bit, two Negroes pulling corn stood watching the scene.

I walked in ahead of Ticket, and a cock bird buzzed to my left. The two dogs stood to shot like statues. I clucked softly, and Ticket pussyfooted to the fetch. Dilating with intensity, Flash's gaze was still "eyes right." I swung into firing balance just as a jack snipe floated from the muck. Flash's optics popped, but he held his ground. Over went *Scolopax,* and the big pointer retrieved at command.

Then, happening to look down, I noticed that my gun was empty and open. I had failed to reload after firing at the bevy rise; so now the weapon needed refueling. I dropped a shell into the carrier and pushed the release pin. Down went the action with a sharp clang. Horace cried out in amazement, for up from a wet corner of the mutton cane and brier patch flapped a mallard drake. What that lone duck was doing in that out-of-the-way spot will forever remain a mystery. Almost by instinct I bowled over the fellow, and Ticket fetched at a lope, head high with pride at this unusual package.

I made a present of the mallard to one of the corn pullers.

"Cap'n," he said in thanking me, "whut kinda funny li'l ol' long-billed bird wuz dat you jes' kilt?"

I told him it was a snipe.

"Shucks, Cap'n," he replied, "ef you laks to shoot dem things, dey's er whole passel of 'em uses not fur from heah. Whin you an' Ho'ace comes roun' de lane pas' Aun' Molly's cabin, why jes' look in dat wet place out in her cotton fiel'—hit's plumb packed wid dem fellers."

I thanked him kindly for the information, but with the mental reservation that he had merely noticed a lot of killdeer.

For two hours or more Horace and I rode through cornfields, sedgy new-ground tangles and weedy bays. The work of Flash and Ticket was superb. Conditions couldn't have been better, and by eleven-thirty Horace's pouch was puffy. We turned homeward across the corn and, by sheer accident, found ourselves passing Aunt Molly's domicile.

Remembering what our friend had said, we dismounted, put Flash and Ticket at heel, and went over to have a look at that wet place in the cotton patch. A hundred yards from the house we struck it, just a jelly-textured depression among the bare brown stalks. But out of it whizzed clouds of snipe. I sent Horace scurrying to its far end to keep the birds from pitching there, and hunkered down in the scant cover.

Ticket and Flash, flat on their bellies, looked on in amazement. Snipe hung over the area like a locust swarm—a sight I shall always remember.

I fired away as fast as I could cram quail loads into the new fowling piece. Had the gun jammed, I would have gone stark mad, but it functioned perfectly. Hal said later he never heard such a bombardment. And before very long Horace and I and the dogs gathered up twenty-five snipe that further heavied the sack.

Hal hadn't been in very long, with a limit of ducks and three geese to show for his forenoon. He hadn't taken a stand and put out decoys; had just eased along, shooting at leaping or overhead birds. Horace strung up the entire bag for a snapshot just as Aunt Molly came out on the porch to ring her dinner bell. I can see her standing there right now and hear her admiring cry of "Great day in de mawnin'!" There were seventy ducks, six geese, twenty-five quail, and twenty-five snipe.

Don't bawl Hal and me out for a pair of law violators or unmitigated bristle-backs. Don't wire federal and state enforcement agents to hop on our trails and track us down. The old club's record book and my private shooting diary of decades' standing remind me that our bag of seventy ducks, six geese, twenty-five snipe, and the same number of bobwhites was made one rare morning in early December of 1909, just thirty-five years ago, come next gunning season.

I can even tell you exactly where all that wild game went. Three honkers went to the Old Men's Home, and the other three went into cold storage for the Christmas quail hunt at Hal's home in Aberdeen. Most of the ducks went to the Church Home and St. Agnes Hospital. And Hal and I worked on the quail and snipe aplenty when Marion and Irma gave their big dinner party. It came just before the debutantes' ball at the old Chickasaw Guards' Club, and I can shut my eyes and see those two lovely girls who later became our "missuses" standing on the grand staircase with their arms full of long-stemmed American beauty roses.

In 1909 there was no Migratory Bird Law; and in Mississippi there were only county game laws, and those wholly uninterested in waterfowl. In fact, most of the duck clubs of that region were shooting daily limits of from forty to fifty birds. But at Beaver Dam there was a self-imposed one of thirty-five ducks.

There was no limit, for instance, on wild turkey. But those fellows were none too plentiful by 1909; nothing like the late '80s and early '90s, when I first began hunting the big gobblers. We had a rule against more than twenty-five quail, snipe, or woodcock per day per gun.

Our hotels and restaurants served wild game openly and legally. And be it remembered that when the Migratory Bird Law did set a Government limit of twenty-five ducks and eight geese per day (a very generous one, if you're asking me) it was, to all intents and purposes, eighteen years before obvious impairment of basic stocks necessitated the lowering of those figures.

Recently, when I had a friend stop our automobile for me to look around, I figured that where we sat was just about in the middle of that patch of snipe bog in Aunt Molly's cotton field. But there was no distant Owen cypress brake in sight, and I guess the bear and wild turkey that we used to hound through the big woods are about things of the past. Beaver Dam Lake took its name from beaver colonies that kept the forests wet before the railroad went through that country. And that clear, deep bayou overhung with cypress and full of game fish is now a silted and muddy drainage ditch.

Today, everything is pretty much cotton; mighty little smoke drifts off new-ground burnings, and the homey smells and sounds of a pioneering backwoods country are missing. But strange to relate, there are fallow fields and woods pastures where some pretty fair quail shooting can still be had if the cornfields and pea patches help out. Most plantations are now posted, and their owners cooperate with the State Game and Fish Commission to restore and maintain well-fooded habitats for wild life.

Beaver Dam Lake still has a goodly skyline of timber. Even some of its saw-grass rim is intact. But drainage and varying water levels have hurt its once magnificent fishing, and at times endangered duck shooting because of drought. Gone are the coontail moss, duckmeat, yonquapins and other aquatic naturals which once fed the migrations. For many years the old club baited the lake, but a federal edict stopped that and hurt the gunning to some extent. The members shot over live decoys, too; something we of the older times didn't have to worry with particularly.

Somehow they still have pretty good shooting at old Beaver Dam, and occasionally, on a right water stage, the bream, crappie, and bass fishing picks up. But there is no huge pecan tree sheltering a moss-shingled clubhouse.

A cyclone bowled over the patriarch and crushed the building. All I salvaged were some English sporting prints, deer antlers, pictures of the club's founders, and the historic log book.

There are probably two thousand "Beaver Dam Clubs" in this country today, exclusive of the commercial gunning places. Mighty few, however, have been steadily shot over for more than sixty years and survived to offer sport. Some of the largest have been sold to the government for wildfowl refuges; others couldn't stand the pressure of drought and restrictions, and folded up.

If, during the droughts from 1929 through 1934, the majority of the worthwhile duck shooting clubs of this country hadn't, at great expense, cooperated by hoarding water and feeding highly concentrated migrations, we would have closed seasons quite a while ago. The most wretched move was that propaganda which branded all duck club members as wealthy game hogs and, in setting class against class, dismembered our union of sportsmanship and set back wildlife restoration at least two decades. There is good, sound restoration work going forward. But one major waterfowl problem remains, and that is the adjustment of commercial shooting's status.

It's a far cry back to that lovely forenoon of December 1909, when Hal and I had our great-day-in-the-morning at old Beaver Dam. Writing this, there is a true prayer in my heart that the old club's members of today and their sons, too, will in some measure relive Hal's and my good times there. What wouldn't I give to see those gorgeous mallards floating over the lacy cypress tops and hear Aunt Molly ringing her dinner bell and calling: "Great day in de mawnin'! Come an' git it!"

Comin' Twenty-One

This is the opening story in Hallowed Years, *the collection published by Stackpole in 1953. In "Lay of That First Goose" in* Ole Miss' *(1937), Nash described an earlier trip to Wapanoca Duck Club in Arkansas, across the Mississippi and upriver from Memphis, telling how it was reached:*

> Away back yonder we entrained for Wapanoca at the old Kansas City, Fort Scott & Memphis depot. There was no bridge across the Mississippi at Memphis then, so whole trains were ferried on a gigantic towboat. Transfer was a fascinating, ticklish piece of railroading. For safety's sake we perched on advantageous jumping-off places, lest snapped brake chains or a pulled coupling send the whole shebang into the river. Reswitched to the main line, the train hooted a slow schedule through the tall and uncut wilderness of eastern Arkansas, gorgeous gameland of the lush St. Francis Basin. Deer and wild turkey flocks were constantly seen crossing the tracks. Save for an opening or two at villages, the twenty-odd miles to Wapanoca's whistle-stop at Big Creek water tank was hewn from primeval jungles.

On that same hunt: "Captain Austin said at breakfast that first morning—'I lay awake half the night trying to decide what Bun Price's snoring sounded like. Finally the answer came—two big hogs fighting.'" No man who has shared a hunting cabin more than a few times can be unmoved by that.

In "Comin' Twenty-One," the old Wapanoca Duck Club (Nash always spelled it with one c) still offered magnificent shooting. "Cypress Island" and "Aconapaw" are Nash's fiction versions of Wapanoca in some of the stories. Today it is the Wapanocca National Wildlife Refuge, one of the Department of the Interior's Bureau of Sport Fisheries and Wildlife refuges, established in 1961. There is the 600-acre Wapanocca Lake, and 1,800 of the 4,900 acres in the refuge are managed as supplemental foodland for ducks, with wooded areas flooded in winter for "feeding flats." There has been no wildfowl shooting in Wapanocca since it was purchased by the government. Nash had a part in the transaction.

The refuge manager at Wapanocca tells me that "approximately one half of the clubhouse, which I understand was built around 1912, still stands today and is used as the refuge headquarters. . . . The auditorium, as we refer to it, or lodge room serves now as our workshop and contains the fireplace." This, however, is not the "comfortable white cottage" Nash describes "with its main dining and locker room, giant fireplace" where he watched his father and George Gilham, for in "Lay of That First Goose" he wrote that the "old white cottage has long since passed away."

John Bailey enlightened me as to "Reelfoot's limber jacks": "A limber jack is a small tree or bush just under water level, usually cut off by beavers. It's no fun to hang a boat on one."

Nash's description of his shooting companion that day—Mister George Gilham —is enhanced by a photograph of the Confederate veteran (probably taken about 1900) with the caption "The Judge," that was among Nash's things. This should not be construed to suggest that he was "The Judge" in "De Shootinest Gent'- man" (that individual has been identified as Judge Greer) but is an example of the wide use of the term of address in that period, like Colonel or Captain. Re- vealing a substantial-looking man in his well-larded fifties, the photo shows the blinded right eye with an irregular cast, accentuating the piercing expression of the other, which appeared quite capable of focusing on a fleeting pintail.

A photograph of the 1893 Model Winchester pump gun Nash was shooting when he became twenty-one appears in the Putnam edition of Ole Miss', facing page 141.

Nash caught the color of the old members at Wapanoca, and the scene at the end of this story is top Buckingham.

TURN OF THE century found me at home, in Memphis, Tennessee, ahead of college schedule for Christmas holidays. Recurring "chills-and- fever" had struck me down in mid-football season; a carry-over of malarial parasites from summer baseball in the Deep South's busher circuits. Some- how, medicos in Cambridge, Massachusetts, just hadn't been able to check those debilitating "shivers-and-shakes." From a few pounds under the two hundred slot raw, I scaled a lean and hungry Cassius by early December.

Discouraged, I reported to our family physician down home in Dixie. That handsome and cultured old gentleman, who, incidentally, had fetched me into this world, listened quizzically to the course of treatment prescribed for me in the East, then pricked a bloodsmear, wrote two prescriptions, gave me a weight-building diet sheet, and told me to have the prescriptions filled at Robinson's. Quinine, iron, lemon juice, something winey to make it taste good, and, somewhere along the line a mere soupçon of shot-in-the-arm! But it worked! By Yuletide I was, socially, all but whole again yet strictly aboard Dr. Richard Maury's and Mister Jim Robinson's regimen. And I was told to remain South until they gave the word to return to bleak New England. All of which gave me time to hunt. So gun I did, thither and you until nearing the Ides of March.

Much of my game and wildfowl shooting was in Mississippi and Arkansas at my Dad's two famous duck clubs, Beaver Dam and Wapanoca. Both these magnificent properties spread their waters (gently renewable through multiple effluents of Ole Miss) amid still virgin timber, canebraked ridges and smallish plantation clearings torn from a wilderness. They could be reached only by rail; the threat and eventual carnage of motor travel was still no hot breath upon the back of wildlife's neck.

I had gunned the Memphis areas since boyhood; from Arkansas's Grand Prairie up through Big Lake and across to Reelfoot's limber jacks. Earliest of recollection were Grand Prairie's tawny vastness and gunners in buck-boards following pointers and setters for prairie chickens. As to Wapanoca, my father doubtless sensed the fact that my enforced stay at home would be the last year I could use those glorious waters for shooting and fishing as a minor. For on the last day of May 1901, I would obtain majority, when shooting privileges as a member's son, under-age, ceased.

My diary tells me that we were seven aboard the 'Frisco (K.C.M.&F.S.) local late the afternoon of Thursday, February 21, 1901. Friday, Washington's Birthday, would, of course, be a bank holiday. So, as a special concession to Dr. Richard's having ordered me back to Harvard, father was making it a farewell, two-day shoot at Wapanoca. Step by step from those yellowing pages and pictures, I can retrace those hours almost in detail; diaries can be the happiest of companions. There was always lots of fun in the local's smoking car. That afternoon there were Dad and I, Mister George Gilham, Mister Arthur Wheatley, Colonel William H. Carroll, Mister Treadwell, and youngish, handsome Mister John Price Edrington. Few better all-around game, wildfowl and trap shots will ever stare down a shotgun's tube than "Mister Jack." Most of the time he shot a handsome Colt double-barrel, but he could operate a Winchester pump gun with the chatter of a Gatling. Nearly twenty years later he came from retirement to shoot next to me in a Gun Club Memorial Trap Championship. With that old Colt double he accounted for 95x100; high gun on his squad of "Old-Timers."

Sometimes the local's smoker and coaches would be packed with timber cutters bound for far-off-the-railroad lumber camps. Mostly rough, bearded foreigners with their precious glistening axes strapped to their packs and munching black bread and bologna cut with long-bladed knives and washed down with raw vodka that set some of them crazy. It took conductors with brains and brawn to handle such mobs diplomatically, and many's the incipient riot I saw quelled. Wapanoca was a "flag-and-whistle-stop" cinder platform just across the trestle over Big Creek. And what a lovely little river it was then! Gushing, clear brown water hiding game fish galore and tons of succulent "cat." Big Creek is now a narrow, silt-jammed, polluted drainage ditch writhing with snakes.

I can still see the comfortable white cottage with its main dining and locker room, giant fireplace and two lamp-lit bedrooms of great cheer. Blazing logs took chill off the bitter outside, for a high wind rose to howl through a moonless night. Henry Douglas, the colored clubhouse keeper, reported the lakes covered with thousands of ducks apparently concentrating for a flight northward. The water was low but shooting conditions in general were well-nigh perfect. Wildfowl movement depended, said Henry, upon how the wind held. If against them, they'd stay awhile and wait for a tail breeze.

Steaks and oysters to supplement Henry's game and fish provender were spread across the linen-draped board during our stay. Gentlemen fed well and more than aplenty in those times. There was no "cocktail hour" at turn of the century, but time enough for a round of toddies or the rite of a Gin Fizz containing the mysterious fifth ingredient without which no Gin Fizz may ascend to the Pearly Gates. To name it here would be disloyalty wasted upon an ungracious modernity. Drinking? In Heaven's name—yes! But like the gentlemen they were.

The first draw was always for "paddlers" and then for "stands." With an odd number present that evening they flipped "first jack" to see who shot as rover next day. Mister Treadwell drew that assignment, and invariably delighted in it. The old gentleman had a peculiar habit of arising around three a.m., building up the fire in the clubroom, girding himself into a claret-colored quilted robe and napping in a big rocking-chair until Henry came in to lay breakfast. Wildflowers shoved off early in 1901. But later the club put on a rule that no boat could leave the platform before seven a.m. I always regarded that regulation as a concession to laziness. But at Wapanoca it made little difference; you could have postponed your start until noon and killed about as many ducks.

Mister Gilham and I left Dad and Mister Jack behind us in Cross Arms and seemingly being covered up with ducks. Out upon the vast reaches of Big Lake we swung toward Trexler's Corner and wavelets from the heavy north blow began slapping our prows. Through lifting haze we raised the brush blind and Aaron opined that the wind would probably blow a deal of water out of the Corner and leave us on the mud. But, somehow, there was water enough to float the decoys, and, in a jiffy, with all hands at work, the stool was spread. Predominantly pintails, the set was pear-shaped; with a lead-in out front, but the main set in back, to get the bunches well over us. Our flat-bottomed boats sat firmly upon the mud and with surrounding willow brush at just the right height to shoot standing. Thousands of birds streamed out of Trexler's as we poled in, only to return and try to light on us while putting out the blocks.

The Civil War had taken toll of Mister Gilham's right eye, but he had done a remarkable job of gun shifting to his left shoulder. His was a beautifully cool mount, and his swing revealed carefully coordinated value in barrel levels. All he ever said to me was—"You to the left, son, I'll take mine on the starboard out of respect to this blank peeper." I'll never forget that long-gone forenoon; the last of my youth on old Wapanoca. The disturbed sanctuary was bedlam in sonorous waterfowl cacophony, a wind-tossed living pall of wildlife curtaining off vision's half circle. From it, twisting tendrils of geese fought eastward toward the Mississippi's sand bars. Guns were already thudding to right and left of us and whistling sprigtails pitched in among our decoys like white, wind-driven slashes of sleet against murky clouds. Little did I ken that in the next three decades I would gun ninety percent of the continent's worthwhile wildfowling areas, but to this day, for its size, I have never seen waterfowl life as it used to be at Wapanoca.

Mister Gilham shot a Westley Richards double and was one of the coolest hands at a right-and-left I've ever known. Rarely did he ever fire at a duck or goose until he had it right where he wanted the load to be. Apparently impervious to excitement, due mayhap to both battle command and legal suavity under fire, he stood immobile and with that single piercing eye narrowed to match the hairline of reflex in trigger finger. I was firing with a thirty-two-inch solid-frame 1893 Model Winchester pump gun.

During the ensuing three hours Mister George Gilham and I were kept busy trying to decide which bunch of ducks over our stool had best be taken. From off the Big Lake's sanctuary a mingling of mallards or gadwalls would rise and buffet a way into the protection of Trexler's, see our spread and make but the one-circle maneuver before winging in on the wind for a light. Or, from over Little Lake and the timbered Cross Arms a cloud of voyaging, lilting sprig would suddenly fold and fall from the heights only to find themselves fouled by the mallards applying for seating space. Mister George was a careful, methodical wildfowler who got as much thrill from watching such a sight as I did out of gunning.

I had been force-broken to mind duck shooting's P's and Q's with my elders, with instructions from my father to never, when shooting with a member using a double, put more than two shells into my own pump gun. My attempts to sell him on the idea of at least three (one for a cripple) met "no sale." Said he—"I'll admit that when birds are scarce you can get your limit more readily, and if you're shooting alone what you use is your own business, but, in a blind with a gentleman using only two shots, check your vanity at the clubhouse, don't try to show off, much less ever give anyone the impression you're trying to beat him—nothing more clearly reveals hackles around one's ankles."

It was finally decided that we would try to bag only drake pintails. Just how many greenheads, Susies, gadwall, shoveler, scaup and teal pin-wheeled into and were "shooed" from our decoys, I hesitate to say. But I do know that no four wildfowlers ever enjoyed a more wonderful sight than did Mister George, Aaron, Osborn and I that glowering forenoon. The two colored men and I were to recall it twenty years later. Completely around the blind, white spots marked fallen birds, some half-buried in the mud. Several times Aaron and Osborn "counted up" and it was just a bit past eleven when Aaron, finishing a finger-checking tally, shouted, "les' quit t'well us picks up." Mister George and I squatted on our live-decoy coops while the boys waded behind the boats, shoving them across the muck and picking up both ducks and decoys as they went. The muddied birds were neatly wrung out and carefully stacked. There were eight mallards and ninety-two drake pintails split between the two boats.

Then it was that Mister George suggested going ashore on Trexler's ridge for coffee and lunch with a turkey hunt that afternoon for good luck. Osborn could use Mister George's second gun because, frankly, Mister George intended taking a snooze. Three-thirty would be the hour for starting clubward, providing the weather, which was thickening, didn't break up the expedition. Our boats were mucked out to paddling water and by noon we had a fire going in the big woods. What a primeval forest lay about us that rough afternoon some fifty years ago! Pristine turkey woods that could have been seedlings when Hernando de Soto crossed that very way three hundred and sixty years agone.

We lunched heartily and then, with Mister George lying amid our great coats and slickers with his head pillowed on a boat cushion and a long cigar drawing, Aaron and Osborn and I set forth for gobbler land. The great forest laid the wind somewhat but a break in the weather impended and the paddlers debated that turkey travels might be hurriedly off-schedule ahead of the cold or rain. "Us'll go to d' big cross-slough canebrake in behind'st number twelve blind," surmised Osborn. "Let Mist' Nash stay at d' haid o' d' brake—den you an' me—Aaron, us'll drap off first an' git on each side o' d' cane an' com' on thu'—I got an idea dem turkeys 'll be in d' cane an' outa d' wind dis time o' day—if dey bees, somebody'll git a shot at sumpn'." I knew that strip of tall cane like a book.

We split; Aaron and Osborn circling off to the left while I held on for a half mile to where I struck the brake's end toward the Big Lake. What a sight it was, out across the sanctuary. We'd had no geese into Trexler's that forenoon—the wind was strong and baffled them out of Little Lake and Price's. But now, by the thousand, they streamed in from the river and you could hardly hear for their din. At its lake end the brake narrowed to a fifty-yard width. Aaron and Osborn would be three hundred yards to my left, skulking either side of the cane with a pincers movement. It would all be just a matter of chance—either way—so I edged halfway across the barrier into waist-high switch cane. Alerted, I could shoot in either direction. A half hour dragged by and, a bit noddy, I sank to the leafy mold.

Two seconds later a shot down through the forest brought me up with a bound. Then another shot, and, off across the brake, two more—in quick succession. Coming up the brake clearing toward me was a fan of giant birds. My heart pounded and I sank into the stems. Suddenly the line of turkeys wheeled as though by command and swung toward Trexler's. Then I sighted a lone turkey—huge, bearded, with red-and-purple mottled head —holding to the bunch's original flight line and coming over me not thirty yards high. I led him like a slowing mallard and the impetus of his crash carried him into the cane fringe. In fact I all but caught him as he fell, and stood there winded by sheer excitement as the battering wings stilled in death.

Aaron had first flushed the bunch, killed a fine gobbler and spread part of the birds over Osborn for a double. My chance was sheer luck. We set off down the trail along the lake's shoreline of matted cypress. In single file and chatting, a sudden blare of goose alarm sent us whirling. They were silently skimming the stunted cypress, and saw us—too late. I was the only one loaded and two shots from the old Winchester dropped a fat goose.

The heavily laden boats shoved off under the exhilaration of happy hunters. I helped paddle down the Bayou with gratitude in my heart for a decade of days amid Wapanoca's joys. Hoping, too, that someday I'd see again those sunrises past the entrance to Big Lake. Nineteen years were to pass before I saw them, however; until father, like Mister George and Mister Arthur and many another of Wapanoca's Old Guard, had taken up his decoys for the last time and willed his membership certificate to me.

We gained the boathouse just as darkness closed down with a rush. "H'it'll be rainin' befo' mawnin'," prophesied both Aaron and Osborn, "d'wind's fixin' t' git roun' in d' souf' an' t'morrer us'll see dem ducks gangin' up, gittin' high an' leavin' d' laik—dey'll hav' d' wind on dey tails an' goodbye t'well nex' year." How right they were—those black children of Nature! For next day we witnessed a sight vouchsafed only to those who live closest to happenings amid the wilds. The wind had whipped around to the south and a gentle rain fell at intervals. The vast sanctuary was in turmoil as platoons, companies, divisions and corps of fowl circled to the stratosphere and bore northward. By nightfall not a corporal's guard of yesterday's mighty host roosted upon the broad waters.

We had a wonderful supper and evening that Washington's Birthday of 1901. Mister Arthur made a little talk and wished me well for the long road past "twenty-one." Thanking God for the likes of him, it has been so. I turned in with all my young gunner's plunder readied for the five-a.m. train, and a farewell handclasp with Aaron and Osborn. Lying in my favorite big bed that had refreshed my childhood and youth (and comforted many a bad miss), I could see Dad and Mister George Gilham sitting there talking in front of the dying embers. The clubroom was in darkness and flickering winks from the cavernous fireplace embossed them with a patina of endearment. All were abed save them.

A drowsy pause, and I heard father ask—"How does the boy shoot, George?"

Mister Gilham pondered. "He's coming along fine, Miles; he's observant and a first-rate judge of range. Not a fast shot yet, but a steady one."

Father remarked that by now I should be arriving.

Mr. Gilham added—"By the time you and I are ready to 'lay down the shovel and the hoe,' Miles, that boy will be ready to 'pick up the fiddle and the bow.'"

Dad remarked that I did a good deal of beauing-around now and was inclined to fiddle.

They chuckled and there was a long pause. Dad spoke.

"George, I'm constantly reminding my lads of how thoughtful all you fellows have been in helping them toward enjoyment of the outdoor life. My littlest fellow is on his way up and the older boys can pass such on to him."

Mister George Gilham thought awhile and said— "Keep the youngsters at their duck shooting; they could do worse."

Dad rose, patted Mister George on the shoulder and stepped toward the table for the toddy.

"Thank you, George," he said, "I shall. It's bedtime—may I fill your glass?"

Wapanoca's forests have fallen, concrete highways and gravel roads encircle its sparse rim of woods. Of all the group gathered there so happily that evening, I alone am left to tell of Wapanoca as it was.

How Come?

"How Come?" appeared only in Ole Miss'. *Hugh Evelyn Buckingham—Nash's "Cousin Ev" in the story—informs me that the hunt took place about 1930. Two guests Nash mentions were Burr Chapman and Lemmon Buckingham, Hugh's brother. "I know little about the origin of Lake Arthur Club," Hugh wrote, "but thought it the most deluxe club you could find anywhere. The clubhouse was a very large houseboat—practically no land, just canals and saw grass. It was so isolated they did not need to own acreage. I think our membership was twelve or fifteen, and you could bring guests. Wonderful service and food prepared by chefs from New Orleans. The guides were native Cajuns who certainly could bring the ducks in with their funny little homemade duck calls. I think Nash enjoyed this trip, especially stalking geese one day after he had finished his limit of ducks."*

"How Come?" is an inside glimpse of a plush duck club—the exotic houseboat, white-jacketed attendants, and, as always, Nash's preoccupation with gourmet food. Pre-dawn arisings, which would have crumpled an ordinary man of fifty, which he was then, but seemed to keep Mr. Buck in shape into his eighties, are described with affectionate attention.

Nash's flair for becoming friends with almost any man within minutes shows here in his relations with the Cajun guides, colorful foils to the usual Negro duck-boat paddlers.

In the episode with the raccoon—a beautifully touching passage—I discover evidence of empathy with game that I have not observed elsewhere in Nash's writing, as though in quarry he is not pursuing he can see tragedy in dying. The duck hawk (peregrine falcon) turns this strange inconsistency among us shooters into another perspective—that the other fellow, who is pursuing the same quarry as we, especially if he is of another species, is "the killer."

I am fond of this story because it shows up Mr. B. as human. No one grieved more deeply over a miss—in this case, a missed chance—which makes him one of us in a field where I, at least, have had fuller experience than he. And no gunner who has leaned into a recoil that wasn't there has not agonized through the memory of it, more than once, in the stillness of the night.

BURR, LEM AND I went to Lake Arthur as my cousin Evelyn's guests. The memory of it is a full spectrum of wildfowling emotions. An overnight ride from our homes in Memphis; several hours convivial gadding about in picturesque New Orleans with old friends, and a near-dusk detrainment far westward at Jennings, Louisiana. Thirty minutes via automobile landed us at Port Arthur, point of embarkation for the Club's palatial houseboat. Other arriving members and guests swelled our company to nine. Licenses were issued and baggage holed. After our captain-helmsman and his crew of two were aboard, twelve of us were sardined into the low-roofed cabin of a high-speed gasboat.

Booming thunder, jagged lightning and a high wind added nothing to that situation and by now, most of us realized that with thirty-five miles to voyage, we were facing an "out yonder" capable of maturing into an extremely sloppy business. Nineteen miles of tortuous channel until the storm's fury forced anchorage in the lee of a last lighthouse mainland. Sixteen miles of tossing lake ahead.

Then, abruptly, the lashing rain drew off. Puffy whorls sent fog scuds scurrying. Friendly stars twinkled apology. A timorous moon rose over the ribbonlike shore line, and suddenly we were off like a greyhound across untroubled waters. Winding lagoons eventually led us toward a glowing patch on the horizon. The clubhouse! Two hours overdue, we docked to relieve considerable apprehension. Welcoming hands! An open fireplace! Bright lights! Food and more of it! Drink and what of it! We were safe and whole again. To the duck hunter, danger past comes under the head of "old business."

Lake Arthur's clubhouse boat is moored to a small island cast away amid an apparently limitless vista of sere coastal marshland. What with the guides' home, boat sheds and servants' quarters, the beautifully landscaped outfit is a community for sport royal. At most duck clubs the "draw" for stands and pushers is an event. At Lake Arthur it is ceremony. Each guide rules an individual domain. Assignments of each day and "bags by species" are recorded in the club's game register. At the season's end their total "kill-by-species," together with all additional observations and data of value, is reported to the United States Bureau of Biological Survey at Washington, D. C. Such information, incidentally, should no longer be *asked for* cooperatively, but *required* from every duck club and commercial shooting resort in the country.

"Your guide tomorrow will be 'Joe,'" my old trapshooting friend, manager Bob Worsham, tells me after the draw, "and a fine lad he is, too. Coffee at three-thirty sharp. Buck—your duffel bag is up in the 'dorm'—grab a bed; you can't go wrong, they're all mighty good sleepin'." Rough-weather rubberalls, and other comfortable if odoriferous ducking duds, are piled handy. Alongside are stacked my favorite three-inch shells loaded with copper-coated fours. And towering close by is "Bo-Whoop," as Hal Sheldon dubs my ten-pound, overbored, Burt Becker twelve-bore Magnum.

White floodlights startle me awake. My wrist watch dots three-thirty. Grinning Granville, an ebon study against cook's frills, slippers into view via the stairhead. He offers us cups of stygian Louisiana "drip." Reluctance to desert Morpheus gets a kick in the pajama pants shortly after the first intakes of that rowdy fluid. The "dorm" becomes vigorously astir with cheerful salutations and matutinal tubbings. Shaved and in utter sartorial discord, we troop to the breakfast board. Jocose black boys thrust fresh "drip" before us; bend attentive ears and scuttle kitchenward flinging advance orders in chaotic patois. These reappear as *fruits en saison,* eggs *au beurre* something or other, girdles of bacon, and relays of thin patties with ribbon cane sweetening.

Finally, we nondescripts of the duck blinds are herded toward the boat-house. To the accompaniment of smoky lanterns, prying flashlights, inevitable "where's-where" and "who's-who," boat quotas are handed into shallow-draft motor craft; while balky engines gulp, Cajun invectives sputter, and caged live decoys writhe and squawk. A stocky, clean-cut chap locates me amid the confusion and grins as we shake hands—my guide, Joe. I hand over part of my equipment (habit forces us old-timers to hold onto gun) and follow him into a boat with two other sports going our general way. Someone spins a wheel; we clear the boathouse, and head out across a choppy bay. In the damp, inky chill a heavy coat is comfortable. The sky brims with stars. Grouped on the motor housing, our Cajun guides patter away in jerky marsh jargon. We gunners appraise the morning's prospects. Twenty minutes eases us into a pocket that narrows rapidly into a ribbon-like canal. Up this a piece we stop at a small planked dam, shutting off a ditch through the marsh wall. Joe bestirs himself. "Eef yu plees, M'sieu, we go obode heah—yu an' me—there—steady, M'sieu—das eet." We call "good luck" as the motor picks up and slips away around a bend.

Lifting our cockle shell of a pirogue across the barrier, we relaunch and effect a delicate entry. Shift your chewing gum or change your mind in a "pee-roog," and see what happens. The slit is not five feet wide and its few inches of water make tough poling for Joe. But we slide along as he puts arms and back into his crutch-ended prod pole. Our whole world is suddenly pulsing with the thrummings and rustlings of nomadic wildfowl life. There are distant roars from duck rafts. Nearby alarm calls are passed seaward and fade into the distance.

"Heah we are, M'sieu," Joe whispers. "We be right dere pritty queek." Joe pushes his pea-hull steadily ahead with his long paddle. A hundred yards of slog through matted growths, and I sense that a clump of "cut" grass showing up dead ahead is Joe's objective. Built into its center is a four-foot platform. Joe quickly arranges the stool to suit himself, stakes out three live callers, and hides his boat in an adjacent grass mat. The sun is about to crash a suffused East. Sinuous lines of ducks weave the horizons; wispy bundles high overhead burst into rocket-chaff. Their subdued chatter comes down to us. I cram a pair of shells into the big gun's breech and estimate yardage to a passing flock. "Too high, M'sieu," whispers Joe, "motch too haut." And Joe is right—this time.

"Almos' too bright t'day, M'sieu; de dox dey see longways—but maybe pritty soon som' foolish fellas com' 'long—ah! To de right, M'sieu—queek —I call dem." I've picked them up by now—eight lugging mallards, five drakes and three tagging hens. Joe claps his tiny cane call to his pursed lips, grunts a tune-up, and turns loose a hail, then switches abruptly to the "tuc-atuc-atuc" feeding chatter. Joe's talk is crudely unlike the almost too-perfect duck lingo of my native ponded tall timber. Sounds odd, but by Jove it works. My own Hooker duck call stays in my pocket while I listen intently to the other fellow's racket. From a distance, it must be nigh perfect in quality. Four of the mallards break sharply away and circle toward us. "Down, M'sieu," hisses Joe, "dey comin', sho'." He couldn't have "worked" them more satisfactorily. Letting the two lead birds light, I crumple a right and left above them. Carrying a third shell in the corner of my mouth is an old double-gun reloading trick—providing you can concentrate solely on shoving it into the gun before looking up to locate the third chance. But I manage it, and annex a third drake from the bewildered, leaping pair.

Joe is all smiles and enthusiasm. "Fine beeginnin' we mek, M'sieu, dose shots ver' fas'—pouf-pouf—*pouf*." He searches the reeds for my three ejected shells. "Deese hulls wid d' extra long brass ends—I ketch dem all when d' gun fly open—we use d' brass f' mek dock-call—yu see?" He shows me his own, fashioned simply but neatly from marsh cane, based with shotgun shell brass, and equipped (most important) with a reed filed from a rubber comb. Joe twigs out our three victims as decoys.

The sky is now rarely void of traveling waterfowl. An occasional goose note drifts our way. One moment our immediate vicinity is bare of ducks, while the next, one scarcely knows which shot to take first. The "limit" means merely making one's choice of species—mallards—teal—or what have you. Now Joe produces a jug of fragrant, hot *café au lait,* and over it we become better acquainted. He is exceptionally intelligent and well informed on regional wildfowl conditions. Comparatively young in years, Joe is an "old head" at the guiding and shooting business; born to it on an old farm down Grand-Chênier way. His eyes light with joy while we discuss respective home lives. There are the *grandpère* and Joe's blue-eyed baby daughter. "Bot," he adds, "eet ees so lon'lee whin I com' heah t' guide in de winter—lon'lee widout dem two, but, M'sieu, work ees work an' mo' monny f' take back—she ees so lov'lee, M'sieu—golden hair—t'ick lak d' moss—an' soch blue eyes—ah, M'sieu—so lov'lee." And I tell Joe I have such a one at home, too.

Before we know it, ten o'clock has drifted around, and ten a.m. at Lake Arthur means quitting time, limit or no limit. We start the long shove to our motorboat rendezvous. Ahead, on the ditch bank I sight a trapped raccoon intently watching our approach. Joe traps "partners" with Gabe D'Aquin on this particular sector. "Now, M'sieu," he grins, "I show yu how we dooes business wid d' coons. Regardez, M'sieu." Stepping gently from the pirogue, Joe snaps open a long-bladed, keen jackknife and approaches "Cooney." "Pauvre p'tit—d' lil garçon in Joe's trap—eh?" The glistening blade is whetted for an instant on Joe's palm. "But d' dollar ees d' monny, mon ami. Maintenant—regardez bien, M'sieu." The raccoon, a roly-poly fellow erect on his haunches, looks upon the proceedings with half-furtive belligerency. Joe fences with him, using a bit of cane switch to gradually elevate the animal's guard. Feint after feint. Black-fingered paws warding off pokes higher and higher! A few low snarls. Then—"Z-i-t." Straight down into Cooney's heart darts Joe's slender blade; an oft-practiced thrust so deft as to almost foil the eye. A look of wondering, agonized surprise leaps into the coon's troubled, stricken eyes. "Why," he seems to gasp, "why, fellows, I wasn't really mad at you—you've—you've—got me all wrong—you've—!" In exactly eleven seconds I count there, he is dead from the lethal stroke—and boated. We push along, and Joe whistles. "Mo' monny, M'sieu!" And why not? Toll of life in the great marsh, and at that a merciful end, far better than shooting or battering. Just another coonskin coat for some campus waster.

Good luck has attended each of our party's efforts. And such a lunch when we have napped, tubbed and tidied. Peeled duck gizzards with gravy in a sizzling curry; mallard breasts grilled, sauced fish cutlets and fresh vegetables. Then, following renewed siesta, Evelyn and I put in an afternoon of furious sport with fly rods and big-mouth bass. The sun rims the sedge as we paddle from a chain of lakes down to the main canal.

I am drawn next morning with Emory, a husky Cajun, whose shooting is noted for canvasback flights. Our motorboat drives breakneck into and through a long, narrow chute; skidding corners and cutting across wide lakes. Some higher intelligence seems to guide and guard our destinies. Emory deposits me at the very tip of a grassy point, hides the gasboat and returns in the pirogue. I sit in near reverie as another grand day is born.

"Voilà," explodes Emory, "vite, M'sieu!" I wheel to see a bunch of cans flaring off the stools. I catch up with them a bit tardily—for all save a tail-ender. Emory peeps through the rushy rampart and points a questioning finger waterward. "Heem—daid?" One must converse somehow. "Oui, mon Emory—là bas—bien mort." My towering friend grins widely—"A-h-h-h —s-o-o-o—on parle français—oui?" Torrential Cajun. I've let myself in for it now. "Un peu, mon Emory, très peu!" But I am saved immediate exposure. A mass of birds slithers suddenly among the shadows. Teal—by Jove! Follows a rush of cans, with just enough wait in between shots. I slice down a tall voyageur, and, getting cocky, ingloriously muff an easy decoy shot. Considerable questionable conversational French that somehow gets by on my part. A good scout, Emory.

Again the motor craft reunion and luncheon that overtempts one. A crab gumbo, broiled snipe, and a challenging array of side dishes. After the inevitable nap, we cousins unlimber twenty-bores and fill our pockets with snipe loads. A short run across the bay and we tie up at quite a chênier. With Emory to help retrieve, I go my way and skirt a damp palmetto patch. Distant shots begin mingling with my own. What a bird dog this Emory. Cattle have gashed the soft soil and frequently a double on the long-bills sends the birds headfirst into hoof holes. But the gigantic, black-haired Cajun's eyes dart from bird to bird unhesitatingly. The circle of a mile or so is all that is required for a limit of the snipe. And along with a lowering sun we chug peacefully home to the houseboat.

That evening Evelyn makes the "draw" for which he has been hoping, so, with characteristic generosity on my kinsman's part, I am turned over to Adler, a springy, well-knit Cajun of about my own age. His is a merry smile and happy disposition. His territory is far distant, but noted for its chances at both blue and Canada geese. It is still pitch dark when Adler and I tie his gasboat at the end of a long canal and clamber over into the marsh. Salt air from the sea is almost like vapor in our nostrils. A full mile of "mud-planing" lies ahead, so two push faster than one. The coastal pampas suddenly level off into a series of meandering ponds, and these, in turn, widen into grass-splotched spreads. Distantly disturbed geese swell the chorus of departing ducks. "This," I say to myself, "is just about the finest gunning lay I've clapped my eyes on in many a moon."

We round a grassy point and slosh in among some scattered wooden decoys; this is the set. The boat is lifted into a clump, and shooting preparations oriented. How many hours of my life, I wonder, have I passed in such reedy nooks? A bit of rest while we swig the inevitable *café au lait*—and plenty of it. I load my gun and look about. Plenty of high birds crossing, but why gamble at this stage? Unlimbering his call, Adler does some throat-clearing and note-fingering before cutting loose an alluring overture of the marsh.

Two sailing mallards, well to our left, dip at the hail and sweep toward us just as the rule book says. But one of them suddenly veers and climbs for dear life. Gets away with it, too. As for his buddy, a storm of fours clips him and he lies "tummy up" with his pink toes going gradually out of control. Adler is still offering congratulations when a flash of color slants from above and a wary duck hawk drifts into focus. Evidently he likes the look of our peaceful live decoys. Watch this fellow; he is a killer! He circles cagily; a few lazy turns to satisfy himself that the coast is clear. A bit of a rise and dip to one side for favorable air; then down he knifes with plummeting velocity. Decoys scream and tug at their tethers. Poised for a kill, shins extend, hackles fluff in the sunlight, and razored talons are hair-triggered. The big gun bellows and atop a lily-pad hummock, Mr. Hawk crumples to a well-merited end.

Forty minutes later Adler and I have become buddies; who wouldn't with this infectious, hard-working fellow. "I t'ink now, ol' fren', I mek peek-up, we got mebbe few mo' t' git—not manny do'h—you stay—pretty soon we tek mo' coffee." But I'm hunting exercise by now, and clamber after Adler. Final count shows three ducks needed, but these are soon added. Adler grins as he uncorks the thermos. Meanwhile, far behind us and seaward, gabbling geese have been trading—trading—drifting at times almost within good gunshot. There must be some way to get at them. A wave of talking Canadas rises from the concentration, circles enticingly and resettles something over a quarter mile away. Adler watches them down hungrily.

"Manny ol' goose ovah dere now—by golly—yaas, suh!"

"Adler," I query, "why can't you and I wade over yonder?"

Adler sizes me up about the waistband. "By golly, ol' fren', you tink you kin mebbe pool troo d' mod—meks d' laigs ache—long way—ol' fren'—but you ain' got hardly no belly—no?—an' we needs d' gooses mighty bad —yaas?—so by golly damn yaas—le's go."

The stalk begins. Adler threads a careful lead from clump to clump. "Tek yo' time, ol' fren'," he tosses over stooped shoulders, "go vairee easy—lak meester mink—I ve'y motch lak knock d' socks plum off beeg gooses dees treep." Compared to some wading I've done through Arkansas "no-bottoms" and boggy elbow brush, this stretch isn't half bad. But it'll be no pushover before the final gong, at that. Gradually we near the marked landing sector of that last big bunch. Like a warpath Indian, Adler skulks from vantage to shelter. Every vestige of cover is utilized. Suddenly, stiff as a pointer on quail, his eyes turn to mine as his lips frame an appeal for extra caution. A nod that spells—"just ahead."

Bent double, I twist in front of him and a bit to one side. We can hear them now—wing flaps, "twits" and an occasional gurgle of discord. Adler whistles shrilly and upward leaps a dinning black cloud. Toward its middle and climbing with one certain black neck, swing the big gun's tubes, sub-consciously toward the touch-off. Just how many will fall to this pair of shots? I lean into the weapon's recoil—a shade higher—*Now!* Then I all but plunge headlong into the muck, a victim of the most awful realization that can stab a laboring wildfowler to the heart. A sharp, hollow "snap-snap"—both barrels—*unloaded!*

Oh, shame! Oh, alibis! Where are you now, in this my moment of agony and hour of high need? And to pull one like this on good Adler—there behind me—looking pitifully on! This is bitter—bitter! Fading goose "razzberries" pierce me like red-hot needles. Utter chagrin and one sickly swallow after another. To miss when one's time comes is bad enough; but this other business—this—this! But as my crestfallen eyes meet Adler's, something in them explodes. Face wreathed in smiles, he claps me on the back. "Why—nev' mind, ol' fren'—you know one tame las' wintah I mek moch longer walk—oh! by golly yaas—ver' moch longer—an' den I dooes de same damn t'ing—just' too bad do'h—I say t'm'se'f—Adler—I bet ol' fren' ruins dem gooses—an' now—by golly—damn—look at dem fellahs." On pour the fine fellow's consolations during my long, sweaty silence. How intolerably hot the marsh has grown. Or maybe it's my red face? But Adler's merry one brings me to life. "Well—com' on—les' git goin', ol' fren'—by

golly—hell dem ain d' onles' gooses in d' worl'—les' mek walk aroun'
awhile—we fool dem fellahs som' mo'—but—" (and this time his eyes
exploded again) "—dees tame plees load d' gun."

We potter aimlessly about the marsh. Not a goose note in the air. All
I can do will be to tell the funny story and go into the routine. Then, just
as even stout-hearted Adler is about willing to call it a morning, comes the
break. A hiss—"Down—down queek—dey com'—in behin'." I collapse
against the base of a friendly grass bunch. There they are—seven of them—
low and straight over us if they hold their line. Wait just three beats more—
if you slobber this chance, Big Boy, why start running. Chug! Wham! One
snaky neck sent sprawling. A second down! Then, completely off-balance
and overly excited, I let nature take its course and sit down in the mud and
water. Feels good, too. Who cares? Adler is rejuvenated as he collects that
pair. "By golly-damn, ol' fren'—didn' Adler tell you—didn' he say giv' d'
ol' fren' tame—das whut I say—jus' giv' d' ol' fren' tame—he git 'em."

Catching breath, we plunge along the home stretch. Within a hundred
yards a second warning from the alert Adler announces another trading
squad of honkers. Determined to make amends, the gun overlaps two long,
skinny black necks and then, swinging, downs a badly scared lunker standing
practically still in midair. We divide the load and stagger onward. Who
cares now for a soupy underfoot and heavy gun? What if it was all *my*
fault? It is a good story *now*. What matters anything when Old Man General
Average and Lady Luck decide to come on the party—arm in arm? Sweating
and garlanded with geese we tumble into the pirogue. Stripped to the buff
we bathe and let the wind do towel duty. We toast the finale in drafts of
"drip."

"By golly-damn, o' fren'," chortles Adler, gesturing a soggy bandanna
flamboyantly at a conquered goose land, "by golly-damn jus' giv' me an' ol'
fren' plenny tame—us gits d' gooses." But, somewhere, stretched at ease and
grateful for that face-saving break, I know full well that I shall endure many
wakeful hours, looking along those empty gun tubes, dying a thousand
deaths, while still wonderingly vaguely—how-th'-*hell?*

Jump-Shooting's Joys

I was surprised to learn from Berry Brooks that in 1950 Nash was planning to bring out a book entitled The Joys of Jump-Shooting, *which would probably have included this as the title story. It had been published first in* The American Rifleman, *January 1948, but did not appear again until 1961, in the Nelson edition* De Shootin'est Gent'man and Other Hunting Tales. *This is an effective manual for this form of duck shooting. To the lay gunner, the duck-shooting scene is a Frank Benson painting—coastal marshes, a string of ducks under clotted clouds backlit with a dull-rose dawn, decoys, a wildfowler in a blind. The concept of shooting ducks from a boat pushed through flooded woods is an unfamiliar experience even to men who have jump-shot mallards from woods holes and beaver dams. As Nash makes clear, it is often fast shooting at glimpses of overhead birds shimmering above tree tops, or at other times at near-vertical rises off an explosion of water.*

I enjoy the closeness of gunner and retriever here and am puzzled, in spite of the efficiency of Horace and Aaron and Jackson Bounds in "picking up," that retrievers were not mentioned in more of the shooting at Beaver Dam and Wapanoca.

Jackson's warning to the young Nash in this story to "watch for water shakin" is picture-making—the ripples through the brush stems, disturbing reflections of overhead trees, even the ducks you can only hear. Nash's mature suggestions as to how to approach unseen feeding wildfowl are the product of the experience of years.

His advice as to guns was always "send a man, not a boy," and after his early shooting with a ten-gauge, he almost always shot twelve-gauge guns on all game. Discussing loads in the next-to-last paragraph, he mentions his favorite ounce and three-eighths of number fours. His shooting friend Bob Anderson corroborates this: "He would only shoot Super X 1⅜ oz. of Lubaloy 4's on waterfowl. Never that silly 1⅞ load. I helped him pattern his second Becker. At 40 yards in a thirty-inch circle, that gun shot 91% in the left barrel and 93% in the right! No wonder he was called the finest long-range shot in the country."

As Nash grew older, I noticed an increasing mention of misses, and I wonder if this was a viewing of the limitations of sight due to the aging process—it comes to every man—or simply a more realistic assessment of shooting, not present in his early writing.

I FIRST WENT JUMP-SHOOTING with my father and club keeper Jackson Bounds in 1891 at Beaver Dam. To start me off right that first morning in the fourteen-foot, double-ender duck boat in the South End trails, Jackson said, "Always keep the muzzle of your gun over and outside the boat's rail—if it goes off accidentally, you don't tear up anything and maybe get sunk. Try not to talk but mighty little while we're jump-shooting. When we're in the trails watch close an' keep your eyes shiftin' an' low as far as you can see through and under the brush. If you notice the water shakin' ahead or off to the sides, somethin' is fixin' to flush."

The jump-shooter, alone or companioned, afoot or afloat, with or without a retriever, should bear in mind the sport's fundamental vigilance. A careless footfall may see lost opportunity, for wildfowl lurk and linger in the oddest of spots and I have turned many a thoroughly unpromising flight day into ample reward in fun and birds by drifting ghostlike through byways of marsh, lake or rising waters along switch-willowed beds of "Ole Miss." Many a day, after moonlit feeding nights and bluebird weather, I have watched thousands of ducks leave an inland lake at the first gun pop. Shorn of prospects, I've either taken a cruise that bagged stragglers here and there, or followed the flight to distant rising rivers and pin-oak flats that could be sneaked afoot.

A twelve- or fourteen-foot, double-pointed, low-raked boat of the old Dan Kidney type, painted a smudged dead black with brown and gray stripes, inside and out, was the best craft for jump-shooting in the old days. But today the twelve-foot Alumacraft Lifetimer Ducker is even lighter and handles easily in weaving through watered forest aisles. Mine has been in use since the mid-'40s; and, well cared for, is as sound as the day it was launched. It can be stobbed down fore and aft if need be, and, for prying through brush and sedges to retrieve, it saves many a push-around and much heave-ho. When jump-shooting with my big Chesapeake Bay dog, Buck, I never forget to make haste slowly while following the admonitions of Jackson Bounds—to listen carefully. And if you think a veteran retriever doesn't duplicate your moods—you haven't your degree in the game's finer arts. Many a time, Pat, Baltimore, Peake or Buck, perched on the forward deck with ears a-cock, would turn their heads, give me a solemn blink and all but ask—"Hear that—over yonderways?" My ears aren't that good any more, but they were then, and between us, my Chesapeakes and I used to get a lot of ducks in trouble.

Remember well Jackson's warning to "watch for water shakin'." And the same, he warned me, could apply to one's own boat. Fowl catch a prow riffle or the scrape of a bush a long way. If in current, let the boat drift and trust to clear steering. If in still water not more than paddle-blade-deep, utilize the bottom for noiseless shoves along rather than paddle dips. But if in deeper water, paddle on the same side, no matter how slow the progress. When jump-shooting with my dogs, or alone, I sit with cocked gun across my knees and the paddle tied to the boat with a strong cord. When ducks flush, I simply drop the paddle, snatch up the gun, and go into action. There is no time for lost motion.

Rising water backs into many a shallow flat made to order for hungry ducks, and when well fed, like human beings, they have a way of getting drowsy and careless—and your boat becomes merely some old log drifting into their lagoon. On entering an area of pin-oak flats afoot, size up as carefully as possible the directional trends of its ridges, which, although water-covered or nearly so, may afford wading in comparative safety from "step-offs." And when wading, cut yourself an alpenstock and "shuffle-the-bottom." Take it easy. You stay topside and dry longer.

If ducks are scarce, begin looking in areas where instinct tells the birds they'll be less disturbed. Always stop and listen while sizing up your stalk. There may be a lot of ducks banked in somewhere. Figure the wind and investigate carefully. The more fowl there are, the easier your approach; for unless there are scattered spies out, the duck raft's own feeding rumpus will drown your sneak. Sometimes, by listening carefully, you can get a good idea of the raft's spread. In any case, when sprung—it'll be against the wind.

Never "bust in" on such a situation, firing as you go. After risking a too-far shot at a rise of stragglers, you may find yourself watching several hundred mallards take wing from well beyond in the thickets. If you have heard the "feeding murmur" previously, move in but hold your fire. They'll circle you probably, but if they sweep across, let 'em have it. Then make your kill out of the big rise, which should not be difficult in these days of extremely low bag limits.

If you have a shooting companion, the situation is far less complex. Size up the situation, leave the boat and wade a pincers movement. Correctly applied, this results in a tremendous scatteration when both guns chime in. But with ducks fanning out in all directions, be careful about reckless firing at cripples—you may pepper your partner. And, above all, take your time and shoot coolly and carefully. Pick your birds.

With bag limits having declined from twenty-five to four ducks a day—even three in some states—the thrill of jump-shooting can be stretched over longer periods daily. An example happened to us during the early days of World War II. With Captain George Blagden, we made a two-day hunt at the Section 16 Club's pin-oak flats along Bayou Lagrue near Clarendon, Arkansas. Captain Blagden, who shortly thereafter was to know some good jump-shooting along German waterways during the Occupation, likes to ramble swamps and take his game as he finds it. By early afternoon of our second day we lacked but eight mallards of the number George could legally take to Camp Knox that night. So, we decided to gamble. The water in Bayou Lagrue was deep and swift, overrunning its banks and shoving sluic-ings into innumerable "guts." Except at some U turns, the sun was mostly at our backs. The suck was pretty fast, so my job was comparatively easy. A half mile from the landing we were only two mallards shy, and, had I been of a mind to shoot, we could have bagged two additional limits between us. There came a sharp elbow bend and off it, I knew, spread a long, shallow inlet ringed with high timber and low cane. Above it, I measured the sun-light accurately, held onto a tree and peeped along surface glare dappling the amber gush. That smallish cutoff was literally crawling with mallards, totally unconscious of danger less than twenty-five yards away. We hung on for several moments enjoying the sight. We whisperingly discussed leaving them, but the Captain had duck-eating obligations among an array of Top Brass, so it had to be. This might be his last chance to fill the quota, so, when they boiled out in wildest disarray, he bowled over a pair of green-heads—and that was it. And that raises yet another point as to jump-shooting.

It used to be when two of us had parted to clap a pincers movement on rafted ducks off a trail, back in the days when limits were larger, we deliber-ately passed up the first few overheads if we had sighted plenty of fowl in behind them. In that way we let many ducks fan out ahead of us and relight farther on down the swamp. In fact, we waited for them to do so before moving in on the big spread. We then operated on the big bunch. Had we begun firing on the first ones breaking out, we might have shot the entire outfit out of the area. If you want to make a big kill, never "shoot up" a

big raft in such seclusion. Simply ease them out—no shooting—then make
your set of decoys—and before long they'll come drifting back in small
bunches.

Some of the finest jump-shooting I have ever enjoyed has been along
creeks winding through meadowed valleys from Colorado to Saskatchewan
and Manitoba. And the more unknown one's territory ahead, the more
thrilling the gunning's suspense. Here, the services of a well-broken retriever, even a good setter or pointer that will "hit the water," are simply
beyond estimate. Such gun dogs come to realize the occasion's problems
and become acutely responsive to hand signals. Sneaking creek bends, I
have put my dog at "sit," cut across a bend and then signaled him to make
the flush. I recall two situations along a meandering Saskatchewan creek
when Edgar Queeny's gorgeous setter, Wingmead Billy, and I left off shooting Huns and sharp-tails to bag a limit of jump-shot ducks. No full-fledged
waterdog could have outdone Billy that morning.

The importance of a retriever in jump-shooting is little short of inestim-
able. When either "bank walking" or from a boat, the hunter can leave
the first fall to the dog and center his attention on the second kill, particularly if the current is swift and the second hit be crippled. After delivery
of the first fetch, you are in position to keep contact and give your dog the
line. In jump-shooting give your dog its own initiative under the sport's
circumstances. Let him break to the first fall. Working from a boat, give
your dog all the help you can and don't expect to not get wet when he
shakes water off himself. What the hell? Jump-shooting is one phase of
wildfowling during which no rules apply. And amazingly, many times the
dog outthinks and outperforms his boss.

As to tactics afoot in jump-shooting let me cite a day when Robert
Anderson, a great game shot and photographer, and I, with General L.W.T.
Waller, were shooting in tall timber along Bayou Lagrue, Arkansas. After
establishing Bob and the General at the Brooks Blind, Eddie Hackleton,
our superintendent, and I paddled up the bayou to locate a concentration
and spread it. It was a warm, bluebirdish forenoon but with a hint of
cloud-up in the offing. Eddie and I moved quite a few ducks, but as several
of the other club blinds were occupied, we let them alone and set out to
cross a ridge and explore headwater shallows of another bayou. Suddenly,
Eddie halted and held up a warning hand.

"Hear 'em?" We crouched in the sedges. "There's a slug of 'em in yonder," Eddie whispered. "You ease down yonder into th' wadin' water along
Cook's. I'll wait until I hear you whistle an' know you're all set—then I'll

move on aroun' to th' left an' start proddin' at 'em right easy." Eddie hadn't spent a lifetime along the Bayou Lagrue without knowing techniques of jump-shooting. "I'll try to scare out a bunch or two at a time—when you're through, we'll run'em all out to scatter over as far as Turner's."

I'd hear faintly—a rise. And in a few moments here would come anywhere from a pair to half a dozen mallards floating easily overhead. In less than twenty minutes I had seven birds. Then I heard Eddie shooting and I knew that he not only had his limit, but had started the big outpour. I heard a roar and overhead went probably a thousand mallards clamoring about being disturbed. We heard Bob and the General opening up briskly, and by the time we rejoined them they had their limits, too. A novice wildfowler could get a liberal education watching Eddie Hackleton wading wet woods to sneak concentrated ducks. He never walks through calf-deep water. He just seems to glide from tree to tree and bush to bush without lifting his feet above water; he wades too squirmingly to even trip.

Jump-shooting from a moving boat or walking-up ducks in tall timber is the most physically difficult of all wing shooting; yardage calculations vary with practically every shot and change in the twinkling of an eye. An opening through which you planned to fire may be suddenly obscured by the boat's swing and demand a long try and more forward allowance. Drifting downstream, even with an expert pusher, a too-low boat seat without a back rest can make a sucker out of the best shot in the world. For, believe me, contrary to all popular belief, they all miss 'em somewhere along the line. As long as ducks flush, tower and cross out evenly ahead, it is not too difficult for control of elevations and leads. But when hemmed up or fenced in button willows along a narrowish lagoon, ducks have a way of driving straight at the gun. This is especially true of river ducks with low take-offs. Coming at you head on, there occurs a necessary leanback that overbalances and ofttimes causes a red face. When boat jump-shooting, try to provide a back rest. A couple of sacks of decoys will provide one—in case.

The best gun and loads for jump-shooting? The sport calls for the fastest eye estimate of gun yardage and forward allowance known to wing shooting. Remember that. Easy chances flog from the willows and you can almost take your pick—at times. But next time—in a flash—distance may cause indecision. In decoy, flight, or pass shooting there are elements of warning to control gun swing and stability. But in jump-shooting the element of surprise is almost always present. I've seen many duck hunters, otherwise pretty good shots, score sad averages at jump-shooting. So, approaching the gun and load problem, the most important suggestion I can give here is don't ever go jump-shooting *undergunned*. Jump-shooting's errands call for men —not boys.

True, a stiffly loaded twenty-gauge will do if you'll take it easy, use good judgment and not try to strain the weapon. The same goes for a properly estimated chance with a sixteen-gauge. But for general, all-around duck shooting, full-choked maximum charges of big shot is the most useful and desirable combination. A twelve-gauge using three-inch cases lends an extra margin. For many years I have used a ten-pound, thirty-two-inch Becker magnum, bored to handle an ounce and three eighths of fours coppered, ahead of four drams of powder. The two-and-three-quarter-inch magnums (twelve-bore) packing an ounce and a half of fours coppered, are just about as effective. The use of fours is suggested because game falls hardest hit from absorbed energy. Many a mallard jump-shot at a true fifty yards will take the absorbed energy of a six and keep going. But, shocked by a four, it will come down unless the wound is trivial.

If any areas you visit to gun wildfowl provide opportunity for jump-shooting, have a go at it. Big-game hunting's major thrill is in the trophy's stalk and measuring it off for the kill. No one appreciates that better than the goose hunter who has slithered on his belly through muddy switch willows and then leaped to his feet to score a killing right and left. Or longed for death as affrighted honkers soar away unscathed. I particularly recommend a try at jump-shooting to those duck hunters who lazily idle away a day in a comfortable blind, too unwise or apathetic to get out and hustle.

De Shootinest Gent'man

Nash's most famous story has had a long and glorious career.

1916: First published in Casper Whitney's magazine Recreation, *where the editor, Edward Cave, bought it for $75, a good fee at that time for an unknown writer.*

1927: Reprinted in the first combined issue of Outdoor Life & Recreation.

1930: Used in the anthology Classics of the American Shooting Field *by John C. Phillips (president of American Wildfowlers) and Dr. Hill; 150 copies signed by Phillips, Hill and the artist Frank Benson; also a regular edition.*

Between 1930 and 1934: Used in a gunning anthology by Harry McGuire (son of the owner of Outdoor Life).

1934: Derrydale edition of De Shootinest Gent'man; *950 copies.*

1941: Scribner's edition of the single story, De Shootinest Gent'man; *small issue.*

1943: Putnam edition, De Shootinest Gent'man.

1961: Nelson collection, De Shootin'est Gent'man and Other Hunting Tales; *260 copies signed; also regular edition.*

In Wild Fowl Decoys, *1934, Joel Barber mentions a "Windward House" edition of* De Shootinest Gent'man *that I have been unable to locate.*

Finally, I was presented with a taped recording of "De Shootinest Gent'man," read in 1965 by Robert Reaves of Manning, North Carolina.

Few writers have had a story published when they were thirty-six, used again when they were forty-seven, fifty, about fifty-two, fifty-four, sixty-one, sixty-three, and eighty-one. If "De Shootinest Gent'man" is a true story—and who would doubt it any more than the existence of Lady Luck and the Happy Hunting— then Nash Buckingham has Horace to thank not only for his best title (among some great ones) but for his immortality as a writer. It is by this story that Nash is known to eighty percent of his readers, many of whom think subliminally of Nash, not Mr. Money, as "De Shootinest Gent'man."

Like other stories in that first Derrydale collection, this was written during a period of Nash's life when that rich flow of Buckingham narrative was bursting to pour out under the pressure of his prime gunning years in an environment stiff with game and abounding with opportunity to shoot. Nash being Nash, the story would have to open with Molly's goose stew recipe. Irma Buckingham Witt describes Horace's helpmeet Molly as "the original five-by-five, and, oh, how she could cook up 'vittles'!"

The club is Beaver Dam, identified by Horace's presence and by the "Han'-werker" blind. "The Judge"—James M. Greer—was a charter member of Beaver Dam.

Horace, as Horace always does, approaches perfection. Old photographs show him medium in height, not heavy, with full mustache, dressed not in hunting clothes, other than a shooting coat, but always wearing a vest, frequently a long overcoat, almost invariably a felt hat. But to see him you need no picture other than Nash's words and Horace's mellifluous expressions. I came across a letter to Nash from his literary agent, relaying the opinion of an editor that Nash should simplify the Negro dialect in a certain story. I'll wager Nash's reply was: "But that is what he said!" Horace's difficulty with Harold Money's British accent—so "queer an' brief lak"—and his wistful contemplation of "dat ole big bottle wid de gol' haid" are painted from life.

If Uncle Tomism in this story—and it is there—is objectionable, try to view a parallel situation with a French Canadian or a Swede guide with a weakness for a bottle. I certainly object to placing any man, whatever his race, in the position of a dog performing for a biscuit, and to try to brush it aside because it is funny doesn't work. But the story is so real I end up accepting it simply as what happened.

The legendary Captain Harold Money turns up sporadically in shooters' conversations, especially in the East and South. Nash wrote the story in 1916, but according to his inscription on a photograph it took place in 1908. In his files I found a copy of a letter in which he wrote in 1954 about Harold Money:

Harold Money, younger son of an old and honored British family, came to this country with his father, Capt. E. C. Money, who produced the earliest smokeless powders. They were a wonderful pair. Harold first attracted attention by winning the famous Carteret Handicap at live birds in the East and went on to become a professional exhibition shot for the old Winchester Repeating Arms Co. For several years his ratings head many lists.

When the circuits closed he'd come here to Memphis during the winter to enjoy the duck club life. If there was ever a better all-around game shot, plus unselfish, gentlemanly spirit that endeared him to all, I have yet to meet him. I shot with Harold for many years, until 1908, when he returned to England.

Brilliantly educated, he was as much at home in an Indian wicki-up as at the court of St. James. From Ceylon he rushed into World War I. Years later, he returned to America and was with Abercrombie & Fitch in New York. He married the widow of the late Douglas Franchot and they retired to a lovely home on the Severn near Annapolis. He contracted pneumonia in the Adirondack Mountains two years later and passed on.

John Olin described Harold Money to me as he saw him first in 1913, after John had left Cornell and was working at his father's Western Cartridge plant at East Alton, Illinois:

"Money was tall—six feet four or five—and he had been loading and handling the Velox smokeless powder, which we obtained from his father. It was made with picric acid and he was as yellow as a Chinaman."

A faded photograph in Nash's collection shows Harold Money beside a horse in a sedge field, fondling the ears of a pointer standing with its forepaws on Money's waist; he is wearing a tweed cap and a shooting coat, and his celebrated Winchester Model 97 is in the crook of his right arm. The photo is inscribed in Nash's writing: "Capt. Harold Money, champion gunner and ace sniper in W.W.I, home on a brief vacation. A dear friend."

Describing a live-pigeon match at Rogers Springs, Tennessee, in January 1910, Nash wrote: "I was shooting Harold Money's marvelously choked 1897-model Winchester trap gun that he left with me when he returned to England in 1908." (Nash won the shoot-off with thirty-three straight at thirty-five yards.)

Nash told John Bailey he had met Harold Money about 1905. "Nash told me," John said, "that Money was a superb shot on any kind of game except a quail covey rise. Said he was death on singles but the covey rise always troubled him." (Horace should have been there then.)

Next to his role in "De Shootinest Gent'man," Captain Harold Money was probably best known as a trap shot and third as a personality in Abercrombie & Fitch's gun department. Charles Wicks wrote me:

I worked with Harold Money for a number of years. He came with Abercrombie & Fitch in 1926 or '27. He was typically English, a meticulous dresser and always appeared as if he were scrubbed clean. He was a wonderful mixer, well mannered and liked by everybody. He liked to drink and I think he made bathtub gin and usually had a bottle hidden somewhere in the department, but he never was drunk although the aroma followed him.

He represented A&F at various shoots, New York Athletic Club, etc. and always shot his old Winchester M/97. Why, I do not know (I had expressed surprise that an Englishman did not shoot a double) only that he was a wonderful shot and apparently the M/97 was the gun for him. He told me that he never cleaned it outside of wiping it off. He said that the dirtier the barrel got, the tighter it shot.

Money was a friend of the old actor, Fred Stone, who did quite some shooting himself. Abercrombie & Fitch merged with Von Lengerke & Detmold in 1929 and Money was still with A&F. He was a good friend of a very wealthy man by the name of Franchot—I do not recall his first name. Franchot died and Money married the widow, I think in 1930. After this he did not have to work. They had a big place as I remember in Tulsa, Oklahoma and a summer residence in the Adirondacks. Whenever he was in New York we had lunch together. I do not know when he died but think it was not long after he married. I would guess he was in his 60's.

Nash placed Harold Money's age at one year older than his own. The photo-graph in De Shootinest Gent'man *shows him as suave, with dark hair gray at the temples, mixed-gray mustache and heavy eyebrows, whimsical mouth, somewhat large British nose, a shooter's gray eyes, a cigarette in a hand that had never worked, and an easy manner evident through the camera. His father, Captain E. C. Money, should not be confused with Captain A. W. Money, a live-bird shot who wrote* Pigeon Shooting *in 1896 under the pseudonym "Blue Rock."*

As God made ducks and Horace, here is the story that made Nash Buckingham.

SUPPER WAS A delicious memory. In the matter of a certain goose stew, Aunt Molly had fairly outdone herself. And we, in turn, had jolly well done her out of practically all the goose. It may not come amiss to explain frankly and above board the entire transaction with reference to said goose. Its breast had been deftly detached, lightly grilled and sliced into ordinary "mouth-size" portions. The remainder of the dismembered bird, back, limbs and all parts of the first part thereunto pertaining, were put into an iron pot. Keeping company with the martyred fowl, in due proportion of culinary wizardry, were sundry bell peppers, two cans of mock turtle soup, diced roast pork, scrambled ham rinds, peas, potatoes, some corn and dried garden okra, shredded onions, and pretty much anything and every-thing that Molly had lying loose around her kitchen. This stew, served right royally, and attended by outriders of "cracklin bread," was flanked by a man-at-arms in the form of a saucily flavored brown gravy. I recall a side dish of broiled teal and some country puddin' with ginger pour-over, but merely mention these in passing.

So the Judge and I, in rare good humor (I forgot to add that there had been a dusty bottle of the Judge's famous port), as becomes sportsmen blessed with a perfect day's imperfect duck shooting, had discussed each individual bird brought to bag, with reasons, pro and con, why an unde-niably large quota had escaped uninjured. We bordered upon that inde-cisive moment when bedtime should be imminent, were it not for the delightful trouble of getting started in that direction. As I recollect it, ruminating upon our sumptuous repast, the Judge had just countered my remark that I had never gotten enough hot turkey hash and beaten biscuits, by stating decisively that his craving for smothered quail remained inviolate, when the door opened softly and in slid "Ho'ace"! He had come, following a custom of many years, to take final breakfast instructions before packing the embers in "Steamboat Bill," the stove, and dousing our glim.

Seeing upon the center table, t'wixt the Judge and me, a bottle and the unmistakable ingredients and tools of the former's ironclad rule for a hunter's nightcap, Ho'ace paused in embarrassed hesitation and seated himself quickly upon an empty shell case. His attitude was a cross between that of a timid gazelle scenting danger and a wary hunter sighting game and effacing himself gently from the landscape.

Long experience in the imperative issue of securing an invitation to "get his'n" had taught Ho'ace that it were ever best to appear humbly disinterested and thoroughly foreign to the subject until negotiations, if need be even much later, were opened with him directly or indirectly. With old-time members he steered along the above lines. But with newer ones or their uninitiated guests, he believed in quicker campaigning, or, conditions warranting, higher-pressure sales methods. The Judge, reaching for the sugar bowl, mixed his sweetening water with adroit twirl and careful scrutiny as to texture; fastening upon Ho'ace meanwhile a melting look of liquid mercy. In a twinkling, however, his humor changed and Ho'ace found himself in the glare of a forbidding menace, creditable in his palmiest days to Mister Chief Justice Jeffries himself.

"Ho'ace," demanded the Judge, tilting into his now ready receptacle a gurgling, man's-size libation, "who is the best shot—the best duck shot— you have ever paddled on this lake—barring—of course, a-h-e-m-m—my- self?" Surveying himself with the coyness of a juvenile, the Judge stirred his now beading toddy dreamily, and awaited the encore. Ho'ace squirmed a bit as the closing words of the Judge's query struck home with appalling menace upon his ear. He plucked nervously at his battered headpiece. His eyes, exhibiting a vast expanse of white, roamed pictured walls and smoke-dimmed ceiling in furtive, reflective, helpless quandary. Then, speaking slowly and gradually warming to his subject, he fashioned the following alibi.

"Jedge, y' know, suh, us all has ouh good an' ouh bad days wid de ducks. Yes, my lawdy, us sho' do. Dey's times whin de ducks flies all ovah ev'ything an' ev'ybody, an' still us kain't none o' us hit nuthin'—lak me an' you wuz' dis mawnin', Jedge, down in de souf end trails." At this juncture the Judge interrupted, reminding Ho'ace severely that he meant when the Judge—not the Judge and Ho'ace—was shooting.

"An' den dey's times whin h'it look lak dey ain't no shot too hard nur nary duck too far not t' be kilt. But Mistah Buckin'ham yonder—Mistah Nash he brung down de shootin'est gent'man whut took all de cake. H'its lots o' de members he'ah whuts darin' shooters, but dat fren' o' Mistah

Nash's—uummp-uummpphh—doan nevuh talk t' me 'bout him whur de
ducks kin' hear, 'cause dey'll leave de laik ef dey knows he's even comin'
dis way.

"Dat gent'man rode me jes' lak he wuz er saddle an' he done had on
rooster spurs. Mistah Nash he brung him on down he'ah an' say: 'Ho'ace,'
he say, 'he'ahs a gent'man frum Englan',' he say, 'Mistah Money—Mistah
Harol' Money,'—an' say, 'I wants you t' paddle him t'morrow an' see dat
he gits er gran' shoot—unnerstan'?' I say—'Yaas, suh, Mistah Nash,' I say,
'dat I'll sho'ly do, suh. Mistah Money gwi' hav' er fine picnic ef I has t'see
dat he do m'se'f—but kin he shoot, suh?'

"Mistah Nash, he say, 'Uh-why-uh-yaas, Ho'ace, Mistah Money he's uh
ve'y fair shot—'bout lak Mistah Immitt Joyner or Mistah Hal Howard.'
I say t' m'se'f, I say, 'Uummmpphh—huummpphh w-e-e-l-l he'ah now, ef
dats de case me an' Mistah Money gwi' *do* some shootin' in de mawnin'.' "

"Mistah Money he talk so kin'er queer an' brief lak, dat I hadda' pay
mighty clos't inspection t'whut he all de time a-sayin'. But nex' mawnin',
whin me an' him goes out in de bote, I seen he had a gre't big ol' happy
bottle o' Brooklyn Handicap in dat shell box so I say t' m'se'f, I say, 'W-e-l-l-l,
me an' Mistah Money gwi' git erlong someway, us is.'

"I paddles him on up de laik an' he say t'me, say, 'Hawrice-uh—hav'
yo'-er- got any wager,' he say, 'or proposition t' mek t' me, as regards,'
he say, 't' shootin' dem dar eloosive wil' fowls?' he say.

"I kinder studies a minit, 'cause lak I done say, he talk so brief, den I
says, 'I guess you is right 'bout dat, suh.'

"He say, 'Does you follow me, Hawrice, or is I alone?' he say.

"I says, 'Naw, suh, Mistah, I'm right he'ah wid you in dis bote.'

" 'You has no proposition t' mek wid me den?' he say.

"'S' I, 'Naw, suh, Boss, I leaves all dat wid you, suh, trustin' t' yo' gin'ros-
ity, suh.'

" 'Ve'y good, Hawrice,' he say. 'I sees you doan' grasp de principul. Now
I will mek you de proposition,' he say. I jus' kep' on paddlin'. He say—
'Ev'y time I miss er duck you gits er dram frum dis he'ah bottle—ev'y time
I kills a duck, I gits de drink—which is h'it?—Come—come—speak up,
my man.'

"I didn' b'lieve I done heard Mistah Money rightly an' I says—'Uh-
Mistah Money,' I says, 'suh, does you mean dat I kin hav' de chice whedder
you misses or kills ev'y time an' gits er drink?'

"He say—'Dat's my defi,' he say.

"I says—'Well, den—w-e-l-l—den, ef dats de case, I gwi'; I gwi' choose ev'y time yo' misses, suh,' Den I say t' m'se'f, I say, 'Ho'ace, right he'ah whar you gotta be keerful, 'ginst you fall outa de bote an' git fired frum de Lodge; 'cause ef'n you gits er drink ev'ytime dis gent'man misses an' he shoot lak Mister Hal Howard, you an' him sho gwi' drink er worl' o' liquah—er worl' o' liquah.'

"I pushes on up nur'ly to de Han'werker stan', an' I peeks in back by da' l'il pocket whut shallers offn de laik, an' I sees some sev'ul blackjacks —four on 'em—settin' in dar. Dey done seen us, too. An' up come dey haids. I spy 'em twis'in' an' turnin'—gittin' raidy t' pull dey freight frum dere. I says, 'Mistah Money,' I say, 'yawnder sets some ducks—look out now, suh, 'cause dey gwi' try t' rush on out pas' us whin dey come outa dat pocket.' Den I think—'W-e-l-l, he'ah whar I knocks de gol' fillin' outa de mouf o' Mistah Money's bottle o' Brooklyn Handicap!'

"I raised de lid o' de shell box an' dar laid dat ol' bottle—still dar. I say, 'Uuuuummmpp-huuummpph.' Jus' 'bout dat time up goes dem black-haids an' outa dar dey come—dey did—flyin' low to de watah—an' sorter raisin' lak—y' knows how dey does h'it, Jedge?

"Mistah Money he jus' pick up dat fas' feedin' gun—t'war er pump— not one o' dese he'ah afromatics—an' whin he did, I done reach fo' de bottle, 'cause I jes' natcherly knowed dat my time had done come. Mistah Money he swing down on dem bullies—Ker-py-ker-py—powie-powie--splamp-splamp-slamp-ker-splaash—Lawdy mussy—gent'mens, fo' times, right in de same place h'it sounded lak—an de las' duck fell ker-flop—almos' in ouh bote.

"I done let go de bottle, an' Mistah Money say—mighty cool lak—say, 'Hawrice,' say 'kin'ly to examin' dat las' chap clos'ly,' he say, 'an obsurve,' he say, 'efn he ain' shot thru de eye.'

"I rakes in dat blackjack, an' sho' nuff—bofe eyes done shot plum out —yaas, suh, bofe on 'em right on out. Mistah Money say, 'I wuz—er-slightly afraid,' he say, 'dat I had done unknowin'ly struck dat fellah er trifle too far t' win'ward,' he say. 'A ve'y fair start, Hawrice,' he say. 'You'd bettah place me in my station, so that we may continue on wid'out inter-ruption,' he say.

" 'Yaas, suh,' I say, 'I'm on my way right dar now, suh,' an' I say to m'se'f, I say, 'Mek haste an' put dis gent'man in his bline an' give him er proper chanc't to miss er duck.' I didn' hones'ly b'lieve but whut killin' all four o' dem other ducks so peart lak wuz er sorter accident. So I put him on de Han'werker bline. He seen I kep' de main shell bucket an' de liquah, but he never said nuthin'. I put out de m'coys an' den cre'p back wid' de bote into de willers t' watch.

"Pretty soon, he'ah come er ole drake flyin' mighty high. Ouh ole hen bird she holler t' him, an' de drake he sorter twis' his haid an' look down. I warn't figurin' nuthin' but whut Mistah Money gwi' let dat drake circle an' come 'mongst de m'coys—but aw! aw! All uv' er sudden he jus' raise up sharp lak an'—Ker-powie! Dat ole drake jus' throw his haid onto his back an' ride on down—looked t' me lak he fell er mile—an' whin he hit he throw'd watah fo' feet! Mistah Money he nuvver said er word—jus' sot dar!

"He'ah come another drake—way off to de lef'—up over back o' me. He turn 'roun—quick lak—he did—an' ker-zowie—he cut him on down, too. Dat drake fall way back in de willers an' co'se I hadda wade after 'im.

"Whil'st I wuz gone, Mistah Money shoot twice—an' whin I come stumblin' back, dar laid two mo' ducks wid dey feets in de air. Befo' I hav' time t' git in de bote agin he done knock down er hen away off in de elbow brush.

"I say, 'Mistah Money, suh, I hav' hunted behin' som' far-knockin' guns in my time, an' I'se willin, sho—but ef you doan, please suh, kill dem ducks closer lak, you gwi' kill yo' Ho'ace in de mud.' He say—'Da's all right 'bout dat,' he say, 'go git de bird—he kain't git er-way 'cause h't's daid as er wedge.'

"Whin I crawls back to de bote dat las' time—it done got mighty col'. Dar us set—me in one en' a-shiverin' an' dat ole big bottle wid de gol' haid in de far en'. Might jus' ez well bin ten miles so far ez my chances had done gone.

"Five mo' ducks come in—three singles an' er pair o' sprigs. An' Mistah Money he chewed 'em all up lak good eatin'. One time, tho'—he had t' shoot one o' them high flyin' sprigs twice, an' I done got halfway in de bote—reachin' fer dat bottle—but de las' shot got 'im. Aftah while, Mistah Money say, 'Hawrice,' he say, 'how is you hittin' off—my man?'

" 'Mistah Money,' I say, 'I'se pow'ful col', suh, an' ef yo' wants me t' tell you de trufe, suh, I b'lieves I done made er pow'ful po' bet.' He say, 'Poss'bly so, Hawrice, poss'bly so.' But dat 'poss'bly' didn't get me nuthin'.

"Jedge, y' Honor, you know dat gent'man sot dar an' kill ev'ry duck whut come in, an' had his limit long befo' de eight o'clock train runned. I done gone t' watchin', an' de las' duck whut come by wuz one o' dem lightnin' express teals. He'ah he come—look lak somebody done blowed er buckshot pas' us. I riz' up an' hollered—'Fly fas', ole teal, do yo' bes'— 'caus' Ho'ace needs er drink.' But Mistah Money just jumped up an' throw'd him fo'ty feet—skippin' 'long de watah. I say, 'Hol' on, Mistah Money, hol' on—you don' kilt de limit.'

" 'Oh!' he say, 'I hav'—hav' I?'

"I say, 'Yaas, suh, an' you ain' bin long 'bout h'it, neither!'

"He say, 'Whut are you doin' gittin' so col', den?'

"I say, 'I spec' findin' out dat I hav' done made er bad bet had er lot t' do wid de air.'

"An' dar laid dat Brooklyn Handicap all dat time—he nuvver touched none—an' me neither. I paddles him on back to de house, an' he come a-stalkin' on in he'ah, he did—lookin' kinda mad lak—never said nuthin' 'bout no drink. Finally, he say—'Hawrice,' he say, 'git me a bucket o' col' watah.' I say t' m'se'f, I say, 'W-e-l-l-l—dat mo' lak h'it—ef he want er bucket o' watah—you gwi' *see* some drinkin' now.'

"Whin I come in wid de pail, Mistah Money took offin all his clo'es an' step out onto de side po'ch an' say, 'Th'ow dat watah ovah me, Hawrice, I am lit'rully compel,' he say, 't' have my col' tub ev'ry mawnin'.' M-a-n-n-n! I sho' thow'd dat ice col' watah onto him wid all my heart an' soul. But he jus' gasp an' hollah, an' jump up an' down an' slap hisse'f. Den he had me rub him red wid er big rough towel. I sho' rubbed him, too. Come on in de clubroom he'ah, he did, an' mek hisse'f comfort'ble in dat big rockin' chair yonder—an' went t' readin'. I brought in his shell bucket an' begin' cleanin' his gun. But I see him kinder smilin' t' hisse'f. Atta while, he says, 'Hawrice,' he say, 'you hav' los' you' bet?'

"I kinda hang my haid lak, an' 'low, 'Yaas, suh, Mistah Money, I don' said farewell to de liquah!'

"He say, 'Yo' admits, den, dat you hav' don' los' fair an' squar'—an' dat yo' realizes h'it?'

" 'Yaas, suh!'

"He say, 'Yo' judgmint,' he say, 'wuz ve'y fair, considerin',' he say, 'de great law uv' av'ridge—but circumstances,' he say, 'has done render de ult'-mate outcome subjec' to de mighty whims o' chance?'

"I say, 'Yaas, suh,'—ve'y mournful lak.

"He say, 'In so far as realizin' on annything 'ceptin' de mercy o' de Cote'—say—'you is absolutely non-est—eh! my man?'

"I say, 'Yaas, suh, barrin' yo' mercy, suh.'

"Den he think er moment, an' say, 'Verree-verree—good!' Den he 'low, 'Sence you acknowledge de cawn, an' admits dat you hav' done got grabbed,' he say, 'step up'—he say—'an' git you a tumbler—an po' yo'se'f er drink —po' er big one, too.'

"I nev'uh stopped f' nuthin' den—jes' runned an' got me er glass outa de kitchen. Ole Molly, she say, 'Whur you goin' so fas'?' I say, 'Doan stop me now, ol' woman—I got business'—an' I sho' poh'd me er big bait o' liquah—er whol' sloo' o' liquah. Mistah Money say, 'Hawrice—de size o' yo' po'tion,' he say, 'is primus facious ev'dence,' he say, 'dat you gwi' spout er toas' in honor,' he say, 'o' d' occasion.'

"I say, 'Mistah Money, suh,' I say—'all I got t' say, suh, is dat you is de king-pin, champeen duck shooter so far as I hav' done bin in dis life—an' ve'y prob'ly as fur ez I'se likely t' keep on goin', too.' He sorter smile t' hisse'f!

" 'Now, suh, please, suh, tell me dis—is you *evah* missed er duck—any whar'—anytime—anyhow—suh?'

"He say, 'Really, Hawrice,' he say, 'you embarrasses me,' he say, 'so hav' another snifter—there is mo', consider'bly mo',' he say, 'in yo' system, whut demands utt'rance.'

"I done poh'd me another slug o' Brooklyn Handicap, an' say—'Mistah Money, does you expec' t' *evah* miss another duck ez long ez you lives, suh?'

"He say, 'Hawrice,' he say, 'you embarrasses me,' he say, 'beyon' words—you ovahwhelms me,' he say—'git t' Hell outa he'ah, befo' you gits us bofe drunk'!"

Opportunity Flies But Once

This revealing view of goose hunting from a pit in the broad sand flats of Ole Miss appeared in Mark Right! *Nash's comments on precautions and strategy— from frost on decoys to avoiding more than the minimum of tracks—could fill the notebook of a novice goose shooter who had the wisdom to listen.*

Nash leaves doubt as to which of his two close friends named "Henry" is in this story—Henry Bartholomew or Henry P. Davis (for years, dog editor of Sports Afield).

It is unlikely that Henry Bartholomew would not have "as yet bagged a wild goose," having gunned wildfowl for years from his own blind on the Potomac with the aid of his personal strain of Chesapeakes. A letter to Nash, dated October 29, 1964, from Henry Bartholomew described "over one hundred Canadian geese feeding on my corn—within gunshot of my front yard! Some days last winter I had over 500 of them flying all over my yard. I've raised food for them for the past ten years. They all roost on the river even when it freezes over." Mention of "Mrs. Henry's" spick-and-span sedan implies the Davis couple, who lived at one time in Memphis, and not Henry Bartholomew who would scarcely have brought his wife's "sedan" from Maryland. Nor did Nash in this story use the term "Marse Henry," as he almost invariably did when describing Henry Bartholomew.

Mrs. Henry P. Davis (Almyra McCreary Davis), called "Mack" by Nash, answered the question for me:

"Henry and Mr. Nash shared many a goose pit and duck blind. 'Opportunity Flies But Once' is devoted to a hunting trip Mr. Nash and Henry took together."

HENRY WAS EXPLAINING, almost tearfully, how come he hadn't as yet bagged a wild goose. He had told of going places and doing things in the attempt, how close he had come, how something always happened. His dissertation was a sort of hypothesis of failure—and he was dissertating in low, morose tones while we sat in a duck blind on Mill Bayou.

"Henry," I comforted, "dry your eyes. Tomorrow is another day, and this world thrives on hope."

"You can't eat hope," said Henry. I sat back and looked wise, which is a fine method of comeback when you can't think of the right words.

At length Henry said: "Where?"

"An old friend's place," I resumed impressively. "On a wonderful sand bar downriver. We'll drop in on him before long. It'll be as easy as sitting down in a tub of honey."

Henry whisked his eyes suspiciously my way.

"All you have to furnish," I said, "is transportation and moral support. I have the spade and the decoy set. You can dig and I'll set."

I was launching into a more detailed plan of strategy and exposition of the hardships and disappointments of goose shooting, when four fat green-heads whipped over to flirt with our "Susies." We got three of them, which interrupted further conversation but served as a prelude to a later December afternoon which found Henry and me rolling along a corn- and cotton-lined plantation road in eastern Arkansas. Henry, who was driving, took a long glance at the scenery and sighed: "Dark o' the moon. Clear, crisp, an' gonna be a flarin' red sunset."

We were traveling in Mrs. Henry's spick-and-span sedan. Henry's battle-scarred hunting chariot had suffered some sort of spare-part infection and was holed up for rejuvenation.

"We gotta be doggone careful of the Madame's bus," admonished Henry. "Anything happens to it, the roof'll sail off our house."

"Same way at my house," I said. "But the road isn't overly mucky. Uh— that is, until we cross the levee and light out across no man's land. If the turn-row mudholes are even half dry, we'd ought to be able to make the bank timber."

Henry groaned with premonition. Then we were in Lamar's pecan grove, and there was Lamar himself—huge, hospitable, and cheery. Lamar admits to being no goose hunter, but is a goose eater from Who-Laid-the-Rail! What a place. Ineffably Southern. Mississippi River plantation. Serene. Spicy with wood smoke spilling from homey chinked cabins. Panting cotton gins. Timber belt and cane brake. And often wedges of geese and files of ducks winking 'twixt you and cloudland.

Goose hunter or no goose hunter, Lamar offered a sensible program. One of his boys saddled our mules. "You scram up on those donkeys," Lamar said, "and let Jembo, here, show you a shortcut to the sand bar. He can pack decoys and do the pit-digging while you-all look around. It'll give you a workout and bring you in with an appetite for supper." Lamar scanned the west. "Clear weather. Early morning you can run your car over the levee ramp and out to where Jembo'll meet you with the mules."

Shortly thereafter, our three-donkey expeditionary force was hitched and unlimbered in a slumbering cluster of cottonwoods commanding the Sahara-like expanse of the Phil Allen bar.

I told Henry to locate the wind and listen carefully before venturing onto any goose bar. Old Boreas has a way of tattling all over sand bars. Many a breeze-borne goose note leads to a successful stalk, or betrays some distant hide-out. Next I told Henry to sit down and sweep every nook and cranny of outlook with my high-power glasses. A sand bar needs as careful searching as an Alaskan mountainside or moose meadow. A good glass is the hunter's other gun.

Listening post and inspection finished, we sized up the lay of the land. One season's high water can completely change last season's terrains. But river knowledge helps as to judging likely flight lanes. To our right, two miles square of apparently clean, open sand bar. Above, it narrows gradually to hard, steep, mud banks, thence to wooded mainland. Then, across a chute and island, the river circles eastward. At the foot of our bar is another opening, shielded riverward by a towhead. Chances are, what we get from the South will haul through that opening. And all the while Henry is a good listener.

Twenty minutes of hard going in the sand: Henry was "wised" to the importance of clocking time around a sand bar. Saves a lot, knowing just how long from camp to pits, or across the river and home again. We topped a little rise, and full twenty honkers took wing from a mud flat concealed beneath a five-foot reef.

"Out of gunshot," I explained. But that just shows that on a goose bar your gun should never be out of hand. When you think you've explored far enough, go on a piece and be ready to shoot always. "Geese," I told Henry, "have two well-nigh infallible bar tendencies. Lighting near a river's edge, they walk steadily toward higher ground." For proof I pointed to a maze of tracks all headed the same. Flying in, they usually point and pitch for a high spot and avoid snags or big drift that might conceal an enemy. Against better judgment I decided on a double pit for the morrow. Henry would need coaching. But I figured we had ample profiles to do a bully job of pit masking. Jembo had been putting his back to the spade. Widely scattered wet sand soon dries to bar color. Before long he had hollowed a breast-deep hide; and, climbing carefully out, he looked for all the world like one of Captain Kidd's minions leaning on his shovel after treasure-burying. The decoys were left sacked. Early-morning frost and dew would turn them white in the sun. Bad business. We'd have them up in a jiffy tomorrow. Then, single file, to keep down tracks, we hiked for the donkeys. Two bunches of geese, high, traded past, bound downriver. They chose the chute, as we guessed. "Looks like we've dug in the right alley," smiled Henry, waving at the talking parties. "Come back in the morning, and we'll say hello to you."

It is my contention that no gunning period approaches that moment of ease just before and after a perfect meal. Sitting about in our moccasins and loungy duds, sipping Lamar's masterpieces, painted glowing borders about our perspective. Then the summons from our host's charming consort. When it comes to carving a puff-bosomed wild goose, Lamar's sharp blade knows its way, hip, thigh, and cheerio.

"My agent knocked this fellow out of a flock five days ago," related Lamar. "He sho' oughta eat right where you hold him."

What a meal! Real oyster stew, winter-garden crispies, an apple pie that was a passport to heaven, and afterdinner coffee with ol' N'Awleens flavored all over it. Henry offers to lay a wreath on the unknown gander's grave. An hour later and bedtime. I am no match for Henry's lusty snores, so promptly beat him asleep.

In the morning we dressed by the fireside while the "ring out" bell still tolled. Gunner's breakfast in the kitchen. The black girl really came from Louisiana. No wonder such Java, with toasted biscuits and an egg-and-bacon flurry, reminiscent of Antoine's. We shouldered the guns, pocketed some shells loaded with coppered fours, and found Jembo at the sedan. He gave us our route: Up the levee to the big, white Haunted House. Over the ramp, straight out, turn to the right, then the left.

"W-h-o-a—hu'ah," from Henry! At the road forks, the headlights swept a watery mudhole. We investigated. By backing, taking it on the run, and holding well to the right, we might make solid ground. A cascade, some skidding, but we made it. Henry groaned. The car was a sight.

Five minutes and we were amid the cottonwoods, and our flashlight picked up the tracks. Hereafter, not a sign of a glim. Some silent hoofing. Decoys arranged to hide the pit and yet give every indication of a goose convention. Carefully, to avoid a cave-in, we jumped into the hole. Henry was instructed as to peeping space 'twixt sand and decoys close to the pit, and why the shadows are headed upwind to maintain angles of view from all points, to circling birds. The spade, crossed wall to corner, made an excellent gun rack free of sand litter. Seats had been dug into the walls at opposite ends of the hide. But we stood awhile, watching the east for fiery spear points of dawn. Half an hour and the bar frost would be steaming.

Suddenly I picked up a wide line of rushing black dots swarming through the lower slough. Mallards! Now they were over the mud flats, but climbing as they passed the main-bar rim. Another bunch cut in with them, disorganizingly. They were a tempting flock shot. We let loose two tubes each. From opposite sides of the flock plunged two birds, one stone dead, the other hard hit and killed by the fall.

Henry's mouth flew open. "Do you reckon I knocked one of them?"

"You're bound to have," I replied, "mine fell to the right."

"Well," mused Henry, "I've got my Sunday clothes on after that performance, and I'm now ready to do first-class work for the Big Shots."

A smoke smudge over a bend spelled river steamer—it might put some geese out of the current. By George, it had. We heard them before spotting their outfit; talking like a lot of market wives and lugging indecisively through the chute. Henry licked his lips and became wide awake. All at once the gabble ceased.

"Sighted us," I warned Henry, "and if only they were lower." Henry inspected his gun loads.

"Just keep still," I advised, "and when I say okay, why, come out shooting on your side."

Henry swallowed convulsively and nodded. "Sister Anne," he grinned, "don't you see no dust arisin'?"

Through a slit, my eyes were clamped upon the flock, following their every move and intonation. They veered between us and the river. Damnation! They were arguing again. Some want *down*. Others to pass us *up!* They actually split. An insurgent group volplaned decisively down and to our rear. But no! The Head Goose bawled them back into line. There was considerable confusion, and to my disgust they lugged off toward Rabbit Island.

"Too bad, Henry. Their leader simply had a better bar in mind. The set is all right."

A vacant hour passed, two! Away up high, their calls indistinct, two or three flights have come south.

"Where are all the geese who track up this bar?" asked Henry.

"Oh, they'll be in before long," I promised.

By now the pit was sun-warmed. We slipped gradually down into our seats.

"I've been dreaming like this many a time," I told Henry, "and been brought to by geese lighting among the decoys."

Henry yawned. "Oh, yeah? For two cents," he sighed heavily, "I'd do a little bunk fatigue."

A bit later he asked: "What do you say we take our guns and walk away up yonder to the head of the bar and explore a bit?"

Rank amateurism, this careless bar-walking; but, after all, I must break the restless fellow in gradually.

We'd trudged half a mile when, behind us, faint honkings. We dodged for a near-by snag root. Just as I thought: a nice gang circling and lighting in our decoys. Henry gritted his teeth.

"My fault—you told me right."

"Well," I said hearteningly, "let's let them get settled, and we'll try to make a sneak."

We gained the mud bar's tip. "Now," I explained to Henry, "I'll drift down the treeline to a point opposite the set, if you can, make it to the river side reef without scaring them. You can hold that undercover to within two hundred yards of the layout. Then I'll ease over into sight and try to drive them out over you. Try to make the head of that little switch willow draw. And, remember now, if they come over, don't move or stand up until they pass your hat brim. They're too late then to flare, and you've got a direct overhead shot into a wide-open bird."

Henry dwindled to a crouching dot and gained his objective. If I could do my part, it would be up to him to connect. Twenty minutes, and, glasses in hand, I sauntered out upon the open sand. Old watch-goose stabbed the "alarm clock." Heads snatched from under wings. I was under attentive scrutiny. A wave of discussion. The thing now is not to advance. They don't want to leave unless pushed. Back and forth I slowly tolled. The flock left the decoys and, as I thought, began a steady march toward the river. Somewhere behind that rampart lurked Henry. He could govern his position by listening for their talk.

I advanced slowly. The game continued. They didn't really know whether I was coming or going. They were within a hundred yards of the rim. Then I went for it on the run. The bunch gabbled, scratched sand, and was up. One off-sider swung very wide. The main outfit barely cleared the wall.

My glasses searched: There was Henry, a crouching figure in the switch willows. Henry would have his smack at the single bird if—if—he would only stay down—*stay down!*

But up jumped Henry. The big bird flared, and two thuds followed. Mr. Gander swept on after his comrades.

Henry hurled his hat upon the ground and jumped on top of it. A gesture of despair answered my hail.

"If I had some prussic acid I'd sure commit suicide," said Henry as we met, laughing, at the pit.

"All you did," I told him, "was to shoot a fraction too soon. He beat you to the jump. You were a bit unsteady—or he'd have been on the spot."

Lunch was a more or less blue function; herrings, hardtack, dates, and river water, taken in the lee of a drift log under the reef. There was a faraway note, at times, in Henry's conversation. But the party picked up spirits and re-entered the trenches full of fight. An hour dragged by. Problems of vast moment to the nation were discussed and solutions voted. Henry produced a national weekly from his "possible" sack and prodded me on its list of "questions and answers." Ignorance put me on the defensive with: "Why don't they ask something about ducks and geese and guns—I might get a break then." Gradually we sank lower in our seats, until, feet to head, we lay side by side on the pit's warm, sandy floor.

A faint *unk-ah-lunk-ah-lunk* hammered through deep slumber. It grew louder. My eyes fluttered. Henry purred gently. Now the call was clarion, and my eyes roved skyward. Directly overhead, not thirty yards aloft, sailed a fleet of gorgeous geese, their black necks writhing to scan our decoys. Hazards raced through my mind. Have they seen us? Had I better let Henry be, and risk a solo performance? One thing is certain, the boy has it coming, and we can't kill geese on our backs.

"Henry!" My tone startled him into a wide-eyed daze. "Quick—geese!"

In trying to bound erect, my boot heel, somehow, got across Henry's neck. He retaliated by clamping on a scissors hold and attempted to climb up and apply a body lift. We went figuratively to the mat, grabbing for the guns, when both side walls of the pit caved in thunderously. We dug out furiously and hurled four barrels at some disappearing phantoms. Away they soared, with Henry shaking his fist and breathing about Lady Luck. The whole business was, I claimed, my fault. But Henry, good sport that he is, overruled my motion. He might, he added, have put in a shot could he have dislodged my boot heel from his ear in time. We resurrected the spade and rehabilitated the pit. "No more snoozing for me," vowed Henry. "I'm going to stare the horizon down from now until night." And that is what happened. Two elusive flights beat upriver. Our Big Moment had come—and gone.

"Well," reminisced Henry a few hours later, as we left the viaduct and recrossed the dark and mighty river far below, "as a goose hunter I am still in the maiden class." He sucked loudly on the inevitable pipe. "Let's stop in somewhere an' git us some ham and eggs. We can have the car cleaned up in the auto laundry while we're eatin'."

At table, Henry's countenance again grew reflective. "No man will ever have a prettier chance to kill a goose than I did on that overhead shot—I don't see how in the name of—!"

I told him, in turn, that there were two absolute essentials for the goose hunter, and that they were acquired only by long and arduous experience. Trimming up a one-eyed fried egg, Henry's look was inquisitive. He must have, I said, first, an enormous capacity for infinite patience. And, second, a decided sense of humor.

"In which case," said Henry, with a quirk at the corners of his blue eyes, "I've got a question I'd like to ask you: You've been all through the mill and killed many a goose. But the thing I can't understand about it is—" he rubbed the side of his neck tenderly—"why you ever let goose-shooting spoil a great wrestler's career."

Recall to Eden!

Published first in the Nelson collection De Shootin'est Gent'man *and Other* Hunting Tales *in 1961, and later in* The American Field, *December 1, 1962, "Recall to Eden" embodies a mellow experience—begun in 1890 and continued to be savored through 1956 (when this was written) and on to that last time Nash Buckingham shot ducks, the first two days of the 1968 season.*

Bob Anderson told me that Beaver Dam Duck Club ceased as such "about 1941 when they lost their lease on the Owen property. Nash sold his membership long before. Sterling and Richard Owen are both dead but their wives live there. The Owens were always friendly with Nash and allowed him to bring one or two people to shoot. When the Mississippi season stayed open some weeks longer than Arkansas, we would go down there."

Dr. William Andrews wrote me about the period during which he shot with Nash at Beaver Dam:

> My first real experience hunting with Mr. Buck was on December 20, 1958 when, with a Mr. Bill Day (whose name appears in "Recall to Eden") and Mr. Tommy Frazier, I hunted with him in the famous old Round Pond in the north woods of Beaver Dam Lake, the first of many experiences we shared both as hunts and as memories of his days in those areas. He had almost total recall and, even as an octogenarian, he rarely repeated himself.
>
> My father, encouraged by Mr. Buck, became a member of Beaver Dam about 1921. The old clubhouse was destroyed soon afterwards and Dad and Lemmon Buckingham had the present clubhouse built in 1925. It has been remodeled and is the home of Octavia and P. W. Alderson, where Mr. Buck and I have many times enjoyed the fine food that Mrs. Alderson so graciously prepared. On mornings I used to hunt with Mr. Buck, I would pick him up in front of his apartment, have breakfast, and drive fifty miles down to Beaver Dam. We used a small double-pointed aluminum duck boat given to Mr. Buck twenty years before. We would paddle to our blind—as much as forty minutes if the wind was heavy out of the north—with Mr. Buck on a Canada Dry wooden box in the bow. Quite often we would jump-shoot the circumference

of the open lake, with a variation of mallards or gadwall or baldpates over decoys from our blind.

Dr. Andrew's color slides and movies, taken shortly after the hunt Nash describes, show gratifying numbers of wildfowl. In "Recall to Eden," Nash was seventy-six, an age when much younger men would have been sleeping soundly at five a.m. of a January morning, not out smashing a duck boat through ice. In photos taken at this period and with Nash as late as 1968, P. W. Alderson looks much the same—a wiry gamecock of a man with an apparent aversion to wearing dentures. The subjects are, as usual, holding bouquets of ducks and looking directly at the camera. After 1963, Nash was shooting with the impressive handicap following a cataract operation—a grand and game old sportsman, deserving an Eden to go back to in a bewilderingly altered world.

THIS LAST WEEK of the 1955-56 waterfowling season in the Mississippi Valley Flyway had become spotty. Bob Anderson and Bill Day and I hadn't done any good in Arkansas. Bluebird weather plus foods on Grand Prairie's riceland that seemed to have run low probably accounted for that unusual situation; concentrations were scattered. Then, overnight, old man General Average, Mother Nature and Lady Luck got their heads together in our behalf.

No moon! Cold wave flags breaking out and mercury tumbling. Radios blaring predictions of freeze warning to produce shippers. Even then business pressures bore down too heavily on Bill and Bob. Sic semper the fast buck! Growing restless by Thursday evening because time was running out, I telephoned another favorite gunning buddy, Captain Ben Tyler. Two weeks agone Ben and I enjoyed a forenoon's wonderful mallarding at the old lake, thanks to the hospitality of its owners, Richard and Sterling Owen of Evansville, Mississippi. This sporting benefaction is generously extended to a few old friends whose pioneering of the former club's halcyon days still lives in memory.

Ben's car was afront our residence at three-fifty-nine the next morning. Friday the thirteenth or not, this was a real duck day. Bitter, gusty huffs and puffs that razor-bladed nose tips and reddened ears. Forty-five minutes later we ducked into the cozy Blue Front restaurant on Highway 61 south, at Tunica, Mississippi. We made strong medicine with as real good coffee as this broad land affords, country ham and eggs with fluffy hot biscuits. Ten minutes south from Tunica we crossed the railroad and a mile later swung from the blacktop into P. W. Alderson's homeclose. P.W. is guardian of old Beaver Dam's *lares* and *penates* in every sense.

Exactly here and amid virgin timber, the old duck club, with leases from Mr. Owen had taken root first in a tent and then a dogtrot log cabin. I first saw it in 1890 and even then the original clubhouse was but five years built. And there the old club stood for nearly forty years until a tornado wrecked it.

P.W.'s curtained kitchen windows showed a light; he was up and readying to run his trap lines. Were it a summer morn, he'd already have been in his paddle boat easing along the willow line offering roaches, worms, crickets, minnows, spin-baits, flies or plugs to scrappy bream, slab crappies, fighting shellcrackers, walloping bass or an occasional bull-shouldered catfish. Just as Ben began pulling on his slipover boots, P.W.'s door opened.

"Mawnin' gents, advance an' giv' th' countersign."

"*Zero*," yelled Ben. "Any ducks, P.W.?"

"There's more ducks here than I've seen in the last five years put together; but you're going to have to bust some ice t' get at 'em. Th' whole countryside began freezing yesterday afternoon. There's still some open water for the geese, and ducks have piled in and kept some open for themselves." Ben all but yanked off a bootstrap.

At the boat landing we tramped out an icehole roomy enough to give us launching space and a running dive at the ice barrier. But first we put half of our four dozen mallard decoys into P.W.'s boat and the rest, all rigged and ready to toss out, into ours. Years ago we learned better than to invite disaster by taking out sacked decoys for attempted placement in the black dark. It's the best way we know of to lose time and religion—picking knots and untangling frozen cords and anchors. Get everything ready before you start racing shooting time.

By mutual consent, two about-bushed wildfowlers ceased smashing ice at precisely five-twenty a.m. It was too dark to see a black cat—and cold. How many times, I reflected grimly, since my first solo duck hunt began right here, had I pulled this same dense-headed stunt on old Beaver Dam Lake? With sixty-five years' actual wildfowling behind me, common sense should have kept both us oldsters between the blankets. Now look at us! Here we were trying to head for that same bunch of saw grass just south of the Oliver Hole's entrance from which I fired my first shot.

In the stern of the twelve-foot aluminum boat Ben was puffing and sweating like a country boy writing a love letter. At Beaver Dam, during duck season, outboard motors are ruled off limits—and rightly so. Rafts of fowl and geese will take just so much of that. As in the old days at Beaver Dam, it's paddles or oars. Ben groaned, "Just like P.W. said—there are jillions of ducks on yon west side—they're roarin'—just listen."

I replied that I couldn't seem to get my better ear into action but I didn't doubt it. Suddenly the prying beam of P.W.'s torch spotted us from the dock. Then his hail: "Hold the line—reinforcements are coming up." We could hear P.W. crashing through the splintered debris of our meandering ice trail. A few moments later he skidded past us. Paddling furiously from the reversed prow of his light, square-sterned breaming craft, he shot its elevated end out over the ice, let it smash down and through, then backed up a bit and renewed the assault.

"I think that white line out yonder is open water," shouted P.W. "Come ahead—we'll make it."

Gruntingly, Ben and I took off after him. Suddenly, plying the stubby oars as paddles, we noticed we were smashing the ice more readily and slid noiselessly into open water. I swung around, oar-locked the blades and took out after P.W. "For Heaven's sake," called Ben, "look yonder at the ducks rising off the willow flats south of the Oliver Hole." Pulling hard on my left oar, I swung our nose northwest.

"Ben," I said, "hold me dead onto that dwarf cypress you'll pick up in a few moments off the saw-grass point ahead. I want to just miss that tree— our bunch of grass is about two hundred yards past it." By now, even I could hear roar after roar as thundering clouds of wildfowl rose from the timbered west shore line. Glancing hurriedly, I could see them now, faintly, like clouds of gnats against a swamp's twilight. A good navigator, Ben skimmed me past the dwarf cypress and we all but ran down a raft of coots emerging from the saw grass and button willows. Lines came back to me from dawns of the long-ago:

> The sky now turned more softly gray
> The great Watch-Stars shut up their Holy Eyes
> The East began to kindle.

P.W. was already tossing out decoys afront our hide. We were shooting over an apparently long strip of slowly freezing open water. We added our stools to the set with a sort of "lead in" effect to P.W.'s. With the northwest wind at our backs, flights working north and south could glide in.

"I'll ease on up the open water," called P.W., "and see what's happening in the North End. You-all ought to be getting through in short order. Don't be missing too many. I'm sort of craving mallard meat with dumplings, gravy and a covey of cathead biscuits."

We drove the boat behind the saw-grass clump and lashed it into as perfect a shooting niche as nature ever provides duck hunters, our prow wedged and roped between two button willows, head-high buckrush at our stern. We blew through our gun tubes for luck and safety and knocked ice particles from outside. Then we checked shooting time; so few moments can mean so much in life or death to wildlife—to humans, too. Ben was using the new combination of an ounce-and-a-half of coppered fours. My ten-pound Becker twelve-bore magnum carried an ounce and three-eighths of Lubaloy fours, in three-inch cases. Ben stood aft, and I, amidships.

"Watch sharp to your right and from behind," I warned. "They'll come up on you all of a sudden—remember that susie that almost knocked your hat off last week?" Ben grinned. We could now see three-fourths across the frozen lake and spot P.W. just rounding a cypress point to the north. Clouds of ducks suddenly began milling as far south as we could spot them past the headland. Skeins of quick-winged divers began scraping past our decoys' heads. From farther south we caught the faint gabble of voyaging geese. The east turned rosy. Ben gently tuned in his call and then sent forth a tremendous notice to the effect that we were in business. I turned for a peek southward. From nowhere behind Ben, three gorgeous mallard drakes whisked waterward, banked steeply into the breeze, and, with hissings of salutation, braked over the decoys. They hadn't missed Ben's hat twenty feet. He spat out his call, glowered at the now serenely seated drakes and grinned at me sheepishly.

"If you knock over all three of them on the lift," I warned, "you'll be three-fourths of your way through the limit. Take it easy or you'll be meeting yourself coming back." Gun below his elbow, Ben sounded a loud "S-h-o-o-o!" The three visitors spun like humming tops, slammed their curved and thrusting wing tips against the water and left amid vast splutteration. The center mallard crumpled. "Those coppered fours," Ben remarked, "are very, very strong medicine; remember when you began breaking me in on them—years ago?" Then we both shrank into the hide, eyes bulging with astonishment.

Overhead a mantle of wildfowl suddenly blotted out the dawn. That crashing shot of Ben's must have disturbed the willow flats' unsuspecting populations. Thousands of mallards, pintails, gadwall, widgeon and lesser fry were smothering our decoys. You could hardly see through the mass. "Hold onto your hat," whispered Ben. "This is worth sitting up all night to see—let's let them all get down—then we'll move them out carefully and they'll come drifting back. Let's not shoot anything but mallard drakes—pick the fat ones—too." Ben mounted the seat and waved his hat. It was fully five minutes before order was restored. "My kingdom for a camera," mourned Ben.

Cruising from downlake six mallards swung in low from the right. Four drakes and two susies. Ben appraised this situation through slitted eyes. With lowered flaps and throaty hissings sent on ahead, the visitors were definitely bordering "borrowed time." Ben let the two leading drakes slither past and into my swing. My big gun lowered the twain, and Ben's ensuing two shots rubbed out the followers. The hens leaped sky-high and departed the scene. Our limits of four each were now on a three-two basis. P.W.'s boat was spotted curving across the northern open water, and almost immediately a swarm of fowl appeared from that direction. They swept close overhead and behind us, but there was no use shooting; open water out front made easier pick-ups. Ben couldn't resist picking off a high-flying drake perfectly etched against a slowly smoldering east. My next two victims swung in from the north; a pair of drakes answering Ben's clucking call. "That does it," said my companion, taking the shells from his gun and blowing through its tube. "I'm not too sure we've even been duck shooting." He raised a war whoop for P.W.

We had the ducks picked up and about half the decoys in by the time our host made contact. "You boys sure minded me about not missing too many—I could see 'em tumble before I heard the guns."

"What's in the North End, P.W.?"

"The trails are frozen, of course, and the open lake is black with ducks on the ice. Let's beat it across before our back trail freezes, too." At the pier, while I tied up the ducks and sacked the decoys, Ben went to the automobile and returned with a big thermo-jug. Setting out three large-sized paper mugs, he unscrewed the jug's top. Steam from a delicious tomato fragrance— or was it—turned whiter in the icy air. P.W. and I had come on point.

"Here," announced Ben, "is the tomato bouillon that Captain McCutchen of the U.S. Marine Corps made famous when he won the 'Menu' sixty-four-thousand-dollar question. I made up some from the formula printed, in, I think, *Collier's* magazine. You put water and cloves into a thinned juice, add lemon, bile and rebile, imbibe and come out fighting." We sat there sipping the delicious concoction and watching great streamers of wildfowl passing in review over the ice. It was five minutes until eight o'clock.

"This stuff takes a powerful holt on you, don't it?" asked P.W. "I've got to run my traps an' git me four ducks while I'm about it. You-all come back tomorrow for the last day." Ben said he couldn't make it, but I told P.W. I'd be there with two friends who wanted to stage a calling contest.

"Better get here earlier than you did this morning," P.W. called from his boat. "She's gonna freeze plum across an' we'll be in for some plain and fancy ice bustin'."

Ben and I put up a job on Bob Anderson and Bill Day. Told them that there were a few ducks around but limits couldn't be guaranteed. They were desperately afraid of missing that last day, so next morning, equipped with plenty of hot coffee and sandwiches, and after another and earlier breakfast at Tunica's Blue Front, we were there on schedule. P.W. was ready.

"You might as well know the worst," he announced. "She's frez' tighter'n Dick's hatband, but maybe not quite so solid on yon side—here we go."

P.W. was right. Toward the west bank the ice thinned enough to crash with oars. When we passed the dwarf cypress, Bob Anderson remarked, "Something tells me that Tyler and Buckingham have been withholding valuable information—I'm seeing, hearing and smelling scads of ducks— just look yonder." The breeze was bitingly northwest. We crashed out a hundred-foot-square hole for the decoys, shoving big sheets of ice under the pool's sides, thus leaving the water clear. Then we lashed our craft into its hide. Today I was shooting my Model 21 magnum; Bob, his heavy over-and-under; and Bill Day, his magnum repeater. We had a ten-minute wait before time.

"They'll gang you very shortly now," P.W. announced, "and good luck to the winner of the calling contest."

While my companions first cleared their throats and then gently huffed soft, chuckling notes into their calls like musicians warming up their orchestral instruments, I could see a lot of wildfowling ghosts out yonder through the freezing murk. Eastward, across the ice-bound expanse, a splinter of light began prying through the bank's latticework of willows and towering cypress. Northward, on the east bank, too, once stood the famous Handwerker blind where Mister Harold Money of "De Shootin'est Gent'-man" fame held forth to birth Horace's tale of the sips of Brooklyn Handicap he nearly never got. Diving ducks were crossing and lighting in our decoys. Somewhere in this tremendous panoply of *Anatidae* were twelve succulent mallards bound for freeze-boxes and platters. Where were all these ducks and geese feeding? Just westward of the lake amid an amplitude of soybean and corn fields.

Then, somehow, that long-gone November morning of 1890 became a flashback. Young eyes peered through these same saw-grass tops sixty-five years agone, a keen-visioned Jackson Bounds, giant Negro keeper of the original long clubhouse, shoving our boat into this same nest. I even hear Jackson warning the little lad in his care to not grab at the grass stalks barehanded; they would cut worse than knives and take a long time to heal.

Dad had sent my older brother, a visiting boy friend and me to Beaver Dam with two hundred hand-loaded shotgun shells. My peers-in-age handed me fifty for my twelve-bore hammer Bonehill double, and beat back demands for a three-way split. I had been warned by Dad that if I failed to bag ten ducks on my own for the first time, waivers would be asked. Jackson tossed out our decoys and flocks of almost every species of wildfowl known to today's Mississippi Valley Flyway (and a few that are extinct) immediately tried to light among them. Ensues a bombardment and all too soon my fifty shells were gone and my gun's tubes hot to a wetted finger tip. The lure and charm of the business had gotten into my blood stream —for life.

"It's shooting time," announced Bill. Bob and I snapped to attention. The next moment we didn't know which greenhead to shoot at first. The boys just stood there, waving their pieces at first one drake and then another; yelling, meanwhile, to remember to shoot only green-caps. As a result of the ambush no one shot at anything. They lowered their weapons and turned to me.

"Let's make a deal," urged Bill. "We've got but twelve ducks to shoot, and we'll never have a better chance to try open-water calling and gun yardage. Let's take turns and call our shots—one at a time. Bob—you go first." Bob's eyes glinted the situation. Ignoring the fact that several hundred assorted ducks sat with the decoys, he blasted his call at a bunch of mallards swinging out over the broad water from willow flats south of us. Right there we were witnessing the most difficult test in real duck calling; to blow so naturally that you don't disturb visitors.

If you've never tried that one, Mister Duck Caller, it will provide evidence that perhaps your education along such lines isn't quite summa cum. You could actually see and almost hear that long hail of Bob's hit target. The dozen or more mallards veered our way. With cupping wings they lost altitude and under the wind fought their way to our stools. Bob switched to a pianissimo chatter, soothing with feeding palaver. "You've got 'em hooked," I whispered. "Pick yourself a fatter-than-average drake— if you miss—take to the ice and start skating." At the rasp of Bob's over-and-under, a greenhead keeled from among its fellows and smashed an icehole beyond the decoys. The shot sent our visiting scaups, widgeon and gadwall into the air.

"Centered," complimented Bill. "I'll go topside now." Several bunches of gadwalls inspected the setup, but were dismissed. Two greenheads accepted Bill's invitation and trimmed the forty-yard deadline. Bill selected a victim and let drive. Once—twice—thrice! Only at the last report did the big bird tumble. Bill grinned. "Pride goeth before a fall—that mallard almost made me do my best." It was now my turn at bat. From the center seat Bob boxed the compass.

"It's a wonder," he reported, squinting through his binoculars, "how these deep-water ducks maintain traffic lanes over the ice—I haven't seen a crash yet—just look at those teal, they twinkle through thick traffic like it wasn't there."

"Let's both bawl at yon bunch of mallards out over the dwarf cypress," suggested Bill. He and Bob made the welkin resound with invitations. The gang luffed. Bill had to stop blowing to catch his breath.

"All right, Mister B.," chuckled Bob, "here they come—how do you want 'em—straight up or once-over-light?"

"I'll try to poach a couple of 'em and get a drake ahead of you two wolves."

With that bunch of mallards crawling across an iridescent east I longed for my old friend Richard E. Bishop, the etcher, to capture the matchless beauty of the scene with his dry points. I chose an end incomer first, collapsed it and then let the Model 21's second tube pass a towering drake before the fatal touch-off. Bill said, "I've read stories of yours about this lake in older years, and I've seen the times elsewhere in my younger gunning life—but I am just now beginning to see how it was possible to bag a hundred ducks in a whole lot less than a day."

Bob asked, "Does a sight like this lead you to believe that there are as many wildfowl in the flyways as there were—say—when you were a young hunter fifty years ago?" But before I could reply that in my opinion there are not remotely the ducks and geese there were then, Bill and Bob called a bunch of mallards into their dragnet and sacked a pair each.

"I move," said Bob, "that we apply the brakes and wait for P.W. to show up; he is going to want some ducks for the season's close, and, besides, you don't get to see a sight like this but a few days in a lifetime." He broke out the coffee jar and some cookies to dull the wind's edge, and asked me about the club's old days, a wildfowl Eden.

"When Beaver Dam was a twenty-member club in a log cabin of the earliest 1880s, there was no limit. But when they got into their own home about 1885, they put on a bag limit of fifty ducks a day and as many geese (or swans) as you could get. There were no state or federal laws as to waterfowl for many years. It was nothing unusual, as old record books show, for an average of six or eight guns a day to be disappointed unless all hands bagged limits. I have lived for weeks in goose camps along the Mississippi—many of them just west of here about three miles along what is now Tunica Cutoff, and watched the migrations stream down in late afternoons until they arched the skies and were still passing at moonrise. You'll never see that again. As many ducks now—as then?" I shook my head sadly. "Look into autumnal skies for your answer. Less than a mere dribble of geese gets past the commercialized areas of Illinois, Missouri and Kentucky. Even the big rivers are changed, and everything along them. There's no longer the corn crops along downriver Ole Miss."

Suddenly P.W. eased into the picture along his as yet unfrozen passageway to the Oliver Hole landing. He had good fur to show from his trap line. "Men," he related, "you haven't seen a tenth part of the ducks this freeze-up has driven into Beaver Dam. Those geese we heard traveling this morning have fed in the oat field back west and have resettled on the ice in the South End. Yep, I'd sure admire a cup of that Java and some cookies."

"P.W.," said Bill, "we each have a mallard drake to bag and you have four ducks to get yourself. We'll do the calling until you catch up. Then we'll take turns again." But P.W. bade us collect our ducks while he attacked the eats—and that didn't take long. Then P.W. brought his Winchester pump-gun into action and, with Bill and Bob sounding off, soon had himself a season's parting feast.

"You know," he chuckled, "those loads you gave me—three and a quarter drams of powder and an ounce and a quarter of number seven-and-a-half shot are powerful all-around game loads. Well—that's about it till nex' year."

Bashing homeward through reglazing skim-ice corridors, goose talk came to us faintly from the far South End. The sun had lost its battle for the day and a snow ceiling was settling ominously. On Beaver Dam's Eden certainly, were countless migrants freed from gun perils until confronted with even graver dangers of droughts in their far northern habitat.

"Men," said P.W., after we'd stowed all plunder into the canvas-battened boat and loaded it onto the car's trail-rig, "in my opinion duck callers who really know how to hunt—and by that I mean when to blow and when to *not* blow—can call 'em anywhere. Bill and Bob qualify. Good-bye, good luck and God bless all three of you. Come back this spring when the bream and crappie are on the prod."

Part Two:
BOBWHITES

Brick House

I FIRST READ of Brick House in "Bob White Blue! Bob White Gray!" in *De Shootinest Gent'man*. Through the years, although there were long periods during which I did not reread this story, one thing remained tantalizingly with me—Nash's description of Brick House and the quail shooting he enjoyed there. I have never lost my desire to go. That I haven't, in a life shaped by self-indulgence, at least gone just to see the old place is perhaps because I live in a similar place of my own.

During World War II, Nash wrote me in January 1944:

> I was at "Brick House" in mid-December while making some scenes for *Life* magazine with a photographer they sent down. He took several shots of the old place (Cousin Charley Hall now lives there) and also Hunt House, Beasley House, the old church, etc. of that grand and birdy terrain.

The *Life* pictures were disappointing to me in terms of dog work and bird shooting and of Brick House itself. In the captions, a setter was designated a "retriever," and table qualities of quail described as "the best of all wildfowl." Poor Nash. But nothing can dim my image of Brick House as Nash tells of it on a New Year's hunt in "Bob White Blue! Bob White Gray!"

> They built the Brick House, so Aunt Dora's crone of a black mammy told me in her cabin one night years ago, "long 'bout som'time befo' ol' Cunn'l hisse'f clamb up on he big white hawss an' rid off t' fight wid d' Mexicums!" Granny Captola inhaled three sucky draws upon the sparky dregs of her corn-cob pipe. They called it the Brick House then, and the name has stuck right down to this day. . . .
>
> Well, then, you drag gradually uphill for a couple of country miles and pop out all of a sudden right in front of Brick House. A formal front yard, palisaded with hand-drawn white oak staves; a limpety-

crackety gate and a shrub and flower-bordered walk of curiously cobbled squares. An alleyway, overhung by stately oaks and fringed sweepingly with interliners of gnomelike, berried cedars. . . .

Clump into its austere but welcoming center hall. Never mind the mud on your boots and leave the dogs be! Pile your bird hunter's plunder in Captain Ev's bedroom—it used to be the parlor, when crinoline waltzed to the "Mocking Bird"! Now look about you.

Rare old furniture everywhere. Thump those paneled doors and toe those hewn floor boards—wide as your forearm is long. What massive sills and beams, and such plaster. You'll notice bogs of brick and mortar gouged from outside walls, and some of the windows have splintery holes drilled through the panes and ugly slug cavities in the shutters. Aunt Dora tells "outside folks": "Dem wuz done du'in war times, yaas suh— when us fit wid d' Yankees—ol' Cap'n ain' nuvvr 'lowed nobody t' put in no new glass—says he want 'em t' stay jes' lak dey wuz made—an' ef nobody don't lak de wind whistlin' thu dem bullet holes—den dey kin jes' buil' up de fiah an' git closer to h'it." . . .

Brick House smiles a rare and all-embracing welcome the full width of its classic facings. It seems to say: "Come along with you, young folks —I've minded generations of you through sunshine and shadow. Light down and hitch, you fox hunters and bird shooters—I know every one of you—sweethearts and wives and good old dogs and jumpers, aye and your daddies and gran'daddies, too. Come on in he'ah; I miss you and I'm getting along. I'm yo' *home!*"

So, look affectionately if not reverently upon Brick House. Go close to it. Feel of its oddly shaped, time-dulled red bricks patted into shape and burned by slave hands that were such in loyalty only. Do this as I am not ashamed to confess having done, with a comforting sense of pride in heritage.

Hugh Evelyn Buckingham ("Cousin Ev") recently wrote me, describing Brick House:

It is situated about six miles south of Saulsbury, Tennessee, and is reached by an unimproved sandy road. Built about 1850 by my grand-father on my mother's side, it was left to his granddaughter, Emma Lou McClellan, who married Charley Hall. While the Halls were living in Memphis I leased this place and used it for a shooting preserve for about ten years. The Halls decided to move back to their farm, so I bought some acreage adjoining them, built a house, and it was from there that Nash did most of his shooting and would visit with Cousin Charley.

Brick House is in the vicinity of Grand Junction and the Ames Place. A photograph taken in 1969 shows it as an antebellum house with rather flat-looking roofline, a simple cornice, and a chimney at each end. Its broad two-story expanse has nine twelve-paned windows—one of them centered above a classic white entrance (two small pillars on each side) with a wide doorway framed with rectangular lights. At a distance in the photograph, the house appears deceptively small, the only clues to its size being the size of the bricks, which seem almost tiny, and the multiple-paned windows, which by their size indicate high-ceilinged rooms. The "formal front yard, palisaded with hand-drawn white oak staves" is missing, as is the "alleyway, overhung by stately oaks," but there are several evergreens that appear to be remnants of the "interliners of . . . berried cedars" standing before the house, and I see one very large tree stump, a reminder of the oaks. No matter, they are all there in "Bob White Blue! Bob White Gray!"

In the title story of *Hallowed Years,* Nash takes you again to Brick House, this time in 1908, with Cousin Charley Hall living there. The furnishings could, perhaps, have been in another fine old Southern house, but you know that this was at Brick House because—you almost tell yourself—you were there.

> Cousin Charley unlatched a tall, mirrored cabinet above his chunky, mahogany secretaire, lifted out a quart-capacity, hand-hammered silver cup and sent black Qno to rinse and scald it in the kitchen at Brick House. Then he reached back into the cabinet and handed down to Hal and me two wonderfully preserved and exquisitely engraved muzzle-loading, double-tubed shotguns, with richly stamped, brass-nozzled leather shot pouches and their paper-thin powder horns through which, when shaken, could be heard the soft rustle of fine-grained propellant.
>
> "They were Colonel Bourne's and Grandfather's, a matched pair of guns for as finely a matched pair of gentlemen and real sportsmen as the world ever saw," he added pridefully. "I still shoot them for what little hunting I do. But I manage to keep in ducks and squirrels, with a wild gobbler now and then. And when I score a right and left on quail with one of these old boys I'm so tickled I quit anyway and ride on to the house."
>
> Hal and I were still exclaiming over the fit of those burled stocks, and mounting and swinging the gorgeous pieces at imaginary quarries flitting about the high-ceilinged library when Qno returned. Charley handed the cup to us for reading of its legend: *From Dunbar Bourne to Dall and Worship Auburnton for their Crusader's beating my Roland— December 1840.* I put the cup on the firefront's broad shelving while Charley swirled bouqueted brandy into our crystal cones. Qno retired to hearthside with a switch of same for his own personal consideration from a double-duty shaving mug.
>
> I sat there on a triple-backed chintz sofa, palming my brandy cone and figuring that 1840 would be sixty-eight years ago to the very month. The guns, fifteen years younger, were percussions of the mid-1850's and by one E. Smith, the same make as my own double-barrel, twelve-gauge, breech-loading hammer gun standing in the corner in its oiled saddle scabbard.
>
> For now it was the Year of Our Lord 1908, and my voluminous diary states that Hal and I and Cousin Charley, about of an age, were in the fag-end of several grand quail-shooting days during mid-month's frosti-ness. At least Hal and I were doing the gunning and dog handling while conscientious Cousin Charley plantation-managed and horsebacked to the railroad village ten miles north over parlous roads.
>
> Our two braces of dogs (three setters and one double-nosed pointer)

thất we put down for alternating hour-and-a-half heats were long since burred, fed to satiety with buttermilked corn pone and braised beef choppings, and bedded down snugly in the cottonseed shed. That day's legal bag of bobwhites, twenty-five each, drawn and strung, accumulated frost shrouds on the back gallery. Ourselves, laved with sweet soap amid hot waters fetched and poured into ancient, high-backed tubs by the indispensable and indefatigable Qno, were in trenchermen's finest fettle.

Next, in that pre-cocktails era, Charlie observed with ritual his chef-d'oeuvred version of the personalized absinthe-anisette. Dripped slowly off an upturned soup spoon onto ice shavings coated with (whisper it not in the streets of Ascalon) powdered brown sugar; the brandied wormwood, titillated with never to exceed two drops of bitters and shaken to chilled froth, not only lent wings to jaded reflexes, but sometimes alerted appetites to injudicious horizons and nightmares.

My diary even records our supper's menu, served from a vast, marble-topped table with massive oaken props in the wainscoted butler's pantry. We were just the right distance from the warmth of an open hearth that aided the four tall, yellow candles lending an enriched patina to the two-century-old, French game-bird oils in their pressed-leather frames. If such could only speak! "Lord," graced Cousin Charley, "make us truly thankful for this manifestation of Thy bounty, and pardon our sins, for Christ's sake—Amen!"

We ate, so the diary's embrowned pages depose, barbecued breast of lamb, with red-hot brown gravy, smoking baked potatoes suffused with country butter and sprinkled with flakes of freshly ground coarse black pepper. Cornfield peas, stewed apples, Sally Lunn, and a coconut cake five decks high and as white and broad as Abraham's bosom. Fetched hot, was a kite-paste pour-over that undoubtedly earned Captola her Golden Slippers.

Now and then the watchful Qno deftly boxed the board's compass with replenishments of dripped coffee whose reputed alliance with insomnia held no terrors for the company. Table talk was of the superb dog work, and it was agreed that by season's end our two derbies, Flirt and Flash, would be pushing veterans Tom Cotton and Leo. Thirty bevies in six hours down-and-up, meant bird work galore and little gunning save on the rises. Singles were mostly for photography, a must even in that long-gone day.

God's being kind, Charley and I were back in Brick House's library one evening of December 1949. Forty-one years since Hal and I first saw the silver cup, the matched "E. Smith" percussions, and listened to Charley's tale while he examined old records. Heaven rest their souls! Hal's and Qno's and Captola's and those of the dogs, too.

Flamboyant, but how could it be better? Nash mentions a diary in those days. I wish I could find it. It may seem odd that I do not include "Bob White Blue! Bob White Gray!" and "Hallowed Years" in this book. The morsels I have used should be enough to move readers to go back and enjoy the complete stories in the original editions.

The Harp That Once –

Nash Buckingham wrote with special charm when writing of bobwhite shooting over bird dogs on old plantation lands. A few of his stories—some fiction— dripped with atmosphere of the War Between the States, and readers who delight in Civil War history will find satisfaction in the title story in Tattered Coat *and most of the title story in* Blood Lines. *For those of us to whom shooting is everything, two of the stories I've chosen, "Play House" and "The Harp That Once—", have a toothsome amount of butternut and Stars-and-Bars, but not so much that it smothers the bird-shooting flavor.*

"The Harp That Once—" was in the Derrydale and Putnam editions of De Shootinest Gent'man. *That it appeared in some form about 1921 (so far, I've been unable to learn where) is indicated by a letter I discovered among Nash's papers under the letterhead* Robert Frothingham, 8 West 40th Street, New York *and dated "Friday evening, at home, August 19th, '21."*

> Dear Nash Buckingham:
> It is 10:30 and I have just finished reading "The Harp That Once—", first to myself and then aloud to Mrs. F., who is one of the few "men's women" I have ever known. My dear fellow, I don't know when I have read anything that has gripped me so. If you never write anything again as long as you live, you have built a little monument for yourself that will be unction to your soul up to the last hour. It calls to mind those lines of an obscure British poet, John Clare, who died 100 years ago—

I hope Nash remembered that letter in his last years when he was experiencing anxiety about his work in a world that had changed. The letter obviously impressed him at the time, for he opened the book version of "The Harp That Once—" with the John Clare poem quoted by Mr. Frothingham.

This story is Buckingham rich in mood and character, with passages you could wish to have written yourself. Mr. Arthur Wheatley, who used the name of his dog Guido—a dropper—as pseudonym for pieces he wrote for early issues of The American Field, *died between February 22, 1901, when Nash wrote of him in "Comin' Twenty-One," and May 18, 1901, when his death was mentioned in an entry of the Beaver Dam Club logbook.*

The down-South form "Mr. Arthur and Miss Laura" confused me as a boy and I considered there to be an abnormal number of Southern bachelors whose maiden sisters kept house for them, until I grew to learn that, as in this case, "Miss Laura" was Mrs. Wheatley—the South's clinging to its women's years as belles.

The Master of Game, from which Nash quotes in the next-to-last paragraph, was, as he stated in "P-o-i-n-t Judges" in Tattered Coat, *begun in 1387 by Gaston de Foix, translated and added to by Edward II, Duke of York—the oldest book on venery.*

The scene with Arthur Wheatley and the old slave, Landom Harris, is superb. No one could have written that who had not observed, and felt a wince of pain, as an aged man struggled to rise with a hand shaken by intention tremors. This ranks with "Thou and Thy Gun Bearer" and some episodes with Horace Miller in revealing the warm affection that existed between the gunners of that period and the Negroes with whom they shared their sport. Who but Nash wrote lines like: "Long, as long goes to tired hunters, we sat by the fire," and "I looked out upon night frost and our string of bobwhites hanging high against the moonlight"? And who but a shooting man can know fully what they mean?

"O had I known as then, Joy would
  leave the paths of men,
I had watched her night and day, be sure,
  and never slept agen.
And when she's turned to go, O I'd
  caught her mantle then,
And gave her heart my posies,
  all cropt in a sunny hour,
As keepsakes and pledges, all
  to never fade away."

—JOHN CLARE

THE DAWN OF youth's call afield brought to me our comradeship, and an abiding affection therein for him. Somehow, he seemed to happen rightfully into my life; an upstanding, wholesome man's man, with booming, resonant voice, humorous hair triggers in his keen, tender gray eyes, and a heart, God guard his destiny, as big and as stanch as a barn door. To my dear father he was always affectionately "Arthur," and Dad to him was "Miles"; and their tracks ranged trail side by side. So, Mister Arthur became by that vaguely intuitive diagnosis of boyhood, my ally, confidant and hero. There was but one Mister Arthur—"Guido," whose facile pen traced magic, helped pioneer American field trials, and lived, unselfishly, incomparable joys of the chase.

In the period of which I write black powder was but sensing encroachment of a smokeless product. Repeating shotguns were tricky novelties. Auto-loading weapons were mere dreams of a Jules Verne vintage. Our old-fashioned street was almost out in the country in those days. Mister Arthur and Miss Laura were our neighbors; their antebellum home set well back among oaks, maples and magnolias. It was approached along a square-bricked promenade hedged with ground-sweeping cedars beautifully inter-spaced with magnificent hollyhocks. Miss Laura, all in white and a charming picture of wifely devotion, knits amid the shady aloofness of a broad col-umned veranda. To me that playground is a memory of droning bees, humming birds and scents of mingled rose and honeysuckle.

Down in the woods lot was Mister Arthur's kennel. In those days gentle-men trained their own shooting dogs. Whip, forerunner of the mighty Gladstone, had gone the way of all dogflesh. Mister Arthur's full gun-dog string was an assortment of bird and water canines, with hounds and beagles thrown in. I've spent whole afternoons searching for and dragging puppy scions from beneath cobwebby house-sills. And evenings, figuring pedigree papers and choosing names for future challengers to title in pointer and setter Halls of Fame. Many a night, lodging with some crony at Mister Arthur's we fought field trial winners for a fair share of bedcovers.

And oh! those pioneer bobwhite hunts when I first followed Mister Arthur and Daddy. Friday nights, in wintertime, we youngsters were taken to a duck club to which Father and Mister Arthur belonged; a preserve of some five thousand acres. What jolly nights those old-timers had! How they loved their weapons and every detail of gunning! The first repeating shot-gun I ever saw was a Spencer, operated by Mr. Bonnie, a famous shot from Louisville, Kentucky. But for the most part our fathers clung to works of art by Greener, Scott, Smith and Westley Richards. They believed in stiff powder loads, plenty of big shot, and devil take the recoil. They made an early start for their blinds, worked like Turks for their game when need be, and took toddy as often as they frequently felt so inclined. Sterling shots they were, too. We lads were kept well at heel, and were warned to talk short unless otherwise bidden. Wretched the youth who blabbed of how many "snorts" Mister So-and-So took. Or how much changed hands in the poker game we peeped at from a sheltered observation post around the chimney corner.

Some of those mornings are priceless memories. At the entrance to Big Lake, the sun's curtain of fire enfilading jagged skyline; filmy cypress tops etched against blue satin; countless thousands of ducks booming from spray-flung wave jets! Swan gangs blaring! Clanging files of disturbed geese, muffling the drum-fire of one's pulse.

On any hunt Mister Arthur was the life of the party. His locker at Wapanoca, or trunk at Beaver Dam, literally a gunner's treasure trove to a boy. He preferred having us lads help him paw over old shells and hunting gear which he tumbled promiscuously from his helter-skelter plunder abodes. He rarely joined the poker game, but told us stories of his boyhood home in the hill country; tales of bear and deer hunts with his Civil War body servant, Landom Harris, handling the strike dog and packs. I can see Mister Arthur, in a stained dressing robe, and, from a rocking chair just off the huge fireplace, punctuating the dramatics of recital with flourishes of his glass of heady punch. Intent little faces drinking in the thrills of the battles and death of his two greatest hounds, Rambler and Bugler Ben, slain together in mortal combat with a gigantic panther. We usually slept three in a bed after that yarn. Once in a while some reference was made to his own son who had died a mere boy. We always wanted to hear more about him. But somehow when Mister Arthur started on that, a wistful shadow settled about his fine eyes, and off he branched into hairbreadth forays and brushes with the Yankees. Ofttimes our dreams, reeking with powder smoke and saber charges, to say nothing of too much supper, took a nightmarish turn. But in moments of quiet in his office, when he let business slide to write gunning essays for the few outdoor publications of that day, Mister Arthur, like some men, had a favorite tune which he whistled or hummed during particularly happy interludes. His was that old Irish lay, "The Harp That Once Through Tara's Halls." He rarely ventured beyond its first line or two before branching off into "Old Dan Tucker" or "Annie Laurie." But all in all "The Harp That Once—" was his heart's melody.

Then, just as the glory of October days gathered for the first shock of killing frost and made it high time to begin decoy painting, the crash came. One evening, home from the bank, Father was very grave and not quite himself. After supper he and Mother talked alone in the library, while we boys, a most extraordinary proceeding, were sent upstairs for lessons. Mister Arthur and Miss Laura called and it was past midnight when we heard them leave. Next evening a similar conference occurred, with lawyers present. Mister Arthur had grown suddnly haggard. Mother spent much of her time at Miss Laura's, and three days later Father informed us that our neighbors were going out West to live. There was talk of a will, a relative's deed, heavy endorsements and suspicion—terms wholly impenetrable to children other than their terrible import of parting with Mister Arthur. Real estate agents tacked "For Sale" signs upon his oaks. Vans bundled off loads of priceless furniture. The shooting dogs, one by one, disappeared mysteriously. All we sensed was that direful misfortune had befallen our hero. But he laughed at us as of old. Made jests of his leaving and how he and Miss Laura would come home from Texas with a cattle fortune. I heard Father tell Mother that "chickens would come home to roost and a day roll around when Arthur would be vindicated before the world." Whatever that meant, I believed and remembered it, knowing Dad.

Came pangs of farewell. When the carriage came to carry Mister Arthur and Miss Laura to the depot, my hero, leading Barney, his favorite setter, and carrying his imported double bird gun, came striding up our driveway. When Dad and I met him, he said, "Buster, here are Barney and the old gun for you. I want you to have and keep them all for your very own— to remember me and our good old times by—I know you'll take care of them—and—and—always try to live like a good, clean boy." But he sort of choked. Father cried out, "Arthur—Arthur—my dear fellow," and putting an arm about his shoulder turned him away. While I, with my whole world black and crumbling, burst into tears and walked back along the rose hedge, leading Barney and sobbing.

Lad that I was, I never saw Barney on a point, or cocked an eye down that treasured gun's rib, without thinking of Mister Arthur. Many an enthusiastic letter I penned to my old friend; of my hunts, school progress and how much I missed him and Miss Laura. Invariably he replied promptly, telling me of the great new country, its wide plains, hard work, buoyant life and game. Schooldays swept into college years. Barney passed on. Dad heard off and on from Mister Arthur, while Christmas seasons brought affectionate little tokens and pledges of gentle faith. Thus nearly twenty years sped away. Then, as abruptly as came that thunderbolt of earlier days, my father's prediction came true. A sinning relative's death-bed confession righted a great wrong done Mister Arthur. The fields of his forebears, estates and holdings, swept away by false signatures, were his again. And for the first time I discovered that it had been Dad who stood by Mister Arthur in his hour of need and staked him west until a fresh start could be made and the debt be slowly but meticulously repaid. Mister Arthur's response to the good news was characteristic. He and Miss Laura would close out their holdings at the earliest moment possible and return.

A better storyteller than I should describe that reunion. I remembered Mister Arthur as above six feet, a wedge-shaped chap with a thatch of thick brown hair. He could ride as only one of Bedford Forrest's cavalrymen. And Lord! how he could shoot. At last they were home! Miss Laura, but for her silvered locks and "specs," the same beauty. And Mister Arthur? Brown thatch a white mane. Broad shoulders a bit sagged. But tender gray eyes still at hair trigger, and his deep voice still vibrant. Beyond repressed emotion, and a necessary discussion of the important business in hand, a main phase of Mister Arthur's visit bore upon quail-shooting prospects. I told him everything I could recall of lapsed years, but when I put back into his hands that handsome bird gun he had given me so long ago—still flaw-less—the old gentleman all but broke down. He would fancy, he allowed, "slipping away with you on an old-time bird shoot and, incidentally, a scouting trip around my old diggings."

Next afternoon a local train set us down in the gleam of a December day at his old home town. It seemed strange that I, who, as a mere lad, had followed this man afield in the days of his power and glory, should return with him after so many years of denial and hardship, but with his feet set once again upon a better road down the far slope. As though he had been gone since but yesterday, he turned toward where the tavern ought to be. Trudging a Main Street now gaunted into sere oaks and sycamores, toward Court House square, he pointed excitedly to spots from his youth. Yonder he had gone to school—where that tumbly brick building stands; there old man So-and-So had kept a trading post—over that way, across the hitch-ing lot, his company had formed and ridden away to the War. Names leaped to memory; war flags arrayed themselves company by company. But no one recognized in us any part of a malady that had previously racked a country-side. At the old-fashioned livery stable we arranged for a double rig and two saddles. We breakfasted by lamplight, just as we had done so many times before. And again a jolly sun stole up and set village roofs asmoke with frost mist.

I was proud of my dogs, Jimmy and Don. Fit for even Mister Arthur to pull a gun over. We clattered the rig up a hill and from a scrub oak ridge a wonderful valley opened, with river bottoms in the distance. Crossing those Mister Arthur showed me where, as a laddie-buck, he had shot his first wild ducks. His delight knew no bounds, he was young again, searching

for landmarks, clucking and sighing with disappointment when some mem-
oried vantage point failed to materialize. Recalling folks from his old days
hereabouts, he wondered if, by any chance, any of them could still be alive.
Knowing the lay of the land so well, Mister Arthur finally drew rein at a
crossroad, suggesting we saddle up and hunt cross country the rest of our
way. A farmer gladly ran our conveyance under his shed. At a fence gap
Mister Arthur turned into an expanse of sedge, post oak and pine islands.
Jim and Don had long since been whipping off their wire edges. Now, far
ahead, they were cutting up respective territories; the noble setter's feathered
plume switching merrily. Don's black and white showed clear-cut as he
raced a brambled bench. Mister Arthur sat his horse like a knight of old.
At that moment he was nearly seventy-five years young.

Suddenly Mister Arthur, watching keenly, tossed aloft an arm—
"P-o-i-n-t!" Three hundred yards away, where a mock-orange row whittled
off downhill to meet a belt of ragweed, Don, striding full blast, endeavored
frantically to check, turned sidewise and slid into as stylish a point as any
bird dog ever contrived. Jim, catching his pal's curved posture, honored
it a hundred feet away. No mounted skirmisher could have quit his steed
with the graceful alacrity of Mister Arthur's departure from that livery
stable nag. He might have been taking cover from a hot corner in cavalry
days. Opening his old gun, he fumbled the flap-pocket of his faded corduroy coat, produced two shiny red shells and walked crisply toward Don.
The Lord was gracious, I said to myself, to have spared us both this moment.
No admonition as to shooting positions, right or left, was needed. Hadn't
he raised me?

With a dynamic buzz and swirl, a bevy exploded just beyond Don's
pop-eyed stare. I couldn't shoot; I just had to watch Mister Arthur. Could
he "come back"? There it was again! The same fractional pause; then up
came his weapon—hitched quickly, but steadily. His eyes handled the
covey, the gun itself. A husky cock-bird, skimming the briars for an opening
higher up, wilted at the fringe of mock-orange and tumbled into the weed
tops. A second fugitive, arcing over sassafras tippets, was sent hurtling. A
clean, beautiful double. Would that I could see him now—just as he stood
there! Boot tops flipped with frost dribble from the sedge. Stained, bottle-
green shooting coat sharp against the brilliant sunlight. Hair, mustache,
weatherbeaten tan. "My boy"—there was an excited quaver in his voice
—"my boy, I'm a very, very lucky old dog; I have made a sure enough,
old-time double." And while I was lying as to why I hadn't done a share of
shooting, in came Don and Jim, each trying to nuzzle a bird into my old

friend's trembling hands. I consider that moment one of my life's great reunions. Then a second nature called us into pursuit of singles. Down a branch bottom, where escaping birds had straggled into tangleweed and blackberry bushes, first Jim and then Don gave exhibitions, and we were again in the saddles. A few wide casts and three or four more covey finds were behind us. Thick woods and creek beds; acorns crunching beneath horses' hoofs, the spice of herbs and acrid tang of dying timber in our receptive nostrils. At noon, still a few miles, Mister Arthur said, from his old plantation, we made a happy meal. Jim and Don nosed their fair share, and rolled in beds of warm leaves. We followed suit, a field custom Mister Arthur hadn't forgotten. With saddles for pillows and our slickers and saddle blankets for cover, we napped.

I wish you had been with us that afternoon, across plateaus rich in peas and hollows sweet with sorghum. Everywhere, daggers of corn were driven into cotton lowlands. And how those dogs of mine did handle the birds! Late afternoon brought us to the rim of a bluff overlooking a considerable stream that Mister Arthur called Big Black. "Yonder," said he, pointing to a chalky bluff, "at the foot of that lower knob, I learned to swim—so did my brothers and Landom Harris—the whole countryside, for that matter. Ed Daniels was drowned there, and for a long while we wouldn't venture in." Fording the river at a crossing well remembered by Mister Arthur, we trotted a worn bridle path skirting the clear, green water. Atop a commanding ridge we came suddenly upon an old double log cabin, its "dogtrot" sheltered with vines and hung beneath with gourds and red pepper strings. A bundle of fishing canes leaned against the caves. A freshly killed hog, with turkeys and chickens in the background, told a story of plenty. Cur dogs and hounds gave us noisy welcome and a fat colored woman answered our hail. Silencing the din, she herded behind her a bunch of pop-eyed children and came toward us, grinning welcome.

"How do you do," said Mister Arthur. "What is your name?"

"Angeline Downs, suh."

"Have you lived around here long, Angeline?"

"Yas, suh, Cap'n; I wuz borned right back o' de big house up yonder—Landom Harris is my gran' papa, suh!"

Mister Arthur started, almost violently. "Landom Harris—your grandfather—he—he—is—alive then—why—you are fairly well along yourself, woman, and I figured Landom long since dead." But Angeline reassured him.

"He ain' daid, Cap'n, but he's mighty ole—he's in yonder now—settin' by de fi'ah—but he fishes er little an' gits aroun' tol'able."

Off his horse and into the dogtrot stalked Mister Arthur, with Angeline and me following. In a spacious, low-ceilinged room, spotlessly clean, with two four-poster beds, sat an old grizzled Negro, close to a log fire. His wrinkled face wore an air of resigned placidity, almost as though he listened, or tried to read in the flames memories from long ago. Mister Arthur went quietly up to him and said, "Landom!" The old man lifted his gaze, and, without a word, looked long and earnestly. "Landom," repeated my companion, "you don't remember me—I am—Mister Arthur, Landom."

Gradually, as reason fought its battle with the years, understanding came. Landom's eyes slowly blinked full of tears, and his lips moved, inarticulate. Seeking to rise, his hickory cane beat a tattoo as he struggled up to attention. He knew now, just as Mister Arthur had looked past the mask of infirmity and seen a stalwart slave riding with him to the War again. Then the storm broke. Their hands went groping to clasp in as honest and heartfelt affection as God's people ever feel. The slave's hoary head bent slowly upon his old master's sleeve. And Mister Arthur's arm went round those bent shoulders. How long they clung thus I cannot say. I remember crossing quietly to the cavernous fireplace and looking down into the flames until my own eyes dried.

It would be romancing to prolong this story—a plain little true story of the quail fields. It is told now—almost. Under Angeline's guidance, Mister Arthur and I rode on to the Big House, a pile of brick, ivy growth, white columns and melancholy. An ensemble of pre-war grandeur long lost in gloom and given over to some sleepy caretaker. The last named, awed in the presence of his new master, showed us through. Our footsteps rang hollow through wide halls and lofty chambers. Dusty portraits of gentlefolk in ball gowns and regimentals looked austerely upon us. Musty gloom hung heavily over the premises.

"Sleep here?" replied Mister Arthur. "Not this night, my boy." He headed for Landom's cabin. We supped at the old slave's bounteous table; off country ham, fried rabbit, hot biscuits and a sweet potato pie. Long, as long goes to tired hunters, we sat by the fire. Mister Arthur and Landom went back together across years—swam under the chalk bluff and hunted grounds that had been lost but were found again, "re-jined" the cavalry. Angeline smoothed our beds, and moved Landom and the youngsters into a room across the dogtrot. Later, I looked out upon night frost and our string of bobwhites hanging high against the moonlight. The note of a running hound mellowed distant bottoms. Was it not, I asked myself, the Master of Game, who wrote: "Now shall I prove how hunters live in this world more joyfully than any other men. For when the hunter riseth in the morning and he sees a sweet and fair morn and clear weather and bright; and he heareth the song of the small birds the which sing so sweetly with great melody and full of Love each in his own language in the best wise that he can, according that he learneth of his own kind. And, when the sun is risen, he shall see fresh dew upon the small twigs and grasses, and the Sun, by His virtue shall make them shine. And that is a great joy and liking to the Hunter's heart." Truly, we had had His proof, that day.

Through the door of our room I glimpsed Mister Arthur. He was seated in front of the fire, removing his boots and crooning softly—"The Harp That Once—"

Pipeline "Pottiges"

Nash wrote two stories about quail shooting on John Bailey's plantation in Mississippi. The first appeared as "Valley of Contentment" in Field & Stream, *December 1943, and as "Castle Tomorrow" in his book* Tattered Coat (1944); *the second, "Pipeline 'Pottiges,'" was published in* The American Field, *December 5, 1959, and again in* De Shootin'est Gent'man and Other Hunting Tales *in 1961.*

John Bailey's gun diary, begun in 1921 when he was fourteen, shows that the "Castle Tomorrow" hunt was on February 2 and 3, 1943, and that the two days described in "Pipeline 'Pottiges'" were January 26 and 27, 1959.

"In 1943," John said, "Nash was still an excellent quail shot. In 1959, at seventy-nine, he was an old man trying to hang on. This hunt was his last quail limit. I have pictures of this hunt, and I have a sign where he killed the last bird of his limit, eight quail at that time—Nash always called it the 'trampoline.' He came back in 1964 and I got a picture of him approaching a dog on point for the last time. He didn't get to shoot—the dog so-and-so ran the birds up."

In both stories as well as each time Nash mentioned John Bailey to me there was evidence of that relationship that probably exists only between a shooting man in his later years and a younger man, bringing new enthusiasms—even a little awe—to the friendship, and it is something to be cherished. There is no doubt that Nash's life was enriched by knowing John, twenty-seven years younger, who obviously was devoted to Nash. John wrote:

"When Captain Paul Curtis, gun editor of Field & Stream, *reported Nash's breaking 49 x 50 on his first try at skeet using his 90% Burt Becker magnum, I made up my mind to meet Nash Buckingham. My first hunt with him was on November 24, 1933."*

Nash spoke of John Bailey's Quail Hills Plantation as a showplace managed for ideal quail shooting. It is over 1,900 acres with an additional 1,500 acres leased for shooting. There is regular controlled burning, and miles of strips through woods and fields are disked and planted to millet (peas, before deer raids forced a change).

John told me that Nash used his Burt Becker twenty-six-inch quail gun on his first hunts at Quail Hills. "Am most sure this is the gun he is holding accepting the retrieve in the frontispiece in De Shootinest Gent'man. *He liked that gun. Once told me you could lay that gun down in a field and walk off and when you came back it would have killed a quail!" Down there he also shot a Greener hammer gun, a gift from Ira Richards, and several Winchester Model 21's for quail. "Nash usually wore a sports coat and tie on any kind of hunt—sometimes a white coat while quail hunting. On my first hunt with Nash (1933) he was experimenting with glasses. He would shoot at a few quail with them on, then take them off for a few shots. After that first hunt he always shot with glasses. Nash said, 'When you suspicion that you need glasses to shoot quail, you sho' do.' "*

Nash gave John his old saddle gun scabbard. "I think he enjoyed giving me that more than any one thing. He said, 'This scabbard has been in hunting fields in the U.S. and Canada, on field trials, rich estates and on forty-dollar mules on po' farms.' "

I saw the letter Nash wrote at the time:

> I had it made in 1910 by Abercrombie & Fitch on a pattern I sent 'em; big enough to really take a gun or rifle. I've been using and oiling it ever since. I've hunted it at Grand Junction, the Continental and other stakes; and now it is going home to your lands where it has been many times. Use it and pass it on to the young 'uns. Always sling a gun scabbard stock foremost, with the stock a shade higher, so that as you alight you can slash it out with your left hand.

The Buckingham touch is on "Pipeline 'Pottiges' "—". . . my old dog running sideways because he was so tired . . ."—and in "Castle Tomorrow" there is one line worthy of Masefield: "Queen, whipping into sight from her distant questing, strides in, stiff-legged, to honor the find." Nash wrote elsewhere of the amazing rapport between Queen and John Bailey; as for the setters Billy and Rex, I felt I knew them long before John showed me their photographs on point.

One last bit of "Castle Tomorrow" I must quote here. Nash misses a bobwhite, an incident that comes as solace to us ordinary wing shots:

> . . . an inglorious miss. To cover discomfiture, I tell Hal Sheldon's story of a like terrible moment, when, after a long run of goose eggs, he scored a complete Dutch double without an alibi left to command. Slowly he unbreeched his gorgeous Owen twenty-bore and the ejector flung the two offending hulls far behind him. Three pairs of eyes burned into his back, and then Lucius Waldrip's voice arose in comfort. "Colonel," he commiserated, "that little gun sho' throws its shells further 'n any gun I ever saw."

Of these two stories, I have chosen "Pipeline 'Pottiges' " because it reflects both hunts, and the other times Nash gunned Quail Hills with John. Nash, at seventy-nine when most men are practically immobile, dismounts to go to a pointing dog and takes "a neck-crunching tumble," dismissing it with "apparently no harm done; in fact later on I'm inclined to think it's done . . . more good than damage."

Mr. Buck, as always, dwells on the food at dinner with a verve bespeaking an appetite far younger than his years, ending with "a muscadine pudding . . . very few folks have ever seen or will taste."

His statement at the start of the second day's hunt that the quail "heard the truck, the ensuing talk and backtracked down through the woods" is worth noting for those who think that noise and voices have no effect on game birds.

The old home site with its sentinel chimneys on a hilltop is where John and Catherine Bailey built their lodge at Quail Hills, a dream Nash can't help have taken pleasure in seeing come to form. For along with a sign "Nash's last limit" and "The Nash Buckingham Pine," there is much of the man enshrined there, no small part being in the 350 letters written between 1933 and February 13, 1971, that final letter probably the last that Nash Buckingham wrote to anyone. John said, "Nash usually wrote long newsy letters—field trials, football, hunting, politics, etc. That letter was very short. After only a few lines he closed with 'Cheerio, Nash.' I think he became sick while writing it. He had never signed a letter 'Cheerio' before."

Nash gave something of himself to every person he knew, but I believe a very big part of Mr. Buck is there at Quail Hills.

JOHN BAILEY BRAKED his mud-tractioned truck with its compartment for four bird dogs. He pointed into an open field below us and east of the highway. Distant woods formed a jagged skyline. We were en route from Grenada, Mississippi, north through the Torrence and old Bryant Station area to John's farm-lodge and shooting leases about four miles south of Coffeeville.

Said John: "See those four wide concrete steps sitting in the open pasture over yonder? Well, they're all that's left of the Dailey plantation home where you stayed in 1911 and found thirty-three bevies of birds one day and twenty-eight the next—walking." Staring into the dusk I could hardly realize the changes demanded by progress in forty-eight years.

"When Grenada Lake's impoundment is carrying a full load of water," continued John, "it is eight to ten feet deep where we are sitting and a good way from the dam. Water comes to within half a mile of our lodge. As the uppage ebbs and exposes it, thousands of fishermen launch their boats from this old highway. Automobile bumpers touch from here to the dam. See those woods over yonder? During duck season I bagged several limits of mallards in pools the rise left behind in them."

As John resumed our way I caught a flashback of that 1911 bird hunt John mentioned. He was but four years old at the time and I was thirty-one. At Mister Bill Dailey's, John Bourne, Brodie Finley and I had wagoned ourselves and four crackerjack bird dogs from Grenada to Mr. Bill's manor and found so many quail in its vicinity that sometimes I have doubted it myself. Those rolling, pine-clad and sequestered creek bottoms with natural partridge foods and cropped coverts were chockful of zooming bobwhites. And Mr. Bill guarded 'em—plenty—although he wasn't much of a hunter himself. We walked because it was too cold to ride. But the worst was over and the ground was just beginning to exhale moisture as sunlight flashed against it. Two little boys, "Parched Corn" and "Puddin'," carried lunches and extra shells. The provender provided by our genial host—turkey, pork hams, vegetables galore, hot biscuits, cream gravy, milk and pies always groaned the boards. The old home, with its completely encircling upper veranda, had no central heating. So the yardboy left extra pine knots and we took turns refueling and diving back under the blankets of the huge mahogany four-posters. I don't recall state game laws in those days but we had county licenses and the bag limit was, as I recall, twenty-five birds a day.

By now we had turned off the old highway, climbed a winding eminence to a forested plateau facing eastward toward what John termed "Baskerville Mountain." Off through the gloaming flashed distant farm buildings. At the lodge's cheerful settlement we were greeted by dogs' shrillings and welcomings from the helpers. A cavern of bright logs. Walls burdened with oils and etchings of dogs and scenes familiar to John from forty years' roaming of hills and dales. Portraits and enlarged photographs of his greatest dogs on point recalled thrilling moments.

Long known to lovely Catherine Bailey as "meat and potatoes men," picture John and me "setting over" country fried steak, vegetable delectables and apple pie that curls toes and sends glances to rafters. Then John's diaries, dating back to first outings are studied; while we retrace steps leading to the time when the off-mainline railway of some twenty-five miles was built, beginning 1925, from Bryant Station and the Illinois Central eastward to what became the town of Bruce, Mississippi. It wound through the Scuna River Valley, now a tributary of Grenada Lake. I was then looking over the area for a township-size tract for a quail management experiment by the Western Cartridge Company of East Alton, Illinois; now Olin Mathieson Chemical Corporation. John's stack of diaries, over a foot high, probably hold more studies and experiments with Nature's proceedings and have done more to stabilize his prodigious memory of farming and its cultures than college courses encompass today. An entry gives us pause— "November 22nd, 1934. Nash Buckingham and I hunted together; had a wonderful long tramping hunt and discovered during lunchtime that he was double my age—54 to 27." That year, too, was when John began active management of his farm and several thousand acres of surrounding lands for the Webber Brothers, of Detroit, who bought the lodge from the late W. B. Mershon of Saginaw, Michigan.

It's "befo' daylight" when a light tap on his door brings an old bird hunter alive for ablutions and accoutrements that fetch him again to the snapping fire and strong black coffee and a later leisurely breakfast. Thence to feed setters Billy and Rex.

So, all hands into the truck again and off to John's farm with thousands of acres of "Government Land" to its north. At the tilling of John's straw-boss we find the horses saddled. Day is coming in far too warm and with little squilly winds along the ground. Billy and Rex are in for it.

Billy hightails slashingly to the left across weedy stubble alongside the road. Rex sweeps pasturage toward a thinly sedged post-oak ridge and suddenly slows to feather its edges. Just then John calls, "Billy's on point at that tick-grass patch; you can hardly see him in the shadow of the woods —let's go." Dismounting, John has already surveyed the situation. "These birds are scattered feeding and chances are they'll climb for the timber— every whichaway, too."

We attempt a pincers movement and there's a roar from behind us. All I see are bobs getting themselves lost in dense woods. But John's gun yapped down a straggler. We remount and John sights across the pasture. "Yonder go Rex's birds," he shouts. "They are a tricky bunch, too, and have left the old boy flat-footed." We ascend the ridge and pad along a forest dirt road. The dogs are casting on either side and below us.

"Right yonder," I tell John, pointing on ahead and down into a narrow valley headed by a food patch, "is where we found the first bevy two years ago."

"Correct," rejoins John. "Your memory is definitely still good so now we'll see about your reflexes." Shortly thereafter a third bevy tricks our scouts with a wild flush far ahead. Billy nabs a single farther on and in attempting to dismount I managed to step into a leaf-covered ruthole and take a neck-crunching tumble. But apparently no harm done; in fact later on I'm inclined to think it's done my backbone's piano keys more good than damage. A creek bottom and away go two more bevies; this hot wind is playing the wild with us. But finally the dogs hem up a covey in regal fashion and we take heartening toll. "That's better," laughs John. "We're on our way."

"Today," I reminisce to John, "is a dead ringer for one the great Ariel had to face one morning in his National Field Trial Champion's stake heat. We judges sympathized with both dogs because anything can happen, especially when moving single birds have to be literally rooted out. Handlers cringe from puffy hot winds. But old 'Fred' [Ariel's kennel name] made it that day and is one of our Triple National Champions. On his last try he outlasted the magnificent Tarheelia's Lucky Strike." It's getting too warm for comfort and coats come off when we get down to shoot. But we don them when we ride; there's a hint you'd best remember. Again we score on a woods bevy. Pursuit of the singles yields a bird or two, and John, finding a convenient log, produces our lunches and the good old water bottle. The dogs snug into the warming dry leaves, toothing burs from their hides and between their toes but alert and expectant eyes open for their cut of Catherine's delicious sandwiches and cake slices. They get 'em, too.

"John," I query, "in your years of farm and wildlife management have you been bothered by the current outcry against beetles and fire ants and an equally fiery opposition's crusading against dieldrin and other poisonous sprays?"

John thought a moment. "On my farms and leases we've been singularly free from pests and controls. I've heard of few wildlife casualties in this immediate sector. But I have heard roars of indignation elsewhere and from men who ought to know. I guess insecticides and pesticides are like any other products fighting for sales; they've got to have selling points like power and speed in cars and I think the danger has simply gotten away from the authorities and that the situation is far worse generally as to wildlife losses than they want it known. I ride my places daily and I keep my eyes open. So far, I'm O.K."

"John," I ask, "nowadays in your vicinity wouldn't it be possible to bag limits of ducks, quail and doves in a single day?"

John thinks a moment over that one. "Well," he concludes, "it shouldn't be too difficult in the latter half of our split dove season; that is, if you got a real early start and had a bit of luck with the ducks. I'm often home with my limit by eight-thirty. Then I drive out here, many times without a gun, just to work the dogs and look after things generally. I go home for lunch and as the dove season opens after noon, I go shoot with some friend who has a good concentration on his picked corn, or popcorn and milo maize. The doves are strongly resurgent due to crop turn-overs, farm-pond programs and sportsmanlike ethics afield. By the way, didn't you start that split-season idea up in Tennessee and finally talk them into it for Mississippi and Arkansas to copy?"

We said we did, but it was hard selling. But by now it's one-thirty and the bobs should be on their afternoon foragin's. Says John, "We're halfway through our limits and the balance shouldn't take too long; this is my favorite valley of all—ahead of us." We soon see Rex and Billy frozen tight as Dick's hatband just ahead of us off the woods road on which we're jogging. It's a scattered bevy and while John tallies a right and left, I manage to scrape down a left-angling bob that doesn't hit the weed too dead. Rex fetches John a bird, and Billy, after considerable flurry, brings in my cripple very gently for John to pouch. Rex retrieves the third victim and John, doing a "rock an' roll," turns to me.

"That crippled bird of yours has crawled out of my sack and is running around all over my bare back up under my shirt—it's the first time in history I've ever had my back scratched by a quail—catch him for me."

John's shirt back is heaving with the struggles of the brave little bird. I gradually work the moving bulge toward John's waistline. "Let it drop into my hand," laughs John. The bob bounces off John's clawing hand and takes wing with Billy in hot pursuit. The last seen of it was a hundred yards across the sedgetops and rising. We search but never pick up quarry scent. "All I hope," says John, "is that the brave little rascal lives to a ripe old age—he's a game bird all right."

By the time we leave John's dream valley we have the limit and cut across hilltops toward the unsaddling barn. But meanwhile Rex and Billy point three extra bevies just to heighten their own batting averages. Horses curried and fed, we truck to the lodge for a bath and a snooze before welcoming Catherine's dinner guests from Greenwood. Old friends Kirby Sabin and Dr. Ira Bright with their lovely wives and Mr. Provine; the last named a Nestor of old-time woods lore. Kirby and I have spent many a pleasant afternoon together after bream and bass, while Dr. Bright, the great heart specialist, writes wondrous tales of the shooting fields and follows pursuits of happiness over bird dogs and retrievers with his Magnums and Purdeys. Platters of smothered quail in gravy for hot biscuits and pone that only an older generation of Deep South cooks understand. Dove pie, creamed spinach and a dish of eggplant, shrimp, crabmeat, crumbs and cheese in profusion.

We've hardly the nerve to mention a muscadine pudding because very few folks have ever seen or will taste such a dainty. It's as rare as the Wine of Shiraz.

Next morning comes in cloudy, much colder and with a moist underfoot lending scent-sniffers a big hand. At the schoolbus fork of two dirt roads, we find the colored urchins with our horses as instructed yesterday by John.

"Now," says John, handing each a two-bit piece, "when you get home, send someone to drive the truck to your daddy's. Got that? Have it there by two-thirty."

Grins and promissory nods. John and I mount, give Billy and Rex the whistle and start through a woods road—but not for far. Both dogs are pointing just ahead. But they cannot produce and patient relocation is in order. Those birds heard the truck, the ensuing talk and backtracked down through the woods. Sure enough, Billy and Rex soon pick up the scent and follow it two hundred yards down into the hollow and out its far end into the field. The rise is a bit distant, but two bobs stay behind. It is quite a climb back to the feeding horses.

"Now," says John, back at the forks and taking the left one, "see that old post with the sign tacked to it that's caved into the gulch?" I could see the forlorn landmark all but buried in the red clay. "It says," continued John, " 'Coffeeville four miles.' In my young days I used to leave home right after daylight and hunt sixteen miles westward to the mainline of the Illinois Central. I'd eat lunch sitting on the railroad track and then hunt homeward. When I'd hit here and see that old sign, 'Coffeeville four miles,' I'd feel that I was practically home. I could smell the steak fat and hot biscuits and coffee with gravy cooking for supper. Nothing has ever smelled so good since."

Leaving the road, we rode down through a vast stretch of piney woods and climbed to a hilltop. Ahead of us suddenly stretched a long, bulldozer cut reaching almost to the horizon. "Here," explains John, "is where the great pipeline crosses my property eighty feet wide." It is quite a spectacle of mechanized progress. "And," continues John smiling, "it's about like I figured—see that white spike down yonder, sticking up on the levee? That's Rex's tail—he's already on point."

Billy, emerging from the woods, sights and backs Rex in a trice. We had a bird apiece and the bevy sprinkles down through the forest. Then the fun started. Uphill and downhill along the pipeway our sure-footed mounts picked their way. The two dogs, working closely, found four bevies. My timing is sketchy but John is always a Stonewall Jackson. Says John, turning

off the pipeline, "We're about halfway through and I have a special spot to
eat lunch." Billy is soon sighted pointing stanchly about twenty feet inside
a tight barbed wire surrounding a climbing pasture. The wires are really
tight and both John and I realize that to climb over means flushing the
scantily covered birds. We exchange glances, lie down and roll under. It
isn't dignified, but it works. John eases around to the right. The birds are
in sort of a hedgy pocket, and sure enough, try to hoist themselves over a
mess of wild grapevines. So I shoot thereabouts and down tumble two bobs.
Another cuts back—and tumbles. We roll back under the fence, ride around
the wire and John picks up a woods single.

Then, crossing a parklike valley we climb into a cedared hilltop, which,
in its heyday must have been a gorgeous home site. Two tall, stone chimneys
tower sixty feet or more apart; moss and ivy-grown battlements of a long-
gone day. "This," says John, "is where I'm planning to build my new home
and use these two chimneys." We eat another delicious, dog-shared lunch,
quaff pure water and corn the mounts. And there are questions to be
asked John.

"How far does that pipeline cross your land?"

"About two miles. Those raised strips across them are called terraces. The
quail find them wonderful nesting places."

"Do game commissions or soil-conservation technicians follow your example of planting pipelines for wildlife resources?"

"Probably so, in many instances; if not, they should. The pipeline people
themselves sow lespedeza sericia heavily as an erosion control. I add my
own assorted quail foods. I've found sericia only fair as a food. I use mostly
Kobe. But I also harvest and use a world of field peas, also wild Kobe and
peas along ditchbanks. I use perennials heavily. You've noticed, too, that
all through our woods and over the cultivated lands there are feed strips.
There's stock corn, maize, and if you like to have doves, try a patch of
popcorn. Droughts have taught us lessons; our farm-pond program and
withheld waterways are well advanced."

"Isn't the old-time quail bootlegging about over?"

"Yes, it's about scotched. Sometimes, due to the rising cost of ammunition, local hunters trade merchants birds for shells. Preserve owners watch
overkilling very closely. And Mississippi's tough on out-of-state hunters
who violate bag limits."

"What's your slant on 'burning' to improve quail habitat?"

"Well," John explained, "it must be done in daylight of a windless afternoon. With an assistant or two mounted, I ride about six miles an hour,

dropping matches from the saddle and starting a lot of little blazes. This way you don't get a wide line of fire and they burn into one another before attaining volume. This leaves areas that don't burn. It's bound to be a carefully planned operation. If you don't burn at all, sprouts and leaves smother your woods food, and field grasses get so long and heavy a dog can't get through it and quail simply don't fancy or thrive on it. Burn only in late February and early March. And, as you burn, continue scattering wheat or chicken feed or hen-laying mash in the thickets so the birds will have food until grass begins coming up and insects start coming out. Of course, any man with any interest at all in his land's game resources tries to keep some sort of population census in mind and comes to know game range. Indiscriminate burning is senseless and dangerous. Properly done it's indispensable to management."

"Have you any solution as to why, at times, the feeding habits of quail seem to change? Like when two seasons back, they simply took to the woods; lived there and ate acorns almost exclusively?" John thought that one over, too.

"From my observation and studies, until two years ago, at least, I thought quail ate acorns heavily only when their field foods—lespedezas, beggar and ragweeds and pottage 'peas'—had not had enough sweetening summer rains to make their foods taste good. Or that the birds, aside from taste impairment, might have passed them up as impoverished nutritional value. That's the way it was in 1930, '34, '43, '47, '52, '53 and '54. A big percentage of our area quail fed heavily on acorns those years. All seven summers, according to my records, were extremely dry and abnormally hot. Field seeds were small and not properly rounded out. I think the birds realized their lack of palatability and nutrition. Two years ago, though, we had nice summer rains and not too high temperatures and lespedeza did well. But the quail ate just about acorns *only*. Post oak ninety-five per cent of my examinations: five per cent, white oak. I still can't solve this mystery. But you have seen the last two days that they are no longer in the woods. So, the foods they're getting in their natural haunts must be suiting them better. I believe the quail's worst enemy is *heat*. And accompanied by real dry winds." All the while, John had been examining crop contents. He spread a handful. "They seem to like the table we are setting—no acorns."

"Now," says John, "we need five—maybe six—birds. Of all my territory, what we are going to hunt is a prime favorite." We headed through a narrow valley and crossed a deep-green swirling watercourse. Rounding a tall thicket corner, three quail flushed wild from under our horses. John blew in Rex and Billy and put them on the case. Both dogs began feathering. "Symptoms," grins John. "I'll follow Rex and you trust Billy." So completely mutual is the confidence and understanding of John and his dogs that they seemed to instantly understand the situation. Billy and I turned left down the scantily turfed rows of tall bicolor lespedeza. I had to speed up because Billy was trusting his nose for some fancy roading. At the patch's end, he hesitated—and whirled to the right. There he faced a peculiar situation; almost a floor of matted-down springy hedges. It was like walking a trampoline. Could birds possibly be hiding or moving beneath such cover? Billy pussyfooted here and there and suddenly squatted in a low-headed point— the only one I'd seen him make. Out of the trampoline's floor sprang first one bob—then another. One escaped. and, as I stood desperately trying to reload the Model 21, birds began spouting in every direction. I heard John shoot twice and heard him calling. Billy meanwhile had been bouncing around on the trampoline and going hog-wild as bobs took flight.

Looking up through the woods I saw Rex, majestic on point. "Come up here and shoot this bird—if there's more than one, I'll take it." I walked in over Rex and three bobs departed. It took composure for John not to sack the third member—and—our hunt was done.

"And nearly as I can figure it," says my host, "there must have been a quail convention going on around that corner when we came along and plumped into it." Between there and where we found the truck at the barn, Rex and Billy stood and we moved five more bevies. I had long since lost track of how many bevies we'd raised that short day—it wasn't two-thirty yet.

John takes a high road home atop a sort of divide. Braking, he looks out across a tremendous scope of country. "Know where you are?" he asks.

"No. I am as lost as the Seven Tribes of Israel."

John's finger points westward. "See that old house away across yonder under the big trees? Well, back in 1934 you and I and Speed Fry ended a wonderful day right there. The limit was twelve birds and you bagged your last one as we came up through the field back of the barn. We're about to come out on Highway Seven—it was part of our hunting country."

"John," I query, "how far are we from Torrence and the old Dailey lands where I gunned in January, 1911?"

"About forty-eight years," he replied. "You didn't think when you moved sixty-one bunches of birds in two days' walking that you'd be shooting nearly fifty years later with the then four-year-old boy in rompers who lived up the dirt road apiece?" He thought a moment and added, "The wonderful thing is that we've both been spared to enjoy it. And we didn't miss our two last shots—did we?"

John eased the truck down to the fork where we met the horses this forenoon. I could see him, a gangling better-than-six-foot stripling, his coat heavy and sagging with a day's kill of quail and rabbits, and, by the signpost, still four miles from home. But he was practically there because he could smell the hot biscuits and coffee and steak gravy. Something my old friend Sigurd Olson wrote me recently came surging back:

"Too much materialism these days. Too little of the depth of feeling and genuine love of the earth that characterizes the things we like to do. Especially out-of-doors. I have always felt that you cannot divorce emotion and feeling and appreciation of the intangibles from Conservation. Those very intangibles are the reasons for all the practical things we do. Without them, life has little meaning."

Just then, in the deep gully, the half-buried old signpost flashed past. The one that heartened young John Bailey by reminding him that he was four miles from home. I, too, had had some tall hoofing homeward with my old dog running sideways because he was so tired. I caught a long-drawn aroma of hot biscuits and coffee and steak gravy from lamplit homes past which I dragged. I'm so glad there are some of John's and my "intangibles" left.

Amid Whirring Wings

Published in Field & Stream, *October 1930, as "Golden Sedge and Whirring Wings," this piece appeared as "Amid Whirring Wings" in* Mark Right! *(1936) and was used again in 1961 in the Nelson edition* De Shootin'est Gent'man and Other Hunting Tales.

This is "must" reading for novices, pleasant and enlightening for the expert. More than how-to, this is a conversation with Nash about how-best-to in the quail fields. In Nash's pouch or "possibles bag" equipment, the wire snippers, I will take the liberty of pointing out, are for use only in emergency with an enmeshed horse or dog. No gentleman ever cut a landowner's fence.

Nash's statement that it requires "continual contacts with [birds] to shape any pointer's or setter's true destiny" is golden wisdom. And those hundreds of coveys found every season had much to do with bird dog excellence in that period.

I would like to endorse Nash's comment about "loose field talk" concerning range of dogs. The mania for wide-moving dogs has been overdone since the first American bird dog trial in 1874. If this had been restricted to field trials, gun dog strains would have been more suited to foot hunting. Nash states this without equivocation, and he cannot be accused of lack of sympathy for field trial dogs. When he and his friends shot afoot, they did not use the wide flashy trial dogs but, instead, shot over Tom Cotton or Lucy, Kate and Don.

A recital of what a shooter should wear can become tedious, particularly if it deteriorates into discussion of fussy details. But if any man was qualified to name what he had found comfortable in the quail field, Nash was. I was interested in his recommendation of a nearly white shooting coat, which I have found an aid to an aging dog in locating me, and nearly as conspicuous as flame orange in most situations except on snow.

"Amid Whirring Wings" was written as a companion piece to "Here's How in Quail Shooting" (the two were placed consecutively in Mark Right!*); I have used "Here's How in Quail Shooting" in Part Three of this collection.*

GUNNERS WHO RELISH searching for bobwhites have doubtless absorbed unnumbered benefits from contact with nature. Age-spotted gun diaries reveal profound thoughtfulness among certain shooting gentry in jotting down seasonal impressions of the family life, manners, and range characteristics of *Colinus virginianus*.

Treasured prints depict top-hatted and velveteened forebears squinting at proper gun play behind clean-limbed dogs. Blood lines, reiterated from obscure hunting strains, are vouched for by today's high breeding in setters and pointers. On occasional manor walls and above sequestered plantation hearthstones, hang rare flintlocks and powder horns dedicated to outmaneuvering Bob's erratic departures. Many a percussion smooth-bore, somnolent in attic rust, is linked in honor to booming yesteryears amid golden sedge and whirring wings. Final verdict is returned, however, in deeply underlying national affection and respect for Bob White as "a fellow of infinite sporting zest."

Among understanding sportsmen the esprit de corps of quail shooting demands unerring fairness to the bird. The hunt itself should be approached in a frame of mind aloof from mere heft of the game bag. Frankly, however, I do not agree with blurbings which sigh that starry-eyed straying through scented countrysides is ample reward for a birdless gunner. If one's mind is receptive to the beauties of frosted pumpkins and vivid sunsets beyond purpling ridges, so much the better. But any hard-going, intelligent shot has a right to fruitful field expectancy. In a vast majority of us lurks an urge for action, an ear for trigger music, and a nose for skillet savor. When those blessings are decently earned, good luck and amen! Let us say, then, that the open season has cleared nature's decks for action. Vernal matings have ripened into strong bevies along many familiar ranges. Beyond wait canvas-coated hosts and eager dogs.

Some days, quail can be found *ad lib*. At other times, the widest casts of your keenest-nosed dogs fail to strike pay dirt. Many factors are responsible for this raid upon the alibi treasury. In field lingo, your dogs may not "have their noses." Warm weather, fatigue, frozen ground, diffused scent particles, or other ills to which dog flesh is heir, may have a bad hand. When such happens, make the best of it.

Through ill luck, good bird range is sometimes missed. At others, bad judgment selects or steers a wrong route. Or another shooting party may have slipped in just ahead of yours. Distant gun reports and scattered single-bird finds tell that story. Yet most hunts are over reasonably familiar territories, with bevy range reasonably well known. Even then, at times, the curse holds. Again, on unseasonable days, birds are raised apparently for the asking, and from most unexpected covers. By all the laws of the quail prophets, they should have been elsewhere. I have even flushed them thirty yards in the wake of a disk plow, widely scattered and feeding peacefully among the hollows of upturned earth.

But before entering unfamiliar territory, the experienced quailer reads sign of sky and wind, terrain and water. Bird country, appearing prime to the novice, may analyze arid to seasoned field reasoning. Waves of glistening sedge and acres of matted weeds may size up beautiful but prove barren; with outskirts of adjacent planted country getting the call. Steady food supplies and coverts affording quick protection from feathered air raiders, are what attract Bob White.

Walking or mounted, the experienced "pott'ige" hunter's eyes rove the ground for vermin spoors. Comparatively fresh empty shotgun shells are clues to prior invasions. Feathers, scratchings, and vocal rejoinders from wood and fields, have meanings all their own. Sandy creek bottoms and moist ditch beds reveal telltale tracks. Overly numerous hawks and owls indicate game country. Many a knowing hunter has some sentinel air inspector to thank for a bevy find.

For instance, Hal and I had followed some singles over a hill into a brambled gully. Arriving first, Hal found Bill dog on point. From the ridge I saw the whole occurrence. A hundred yards below Hal, a big hawk swooped suddenly in, hovered over the thicket fringe, and struck. Ten seconds later he was flapping upwind with a fat quail dangling. Standing like a statue, Hal let Mr. Hawk beat slowly toward him, and, at thirty yards, broke his neck. Alert to a tense situation, he whirled and dropped the flush off Bill's point. Barring a missing head, the robber-bird's victim was intact. With a chuckle about killing two birds with one stone, Hal then attempted to broad-jump a wide sand ditch, and missed.

So then, a quail shoot's scope embraces luck, or lack of it, in judging and selecting routes; dog work and handling; personal equipment; and actual gunnery. Three methods of contact are in vogue. Old-fashioned, all-day hoofing it; horse- or mule-back; and via automobile. The last-named is sinister evidence of gasoline's menace to off-the-road game resources. An hour's horse travel means fifteen minutes with gas. If quick finds fail to materialize, the gang chugs off to more distant but fresher fields.

Once discovered, fruitful but unprotected quail country is soon made barren of birds. Bevies are hunted to the last bob. Along such ranges, decent sportsmen may enjoy a season's tramping, but unthinking irresponsibles and quail bootleggers know no honor or bag limits. Operations begin by the time the bobs are barely on their own. Whole bevies are obliterated when hardly fit for the table.

Noticeably around the larger cities and towns of our deep South, deplorable losses in game stocks result from quail bootlegging. Conniving patrons of such butchers leer over this pitiful, illicit contraband. It is difficult for even trained operatives from state game departments to capture such rogues. Even so, where political pull exists with magistrates, conviction is a joke. Women are often utilized by these game-bootlegging ghouls to make deliveries. Money changes hands later, at the Boss's office. Sharecroppers form rings and deliver to city bird routes, patronized, strange to relate, by people posing as law-abiding citizen-sportsmen. These bobwhite vandals use slow, well-trained dogs and cylinder-bore magazine guns. Bevies are spotted and raked on the ground. Many such miscreants are scattered over the quail's domain. Their nefarious traffic does more harm than all the rest of the predators put together. Cheap fines are of little avail in such cases. The whipping post would prove more beneficial.

For pleasure and physical benefit, no method of quail shooting approaches horseback hunting, more prevalent in the rangier and less fenced Southern areas. Quailing from horseback naturally stimulates one's dogs; they become bolder and more independent on cast, and more readily catch handling signals. Dog-hunting on lost points requires less time. But, walking or riding, dog handling is a one-man job at all times. Nothing more surely mars a shoot than interference with or criticism of the other fellow's dogs.

But not all dogs "savvy" the mounted hunt. I recall the dismay of a friend whose well-broken pointer made a holy show of himself the first time he saw his master in the saddle. He howled, whined, short-cast, and gave every evidence of not understanding what it was all about. His owner suggested every ill from high blood pressure to running fits. Toward afternoon, with Don trailing disconsolately, or pointing an occasional rabbit in an effort to square himself, I suggested finishing the affair on foot. With his Boss down and hustling, Don came to life, streaking out and handling more than his share of business. Such a defect is easily remedied. Three weeks' association with plantation horses and mules, and Don was a seasoned campaigner.

Singles are much more easily marked down from horseback. In the riding shoot, only two should ever dismount for bevy shots. The third man should hold mounts or spot birds. Few men care to gun "three-in-a-crowd" without such a rule in force. One member of the ground squad should remount after flush and permit the off gun to come down for singles. Rigidly rotated, such rule permits matters to progress smoothly, and with reasonable safety.

The thought of weapon safety becomes second nature to experienced hunters. Under pressure, at times, even second nature slips. Many a novice with good, common sense has had his hair permanently straightened through inexcusable carelessness on the part of some uppish veteran. Shooting "threes" is dangerous around thick cover. Two pellets, one in my left cheek near the eye, and a second under my scalp are twenty-five-year-old souvenirs of that remark. Crowding to the shot hampers individual chances, invites ill feeling where it should never prevail, and results in doubled kills.

Too, using horses allows ample foot-rambling without undue fatigue. When riding after Bob White, one should try to reach home around sundown for a bit of rest before the evening meal. Appetite will be toned down, and you'll sleep better for less food. Visiting hunters should realize, also, that in many cases their hosts have farm duties proportionately as exacting as factory and office routine. Saddle inexperience is far better confessed in the barnyard than later painfully remembered. Minor saddle and stirrup adjustments necessary, but neglected, very easily turn an otherwise pleasant jaunt into drudgery. A hard, rumpled saddle blanket irritates a mount's back. Tie carefully, and preferably high. Always ask if your horse will stand shot. If you toss down your lines, see that they are separated. This spares equipment and prevents a trip or hock burn. If you've ever been left far afield, or been interrupted to chase a runaway, you'll realize the value of some of the above remarks.

Watch vigilantly for loose barbed wire, at times rusty and hard to spot in weeds. The tragedy of a frightened horse being carelessly enmeshed and slashed to ribbons isn't a happy sight or pleasant memory. After lowering fence bars, don't make a slipshod job of replacement. And in loosening wire gates and taut fence wires, mind your fingers.

Most important, never mount or dismount with a loaded weapon, or even jam one down into your saddle scabbard. This applies particularly to magazine guns, though no type absolves its owner from such negligence. It is footless to claim there is no shell in the barrel, but in the magazine. You can't continue to outguess memory. Carelessness leads to miscalculation and inevitable accidents. From a lifetime of experience I made just such a slip three years ago, in not checking a friend's gun, handed me just before I mounted. Only sheer luck saved a good dog.

A real bird hunter would about as soon forget his fowling piece, as to ride away minus his pouch, tied behind the saddle. This type of carrier, indigenous to the South, is to the quail shooter what his "possibles sack" was to the old-time mountain man. I have never seen such a bag displayed in any sporting-goods store or catalogue. It is homemade, of waterproof canvas or plantation ticking. A long, center-slit receptacle, flaring into capacious pockets at either end. A pouch rides anywhere, if need be, and packs with unlimited capacity. Mess kit and teakettle, grub and dog food, extra shells, dog leashes, camera, wire snippers, slicker, toilet kit, and even extra clothing, make the pouch essential for any trip. In the field, bird kills are shifted from pockets to pouch, thus lightening shooting coat drag.

Every man to his own method, but I feed my dogs in the morning, in proportion to what I figure it takes to keep me going. Some men expect an animal to burn the wind all day long on a smell for breakfast, and a scrap or two grudgingly tossed at lunch time. Not for mine. Such nonsense and, at times, cruelty, is as out of place today as the energy-sapping routine of ten miles before breakfast and a mixed ale diet of the pre-Sullivan age. Is it any wonder that hungry dogs bolt a bird or two as days wane?

Many advertisements alluringly describe bird dogs that will hunt "all day long for six days in the week." Such individuals may exist. But not when underfed, and even otherwise, not for long. In these days, with well-balanced and nourishing meats and vegetables rationed for dogs, food is as available as one's own grocery stock. No hunter has an alibi for failure to provide well for his gunning stock.

If you are on horseback, with the starting breakaway a good piece off, by all means couple and lead your dogs. This is imperative if the party is to split. Dogs become excited, mix and cast away prematurely. Time is lost blowing them in. And, worst of all, their jumping and barking around horses' heels constitutes liability. Many an eager fellow has been kicked head over heels. If automobiling, watch door closings to prevent paw bruises or fractured dog shins. Never chain a nervous dog in, or to, a car. I have seen one strangled, and two narrow escapes. An ambitious animal, sensing himself marooned when distant guns pop, sits not upon the order of his going. During the ride home, bed your dogs out of the wind. Warm, tired muscles that have gone twenty times farther and faster than yours, shouldn't be exposed any more than a grand athlete's tendons. Examine your animals before and after the shoot. An overlooked limp may hide a thorn-pierced pad or deep burr cut in some tender crease. Don't forget that a real bird dog has all the heart of a game rooster. A substantial noontime rest will profit guns and dogs. A bit of fire, some tea for sandwich company, and a snooze among sun-warmed leaves or pine needles pay dividends in dog reserve and steadier weapon handling. And be absolutely certain that your fire is put out.

In dry weather, carry a flask for your dogs or keep to watered routes. They soon learn to come in for a drink from your hat crown. If running fits occur, shade, rest, water applications, and manipulation of belly and back, toward the tail, are the best first aid that I've found to dogs so stricken afield.

Bottom lands, bayou banks, brambled drains, and new ground around sloughs are the best bets for bevy finds. On the upland, sparse woods with briared borders, weed belts, and outside plantings of grain and lespedeza are most productive. Around lakes and swamps, birds have a way of shelter-ing in the timber and feeding out into the corn. When put up, they sail far in the woods. This is the most difficult going, but sportiest of all bobwhite gunning.

One hears, nowadays, that quail are becoming educated; that they no longer fan out into the sedge and weeds, to be picked off one by one. My hunch is that it is more the lack of cover, than sense. Bob White isn't consti-tutionally a far flyer. But with so much cleared ground these times, watch him have to wing sometimes half a mile across an open stretch to find pitching space in the cane jungles. Fortunately, some such hides are invul-nerable to men and dogs. The dredge-ditch banks of eastern Arkansas are samples of such protective cover. Invariably there is a good carryover of bird stocks in such country. Except in preserves or wide-open territory, a present day's shoot rarely yields more than a bevy or two of good single-bird shoot-ing. Again, a blessing of today's game restoration program is the lowered bag limit on bobwhite. This takes a tremendous strain off hunting singles. Hunters simply take two or three members from each bevy, and are on their way. Thus extra large bunches, found one day or missed another, will afford a full-length program of outings during the season.

Any quail hunt which makes haste slowly will do better, and too many dogs along are worse than none. At that, bevies can be missed by a hairs-breadth. Last winter, I looked fifteen minutes for a lost bitch. About to ride on, after failing to blow her in, I happened to glance aside and saw her stanchly on point behind a big black stump. We had been within thirty yards of her twice. Afoot or mounted, moving too rapidly is bad practice.

Some dogs possess real bird sense. When neither gunner nor animal is so equipped, the trip, barring luck, is in for some tough breaks. But a know-ing bird hunter in good country can, by hard work, impart bird sense to any reasonably intelligent searcher. Constant going over known range reacts favorably upon canine judgment. But of one thing you may be sure: it requires bobwhites, continual contacts with them, and patient work, to shape any pointer's or setter's true destiny.

An ambitious, intent dog is often whistled off productive going through his master's inexperience in estimating signs of game-making or possibility in cover. I have watched good dogs literally stop in dismay, frustrated at the most critical moment by being forced on, or being called off. Give your dog time when a spot diagnoses "likely," and let him work on the case. When he points, get to him promptly. Take your time, mentally; but size up the dog's location, and above all mind a breeze and the probable whirlaway of the rise. Following singles, again take your time. Give them a chance to spread scent.

Another bit of advice: Finding yourself in unproductive country, don't plug blindly ahead. It wears one out, and discourages dogs. Sit down and rest a bit. Read some more sign. On very rainy days, avoid sedges. Bob doesn't care for soppy going, any more than you do. Try ditch banks or spearheads of thicket. On very cold mornings, start later; give the birds a chance to feed some distance from their roosts.

For quail shooting afoot, the overly wide, fast dog, especially in reasonably close country, becomes the hunted, and not the hunter. The merry-tailed fellow of medium range and good nose, that hunts to the gun, fills the walking shoot's order perfectly. Range in gun dogs is usually greatly overestimated. Loose field talk hears boastful terms of "half-mile" and "mile" casting. Barring bolting prairie-sweepers, actual average range, even in field trials, shrinks amazingly. When the smooth-moving searcher works his ground knowingly three to four hundred yards away, nothing more need be asked, even when you're mounted. If you doubt that, sprinkle a four-hundred-yard golf hole with reasonably thick cover, and think it over. Over-range to a foot hunter becomes tiresomely ineffective, and is ofttimes quite unfair to the dog.

Aside from its bearing on field-trial technique, the average quail hunter (or any other type, for that matter) needs and delights in a prompt, tender retriever, regardless of breed. The daring, finished retriever brings a friendly kinship to the gunning theme. Faithful service, understandingly rendered, wins everlasting affection. Many a dead bird is found. And, equally important, countless cripples are brought to bag. The chap who fails to cherish and reward his dog for tackling thorns or dangerous ice and water, simply lacks humanity and sportsmanship. Have you ever sat late before a low-burning log fire, and recalled how the noble animal at your feet risked his life so cheerfully for your fun? If so, then you and I share a sentiment worth owning.

Each bird hunter—and that goes for the breed—secretly dreams and longs to own a royally-bred animal, broken to the queen's taste. But in the end, like most of us, he must be satisfied with plain Belle or Jack, and finds in them traits that can be wine to his soul. As years go forward, quail hunters of this nation will live to thank the men of means, their patient trainers and handlers, and the many field-trial enthusiasts for what they have accomplished in constantly improving blood lines in gun dogs, and, along with them, the movement toward game restoration.

In the average bird dog, stanchness means everything. But it should not in any case be unnecessarily strained. When your dog points, reach him as quickly as possible. He may get a bad break before you can cross a ditch or hedgerow, and be entirely innocent of flushing. Loose stock, a jealous brace-mate, the end of cover, or an inexperiencd shooting companion may be the cause.

My taste, and I'll wager that of many bobwhiters reading this, runs to a big hard-bitten pointer or setter—great-chested, high-headed, long-striding —from a well-bred strain of country giants with verve, hardihood, and courage that blazes the sedges and leaves smoke in the hollows. Fellows not overly friendly, but with a magnificent sense of understanding and loyalty. Fellows that stride up to a weed patch trusting high noses for instant diagnosis. Dogs that spare pace across pastures and then turn loose like coiled springs when their pads regrip bird country. Dogs that cast in reluctantly at nightfall, with vinegar enough left to fight like wildcats, or shake a few curs along the lane. The type that come railroading off a hillside and into an area where potterers are sniffing and creeping, and put them instantly to playing second fiddle. The kind that stalk stiff-legged from point to point among scattered singles, standing like a sentry until clucked on into whatever action is necessary.

Clothing and footgear for quail shooting have long been matters of standardization. Stiff, water-repellent pants, and shapeless coat dedicated to packing off big bags of birds. Bag limits nowadays, however, are such that packing a dozen or fifteen bobwhites requires a minimum of space. For years I have used a combination game pocket and shell pockets slung on suspenders. Riding or walking, the outfit is ideal. It is best, of course, always to select cloths that will repel cockleburs. But in any case, your costume should fit with the best approach to gunning ease. Just as in duck shooting, too much stress is laid on warmth when bird shooting. Riding or walking, one gets ample body movement, and with even a little too much clothing, there is soon discomfort. If your shooting is in thicket country, by all means have your trousers or riding breeches faced with soft, tough leather. And be sure to wear long, ribbed underdrawers in place of shorts. They will save you many a briar cut.

One of the best safety-first measures of quail shooting is a white or light-colored coat, or, certainly, a white hat. The dogs spot them more readily, and around close firing in tight cover, they are marvelous safeguards. Nothing fills the bill when riding for quail, better than a pair of well-cut breeches and soft-legged boots of the Botte Sauvage type. For steady tramping, army-last marching shoes, leggings, canvas or spiral, and, above all, light-weight suspenders are best. In low, swampy country, leather boots of any type are at a distinct disadvantage. There are innumerable rubber footgears on the market today that walk well and keep the feet dry. No leather boot is ever any more waterproof than the greasing it gets. And while quail shooting, use a whistle that has more volume than a peanut roaster, and carry a Scout knife, matches, and tiny first-aid kit of tape, lint, aspirin, and iodine. Somewhere along the line they'll come in handy. And last but not least, a pair of well-fitting shooting gloves. How often, in approaching a shot, have you had to remove some barbed nuisance from your path, and gotten a nasty clip in return?

The homeward ride, with its sense of fun left behind and good cheer ahead, is ofttimes a day's most pleasant episode. If you are five miles from home, with hard going ahead and a heavy game coat, a sturdy mule makes a welcome ally. As one's mount constitutes an important item of quail-shooting equipment, I vote for a saddling mule. When a jughead white-eyes an ugly water jump, or woofs some rickety bridge, my advice is yield to the gentleman. Though by nature ornery, a mule's sixth sense for shaky business is uncanny.

A few seasons ago I was shooting birds with Eltinge Warner. We were equerried by Bob Tyson's Arch, a colored servant whose particular duty, among others, made him *chargé d'affaires* of a valuable motion-picture camera. Toward late afternoon, we found ourselves far off the beaten track. Then was discovered the loss of the big camera from its moorings behind Arch's saddle. The catastrophe almost stunned him, looming as a major financial disaster. And, infinitely worse, it was up to him to " 'splain de case t' Mistah Bob." A murder charge would have worried him less. As he took the backtrack, Arch flung both arms about Rat's neck and poured a torrent of conversation into the mule's long, twitchy ears. About moonrise Arch parted our tent flaps and grinningly handed over the prize.

"Where'd you find it, Arch?"

" 'Bout two hunnerd yards f'um whar us et dinner, suh."

"Tough time locating it?"

"Well, suh, I was pussonally in er swivet at fus', but I jes' laid de case befo' Rat. I say, 'Lissen, ol' mule,' I say, 'look 'round hu'ah at me,' I say, 'me an you is bofe hooked up in dis mess, an de devil ain' nuthin' at all t' what us gwi' ketch f'um Mistah Bob.' I say, 'Ef I gits hell f'um him, why I is sho' yo' boss, an', ol' sapsucker, you gwi' git de same dose f'um me.' Den I jes' laid on back. Rat went right on lak he'd comed, an' dar laid de contrapshun."

Play House

"Play House" is a special gem of atmosphere and character, first published in Field & Stream, *January 1929, later in* De Shootinest Gent'man *(Derrydale 1934 and Putnam 1943), and again in the* De Shootin'est Gent'man and Other Hunting Tales *(Nelson 1961).*

In "Play House," most of the characters bore fictitious names, excepting Nash's family and the dogs. Nash's daughter knows of no Cousin Charley Johnson. The setter Leo belonged to Nash's long-time friend Billy Joyner; "double-nosed" Tom Cotton, with a cleft nose like the Papes strain, was Nash's white-and-liver pointer.

That line in the first paragraph about the point "just where a curlycue broom's end of weeds plaited in among thinning stalks" would speak to a bobwhite hunter if he had never read another book, and a hundred years from now those cornstalks will rustle in the wind and those dogs will stand pop-eyed on point, because of Nash's words.

Mr. Pomp Eddins may not have been in the flesh under that name, but I have known that exceptional type of old gentlemen who lived among coveys of bob-whites on their land without having taken a shot at them for years.

Irma Buckingham's family—"Yo' wife's folks . . . th' ol' Cap'n Joneses"—owned Cedar Grove, purchased from them by Hobart Ames to become home grounds of the National Field Trial Championship. Irma's great-uncle John Jarratt—"with Forrest"—was a keen-eyed lean man, as his photo in Blood Lines *indicates. Nash gave me the original photograph, inscribed in Nash's hand, "he 'fit thru' the whole war, a gentleman and bird hunter to his fingertips."*

The description of the Manton makes you smell and feel it: "—muzzles paper thin, locks that sang like harp strings; stock fit and balance that made shoulder spot and eye all one." When, on occasion and in lesser stories, Nash's writing slips into journalese and adjectives begin to pile up like too much paint on canvas, it is well to recall passages like that.

Now and then a bit of writing comes along that should, in all fairness, be read by anti-hunters, not, perhaps, to dissuade them, but to give them insight into what they seek to eliminate. The scene with the old Pomp Eddins and his grand-son's first kill on quail is such a bit.

"Oh! happy Boy; you have not lost your years,
You lived them through and through in those brief days
When you stood facing Death! They are not lost!
They rushed together as the waters rush
From many sources! You had All in One!
Why should we mourn
Your happiness? You burned clear flame, while he
Who treads the endless march of dusty years
Grows blind and choked with dust before he dies.
And dying, goes back to the primal dust
And has not lived so 'long' in those long years
As you in your few, vibrant, golden months,
When, like a spendthrift, you gave all you were."
—Anonymous

COUSIN CHARLEY AND I had figured to turn the hunt homeward. Quite a piece it was, too, across those hardwood ridges, pine domes and sedge hollows that made a skyline for Big Hatchie basin. Leo and Tom Cotton were off on cast. We trudged across the furrowed aisles of a rustling corn patch, and found them both stanchly on birds, just where a curlycue broom's end of weeds plaited in among thinning stalks.

Leo was strictly in character, head and plume aloft, dog aristocracy posed and poised. Brawny, lumbering pointer Tom, having evidently swung off-hill a trifle late, was bowed into an upstanding study in rigid, pop-eyed liver and white. Since that good day, almost a quarter of a century ago, the memories of those two valiant comrades and that particular happening have never left me. Their like comes about once in a lifetime. and perhaps rightly so.

Leo belonged to Billy Joyner, and Tom Cotton to me. But in those brave days dog sharing was an indissolubly companionate affair. Leo had handled chickens from the Texas Panhandle to the wild-rose hedges of Saskatchewan. Many a time he had stopped to stare at the dust trails of antelope. And fight? He and Tom met in many a sanguinary set-to. But their issue, whatever it was, was never definitely settled. Sometimes Tom took the count and limped pitifully for days. Again, it was Leo who licked gaping gashes in his bur-curdled hide. From kennel to bird field in baggage car or buckboard, the air was electric with intoned mutters and snarled dares. Once thrown down on the job, however, and stretched out for a day's business, no more friendly or loyal brace of comradely co-operators ever spoored an upland. But, their day's hunting done, Leo and Tom immediately resumed their private feud.

When we came on them that particular afternoon, I was on the left, with left-handed Cousin Charley beside me, a segment of tumble-down rail fence 'twixt us and the birds. And a sign "NO HUNTING" tacked to a nearby persimmon tree. Funny how one remembers such things, but that was the setting. It had been an altogether gorgeous day. Lunch time almost before we realized it. We found a sunny spot just off Fish Trap Dam and lazed on the pine needles, while we munched well-browned soda biscuits and lardy spareribs. The Big Hatchie is a rare sight from the eminence of Fish Trap. It comes curving and slushing past an arrow-headed island, above where the darksome Sally Hole Swamp juts its fist of cypress into the river bottoms among the hardwoods. Then it fans into a sheet of greenish black enamel with a habit of switching to lumpy amber when heavy thunderstorms scour the seamed faces of the basin's red headlands.

But up and on our way again! It was ideal bird finding time when we broke out atop that hogback and slanted down in search of our dogs. Our shooting coats were bulging toward completed quotas—larger then. Another find or two meant finis. We paused in disturbed contemplation of the "NO HUNTING" sign.

Cousin Charley grunted. "Got 'em sure as shootin,' but that's jus' exactly what we kain't do—shoot."

"Why," I questioned, balancing gingerly on a rotting rail and peering past him at Tom and Leo, sculptured against the dun swale, "how come we can't shoot?"

"Ol' man Pomp Eddins' place—tha's 'how come'—see that sign, don't you—well, he means it."

"Who th'—who is Pomp Eddins—mus' be hard boiled."

Cousin Charley clucked mournfully. "Ol' man Pomp Eddins," he explained gravely, "is one o' them kind o' ol' gent'mans h'it don' do no good t' fool with—tha's all."

"Bad actor?"

"Well, naw, not 'zactly a bad actor, but if he gits in behin' you f' good cause, he'll jes' natcherly run you right on t' degradation—an' we're a long ways from home t' start runnin'—too."

"Can't we ease around an' drive those birds off his land?"

"Might, but I guess we better not—ou'h folks an' Mister Pomp has always bin ve'y fren'ly—but I ain' presumin' nuthin'—they tell me folks that does don' have no luck."

To the infinite consternation of Leo and Tom, Cousin Charley quietly flushed a bevy that scattered enticingly on a hillside not far away. Cousin Charley, as shooter and host, was using his wits. "Now then," he grinned, "le's go to th' house an' as't his permission to shoot a few birds on his place—I know him well enough t' do that—an' we ought to, anyhow."

We struck off up a winding road. "I know right where them birds lit," remarked Charley. I said I did, too. "I ain' seen Mister Pomp in quite a spell," he went on; "him an' papa wuz in th' Confed'rate Army t'gether—but th' ol' gent'man is mighty queer." Leo and Tom, sensing, as dogs have a way of doing, that the hunt had taken an odd turn, were in at heel. Charley told me more of Mister Eddins. Retired now, he used to keep store in town—president of the bank once upon a time. Knew some of Billy's and my kinfolks in the city. "If he lets us shoot we can git cleaned up all-fired quick," concluded Charley.

The twists and turns of our way mounted higher. "Great folks, them Eddinses," puffed Charley; "th' Civil War 'bout cleaned them up—clan seeded down t' ol' man Pomp; but he kep' things t'gether—don't owe no man—an' had a sight o' cash money an' sev'ul hundred acres—yep—daughter-in-law an' grandson—always been 'folks' an' still are, them Eddinses." We walked out into a clearing. Deeply set amid holly and cedars squatted an antebellum, white brick cottage, its wide chimneys giving off squills of wood smoke into the keen sunshine.

It was young Mrs. Eddins who ushered us cordially into the cozy vastness of a low-ceilinged chamber, filled with crowded bookshelves, hair sofas, armchairs and a grandfather clock that would have made a collector's acquisitive hair stand on end. She spoke gently to a tall, gray-haired, angular old gentleman who unwound from a deep rocker. "Daddy, here's some company come t' see you." Cousin Charley stepped forward: "Mister Eddins, this is Charley Johnson; good afternoon, suh!"

"Yes," he acknowledged gravely, his eyes meanwhile measuring us both in rapid appraisal, "I know you well, Charley; h'its bin som' time sence we met, howsomever. Yo' folks all comin' 'long all right I hope?"

"Yes, suh, Mister Pomp—uh—Mister Pomp—this is—uh—Mister Buckin'ham—from down in th' city—comes out bird shootin' onc't in awhile. Ou'h dawgs got into a covey down yonder on th' brushy side o' yo' place, but we seen yo' posted sign an' come up t' ast if you'd mind us a-shootin' a little if we run into another bunch on ou'h way home—we're meanin' t' head thataway."

Mister Pomp's keen eyes, deeply recessed 'neath shaggy brows, swept me from head to foot. He slowly extended a leathery, man's sized hand.

"Buckingham—is it?"

"Yes, suh."

"Gran'son o' ol' man Henry?"

I nodded.

"He wuz frum th' Nawth—an' sided that way."

"Yes, suh."

"But his brother—yo' great Uncle Fred—he went out fu'st with Walker an' got set with th' Federals—crossed under a flag o' truce at midnight when his term expired second day o' th' battle o' Fredericksburg, an' re-enlisted under Lee—transferr'd later to th' Louisiana Wildcats—they blowed him up on th' *Queen o' th' West.*" I listened in amazement. We had quickly gotten down to rock bottom on party platforms.

A moment of hesitant recapitulation by Mister Pomp.

"Which one o' ol' man Henry's boys is yo' Daddy?"

"Miles."

"Ummm—in th' bank?"

"Yes, suh."

"Th' two younger boys—Gunn an' Hugh—in th' dry goods business —they yo' uncles, o' co'se?"

"Yes, suh."

"Well, I didn't hav' no better fren's than them boys—all o' them—back in th' hard times panic o' '93—they carried me—took care o' me an' mine." His brilliant eyes turned from piercing scrutiny of me off through the window toward the Basin's distant rim. A resurgent sun poured over it. He quidded rapidly. Another line of evidence must be established. He said: "Yo' wife's folks wuz th' ol' Cap'n Joneses, warn't they?"

"Yes, suh."

"Ummnn—tho't I heard tell—Jones wuz my Cap'n—fought all over his own lan', too—Yankees, rich 'uns f'um up Nawth own it now an' fine folks they are, too, I'm told." He spat explosively into the fireplace.

"If I rec'llect rightly, yo' wife's a gran' niece o' ol' man John Jarratt's, ain't she?"

"Yes, suh." No use to elaborate.

"John an' me done some tall ridin' an' shootin' t'gether—we wuz with Forrest. On'ct in awhile we had t' do some all-fired runnin', too." An aquiline nose twisted into a grim snicker at the recollection. Half reverie apparently swept us from his thoughts. Then, "You boys take chairs, git warm—you're welcome t' shoot on my lan' whenever you choose—I'll jes' go 'long with you a piece t'day—I ain't shot at a bird in fifteen yea'hs— John—John Yancey—aw—John Yancey!"

A rough and tumble specimen of shaver hardihood, with clear gray eyes and mop of tousled red hair, darted in from the hallway. The grandfather's eyes blazed with pride. "Say 'howdy' to th' gent'men—say 'howdy,' John Yancey—then run an' fetch Grandpa's gun."

With a whoop of joy the little fellow sprang away and soon returned lugging an old but beautiful muzzle-loading shotgun. It was in superb condition—muzzles paper thin, locks that sang like harp strings; stock fit and balance that made shoulder spot and eye all one. With it was handed up belt, powder horn and shot pouch. A genuine Manton!

"Git yo' hat, John Yancey—you an' Grandpa's goin' bird huntin'—I want you t' watch these good shots an' learn how t' hit 'em, boy—you'll be needin' some such knowledge one o' these days."

There was a method in Charley's madness as we retraced that quarter of a mile to the vicinity of our scattered birds. They had moved around an orchard's rim just outside some splash pine. Tom nailed them tightly. I believe both he and Leo had an idea what was up.

How I wish more of today's "sports" with magazine guns could have watched that old gentleman hustle his percussion Manton into action. In my own boyhood I had, of necessity, performed a like manual, but with nothing comparable to his exhibition of rapid and orderly precision. Nipples capped, he stepped forward and to the left. Charley spun one victim from the rise. But old man Pomp Eddins laid down a bang-up right and left that served notice how he played the game. Congratulations over, we followed the singles across a gully and into a patch of low broom sedge, where we found both Tom and Leo on point.

"Do you boys mind," queried our host, "if I let this little chap try t' see kin he hit a quail on th' wing—he's shot a few rabbits an' some squirrels, settin'—but this'll be his firs' chance flyin'—an' over a dawg?" He turned and smiled at the grandson—"Come on—boy." The Manton, recapped and hammers drawn, was thrust into the lad's eager hands. All must go well with Grandpa there to see it done. Gun below the elbow, keen for contact with a long-awaited moment, he braced for the rise. In every gunner's life, in every father's heart, there should be, at least, one such undying memory.

"Walk on in—walk right on pas' th' dawg—when th' bird gits up—take yo' time." Step by step the child obeyed leadership. "Both eyes open, John Yancey, pick yo' bird an' keep both eyes jes' on him."

Singles took leave on every hand. I can still see that boy, stockinged calves and butternut knee breeches spraddled into a resolute stance among the sedge stems. Determined arms slamming the burled stock—a long pause as the child leveled and swung. B-o-o-m—b-o-o-m. A boy on his knees peering beneath a smoke screen, an old man's shrill cry, "You got him, son, you got him!" A race through the grass as youth and old age broke shot for the retrieve! Oh! the radiance on their faces! Pomp's aglow with pride; the boy's alight with the greatest thrill any possessor of game heritage treasures as no other in life.

For the next half hour neither Charley nor I fired a shot. Then, borrowing the Manton, we took turns at finishing our limits with the tool of a vanished field gentility.

Gulch bottoms were beginning to darken. Shadows thrust claws across the Basin. The crest of a steep ridge split away cleanly, dropping almost a hundred sheer feet to the railway gash. Behind Mister Pomp, we followed a well-defined trail across the hump. It ended in a spacious alcove, swung like a dirt dauber's nest above the brink. I looked about me in wonder! Some grim business hereabouts! Pomp Eddins slackened pace and motioned about him. "I tho't mebbe you'd like t' see h'it." He placed the Manton carefully aside and seated himself on a lichened boulder. "There wuz big doin's went on he'ah—big doin's back in Shiloh times." Mister Pomp smiled reflectively. "I'll bet Charley ain't ever bin in this spot befo' in his life—y'see—from he'ah this height commands th' railroad plumb across t' th' Basin—from whur' th' ol' M. & C. comes outa th' far gap." Somehow he seemed to kindle, take fresh grip on himself. He lapsed into the speech of ancient action; words of almost broad patois leaped from him—"This he'ah wuz an ol' fo'te—I hepp'd build h'it—look yonder at them timbered bastions stickin' outa th' groun'."

He glanced ruminatively at worn, angled earthworks and crumbling casemate, lethargic burrows in their aged blanket of peaceful silt and grasses. "We wuz dismounted an' order'd on detail t' mount two pieces —told t' hold this position at any an' all cost. H'it warn't no easy job, young men, gittin' them guns so high—but h'it wuz wuth th' labor."

His eyes snapped fire; he was at work again. "We come in from behin' —aroun' yonderways—lak we come while ago—with an infantry company in suppote fuh ambush."

I visualized that scene. Gaunt, dog-tired gunners in ragged gray. Slobbery, lathered horses, sputtery whip lashes, straining traces, laborious heaving through steamy morass and unaxed swamp. What a beehive of slapdash, slaughterous activity and toxic hate. A steady voice continued: "I 'member how we stopped 'em th' fust time—a supply train with guard— we wuz hid out an' ready when their locomotive come th'u th' gap and pulled jus' onta that trussle y' see down yonder. We had it blocked with logs; they seen 'em jus' in time as they run outa th' curve. We let 'em git out an' start unloadin'—then we cut that injin' t' ribbons—blowed h'it t' Hell-an'-Gone." He leaped to his feet and almost swarmed to a counter-attack—"Ou'h boys swung ovah th' hill an' flanked 'em—some tried t' make h'it away th'u yon' valley," he chuckled, "but h'it warn't no use—we—we—had 'em—them hillsides yonder wuz strew'd with dead." He was telling it to High Heaven! "We sho' raised Cain in these parts fo' mo'n two months—but fin'lly th' Yanks come in fo'ce with heavy guns an' shell'd th' livin' hide offn us—we—we—had t' abandon th' position and fall back —damn it."

I looked about me more carefully. Through worn embrasures grinned two dummy cannon, fashioned from pine logs painted black and mounted upon hewn wooden gun carriages. About them, in orderly stacks, were piles of round shot—mud balls! As I half grasped all their significance, the flaming realism of this old man's passion and adoration gripped me. I saw sweating, unshaven half-mad men lashing back on lanyards; blistering hands fumbling at red-hot gun muzzles; hell-and-damnation curses turning peaceful quail country into a sudden shambles of thudding smooth bores. Mister Pomp caught my look and smiled grimly. "This he'ah," he injected half fancifully, "is whut me an' John Yancey calls ou'h 'Play House.'" He dropped a comradely arm about his grandchild's shoulder. The child cuddled lovingly against him.

"Y'see," he went on, a proud sort of wistfulness creeping into his tone, "y'see, I had t' raise this chile—me an' his Ma—that is—we come t' this ol' fo'te when he wuz jes' a babe—in m' arms—h'it come t' me one day t' fix things up lak you see 'em—I jus' built it all in mem'ry o' them times—an'—an' as John Yancey growed up, we jus' kep' comin' an' addin' t' things." His jaw suddenly tightened—he spoke proudly: "Anyhow, this he'ah ain't no bad Play House t' bring a boy up in." John Yancey spoke up, softly: "Gran'pa, we hav' a lot o' fun he'ah, don't we?" The old man turned to me. "I fought—we all o' us fought," he cried passionately, "f' ou'h conception o' home an' rights jus' as t' other side seen theirn—my father fought in Mexico, I fought with Forrest—an'—an'—this chile's Daddy—th' only son God Himself could ever give me—wuz killed at San Juan Hill—he couldn't no mo' stayed at home when th' call come than John Jarratt coulda' he'ped ridin' off with us boys."

We shook hands and exchanged "good-bys" and "come agains." He said simply: "Tell all yo' folks y' met ol' man Pomp Eddins—yo' Daddy'll 'member me—sen' me a bird dawg puppy some time—I'll train him an'

John Yancey t'gether—John's gittin' too big f' th' Play House anyhow."
So, leaving them to turn back across their darkening trail through the hills,
Charley and I slid down a precipitous path to the railroad ties and a starlit
trek to home.

Fifteen or twenty years is a long, long time! Again, however, Cousin
Charley and I munched soda biscuits and hog meat at Fish Trap Dam.
The bottomlands still challenged change, but it was there, however furtive. The drone of an airplane might impeach the years, or some raucous
motor change the face of things.

"Charley," I asked, "whatever became of the old gentleman way back
over yonder across the Tubba—Mister Eddins, who knew my folks an'
let us hunt on his land an' showed us his old Rebel's 'Play House'?"

"Daid," responded Charley, laconically. "He lived t' be pas' eighty—but
he passed away aroun' Christmas time—didn' las' long after th' Worl' War."

"And the boy," I went on. "I suppose he turned out to be a bum bird
hunter, like we are, and runs the old home place now?"

"Yep," replied Charley, and something in the way he spoke made me
look up. "There was sho' one mighty fine, honest-t'-Gawd boy, too."

"He's—"

"Yep!" Cousin Charley was a direct narrator. "They hadn' no sooner
started talkin' war with Mexico, back in '16, but what John Yancey an' his
Gran'pa showed up in town with John's gripsack all packed. That kid
signed up an' went on out with th' National Guard—an' I mean he lef'
out right now." I might have guessed as much. Cousin Charley loosened a
sparerib end and kept on with his story. "Then, y'know, come sho' nuff
war—with Germany. By that time John Yancey had turned out t' be a
natcherl born soldier—his Grandad darn near passed out, he was so proud
when th' boy went to an officer's training school an' come out with a commission. I never seen no one quite as happy. Why—why—there wuz times
he'd talk about h'it an' tears'd come to his eyes. John Yancey's wuz a first
unit overseas, too."

Charley paused. Tossed a welcome shred of fat meat to a dog. "Ol' man
Pomp Eddins come t' town a lot in them days—wanted news 'bout th' war,
an' that boy, mebbe. He'd sit aroun' in a big swivet 'till he got his mawnin'
paper off th' 'Cannonball'—talked about how he wish'd he coulda bin
along with John Yancey. That ol' man meant ev'y word he said, whut's
mo'. He'd say: 'This he'ah makes fo' wars f' us Eddins—fo' wars an' th'
Lawd only knows how many mo'. John Yancey—he'll be comin' home befo'
long—an'—an'—marryin' off.' "

A flock of ducks suddenly dipped through the chute and whizzed across the spillway. Cousin Charley watched them dwindle into specks. He went back to his story.

"I happ'n'd t' be at th' sto' th' night th' tel'graf operator brought up th' message 'bout John Yancey. Somebody jus' had t' ride out an' git th' news to his folks. So I run out in m' car—they'd done gone t' bed long ago. But ol' man Pomp he come to th' do'h with a lamp in one han' an' that ol' muzzleloader o' hisn in t' other. He seen h'it wuz me an' says, 'Why—come in, Charles,' says, 'glad t' see you—my daughter'll be right he'ah. Whut you got—a message fo' us 'bout John Yancey winnin' another medal o' honor,' says, 'how many Germans is that boy done kilt this time?'

" 'Bout that time, his Ma, Mrs. Eddins, come into th' room—I guess I musta looked kinda funny—maybe h'it wuz what they call 'mother's intuition'—I don' know—guess she jus' sorter suspicioned—you know? All I could do wuz jus' han' her th' War Department telegram—you 'member how they wuz worded?" Charley looked at me, and remembering, turned quickly away.

"Never s' long as I live, Buck, will I evah fergit th' look that come over his Ma's face. She handed Mister Pomp th' wire—but he didn' hav' his specs, so she had t' read it to him—an'—man—her voice wuz as steady—" Charley clucked into his cheek. "Seemed at firs' lak Mister Pomp couldn't understand—then—all of a sudden, seemed lak, h'it come to him. I wuz lookin' t' see th' ol' fellow bust out—but not a single tear com' down his face—he warn't th' cryin' kind. Naw—he jus' sorter clutched out f' Mrs. Eddins—clasped her in his arms—sorter like he had done 'come to attention'—an' wuz listenin' f' sumpthin'. They both jus' stood there an' shivered. I tried t' say sumpthin' comfortin' like—but th' old man interrupted me: 'I'm obliged t' you, Charles,' he says, 'f' bringin' th' word—hit's sho' bad news,' he says, 'but,' he says, 'on th' other han',' he says, 'John Yancey Eddins has won th' highes' an' mos' distinguished honor that can befall a gallant soldier of our country.' " Charley wiped his greasy fingers on his hunting coat and turned to me reflectively again. "Do you 'member whut an' unreconstructed Confed'rate ol' man Pomp wuz? But in th' end he wuz sold jus' as strong on Uncle Sam." Charley had the thread of things toward the knot. "But about that time," he concluded, "ol' man Pomp raised his face t'odes th' ceilin', an' his whole heart jus' seem'd t' break out in one great cry—'Aw Gawd'—he says—'You know,' he says—'h'it ain't right!' Mrs. Eddins seen he wuz fixin' t' giv' down. She held him tighter in her arms an' says, soothing like, 'There—there—Daddy,' she says, 'th' Lawd giveth an' th' Lawd taketh away, blessed be th' name o' th' Lawd.' Buck, there warn't one single tear ev'ah com' t' ol' man Pomp's eyes. 'I know,' he wailed; 'I take it all back—Gawd—but, oh,' he says, 'John Yancey's th' las' one o' us—no mo' John Yancey—Oh! Christ,' he says, 'no mo' Eddinses fo' th' wars—no mo' Eddinses fo' th' wars!' "

I discovered the following in Nash's things, a photoprint of microfilm V-Mail, the type sent by servicemen during World War II:

> Lt. Col. R. W. Cole Jr.
> 8th Cav APO 201 c/o PM
> San Francisco
> September 4, 1944

My dear Mr. Buckingham:

This being September, although here in the Admiralty Group one would never suspect such to be the case, my thoughts have been turning more and more towards home and the gunning days. My home is in Little Compton, a small fishing-farming community on the eastern shore of the Sakonnet River. In such a location along the Rhode Island coast, the black duck are in evidence the season round and the thought of throwing my decoys on home waters once more makes the months overseas even longer. I know you have shot over the same country of salt marshes and pot holes, of sand dunes and rocky spits over which the long files of coot pass at dawn and dusk, so feel you understand far better than most. To those of us who love the out-of-doors, homecoming means infinitely more than for those luckless individuals whose lives are not in tune with the whisper of wings at sundown.

Have you ever thought of how your books have brought pleasure to us out here? I made a short cruise on a combat mission with the Navy and during lulls in the bombardment and the continuous state of "precautionary general quarters," I found time to read "The Shootinest Gent'-man" for the fourth time. Even the thrill of being at sea on grim and important business was forgotten. This time, I believe I enjoyed "Play House"—"no more Eddinses fo' the wars!"—even more than usual, as it struck a sympathetic note. Thank you for speeding the hours.

The Calvary Division will be hard at it again in the near future and when you read of its exploits, think of it in a more personal sense than might otherwise be the case as I, in my capacity of Executive Officer of one of its fine old regiments, am a very small cog in its wheels.

> Sincerely,
> R. W. COLE JR.

After All These Years

"After All These Years," which appeared in Tattered Coat, *is in the form of a letter addressed to "Dear Noelly," Colonel Hal Sheldon's son Noel, as was another popular story of Nash's, "Surrender to Youth" in* Ole Miss'. *The appeal of this form is that Mr. Buck puts you there beside him "in the attic . . . pawing over worn-out plunder . . . a smelly tattered coat or patched pants." I thought of this line a few weeks ago when examining a whipcord riding coat of Nash's, made for him by D'Elia, Marks & Kines in 1935—hard-worn from many a field-trial stint.*

It is natural for Nash to tell a story in this form, for he was a great letter writer. I first learned of his boyhood association with his neighbor's setter Gladstone in one of his early letters to me. Peep o' Day, whom he mentions shooting over, also belonged to this same neighbor, Mr. P. H. "Pink" Bryson, and was described as a Gladstone-Leicester-Dart bitch by Joseph A. Graham in The Sporting Dog *in 1904.*

The "light, twelve-bore English hammer gun" of his father's that Nash used to bag his first bobwhites in this story was probably one of the pair of six-pound, four-ounce Alfred Smith doubles Nash describes in Part V of the story "Blood Lines." In "Hallowed Years" he describes a pair of mid-1850 percussion guns "by one E. Smith." About 1820, Samuel and Charles Smith of London made flintlock sporting guns. What relation these "Smith" guns bear I do not know, but I trust Nash to hold to facts about guns, even in stories with fictional characters.

The second "red-letter day on quail" was spent with Lucius Waldrip and Hal Bowen Howard, both about Nash's age. In "Buried Treasure Hill" (Mark Right!) Nash describes the Waldrip house, where Lucius lived as a bachelor with his sister Audrey:

> . . . the old house took its name, Solitude, from the inscription cut into the chimney slab over the living room's rock fireplace. *Solitude Is Sweet, Yet Grant Me Still In My Retreat, A Friend Whom I May Whisper—"Solitude Is Sweet."*

In the same story there is an entry from Lucius Waldrip's diary dated October 10, 1893:

Went to Memphis with Papa and Mamma and met two boys named Hal Bowen Howard and Nash Buckingham. They have guns too and like to hunt, but from what they say I think my dogs must set better than theirs . . .

Nash considered Lucius, with his "weatherbeaten Parker that he never cleaned but swore by," one of the best quail shots he knew. According to John Bailey, Lucius in his last years didn't shoot as well as formerly because of weakening eyesight, but was too stubborn to wear glasses. Lucius Waldrip died in the spring of 1934 at fifty-four; Hal Howard died the previous autumn.

The main narrative of "After All These Years" took place at Hal Howard's family home near Aberdeen, Mississippi. Nash indulged in using names such as "Allourn" and "Yosanmine" for antebellum houses, but his daughter Irma tells me "The Shadows" was the name of Hal Howard's home. Bayard in this story was Bayard Snowden, a lifelong friend of Nash's from a distinguished old Memphis family. The girls were Anne Carter, whose home was at Central and Belvedere in Memphis, Mary Anne Robinson, whose father was Mr. Jim Robinson the pharmacist mentioned in "Comin' Twenty-One," Mary Traylor, and Irma Lee Jones, whom Nash married in 1910.

The start of that New Year's Eve hunt, with two men and two girls riding off—each man with a pointer dog across his saddle—is Buckingham. And the scene by full moon at dusk with the little setter Lucy at the old burying ground will bring for more than one man, as it does for me, a vision of a little white wraith of his own.

I place this story last among the tales of bobwhite gunning because it was written with a far look backward, though it took place when these lives were young, and in its last lines lies the beginning of Nash's over-sixty-year love affair with Irma.

Dear Noelly,

MY RED LETTER DAY on quail? The one incident highlighting more than fifty years staring down shotgun ribs at exploding bevies? The one such day I'd prefer reliving? Lad, you almost sent me scurrying to Kodak books and diaries outdating turn of the century. But I've figured it all out now, and I'm really obliged to you for putting the thought on me. It's been like sitting in the attic some rainy afternoon before gunning season; pawing over worn-out plunder you've been, let's say instructed, to discard.

Somehow though, wadding up a smelly, tattered coat or patched pants, incidents crop up about them too arresting to warrant separation. Not right now, anyhow, you tell yourself. So, moths and orders to the contrary, you lie like a gentleman to the Missus, stall the business through with a fake bundle, and gain temporary respite for staunch friends. They get as close to one as a feeble and beloved old dog worth a million times its keep just for association with those golden days some folks accuse locusts of eating.

I've gunned quail with Gladstone, Peep o' Day, and other field trial champions in front of us. And many a brilliant, faithful "potlicker bird dawg" shares my hearth in memory. I've shot from Texas coastals through Oklahoma and the Ozarks at bevies flushing like blackbirds from wintered reed beds. If there's a state in Dixie I haven't dogged *Colinus,* let X mark the unknown spot. But which of all my days after quail would I prefer reliving?

Was it that frost-crisped one I downed my first bobwhites? Daddy and Mister Arthur hunted the Le Master farm, now well within our city's suburbs but miraculously preserved in almost wilderness aspect by that fine old family. Our long, star-spangled teaming before daylight. The warm welcome and shining hospitality awaiting us! My delight at riding muleback behind giant black Dan Bostick. And how we two maintained strict tally on the steadily fattening game pouch.

We shot over Mister Arthur's sterling pointers first, and Daddy's Gordons, Chick and Dee, later. What ground-devouring, keen-nosed, perfectly mannered braces! The hunt moved like clockwork, with lunch in a cheerful holly grove beside a deep, clear bayou and Dan's coffee-boiling fire. I was permitted to shoot at five bevy rises, and managed three birds with Father's light, twelve-bore English hammer gun. Dan boasted vociferously of my skill and produced alibis for the misses with the ease of a magician pulling rabbits from a stovepipe hat.

What a day of breeze-drifted wood and powder smoke; blending scents of wild grapes, persimmons, sassafras, nut mast, and sun-ripened berry jungles of the new ground. Yep, youngster, what with a wonderful country supper and a nap under the buffalo robe driving home to Mother, that was the kind of red-letter day so many, many hunters carry in their souls long after their hearts are stilled.

Or could it be that last day of quail season barely a decade agone? When Hal and Lucius and I swung through a Houston Bottoms, touched at the Big Spring for sandwiches and tea, and shot Newton's section that afternoon? The sun staged a hard battle that bleakish morning, but won out. Bill and Britt found a world of birds, and we were holding it on them, too. Dawss brought along noble Trueboy and Flirt for the postprandial session. But bagging limits was so easy, it became secondary to picture making.

Lucius and I lazied beside Painted Pond while dear old Hal followed the dogs into a blackjack copse after some singles. We talked hopefully of his only-too-apparent slowing down in recent months and agreed that because he was so cheerful and brave, we mustn't let him notice our waiting on him to catch up, or the extra saddling boosts. He was getting a bit suspicious, too, that his turn over scattered points was coming around too fast. And sitting there watching the jays and peckerwoods and listening to the shrillings of a distant hawk, I thought Lucius looked tougher than a pine knot.

Crossing onto Waldrip from Newton a woods road waists steep knolls and winds through silent, brook-worn hollows deep in tawny sedge. At nightfall, riding past that black blob of cedared crow roost this side the family cemetery, we talked enthusiastically of our big-running derby dog prospects. Over our toddies we toasted a glorious season ending—and an even better one ahead.

It never seems possible nor right that shooting pals of a lifetime will ever check out. I still see Lucius and Hal sitting there warming their shins by the open fireplace in the Waldrip guest chamber, little suspecting they'd fired their last shots over Bill's and Britt's and Trueboy's and Flirt's points. How I'd love to hear those old boys sing out "How" at their beading toddy glasses! Even nowadays I rarely say it myself, after a fine day's sport, without listening for their vague echo. That's right, youngster, I started next gunning season alone. God, it puts a crimp in a fellow. Just remembering that last day with a pair of such gallants sets it apart.

When Hal and I were gay blades, he used to entertain a group of boys and girls with a Christmas-week house party and bird shoot at his father's ancestral plantations. That holiday season we were Bayard and Bright and Hal and I, with Wee Anne, the two Marys, and Irma. Some mornings the girls took hunter's breakfast with us and shared a full day. On others, after a dance, they slept late, met us with picnic lunch, and rode out the afternoons. Each fellow brought three braces of dogs, and I doubt if we ever touched the same territory twice, so vast and birdy were those protected holdings. Picture a composite, inside and out, of all the loveliest southern manors you've seen in the movies, and you're still only fairly close to Allourn, Hal's antebellum home.

Away back yonder the state limit on quail was, as I recall, twenty-five a day. Regrettably, but rightly so, it is now less than half that figure. We shot a daily five dollars each per high gun, a similar team race, and high-over-all for the week, on like basis. All ties were split. It meant getting down on your stock, ethical eye-wiping, no quarter asked or given, and no holds barred except trying to handle the other fellow's dogs. That last day, New Year's Eve, was a quail hunter's dream.

Hal and Mary and Irma and I rode to the Gillespie plantation with our lunches saddlebagged and dogs on our saddles. We used Hal's pointers, Flash and Ticket, as first bracemates, and they did a really great job. My overwhelming difficulty was to keep my eyes off Irma. We lunched at Slave Quarters by the free-flowing well atop Piney Ridge, where Anderson met us with my white setter Jim and his consort, Lucy. Memory of that enthrallingly exquisite afternoon, replete with engrossing and outstanding dog work, is as fresh in mind as though 'twere yesterday.

Stealthy shadows infiltrated slopes as we cross-countried to meet the buckboard with its load of Negro jockeys to bring home our mounts. I needed four bobwhites to fill my limit—and never worse. They meant at least an even break on the day's individual race, maybe a team win, and, according to latest figures released that morning at breakfast, a chance at the grand prize. I'd also been worrying considerable about asking a certain damsel a highly important question. In some way the stylish little setter Lucy and I (God rest her brave bones) got separated from Hal and the girls and Jim.

Just as dusk surrendered to full moon, the bitch whipped past me along the fence row of an abandoned burying ground. Suddenly she whirled, flash-pointed, cleared sagging rails with the stealthy grace of a stalking panther, roaded boldly a few paces, and froze. That high-tailed, lofty-headed statue silvered in moonglow will fill my eyes forever. Fortunately there was skyline off an open hillside through the pines, for the blighted straw tops were cloaked in gloom. With gun half-raised to shoulder readiness, I knelt and dubiously knee-wormed to behind Lucy.

My gorgeously postured companion held those roosting birds right under her delicate nose. Away roared a black, spouting mass I heard rather than saw. There was but time for a snap shot. I rose panting. Sitting on a stump, I gave Lucy the green light to fetch dead. Four times that blessed little creature insisted upon searching. And each trip she delivered me a bob-white. Do you wonder I gave her a smothering hug and promised a ride home in my lap, with extra grub?

Yep, I won the day's purse, team wager with Hal, and hit the week's jack pot, thanks, again, to Lucy. On account of seeing to it personally that Lucy and Jim got their promised extra bait of victuals, I was last to tub and dress for dinner. Just as I emerged from bachelor quarters and crossed Allourn's vast upper hall, the door to the girls' apartments opened and out stepped the Vision to whom for so long I had devoted so much tender thought.

We met at the head of the winding staircase, and the loveliness of her melted me down like a candle. I took her hand, but somehow, neither of us spoke. On the landing not a soul was looking except a towering, benevolent grandfather clock. Maybe such sights were old stuff to him, but anyway the gruff old basso profundo had the kindliness and good taste (with surely a great sense of humor) to keep his head shut and give a fellow a break. And there the age-old question was asked, answered, and sealed with a kiss no whit sweeter, thanks be to Him, than its counterpart of this morning.

So there's your answer, and the same to *you* someday, Noelly, with all my heart—and hers.

Part Three:
GUNS & SHOOTING

Mr. Buck's Guns

EDITOR'S NOTE

A GREAT SHOTGUN is close to being alive, with its sensuous form and sheen—
no small part of its appeal being the fascination of deadliness under control.
There are ungainly guns, like gauche women, but the exquisite ones are irresistible
to those of us who love them. Nash's affair with Burt Becker magnums—the "big
'uns" as he fondly called them—lasted from 1921 until the end of his life. He
frequently wrote of his Beckers but in limited detail, sending me on a quest to
learn more.

The name of Burt Becker, the gunsmith, was familiar to the coterie of wildfowlers who orbited around Nash, but it was not celebrated in a broad sense. The
fact that Nash's Beckers were built on Fox actions prompted me to write to
Savage Arms, which took over the A. H. Fox Gun Company in 1930, hoping some
of the old Fox gunsmiths might still be there and enlighten me. The reply made
no mention of Becker:

> We are sorry we are unable to give you the choke information you re-
> quest and believe this work would have been done outside the factory,
> probably using some of our so-called "goose" guns, which had extra wide
> frames and heavy barrels, and were chambered for the 3″ magnum.

Gun editors Warren Page and Jack O'Connor were also unaware of Burt
Becker. Jack O'Connor made an interesting point:

> I have never heard of Burt Becker but when the Fox Gun Company
> was in Philadelphia before Savage bought them at a receiver's sale, the
> company used to make a specialty of "overbored" 12-gauge guns. These
> simply had a larger bore than the standard 12-gauge bore. The theory
> was that they could handle more powder and shot. Just how well this
> notion held water I cannot say, because those guns of Buckingham's
> used 3-in. magnum shells using only 1⅜ oz. of shot, considered a real
> hell-bender. Nowadays they put 1½ oz. of shot in a 2¾-in. shell and
> don't overbore their guns for it either.

John Bailey wrote:

> Nash had two Burt Becker guns when I first knew him—a 7½ lb. 26″ barrels for quail, and the heavy 32″ gun for ducks. They were built on Fox frames. Becker smoothed 'em up and bored one to handle No. 8 shot for quail, and the duck gun for No. 4's. Nash's first duck gun patterned round 90% at 40 yards. Not one gunner in ten million can shoot such a close gun capably. Nash could.

Berry Brooks wrote on August 29, '72:

> I recall that Nash bought the 26″ Becker quail gun from Becker during the 1933 era. It had Ansley Fox action with 26″ barrels bored improved and modified by Becker. Nash never liked open barrels. It had a single trigger designed by Miller who designed the single trigger for John Olin's Model 21 Winchester. It had beautiful oil finished wood with no butt plate. I have just had lunch with John DuPre of Memphis, who tells me his son has this gun now. This is the gun Nash had in hand in the frontispiece in the Derrydale and Putnam editions of *De Shootinest Gent'man*.

The little Becker quail gun has the look of a British gun, with its straight grip and odd fore-end tip, both characteristics of Becker's guns.

Bob Anderson told me:

> Becker was a master gunsmith with Parker before Remington bought them. He made Parker's exhibition guns to go to the Columbian Exposition. But he was an old man when he made #2 for Nash; used a heavy Ansley H. Fox action and made both stock and barrels. Said it was the last he would ever make. Nash said Henry Bartholomew of Washington, D.C. had a collection of them. Nash had a Becker quail gun but I think it got away.

With the Becker story assuming proportions of an epic, I kept digging. I find that Nash's first contact with these magnums came in 1921 when John Olin sent him his own Becker magnum with several boxes of a "mystery" shell just off the drawing board at Western Cartridge. In 1961 in "Firsts and Lasts for Everything" (Nelson edition), Nash wrote:

> Forty years ago the late P. C. "Perry" Hooker walked into our sporting goods emporium in Memphis and handed me eight unmarked boxes of 12-gauge shells and a surprisingly heavy leather gun case. Perry, who represented the Western Cartridge Company of East Alton, Illinois, said, "Buck, here are some hulls and a gun the Big Boss would appreciate your testing on geese and ducks. There's number four shot in all the shells but half of them are regular two-and-three-quarter-inchers and the rest are three-inch shells, all loaded with a new-fangled slow-burning powder that's supposed to give more velocity and shorter, more dense shot strings. Neither shells nor the gun will be on the market any time soon. The gun is an 'overbored magnum.' Give the Boss a full report as soon as you can."

Those shots I fired while my huge Chesapeake, Pat, and I crouched in the head-high willows along old Goose Hole on Wapanoca might have been heard round the shooting world, and their offspring are still bellowing from thousands of magnums. They came on the market about a year later with the label "Super-X." The next step was copper-coated shot.

After writing my report on the test shells and the overbored Fox (Askins-Sweeley model), I lost no time in acquiring a 10-pound Fox magnum of my own.

Here is John Olin's part in the story:

The development of Super-X and its relationship to the Burt Becker magnums I think occurred somewhat earlier than Nash's association with Becker. I still have the overbored 12-gauge shotgun which Becker made when I was working upon the development of Super-X. I am rather of the opinion he made the first one for me. I am thoroughly acquainted with the assistance Charles Askins, Sr., gave me in the development of long range loads which were given the trademark Super-X.

The term "Askins-Sweeley model" used in relation to the Becker magnums refers to the type of boring and reflects the joint work of these men on the design. John Olin advises me that Sweeley had been experimenting with a copper over-powder wad with flexible properties that he felt would contribute toward shells that would produce tight patterns, and that Charles Askins made field tests of the new shells about the same time Nash did.

On September 27, 1972, Colonel Charles Askins, Jr., wrote me:

E. M. Sweeley was a Boise, Idaho lawyer with a penchant for shotgun experimentation. My old man and Sweeley collaborated in a series of articles for *Outdoor Life* entitled "The Ballistics of the Shotgun" and among other things, thoroughly explored the over-bore principle in the magnum shotgun.

Burt Becker was, I believe, an employee of the original Fox Co. I remember during the '20s that my old man loaded up and traveled back to Philadelphia and spent a couple of months with Becker. They were then working on barrels for the magnum 12 shotgun. Becker would make up a set of tubes and my father would test them and then they would make up another set and try them. I assumed at the time and have always concluded since that Burt Becker was a designing gunsmith for Fox.

As to just when the so-called Super Fox was made by the company I cannot say. But I'd speculate it came along after the summer session between my old man and Becker.

"Overbored" signifies a diameter of bore slightly in excess of the standard 12-gauge—what the British indicate by the proof mark 12/1. There is doubt in some quarters as to how much the overboring contributed to producing the impressive patterns those guns threw. What probably was most effective was the long tapered forcing cone from shell chamber to the barrel proper (Nash spoke of it a bit loosely as "cone-less"), and the long leads to the chokes, reducing pellet distortion. Something had to account for patterns such as 91% and 93%, which Nash's Becker #2 threw.

The new Super-X shell drew opposition from competitor ammunition companies and gun manufacturers, the latter perhaps fearing a trend requiring retooling to handle these loads. According to John Olin, it was about this time that Burt Becker left his work as gunsmith in the Fox factory and set up his own shop where he specialized in his custom-made magnums.

In "Are We Shooting 8-Gauge Guns?" (Nelson edition), Nash wrote of shooting in 1928 at the Camp Fire Club, up the Hudson above New York, with "a new 10-pound 32-inch magnum." In "Long-Range Duck Shooting," he says: "In 1926 my first magnum twelve-bore was replaced by one built and bored for big shot by the famous Philadelphia gunsmith, Mr. Burt Becker." This was his Becker #1. I think the "first magnum twelve-bore" that was replaced was the so-called Super Fox, identified in an old photo with his 34-inch Parker—being the one he "lost no time in acquiring" soon after 1921.

A photograph taken in 1934 with Chubby, the springer spaniel, with Nash's inscription "The gun is the famous Burt Becker 3-inch shell Magnum" shows the Becker #1 with a somewhat thick straight grip and a recoil pad. Instead of the typical streamlined Fox breech lever faired into the top of the action, this one had a distinctly un-Fox look about it like the lever on a water faucet, the axis extending almost a quarter inch above the top of the stock. The right barrel had a light spot on the outside, about 13 inches from the muzzle, as though it had been dented and straightened, and there is the characteristic worn area on the barrel blueing near the action, bespeaking a gun well used. This gun, like Nash's Becker #2, had no safety.

In a letter, July 1972, Werner Nagel wrote me:

> Nash didn't believe in a safety; instead, he said one should never load a gun till he was ready to shoot. He felt this was safer than becoming dependent on a safety.

In the undated yellowed photograph with the legend "Heavy Parker 12, Super Fox 12, Over and Under .410 Merkel," the Fox shows the conventional breech lever as well as the typical Fox splinter fore-end tapered to a thin edge at the tip, unlike the big Becker #1, which in some photos shows a metal inlay at the fore-end tip and, in others, an odd little channel with no metal tip. The "Super Fox" in the photo of the three guns is not Nash's first Becker magnum, but probably one of the Fox "goose" guns mentioned in the letter from Savage Arms.

Colonel H. P. Sheldon wrote an introduction for *Hallowed Years* (Stackpole 1953), which he called "The Saga of Bo Whoop," his nickname for the Becker #1. Nash's favorite 3-inch load for the gun was "an ounce and three eighths of 4's coppered, ahead of four drams of powder." (John Olin points out that Super-X shells bore no indication of powder load, a subject of controversy when they first appeared.)

Berry Brooks wrote:

> Nash told me that Becker handmade the entire gun and bored the barrels. It was a very heavy gun and you could always recognize its roar. It made a *whoom,* more like a cannon. Nash would let me shoot at the incoming ducks and after they had flared and were on their way, he would kill two. It really took a man with Nash's build to properly handle a gun like this and he shot it like the master shot he was, making unbelievable kills on ducks and geese.

Nash's last day shooting with his 32-inch Becker #1 was December 1, 1948, at Section 16 Club, near Clarendon, Arkansas, with Bob Anderson and Berry Brooks. On December 2, Nash wrote John Bailey:

> Well, I lost the big gun yesterday—terrible blow. Cliff Green and I came out of our roadway from the club to the highway where the car was parked, due to mud in the lane. Just as we reached the car, a warden's car drove up, two of them got out and began checking us. I handed the gun, cased as usual, to one warden. Then he checked my license and the back of the car to count ducks. Meanwhile, instead of giving me back my gun, the SOB laid it on our car's right front fender. Some other members came out of the lane, there was a lot of talk, Cliff and I drove to Clarendon before I missed the gun. We drove back to the spot—searched —no soap. Met the wardens, and the boy who laid the gun on the fender and not returned it to me was sure sick. We talked to a telephone crew near Roe—said the gun was on the fender when we passed, not 20 minutes before. Another chap, nearer Roe, saw it. It must have finally slipped off in the dips this side of the viaduct and been picked up by either east or west bound traffic—but not too much of that could have passed in 20 minutes on that road. The wardens put in road blocks, telephoned Stuttgart and Ulm, ordered ads and radio. My name on case and also in left barrel of gun. In Clarendon, the town about turned out. If an honest person found it, I'll get it back. If NOT, I hope he gets shot by the missing safety. I feel like I did when Chubby died. It's fully insured, but I'll never get another friend like that gun.

Berry Brooks described the incident for me:

> Now about the day the gun was lost. Nash, Bob Anderson and I had planned the shoot at Section 16 Club, a flooded area in the White River bottoms about ten miles out of Clarendon. Nash and Bob drove down in Bob's car during the afternoon but I had to work classing cotton and could not get off until late that night. It rained hard all night and I pulled in at the old Clarendon Hotel about 3 a.m. and took my gear up to the room which I knew Bob and Nash would occupy. They were both up because the roof leaked and they had to move their beds around often to keep out from under the leaks. We had breakfast and drove on down to the club, as usual, while it was dark. We had no clubhouse but normally used the yard of the caretaker to park our cars. It was about 200 yards off the gravel road and this time, due to mud, we parked on the side of the gravel road and walked in. At the dock, Nash and Bob got

in one boat and headed for BOB'S CORNER, a stand especially located for pass shooting. Nash was a great pass shot and loved this stand. I went alone to BROOK'S BLIND, which was an opening in the pin oaks, made to order for calling ducks. I liked to call and have great numbers of ducks circling me.

There were lots of ducks that morning and we had prearranged to shoot nothing but greenheads. I had counted their shots and knew about when they had their limits of eight ducks each. I was not far behind them but had to pick up my six decoys and arrived at my car to find that Nash had left. After Nash got his limit he was cold and damp and returned to the cars where he found Clifford Green, who offered to drive him to Clarendon, leaving word for Bob Anderson and me. Two game wardens were there, friendly of course, for they knew our members would not break any laws. But one had never seen Nash's gun and the other wanted to show it to him. They handled it, pointed it, and finally laid it on the right fender of the car. Cliff and Nash discovered that the gun was missing before they got to Clarendon and returned just about the time Bob Anderson and I were leaving. Nash got in Bob's car and while Bob drove, I walked about three or four miles to the point where they had discovered the loss, looking in the grass and weeds along the road. Then Bob walked and I drove back. We were terribly disappointed not to find it. Someone in a car that followed or passed must have picked it up. They recalled passing an old truck and later tracked it down but they knew nothing. The area was alerted—game wardens, highway patrols, hunting clubs, sporting goods stores—but to this date the loss of Bo Whoop has never been solved.

Somewhere, someone has that gun. The circumstances of how he obtained it are almost beyond imagining—perhaps sold to him with Nash's name filed off the left barrel. But the gun, somewhere, exists.

Berry Brooks gave me the details of Nash's second Becker magnum:

> In early July 1950, George Warner, U.S. Army Engineers retired, from Lawton, Oklahoma, walked into my office and introduced himself, saying he had been a great admirer of Nash Buckingham, although he had not met him. He knew about the loss of Nash's gun and during our conversation expressed the desire to contribute toward a new one for him. I had had this idea for some time and, learning that he was on his way to Washington, suggested that he get in touch with Henry Bartholomew, who might give us Becker's address.
>
> I invited Nash to lunch and introduced him to Captain Warner, a delightful meeting but with no mention of the new gun. About July 15, I received a letter from Captain Warner, saying he had contacted Burt Becker in Philadelphia and, although Becker had retired, that he had agreed to make another gun for Nash, and that would be the last gun he would ever make. The cost would be $500.00, and Warner paid him $200.00 on account.

Berry sent me a Xerox copy of the purchase order, dated July 12, 1950, and copies of Becker's subsequent letters, written with a monumental disregard for spelling on a typewriter sans comma. Becker's letterhead, *Custom made long range magnum 12-gauge shot guns made to order 8½ to 10 lb. 4531 N. Gratz Street, Philadelphia 40, Pa.,* had a line drawing of a Canada goose in flight.

Mr. George B. Warner
703 "A" Ave;
Lawton. Oklahoma

Dear. Mr. Warner

I have your letter Dated. July. 12th 1950 and you have Purchased"
this Gun on the Installment plan" which is O.K. with me.
now this gun dont want any weight adied. it is wellbalance.
however" if Nas wants any change made with the Gun. that I dont
think he will want. as it is heavy enought. One thing i will say
is" he will never get another Gun like it" as long as he lives.

With Best Wish

BURT.BECKER

Dear. Mr. Warner

Your letter rec: July 31 sorry to learn" that you will or probably"
go into the Army. thats a place i would not send a Dog. dont know how
you feal obout it. however there is no reason to have War at this time.
now that Mr. brooks is agoin to take up where you left off" is O.K. with
me. nowthen" after Nas gets this Gun i hope he will keep it as
no better Gun was ever made. that he knows.

With.Very.Best Wish to
keep out of the Army

BURT.BECKER

Berry Brooks received a letter from Warner, asking that he keep up the contact with Becker, pay the balance, and instruct Becker to ship the gun to him, Brooks, when completed. In a letter dated August 5, 1950, Burt Becker advised Berry Brooks that the gun was finished and could be shipped.

To me, it is incredible that an aging gunsmith could, between July 12 and August 5, custom-build a gun—making, checkering and finishing the stock, engraving the action, and boring the tubes. Other than boring the tubes, I have the impression that at least this gun, he must have subcontracted some of the other work.

Berry said: "The gun was received by me, the balance paid, and the gun was stored at my home to await the return of Captain Warner. I did not mention it to Nash. In September, Warner, now Major Warner, came to Memphis and we presented the new gun to Nash. We let it be known that his friends had tracked down Burt Becker and duplicated Bo Whoop, but only two were involved and that was Major George Warner and me. Nash shot this gun until the last when he went to Knoxville to live with Irma and Roy Witt."

According to Nash, the measurements of his Becker #2 were: 1 9/16″ at comb, 2¼″ drop at heel, 14¼″ pull. Bob Anderson tells me it had ¼″ cast-off, unusual in American guns. It had rather more than normal pitch at heel, as did the Super Fox in the old photo with Nash's Parker. Like the Becker #1, there was no safety. Berry Brooks points out that the Becker #2 was, through a misunderstanding of Becker's, made with a pistol grip—contrary to Nash's taste in stocks. Unlike Becker #1, this Becker was richly ornamented on the action and the barrels had deeply carved engraving for about 2¾″ forward from the breech.

The Becker #2 is the gun shown on the jacket of this book. At my request, it was recently measured for inside diameter of barrels and chokes. Barrel diameter is .750″ with chokes tapering in the last six inches to .700″.

In English gun proofing, bore diameters from .720 to .729 are proofmarked 12, those from .730 to .740 are marked 12/1 (a 12-gauge on the wide side), and a bore just over .740 is proved as an eleven-bore. Nash was, therefore, shooting an eleven-gauge gun. The patterns this gun delivers discredit the notion many gunners cling to: the larger the gauge, the larger the pattern. The eleven-gauge Becker magnum puts its better-than-ninety percent of its load into the same 30″ circle at forty yards as would a twenty-gauge (provided it was bored to throw such choked patterns).

According to all of Nash's friends, this was the last gun Burt Becker made. When "Are We Shooting 8-Gauge Guns?" appeared in *Gun Digest* in 1960, Nash captioned a photograph of the Becker #2:

> Custom built and hand bored magnum 12 double by Burt Becker. Bored for 3-inch cases, it weighs 10 lbs. loaded, and with its F and F 32-inch tubes it swings and balances beautifully. This was the last magnum built by Mr. Becker, now living in retirement near Aurora, Ill. He also made and engraved some of the fine old Remington doubles exhibited at the St. Louis World's Fair in 1904. Later, with the Fox Gun Company, he bored (and helped develop) the Askins-Sweeley magnums. Colonel H. P. Sheldon called him "the greatest borer of shotgun barrels on earth."

In this photograph, the Becker #2 had already earned its service stripes in the form of a worn area in the blueing on the barrels at the fore-end.

In the Nelson version of "Are We Shooting 8-Gauge Guns?" in 1961, Nash refers to "the late Burt Becker," placing Becker's death around 1960. Fitting the pieces of information together, it would seem that Burt Becker made top-grade guns for Parker, beginning in the early 1890s, Remington, and Fox. In the 1920's he set up his own custom gun shop in Philadelphia and made his beautifully bored magnums there.

When Nash was eighty-eight, he was confronted with a step that more than one shooting man has had to take, and those of us who give ourselves to a particular gun can sympathize. He sold the Becker #2. Bob Anderson informs me that at eighty-five Nash found the Becker too straight—part of the aging process—and began shooting several autoloaders because they had more drop and less weight than the Becker. These were a Browning that belonged to Dr. Andrews, and two Winchesters of his own—Models 59 and 1400. But it was from no lack of loyalty to the Becker that Nash let it go—to a man of Nash's pride, a move that was not easy. On February 28, 1969, he wrote Dr. Andrews in East Africa:

Wm. F. Andrews, MD
African Inland Mission
Kijabe PO
Kenya, East Africa

Dear Chub:

I hadn't the slightest idea you'd be interested in the big Becker, and had already told young Bart Cox, down in Washington, about it in connection with his grandfather's collection—some 30 Winchesters, Parkers and Beckers. I knew most of them and helped Bart with them after Henry Bartholomew's death. He had never known that I had dedicated the Scribner's edition of *De Shootinest Gent'man* to him—Bart. He's a PHD with the State Dept., very wealthy, 32, and I doubt if the boy ever shot a head of game, but he looks after the goose and duck ponds we started on his granddad's place. So, when he sent me a check for $850 and hoped it would help, what with having to try to sell the Inness painting, etc., I wrote Roy Witt, who has the gun in Knoxville, to ship it on down. Roy was told it could be done only through a Washington dealer. Then came your letter. There wasn't but one thing to do. I wanted you to have the gun.

So, I wrote Bart and he was just as nice as could be. I sent his check back, and put your check for $1000.00 in the bank. I am delighted to get things in some sort of shape to where I sleep better.

Nash owned and shot a number of guns in his long life, beginning with the 16-gauge Parker double hammer gun, a Christmas present to him and his brother Miles in 1888. Next came a 12-gauge double hammer gun that Nash described as a "bourgeois twelve-bore by an obscure Britisher." There was the 1890 model Winchester lever-action 12-gauge, followed by the Winchester 12-gauge 1893 model pump gun. This looked "sway-backed" to Nash, and he had a gunsmith add a rib—a forerunner of his positive ideas as to gun design. Nash's father, however, appropriated the gun for his duck shooting, leaving young Nash to struggle with his 10-pound Greener double, which Nash finally traded for a light Bonehill 12-gauge double with what he called "rabbit ear" hammers. Nash eventually regained possession of the Model 93 and old photos show him using it on quail. About 1918, he had the durable old pump gun altered to the 1897 action, and I understand the gun is today used by Nash's nephew.

In 1908 he was, in "Hallowed Years," shooting quail with an E. Smith double-barrel 12-gauge breech-loading hammer gun. In "Are We Shooting 8-Gauge

Guns?" he wrote: "Four Wapanoca Club members used 10-gauge and 8-gauge guns by W. & C. Scott of England, all sweet-handling hammer doubles. I was permitted their use when their owners were absent." The 10-gauge he used in "Great Day in the Morning!" may have been one of these. Nash told Bob Anderson he could shoot that 10-gauge seventeen times; if he shot it eighteen, he threw up. In "Great Day in the Morning!" he also mentioned a 16-gauge autoloader with two sets of barrels, a gift from an English friend in 1909.

In 1910 Nash was shooting Harold Money's old Winchester Model 97 pump gun at live pigeons, Money having left the gun with him when he returned to England. During the years just preceding 1920, he shot a 12-gauge 34-inch Parker double on ducks and geese. Then came the magnums, with first the 12-gauge 10-pound 32-inch Super Fox about 1921. His first Burt Becker 32-inch overbored magnum entered his life in 1926 and he and the gun were an entity until it was lost in 1948.

Nash sent me a photo of himself shooting a 12-gauge Hoffman double, "beautiful weapon by the ill-fated Hoffman Arms Co. that got into business a bit ahead of the Depression." About 1933 he got the Burt Becker 26-inch 12-gauge quail gun, which he described as having improved cylinder in both barrels. He was shooting this gun and a Greener 12-gauge double hammer gun, a gift from Ira Richards, as well as "several Winchester Model 21 doubles" according to John Bailey on numerous visits to Quail Hills. Nash described one of the Model 21 doubles on a photo he sent me: "A 20-gauge 26-inch custom-made about 1933 by Winchester's Bob Owen of England, brought over by the Olins. A set of 30-inch choked barrels has been added. It was made to my specifications and is ivory trimmed." He also had a Model 21 in 12-gauge, 8.4 pounds, with 26-inch and 32-inch barrels. When he received the 1962 Outdoorsman of the Year Award, he was given a 32-inch 12-gauge Model 21 by John Olin at the presentation ceremony on January 18, 1963, a gun Nash always called "the Award gun."

I think the second high point in his shooting life was the gift of his second "Big 'Un," the Burt Becker #2. Although he was a friend of Robert Churchill's, as far as I can tell, Nash never owned one of the more famous London bests—possibly because he did not care for light guns and light loads. In later years, he had a Winchester 12-gauge Model 50 autoloader, 9.2 pounds with 26-inch and 30-inch barrels. He also wrote of having "two fine Winchester autoloaders—the new 1400 and the light glass-tubed Model 59. You'll recall, it's the ONLY autoloader up till then that never jammed, and as you'll remember, 'twould kill ducks at ranges equal to the best."

But it was the Beckers that most seemed a part of Nash. That there were such guns, lends romance to shooting. John Olin says that, in light of today's ballistics, overboring did not contribute appreciably to the performance of the Beckers. Something did. Beyond the loving precision that went into the making of the Beckers #1 and #2, there was one dimension that no micrometer can measure, one factor no gunsmith can build in—a man's confidence in his gun. It took Nash Buckingham to shoot those "Big 'Uns" at tall ducks and geese in a manner in which those who saw him do it say no other gunner could. The soul of a gun is of dual essence—its maker and the man who shoots it. In shooting circles, the names Burt Becker and Nash Buckingham may well be spoken together. Not one without the other.

Are We Shooting 8-Gauge Guns?

An interesting concept of the performance of heavy loads as compared with large gauges, this was published in Gun Digest 1960, *in* Gun Digest Treasury No. 2, *and in the Nelson edition in 1961.*

The old 10-gauge Purdey described in the first paragraph was much like the 1868 Purdey shown in figure 83 in Sporting Guns *by Richard Akehurst (Weidenfeld & Nicolson, London, 1968).*

Nash credits choke boring to W. W. Greener in England and Fred Kimble in America "a full decade before I was born (1880)." Jack O'Connor in his The Shotgun Book *(Alfred A. Knopf, 1965) says that Kimble's "experiments were preceded by an English gunsmith named W. R. Pape, who patented a method of choke boring in 1866."*

Nash's self-schooled shooting method—"The last time I saw a chance like you, I shot about yonder"*—didn't mean that the last similar chance he'd seen was two seasons before. The number of shells he fired as a young gunner—sixty or more each day, four days a week from September "summer duck shooting" through January or February—totaled about five thousand shots per season. A man who came through that sort of experience had to be a consummate wing shot or be lacking in coordination. There was something to being in the right place at the optimum period.*

IN JULY 1958, I was shooting at our venerable Memphis, Tennessee, gun club when my gifted gunsmith friend, Mr. H. L. Highsmith, one of the nation's top-bracket riflemen, shotgunners and stockmakers, arrived for a bit of skeet practice with a strange piece. Twelve, sixteen, twenty and four-ten gauges were already rapping on our four fields. Mr. Highsmith's weapon du jour was a 10-gauge Purdey hammer double, exquisitely engraved, with a deft, slide-slip opener beneath its trigger guard. Its stock, a thing of beauty to any gun collector's eye, couldn't have missed my own guns' measurements ($14\frac{1}{4}$ x 1 9/16 x $2\frac{1}{4}$) by more than a skeletal fraction anywhere along the line. The Purdey's 32-inch tubes of lovely flowered Damascus were, of all things, bored true cylinder. Probably made before choke-boring happened in Great Britain. Weighing $9\frac{1}{2}$ pounds, it handled fast.

Mr. Highsmith had loaded himself a bagful of 10-gauge hulls with only $3\frac{1}{4}$ drams of black powder in some, semismokeless in others and the equivalent of smokeless for the rest. Using $1\frac{1}{8}$ of 8s ahead of such propellents was almost too light for a 10-gauge. But Mr. Highsmith's was an investigation of a lot of gunning's adages and priorities ballistically. He broke 23 x 25 at skeet, mixing the loads indiscriminately, to the amusement and amazement of his squadmates equipped with 12-bore doubles, over-unders, pumps and autoloaders. Some were using muzzle gadgets. Mr. Highsmith then turned the 10-bore Purdey over to Robert Sheffield, one of our region's summit all-around shotgunners, and he proceeded to shatter 25 x 25 skeet clays. Messrs. Highsmith and Sheffield are young, strong fellows, so the heavy old Purdey was apparently no adverse factor even at station 8, which, in my opinion, is a silly trick shot. Birds shot at such ridiculous range would be pulped and ruined.

Everybody enjoyed the Highsmith-Sheffield exhibition and quite a few members tried the Purdey just to say that for once in their lives they'd fired a charge of ancient black powder. Mr. Highsmith, a student of magnum shotguns (early and late vintages), has a gift for restoring "Grandpa's" old fowling pieces. Too, aside from his knowledge of ballistics, he can practice what he preaches, from duck blind, a goose pit or in the dove field. When it comes to stockmaking, he is an artist with a deep, keen knowledge, not only of woods and world models in stocks, but of what should be found in said woods; for perfect grains, burls and qualities of inlays that only perfect wood will allow. In short, in his chosen profession, Mr. Highsmith is a delicate and dedicated artist.

Watching him and Robert Sheffield shoot 96 per cent at skeet with that lovely, old-fashioned Purdey recalled for me a Fathers & Sons Day in 1928 at the famous Camp Fire Club up the river from New York City. The late Captain Paul Curtis, then the gun editor of *Field & Stream,* had invited me and the late and equally famous gun critic, Colonel Harold P. Sheldon (then Chief Conservation Officer of the United States Bureau of Biological Survey), to shoot the club's newly installed and freshly discovered shooting game called skeet. Having been Director of Game Restoration for the Western Cartridge Company, of East Alton, Illinois (now Olin Mathieson Chemical Corporation, Incorporated—division), I was in charge of its trap-shooting activities when the originator of skeet, the late William Harnden Foster, of Andover, Massachusetts, brought it to Western and saw it adopted by them first. I had also served a term or two on the National Skeet Board. But I had had literally no experience at the game.

I had been live-pigeon shooting at the Philadelphia Gun Club with Eltinge Warner (then owner and publisher of *Field & Stream*) and had with me a new 10-pound, 32-inch, overbored 12-gauge magnum (with Askins-Sweeley type boring by the late Burt Becker) from which I had been firing Western's latest 3-inch case with copper-coated shot. In 1928 Burt Becker was acknowledged the world's master barrel-borer. Fox-Becker magnums, for which Western developed their first loads and copper-coated pellets, had been in production approximately five years. At the Camp Fire Club, however, I was using standard trap loads. Colonel Sheldon was firing a beautiful 20-gauge double just sent him by Bob Owen, the British gun-maker later employed by Winchester on development of their now famous Model 21. The Colonel and I were patiently briefed by "Cap" Curtis as to skeet's rigmarole; how to swing and lead and behave ourselves at each station; and followed it all with grave appreciation. Then, squadded with the Captain and two other members, we "lit out." There was covert eyebrow-lifting and subtle snickers at my magnum and for the Colonel's 20-bore with quail loads. If I recall correctly, in those days, at station 8, instead of snapping at the incomers, you could wheel and fire at the target as it went away. I broke 98 x 100 and the Colonel (the first time he had ever shot skeet) shattered 97. Captain Curtis accounted for 95 x 100. We got bawled out as "ringers" and thieving ingrates, but we held it over Paul for many a day. Especially about how a magnum 12-bore could be put to a good many uses, on the basis that you have to first hit something no matter what weapon you're using. It is a great satisfaction to me now to recall both Sheldon and Curtis as two of the soundest field and water-fowl shots I've ever encountered, and comradely, unselfish, high-grade sportsmen as well. In after years I wrote a foreword for Paul's book on guns and shooting. And Harold Sheldon did, for me, an inspired foreword to the original Derrydale de luxe edition of *De Shootinest Gent'man*.

From that pleasant yesterday at Camp Fire, I was to shoot that 12-bore Becker magnum at practically every species of continental wildfowl and upland game—except quail and snipe. I shot steadily for twenty-one years until, in 1948, December 1, an examining game agent just forgot to put it back where he found it in our automobile. He left it, lying 'twixt hood and fender; it was never recovered though engraved on both case and steel. With that gun I fired every 12-gauge combination from 3-dram 1-ounce loads to the heaviest charges in 3-inch cases. Long since, I have come to realize that while the good big guns will nearly always beat the good little ones, it is the gunner himself who must toe scratch and swing the weapon with effective timing—or be penalized. You either hit or miss, hit and kill, hit and cripple—and recover—maybe—provided you work hard or have a good retriever. The last named being the best magnum load I've ever seen. When you discuss "long-range shotgunning" with magnum guns and loads (neither is worth a hoot without the other), meaning anything past fifty yards for lethal falls, you had best have a good retriever at "sit" beside you in blind or boat. Or else go over your stock of alibis very carefully.

By the time I was fifteen (in 1895) I was no stranger to the magnums. We didn't know 'em by that name then, such appellations applying to champagne bottles of greater capacities, vintages and voltage. The 20-gauge was practically nonexistent sportingly, 14-gauges were still around, and 16s frequently encountered. In fact, that was our first gun; a 16-gauge double hammer gun by Parker, given to my older brother at Christmas, 1888. Twelve gauge was definitely standard; but for wildfowl there were still many 10-bores and quite a few 8s in use. My father used 12-bore hammer guns by E. Smith of England for quail, snipe, woodcock and doves and plains game. They were probably, as to boring, our today's improved cylinder and modified. For wildfowl, he shot a W. W. Greener side-bolt 11-pound, 32-inch, hammerless 12-bore—with 3¼-inch chambers. Its stock specifications would fit me today. Until a few years ago I had one of those long green Winchester cases he fired from the big Greener. Made with a reinforced base, it was loaded (according to its top-wad) with 44 grains of Du Pont powder but only one ounce of 6s. That was the load made famous by the late Fred (Old Fritz) Gilbert, of Spirit Lake, Iowa. Fred was employed by Du Pont as a professional trapshot, and I have a cup, won in 1915, celebrating his twentieth anniversary with that organization. My parent used many cases of those "Gilbert loads," so, naturally, I helped myself to them and fired 'em from my own double Bonehill. Taking a chance maybe, but what we didn't know fortunately didn't hurt us at that tender age. In those days the loading companies would put up for the ammunition jobbers the favorite loads of "market hunters," duck clubs, and champion clay-target and flyer champions. A favorite load for the Wapanoca Duck Club at Turrell, Arkansas, was 3¼ drams with one ounce of chilled shot. Its members bought them lavishly. Duck bag limits were fifty a day, market hunting was legal, and, with plenty of fowl around it was a pleasant load to shoot from both double guns and the new-fangled and increasingly popular repeating shotguns.

Four Wapanoca Club members used 10s and 8s by W. & C. Scott, of England; all sweetly handling, hammer doubles. I was permitted their use when their owners were absent. I was then five-foot ten and weighed 185 pounds, so recoil was no problem. And I had been taught how to mount a shotgun properly, too. There were worlds of swan and geese available and men didn't have to consider the word "magnum." Big guns for wildfowling were simply a matter of course. There was no specialization for "long-range shooting" as such. There was little of what is known today as "skybusting." There were big bags to accumulate and the good shots and market hunters not only "got 'em where they wanted 'em" before they fired, but everyone tried to make every shell count. There was no need to merely shoot on a chance of crippling.

Use of those 10- and 8-bore guns in my earlier years left me an experience that stood me in good stead in after years of controversial discussion about federally legal aspects of their banning or regulation. There has never been a worse misunderstood nor more humorously garbled ballistic field, from the conservational or industrial slant, than the furored forensics by gun editors (some of whom never fired an 8-gauge and mighty few 10s) and official Washington. One paragraph should cover that historical era of sham and pressures.

In the early 1890s first lever and then trombone-action repeaters by Spencer and Winchester, carrying six shells, made their appearance and quickly infiltrated the ranks of sportsmen and market hunters. About 1905 the first autoloading 12-bore appeared, to further accelerate the pace of national waterfowl destruction. By 1912-13 when the Weeks McLean Bill and Lucy Act appeared, it had become obvious that wildfowl populations (whipsawed by upped firepower and agricultural attritions of northern breeding grounds) were doomed unless remedial measures were taken. Federal bag limits of twenty-five ducks a day and eight geese, with ninety-day open seasons (no "frameworks" or trading with the states—a bit of penny-ante wildlife management inflicted in recent years) were clapped on. To make assurance doubly sure, from the market-shooting slant, the good old 8-bore was banished. The lighter, faster-shooting pump-guns and autoloaders (putting more shot and powder under the trigger-fingers than the 8s) were not allowed to continue, but made the watchword for advertising: "Shoot more, shoot faster and kill more." Putting away the 8-bore probably seemed the right thing to do to disenfranchised market gunners. But what swivel-chair federals knew about real game management then was in swaddling clothes and there weren't many Conservationists around to raise a hue and cry.

This ballistic travesty, begun then, continues—and on a basis of both too-large and too-small bores. A 3-shot magnum 12, pump or autoloader, carrying three of today's maximum charges, gives the user as much if not more firepower than the old double-tubed 8s of my youth. (We'll get into that—later.) Nor, in those early times did we have the tiny .410s with which to cripple game and lose it. Failure to ban those too-little guns on federal migrants has for long pointed an accusing finger at the game management integrity of Washington. Gun editors and ballistic writers have panned this official deviation from Conservational common sense and principles. But there is where we stand today. Many preserve owners and duck clubs rightfully exclude .410s.

Nowadays, using "muzzle-gadgets" successfully designed to permit all degrees of barrel restriction, the gunner, by a mere twist of the wrist or a tiny wrench, can select the pellet density he deems best for wildfowl or uplanders. Or, for the type of game covert he's tramping; thick or wide-open. The mental processes channeled by such decisions constitute a fascination for hunters the nation over. If they miss, the alibi is "wrong choke selection"; not one's own faulty lead. Lakes of ink, mountains of paper, and earth-girdling typewriter ribbons have been dedicated to man's yearning for sporting weapons and their ballistic developments. I have listened by the hour to heated discussions on the "killing power" of guns of varying weights and chokes, on various loads of propellants and shot sizes. Leading and hitting, in such arguments, become rather vague inconsequentials. I have heard more simon-pure bunk about magnum shotguns and their loads!

W. W. Greener (England) and Fred Kimble (U.S.) produced barrel restrictions or "choke boring" in shotgun barrels a full decade before I was born (1880). According to Mr. Kimble's memoirs, it was not unusual for him during his market-gunning days along the Illinois, Mississippi and Little Rivers, to bag and boat as high as two hundred or more assorted ducks per day. He used his favorite, personally choked 6-gauge (Tonks, of Boston, finished up several such weapons for him) with a stiff charge of powder in the piece's single, muzzle-loading tube, and an ounce-and-a-half

of what he called "St. Ouis 3s." In a delightful and voluminous correspondence with me during the mid and late 1920s, when, at an advanced
age, he was living in retirement in California, Mr. Kimble described how
he made his own powder. "It was," he wrote in an exquisite, copperplate
hand, "of a slow-burning texture similar to today's progressive-burning
powder. I cooked it up myself on the back of my kitchen stove, from personally compounded ingredients costing but a few cents per pound." (I
would like to own that recipe today.) He had frequently, he said, made
long runs on single mallards of fifty or sixty straight, flighting timber at
sixty to seventy yards. "I came to realize," he wrote, "that to shoot a long
way it takes a cannon, so, for my duck shooting, I tried to get the closest
thing to one."

To really appreciate such bags and feats of marksmanship, think of the
physical labor expended, not only to paddle or row a heavy boat all day
and gather one's bag, but to muzzle-load for that many shots (many of
which were undoubtedly missed) day in and week out. Such results were
obtained, Mr. Kimble wrote, "by trial and error basis." That means, in
effect, having to learn gun yardage the hard way.

Having sat at Mr. Kimble's knees for fifty years, I know that this means
sizing up an approaching goose, duck or dove and saying to yourself, "The
last time I saw a chance like you, I shot about *yonder.*" And, suiting brain
reflex to action, you try to swing ahead and hit, "Yonder." You're actually
trying to hit a *moving spot* ahead of the quarry—just as you successfully
tried before—at such a distance. The quarry, meanwhile, is carried in your
subconscious vision. You can't intercept it by firing at a fixed spot ahead
—your gun must hit that *moving spot.* You know what happens to your
distance off the tee at golf when your *swing* fails to follow through? In shot-
gunnery that means the same thing: follow on through—or else. And it takes
many an "or else" to make a real game shot. It also takes absorbed energy
to lethalize game and put it on your table. In a gunning way—never send
a boy on man's errand. The use of a magnum shotgun and loads means,
simply enough, "Getting thar fustest with th' mostest—and big'uns at that."
But get it out of your mind that simply because you buy a magnum you
have to shoot heavy loads out of it at everything. If your wildfowling's wild
and rough, select the maximum charge you personally prefer. If the shooting is in the woods—over decoys—the pigeon load of 3¼ x 1¼ x 7½ will
knock mallards for loops. I've killed many a limit of doves with my magnum, using that load or even 3 drams one ounce. Magnum or no magnum,
the gunning law is, "You've got to hit 'em first—and hard."

From a gunning and ballistic angle I am, as the old song goes, "right back where I started from," seventy years ago. I sometimes sit appalled at advertising claiming that clean (worse) consistent kills can be made at a hundred yards with certain 10-bore guns using a heavy powder charge and two ounces of No. 2 shot. That's the length of a football field. Would you try for a goose at such range unless you were starving?

Between early-day big bores and comparatively modern American magnum shotguns lie two main differences in American wildfowling management. During the reign of the big bores (6-, 8- and 10-gauge singles and doubles) there was so much game that the wildlife hucksters rarely expended an unnecessary charge. They water-huddled or "flat-shot" fowl with one or two blasts. Seven-tubed muzzle-loaders hurled thousands of pellets into night-rafted concentrations. I saw the result of such a shot in the early morning of New Year's Day, 1930—when my host and I entered his shore blind near Washington, D.C.—of all places. A northwest gale was breaking up and sweeping ice floes downtide. Henry's binoculars revealed two men in a boat well out and upriver. He sent his helper out to aid them, figuring their decoys were being swept away—but they pulled away into the mist. Awhile later a big ice floe crashed into the shore just below our blind. We picked up 187 dead black ducks. The "big gun" wasn't located for several months, but is now in captivity. Since then, in several states organized rings of wildfowl thieves have been broken up by federal undercover efforts—the only real way to accomplish it. Many of their duck slaughterers admitted using extension magazines on their autoloaders when firing into encircled night rafts.

Wildfowl market hunting stems from earliest shooting on New England's coastal fresh-water ponds. Village shoemakers built camouflaged shore blinds and cobbled footgear behind such brushed-up hides while crude goose decoys floated out front. When honkers dropped in, the cobblers let them huddle and then unleashed hails of hand-molded big pellets, cut-up horse-shoe nails or gravel from their smoothbored, flintlocked muzzle-loaders. Their "Goodies" plucked the slain for feather beds and pillows and spread roast goose around the community.

Later, wealthy sportsmen fashioned elaborate lodges camouflaged seaward to match tidal levels; in adjoining watchtowers gamekeepers released trained goslings to fly out as "greeters" to coastal migrants. With parent geese in restraint (the keepers having sighted flocks headed down-coast) the gaggle of "greeters" winged forth and vocalized welcome to safe harbor. When the visitors were "lit," the trained young decoys swam under the gatepens and rejoined the old folks. Afront the clubhouse blind was a spring-latched window opening onto a big stool of floating lures. The keeper-lookout, pressing a buzzer, interrupted the card game and sent the players to the spring window with 8- and 10-bores. He then sprung the deadfall. Up lashed the window, and there right under the sportsmen were the victims. The bigger the bags the bigger the sports! And I am now talking about what I have actually seen. By the time live decoys were banned, many autoloaders and pump guns had found their way into these shore blinds—and displaced the big bores. Why not: they could throw more shot—and faster.

With pump guns and autoloaders in use (despite the banned 8s) recession came with increasing speed to basic continental stocks. And, insidiously, agricultural attritions on both our own and Canadian breeding grounds were gaining beachheads. Market hunters killed about as much game as they could carry, pack and ship. Some duck clubs, foreseeing an evil day, clapped on daily bag limits—usually fifty ducks and as many geese as one could gun. In the light of today's emaciated bag limits—almost unbelievable.

Today, the sale of other than legally pen-reared and banded wildfowl for public use (in some states) is strictly forbidden. As of now, however, we have not even approached, much less solved, the problem of combining decency afield with game production on a controlled or managed basis. In this country, the public's first reaction to any game regulation is not how it can be best obeyed or enforced, but how it can be evaded, or worse, violated.

Conservation made no move toward the curtailment of magazine gun capacities until the early 1920s. There had been mutterings through the years, but those were stifled by the gunmakers who had seen the big bores banned by the Migratory Bird Act and the Treaty Act with Great Britain. At that time, *Field & Stream* boldly challenged the autoloaders—only to emerge badly beaten. Soon, however, a new force arose which called magazine guns and their manufacturers to an accounting. Begun in 1929 by the American Wildfowlers, a small foundational group that eventually emerged as More Game Birds in America, and later still as Ducks Unlimited, the battle terminated in 1934-35 when an executive order by the late Franklin Delano Roosevelt restricted magazine shotguns to three shots. The various states then passed equivalent legislation, many of them outlawing guns of more than three-shot capacity—on upland game birds. It is now freely admitted that had this not been done we would not, today, be shooting wildfowl. It is also worthy of note that practically every major

benefit attained by this nation's wildfowl and upland-game-bird resources has been due to Conservationists' brains in not only conceiving such measures but being able and willing to stand up and fight for them against lethargic Congresses, faceless officials and exploitative commercial interests.
. Let's examine some of the old big bores, strictly from their own records, then compare them with today's 12-bore magnums, in both doubles and magazined weapons. All targets used in these tests were one foot square.

Fred Kimble's 6-gauge 36-inch barrel muzzle-loading shotgun. Hand-choked by Kimble himself:
6 drams, 1½ oz., #3's at 40 yards. 79 struck—or 44.7%
6 drams, 1½ oz., #2's at 40 yards. 55 struck—or 36.6%
J. Kelley's 8-gauge, single-barreled muzzle-loader. Rugh of Peoria, Illinois —builder; hand-choked by Fred Kimble:
5 drams, 1½ oz., #1's at 60 yards. 40 struck—or 33.75%
Long's 10-gauge double, 32-inch barrels, breechloader. Maker— Schaeffer:
5 drams, 1½ oz., #2's at 40 yards. 58 struck—or 38.6%
4½ drams, 1½ oz., #2's at 40 yards. 59 struck—or 39.2%. Only one pellet struck outside of 25 inches.

These, then, were the guns that made history in the art of choke boring, a restriction that permitted powerful charges of powder and heavy-shot loads for lengthened kills. They were about as close as Fred Kimble could come to a cannon. They, or their likes, endured until 1912-13, when a well-meaning federal assumption of waterfowl protection banned gauges larger than 10s. Now, nearly fifty years later, let's appraise the situation. My own wildfowl and field artillery will suffice.

Model 21 Winchester Magnum 12-bore with 32- and 26-inch tubes, 3-inch cases.
Model 50 Winchester autoloader with 30- and 26-inch barrels, ventilated ribs, 2¾-inch cases.
Model 59 Winchester (Win-Lite glass tubes) 28- and 26-inch barrels, weight 6.4 lbs., 2¾-inch cases.
Burt Becker handmade 10-pound 12-gauge Magnum—32-inch barrels, 3-inch cases; coneless.

This is the last Magnum ever built by the late Burt Becker; described by the late Colonel H. P. Sheldon as "the finest barrel borer the world has even seen." It will shoot consistently better than 90 per cent patterns with 4's coppered.

It is possible from a 3-inch-chambered autoloader to fire three magnum shells, each containing almost five drams of powder and as high as one and seven eighths ounces of shot. Thus giving the user almost 15 drams of propellent and almost six ounces of shot under his trigger finger. If the old big-bore users had had such devastating machines, chances are our waterfowl populations might have been wiped out earlier.

Today, with federal bag limits running from three to five ducks a day in the four flyways, and "goose management" down to one honker a day in some areas, it matters nothing what type of gun or load the fowler uses. Provided it is of sufficient gauge and load to not cripple wildfowl and upland game like the "too little" .410s and 28s. The more (and bigger) shot, the more penetration and lethal absorbed energy and the less chance to cripple (provided the government slackens its decimating practice of permitting too-early and too-late wildfowling). The magnum shotgun trouble is this: the American gunning public has, as usual, been "overexposed," as the advertising trade puts it, rather than "overgunned." The novice hunter (and they not unnaturally increase nowadays) hearing about fantastic "long kills," buys himself a magnum and the heaviest charges available. Expecting, by merely pointing his great gun in the quarry's general direction, to see it collapse and fall from great heights and vindicate the copywriter's claims. If these latter would but stress the fact that a magnum-armed hunter is simply never "undergunned"; that a magnum isn't a special weapon shooting 3-inch cases *only,* but can handle any length hull and bag its fair share of close or distant game—if it's hit—the shooting field would be a better place in which to live. That's the one big important piece of business. You've got to connect—first.

Long-Range Duck Shooting

This was published in Blood Lines *(Derrydale 1938 and Putnam 1947) as "The Comedy-Drama of Long-Range Duck Shooting." At one time I thought it might have appeared in* Field & Stream *as "Judgment of Distance in Wing Shooting," but upon locating that article in the Arms & Ammunition Department of the March 1930 issue, I found no relation between the two, the latter mostly discussing the ranges at which various bores—and men—are effective.*

Nash Buckingham, like Billy the Kid, had a reputation for rarely missing. The young Kid was said to have been deadly, not necessarily because he could shoot more accurately, or even faster, than his victims, but because when he walked into a gun fight there was no doubt in his mind that he was going to kill his adversary. The late adversaries made the mistake of not being certain. With equal conviction, there was never any question in the back of Nash's mind that he would kill a duck, once he had decided it was within the long reach of his big Becker—a point of view that could improve the shooting of thousands of mediocre shots.

This piece belongs in The Best of Nash Buckingham *because in it Nash writes of loads, chokes, swing and leads, not only of himself but of the old duck gunner Fred Kimble, including range, both horizontal and in height. I don't entertain enthusiasm for the market hunters, but Kimble, one of those few who were intelligent enough to write, passed on the color of his era. Nash referred to him in 1938 as still living.*

In this piece, Nash dates the acquisition of his Becker #1 as in 1926, the only specific mention of that date as such that I can find in all of his writing.

Because many of Nash's works appear here for the first time together in one volume, to avoid repetition I have deleted portions of this article dealing with wildfowl conservation and legislation that were in the Blood Lines *version.*

ASIDE FROM Mr. Fred Kimble's published reminiscences of long-range wildfowling with the heavy muzzle-loading shotguns first "choke-bored" in this country by his own tooling, that field of sporting gunnery lacks commentators. I doubt if one half of one per cent of all modern duck hunters ever heard of Fred Kimble, responsible for what is known the world over as choke boring. Financially, he realized little reward from that discovery. Nevertheless, by establishing varying degrees of pellet cluster and distribution through control of tube restriction, this remarkably inventive master wing shot made an important contribution to shotgunning.

Mr. Kimble's famous "muzzlers" were succeeded by heavy ten-bore breechloaders, and their increased rapidity of fire naturally heightened his effectiveness at game killing. From his best-liked muzzle-loader, a six-gauge "single bar'l" (unfortunately lost), he fired six drachms of coarse-grained, slow-combustion propellant differing little, in effect, from today's progressive powder types, burning, so to speak, grain by grain. Ahead of those six drachms of powder went an ounce and a half of shot known as "St. Louis 3's." But Mr. Kimble's records at glass balls, clay targets, and live pigeons were made with lighter loads of smaller-sized pellets.

My wonderful old friend the late Captain Arthur du Bray (real father of the twenty-bore shotgun in the United States) was an all-around, premier wing shot of worldwide field experience. He often told me of gunning ducks from the same boat and blind with Mr. Fred Kimble. He spoke with admiration of the latter's uncanny skill with a ten-bore Parker double and a type of powder Mr. Kimble later manufactured for himself. Mr. Kimble still favors long, heavy guns and big shot for rough wildfowling. He wrote me, in his exquisite, copperplate hand: "The heavy thirty-two- and thirty-four-inch guns you use on ducks would be my exact choice were I shooting under today's law of bag limit. Light, short-tubed guns handle fine in a sporting-goods store, and anyone can bag birds with them over decoys. But for steady alignment and barrel level while swing and trigger press are uniting, give me the long and somewhat muzzle-heavy weapon. I never saw anyone kill really high ducks or distant, crossing chances with a short, light weapon. Now about that powder I made up later. When mixing it at my ranch, I first cooked it on the kitchen stove and dried the stuff on trays in an open field. It wasn't black powder (that kind I afterward concocted). It was very light in color and weight, and was composed from by-products costing only a few cents. In muzzle velocity it was just a trifle short of today's standard progressive-burning powders. Its recoil was easy, breech pressure low, and patterns uniform. I could have run all these tests upward—but played safe.

"I think one and three-eighths ounces of No. 4 copper-coated shot I've been reading about in your articles would be my combination for rough-and-tumble ducking. I read your essays with quite some satisfaction: you've given the boys some real pointers. It is, indeed, amusing to hear some of these modern shooters tell how the birds were so wild they had to kill them a hundred yards off with a twenty-gauge gun and No. 6 shot in order to fetch down a limit. I learn from Colonel Sheldon's article, 'The Big Guns,' that your shooting is not done with six- and seven-pounders and puny charges of shot. In my early days I formed an opinion based on experience that to shoot a mile it takes a cannon. So I tried to come as near a cannon for duck shooting as my size and strength would stand."

In earlier writings, Mr. Kimble states: "I had a double-barrel muzzle-loader built by O. P. Secor, of Peoria, Illinois; and a single-barrel muzzle-loader by Joseph Tonks, of Boston, Massachusetts. My two guns were the first ever choke-bored; Joe's, the second. The barrels on my Secor gun were too thin to stand much of a choke, but the single one had a good thick tube and Mr. Tonks made a great shooting weapon of it. I bought it because it outshot my double. This single-barrel gun would shoot in a twenty-six-inch circle at forty yards and was good for single ducks up to seventy yards. The reason for describing my guns in detail is because our knowledge of choke boring spread from these guns to all parts of the civilized world. I depended on this single-barrel muzzle-loader for all my duck shooting until I got the six-bore one which became so famous. After I finished boring the six-gauge, I found I had a gun good up to eighty yards. I used six drachms of coarse-grained, black powder and one and one-half ounces of 'St. Louis 3's.'"

It is fortunate that such extracts from Mr. Kimble's memoirs are available. A particularly appealing paragraph reads: "Memory takes me back more than fifty years to the Illinois River and the happiest days of my life. I seem to see the old campgrounds, bluffs, points of timber, bends in the river. sloughs, shooting grounds, and everything, just as they were long, long years ago. On certain days the ducks would fly out in the big timber, where most of our shots would be over the tops of tall trees. Shooting mallards in ordinary flight, I held one duck length ahead at forty yards; three ducks lengths ahead at sixty yards; and six duck lengths ahead at eighty yards. Counting a duck length at twenty-four inches meant leads of approximately two, six, and twelve feet at those ranges."

Mr. Kimble tells us how he learned to estimate gunning yardages more accurately by betting with himself and others on distances between trees, lampposts, and street-corner markers. Years ago, after reading Mr. Kimble's writings, I adopted this system, and it helped my marsh and field shooting more than any other one factor in my experience. "In the high cypress," writes Mr. Kimble, "I had a good chance to practice shooting over timber tops with my single barrel and learned to shoot fairly well, killing, some days, as many as thirty and forty mallards without a miss. One day I bagged over two hundred mallards, not more than one to a shot. Such bags as mine look like slaughter nowadays, but in those times there were ducks for all who would work for them."

That last line should bring a blush of shame to the faces of many ease-loving, modern wildfowlers. Nowadays, mobs of inexperienced hunters rattle off magazine guns full of high-power ammunition into masses of ducks lured to the water or hovering close above it. Conceive, therefore, Mr. Kimble's labor and activity in bagging more than two hundred mallards from high in the air with his muzzle-loader, and with even less shot at his command than some of our moderns control. Remember he could fire but once and had to reload his piece several hundred times and, in addition, pushed his own duck boat, set out and picked up decoys, collected his bag, waded swamps, and mushed home to camp chores. Consider the infinite zest involved, to say nothing of patience; charging and recharging that huge weapon.

The Migratory Bird Law bars such weapons as Mr. Kimble's muzzle-loaders. But annually, thousands of ducks and upland game birds are sacrificed to such field toys as the .410-gauge shotgun, in use largely through the vanity of experimentation and the mistaken idea (even among many well-meaning hunters) that the use of so small a gauge gives their game a chance. The shooting field is no place for experiment, if conservation and restoration are to prosper. If a double eight-bore is too large for use on geese and ducks, why reverse the equation by permitting the use of guns and shells too small to be effective? As a weapon for skeet shooting, training beginners and dogs, the .410-gauge shotgun has a use. True enough, expert shots can bag ducks, quail, prairie chickens, and Hungarian partridges with maximum .410 charges. But to score with anything like sporting decency they must be well versed in judging yardage and equally skilled in gun holding to place a shot charge at not exceeding twenty-five yards. I once heard a man who was considered a fine duck shot boast of killing a duck limit with a .410 using extreme loads. "It'll kill 'em," he explained, "but I had to knock down about thirty mallards I didn't get."

Fortunately, I got an early look at the revival of modern long-range wildfowling in 1921 when I was in the sporting goods business. One day a salesman gave me some shells containing what he confided was a new type of powder. I tried them in my thirty-four-inch Parker double and found that I really could cut my lead on higher birds. A year later these loads came on the open market and the sensation they caused is an interesting chapter in the drama of long-range wildfowling.

Later, I was sent some three-inch twelve-bore shells loaded with this same new powder behind an ounce and three-eighths of No. 4 chilled pellets. Also a twelve-bore "overbored" shotgun developed for this particular load by, as I recall, Mr. Charles Askins and an associate. I found this combination, for all heavy-duty waterfowling, to be the superior of any ten-bore outfit of that day. In 1926 my first magnum twelve-bore was replaced by one built and bored for big shot by the famous Philadelphia gunsmith, Mr. Burt Becker. Its patterning power is almost hoselike. Since 1922 I have shot thousands of three-inch twelve-bore shells at geese and ducks the country over. Truth to tell, however, the most important item for all long-range shooting is a good retriever.

In 1925 I was invited to become director of game restoration activities by the company that developed the original "long-range" campaign. And, in later years, I in turn was taken to task by a friendly competitor for my publicity efforts in such matters. "Wrong again," I replied. I have never written a line about long-range shotgun shooting except as applying to a specialized field of "high-fliers" for the heavy magnum combination. And even in such connection I have warned against promiscuous experiment. The whole force behind such tools is to be overgunned rather than undergunned when birds won't decoy, and cannot be called within reasonable range. During that glamorous revival of long-range shooting during the 1920's, I not infrequently suggested to my employers that the hue and cry for excess ranges by the masses was getting out of hand and crippling too much game.

The true basis of skill at what is called long-range duck shooting is little more than trained ability to estimate yardage correctly. Today's gunners will have little opportunity to garner such experience at wildfowl. There are a few passes where scoring at lofty chances is possible for the gunner, but not many. In recent years, however, I've enjoyed some canvasback shooting along the Potomac River that will test any fellow's gun, judgment of distance, and shot-placing skill. But in the main, shortened seasons, lowered bag limits, and generally easier wildfowling methods have reduced necessity for anything much heavier than standard loads. There is, in duck shooting, that happy medium of range that lies between the necessity for reaching out at times and birds at gun muzzle. Truth of the matter is that a real forty-yard chance eye-measures to at least seventy yards for most of today's duck hunters. All of which accounts for the admitted fact that a majority of all ducks killed today are knocked down at under twenty-five yards.

Long-range duck shooting by men qualified to use magnum guns and heavy charges of big shot (and there are quite a few of them) begins at forty yards, the accepted pattern-board test for full-choked guns. And for the hunter, everything above 70 per cent in pattern is choke "velvet." What the average duck shooter needs nowadays is an improved cylinder right tube and a modified left. But even for the better-than-average shot, armed with a full-choked gun and two-and-three-quarter-inch shells containing maximum loads, fifty yards is absolutely "tops" for anything like reasonably consistent kills. With a heavy, freakish gun like mine, using three-inch cases and No. 4 copper-coated pellets which enhance the patterning, single ducks can be knocked cold at what I estimate to be sixty yards. That is when game is scarce and the birds not working well to a call. I've even raked mallards out of flocks I estimated to be seventy yards away—more or less. But when I resort to that sort of thing I am hard-pressed for provender and accompanied by some breed of competent retriever; *not* otherwise!

Waterfowl take on different sizes and colors at varying yardages, differing somewhat with the gunner's natural gift of vision and experience at observation. Wing motion means considerable, too, in estimating speed, and determining species. It all counts where there is a long-range shot to be pulled off shortly. The veteran wildfowler comes to know when a mallard is within a certain zone. If the hunter's only offering is pass shooting, with small opportunity for nearer or circling birds, then is the time for legitimate long-range gunning. But why risk wounding for mere experiment? The whole practice is detrimental to future supplies of wildfowl.

When you have standing timber for comparison in estimating overhead yardage, the job becomes far easier than judging long, angle shots across open water. Yet how few duck hunters go into the timber with the faintest idea of even attempting to figure out the comparison of treetops with their gun patterns! It takes a tremendous tree to reach a height of fifty yards (150 feet) in the lowlands, and a tall hardwood to rear much over a hundred feet. And yet your full-choked gun is tested over a few feet better than forty yards at the factory.

Henry Davis and I were gunning the Arkansas rice fields. One proprietor to whom we were entire strangers took his gun along when he guided us out into his flooded timber. I was shooting my big Burt Becker, and Henry a thirty-two-inch full-choked Parker trap gun. He was using my three-inch shells with an ounce and three-eighths of copper-coated shot. We began dropping ducks from just above the treetops until our guide finally said, "I guess I'll retire this twenty-bore—where did you guys learn your duck shooting, anyhow?" But all we were doing was getting full value out of thirty-five- to forty-yard rulebook patterns, with the punch of big shot tossed in. Remember, absorbed energy is what kills anything, whether struck by pellets, a slug, or an automobile. Henry shot the pin-oak flats until he got the range by judging tree heights. He learned the angles of greatest vulnerability—nearly overhead. But later on, shooting from a stand over open water at Mud Lake, he didn't do so well. When asked the trouble, Henry grinned and said, "Well, over in the woods I got my yardages certified by the trees; but out yonder there was nothing but sky and air, and I just got to trying to do arithmetic in the blind." If you want to miss a lot of ducks, just keep trying to do the mental arithmetic some of these tables of shot and bird speeds involve—the kind some of our most able shooting authorities and advertising men figure out for beginners. Most of them are conservation aids in disguise.

Some seasons ago I joined a friend shooting in the timber. He was using a magnificent Holland and Holland wildfowl gun and twelve-bore express loads. But neither he nor his paddler could use a duck call. Bunch after bunch of mallards winged the cypress tops undisturbed. Unable to fathom it, I said, "Bob, give the next customers a whirl." "They're too high for my gun," he replied. I borrowed it and stepped from my duck boat into the shallow water. A bunch of greenheads sailed over and I dropped a pair. Bob's mouth flew open. Reassured, he began trying and soon took toll. There wasn't a better timber cruiser alive than Bob, but he had just never thought of comparing tree height to duck-shooting yardage. Since that afternoon he has developed into not only a high-grade wildfowl and quail shot, but can blow a duck call with the best of them.

A hint or two for general waterfowling. Over decoys use standard loads —my favorite is the twelve-bore "trap load" of three drachms of powder and an ounce and a quarter of No. 7½ chilled shot. But in another pocket I have a supply of three-inch cases loaded with No. 4 copper-coated shot. Remember: the tighter your gun's pattern, the more ducks you'll miss or mess up at short ranges. The closer they come to such a weapon as mine, the safer they are. But, above all, shoot sitting down or standing up—one or the other. If there's any possible way to avoid it, don't jump up to shoot.

In my very humble opinion, American duck shooting has seen about the last of its glamour days. Gone, perhaps forever, will be baiting and the use of live decoys. Their passing is the direct result of the government's failure to curb commercialism in wildfowling, and sportsmen who fed more birds than they killed have had to take the "rap." Long ago, programs of natural aquatic plants should have been started in clubs and areas when water levels were at the lowest. Commercial duck shooting will either be squelched as a violation of Section 2 of the Migratory Bird Law, or else taxed—like any other business—from every angle. Failure to act on this abortive situation has already cost millions of ducks and valuable tax moneys which state and federal restoration projects could well have used.

Nowadays much is heard and written about a decline in national character. Duck shooting has seen its share. All honor therefore to the fine men and women struggling as conservationists to offset this decline. Theirs is a desperate task involving eternal vigilance. As to long-range wildfowling: common-sense methods, sound sportsmanship, and enforcement that enforces must stay on the job. Or else duck shooting of the future will be viewed at such long range by all as to cancel the sport entirely.

Here's How in Quail Shooting

It is nearly impossible to read Nash Buckingham and not learn something about shooting, but this is probably his most helpful piece in regard to technique. It was in the collection Mark Right! *and was used, somewhat revised in the version I have selected, in the Nelson edition in 1961. In one place it was credited as having appeared in* Field & Stream *but neither the magazine's editors nor I can find it there under any title.*

The richness of years is present in this version—"seventy years actual cap-bustin'" instead of forty-five years in Mark Right! *But there is also the addition of "with the qualification of good eyesight," acknowledging one of Anno Domini's nasty little tricks. Nash had a cataract operation two years after those words were printed.*

His moment of "repression" to focus on the quail singled out is excellent advice for any type of shooting; his version of what to me is mount-and-overtake (passing the bird and firing while swinging through a short lead) is effective in thickest grouse cover—sometimes after losing sight of the bird. But if you concentrate on Nash's "moving spot two lengths ahead of the bob" and "keep swinging . . . a shade ahead of that spot," you are dwelling on that "spot" and your swing becomes sustained lead. This no doubt accounts for Nash's uncanny accuracy on birds in the open where many men become flustered and simply snap-shoot because the shot looks so easy. I asked John Bailey if Nash was actually this kind of deliberate shot.

"On quail," John said, "Nash was fast in a thicket when he had to be, but 'took his time' when he could. I always told him he shot his second shot unnecessarily fast, and he would reply, 'That's because of so much live-pigeon shooting, where it didn't matter whether you shot once or twice, just so that the pigeon fell inside the ring.' "

John Olin told me he saw Nash, with a Model 97 Winchester pump gun, shoot seven quail on a covey rise. Henry P. Davis, according to John Bailey, said: "Nash is not just the best shot this country ever saw, but the best it will ever see." John Bailey also quotes Hal Howard, who probably saw him shoot more shells than anyone, as saying: "Nash's all around shooting is what makes him the great-est. There are quail hunters in this area as good as Nash—maybe a few dove shots —but at long-range ducks he is in a class by himself, and is excellent at all game birds and traps with any kind of gun." John added: "Nash remained a good duck shot and fair dove shot several years after he became too slow for quail in the thickets."

These are opinions of men who shot with Nash over many years. I understand that he was a fine trap shot but not at top championship performance. One phase of Nash's shooting has been discussed almost not at all. Although he listed ruffed grouse among birds to be photographed for the Grantland Rice movie he made in North Dakota in 1944, there was no mention of shooting them. The only ruffed grouse shooting Nash described (although he suggested that he tried it while at Harvard about 1900) was mentioned in a letter to me dated January 4, 1944, when he referred to the old Intermont Hotel near Covington, Virginia, and wrote: "I shot my first Sir Ruffs thereabouts." I later learned that this was in 1892 when he was twelve.

In one of the Tranquillity *stories, Colonel H. P. Sheldon tells of a Southern duck shooter who visited "the Captain" in Vermont to shoot partridge and wood-cock. The implication was that this might have been Nash Buckingham but the shooting and the pseudo-Southern characterization did not fit. However, a New England grouse-shooting acquaintance of mine who knew Sheldon quoted him as saying that Nash had tried shooting Vermont grouse with "a notable lack of success." This would not surprise any experienced grouse gunner, for the deliber-ately sustained lead of the duck blind, dove, quail and trap fields does not lend itself to fast grouse shooting where there is no time to "keep swinging on that spot ahead of the bird."*

In one of his other articles Nash wrote: "The instant you begin figuring lead in so many feet, you are lost, barring luck. Point behind your bird, follow past him, lose him, hitch forward just a bit more and shoot without stopping the gun." This says nothing about clinging to a spot ahead of the bird, and I'll wager that any man who has dropped a bird remembers—if he recalls anything about it— doing much what Nash said in that last sentence.

In the Mark Right! *version of this piece, Nash gave a hint I occasionally find myself following: "Standing ready for the rise, I've acquired a trick, to aid re-pression, of turning my gunstock flat against my right underforearm. This leaves the tubes and action a shade canted. As the birds jump I'm turning the gun while letting the bevy get en route. By the time I've selected my bird, the gun is being lifted in one motion to its shoulder niche that seems to align cheek and comb with butt plate and shoulder simultaneously—a shortcut to 'repression.'"*

Even in that 1936 version, Nash recommended using light loads for better pat-terns and to avoid recoil jump—advice still being given in gun magazines. But as to what to do if you stumble, it is appalling to read: "... don't try to save the gun, just see that it departs muzzle first," and I wouldn't care to be within a hundred yards of the process. One mellow touch in 1961 was Nash's: "I have a bad habit of usually missing the easiest try I have all day," a remark I did not know him to make as a younger man.

Nash's ultimate bit of wisdom re bobwhite and all shooting was: "The only way to learn to shoot is to shoot a lot." If any gunner could speak those words from experience, it was Nash Buckingham.

DISCUSSING SHOTGUN PROBLEMS around our duck club's fire one night, I was asked "In one word, what is your recipe for hitting bobwhites?" I don't claim to know it all, by any manner of means, because I still miss 'em. But if seventy years actual cap-bustin' an' running with th' dawgs counts for anything I can "argufy an' sputify." So, right or wrong, and with the qualification of good eyesight, I had a one-word answer: *"Repression."*

It covers the case completely and controls all the patents of bobwhiting. And for such matter, it'll carry over into gun contacts with flushed game from pheasants to snipe. It means, to you and me, "Steady, you—count one —two—while they're clearing cover and you are picking out one certain bird—got it? Okay—now mount your gun, keeping both eyes glued meanwhile to that bob you've spotted—trust everything to that left hand—let it bring the gun's tubes in from behind, pass the flyer—think hard with every faculty and both eyes, of a *moving spot* two bird-lengths ahead of the bob (if it's an angling shot)—now then—keep swinging and pull a shade ahead of that *moving spot."* Your gun shouldn't have stopped.

Sounds like a lot to mull over during the not more than two-second pause that becomes second nature to the seasoned quail gunner. But that's what happens. When the brain says to trigger finger, "Shoot," the rest of the sequence, hit or miss, is closed faster than lightning. Repression has long since done its bit. It is simply a preliminary mental drill; but the pause that pays handsome dividends in shooting satisfaction.

Repression counteracts an element of surprise present at practically all game-bird flushes, wild or over a point. Caught in mid-step as a bevy explodes, one deliberately readjusts balance and stance. I class flinching at the traps as first cousin to that same element of surprise. Repression comes in handy, too, at Number-8 peg, skeet's bugaboo try. Repress proportionately, and you'll find surprisingly ample time for eye, brain and trigger finger to co-ordinate the gun's fluid upswing instead of turning the shot into mere jabbing guesswork.

In what follows I shall refer to bobwhite as both quail and partridge. There are no real quail in this country. But we of the Deep South cherish the prime little sporter as such and as "pottiges." For all our dialectic swaps and nicknames, however, bob is a partridge clansman, bred, hatched and raised up.

The veteran quail hunter's "zero" moments come at first call of *"Point."* Mounted, or afoot, he goes promptly to his dog, with encouraging recognition of its find, and, if necessary, positive, steadying admonitions. He takes in at a glance every factor of the impending rise—the breeze, escape cover and the dog's covey location—positive or uncertain.

Teaching a novice to hunt and hit quail (two interlocked but separate and delicate operations) becomes, at times, a delightfully hazardous *hell-on-earth*. But, in return, the dogs and the birds teach new and interesting field lessons. I have never gone shooting that somewhere along the line I haven't been taught something—and sometimes the hard way. A quail-shooting instructor's toughest assignment is getting his pupil up to the shot, after point; the next most difficult is keeping order once festivities begin. Fundamentally ignorant quail apprentices, waving loaded firearms around the horizon, afford chances for getting one's hat lifted. All they know is that something is about to come off. They think a bird dog's duty is to hold its point indefinitely—and a well-broken one will come close to doing exactly that, but there's no use to abuse the stanchest dog. What the neophytes know is that when Hades pops, all hands must lay down a barrage, and then, with loud cries, break shot to rush forward and gather up the slain—if any.

I've been amused while quail shooting with a few men recognized as "outdoor writers." Fair shots but shy on the sport's rudiments when put to the test. The rookie is easily and pleasantly coachable, but the reputed expert can get high-hat and difficult. Two such memories are definite. One, of a noted gunning writer dismounting his steed from the wrong side. I saw him open his gun after he had drawn it from the scabbard. It was loaded. With the pointing dogs shown him, he actually stalked them; sneaking catlike toward the two grand and valuable setters, his gun clutched wavering over the low foreground. Henry, my companion, bawled from his saddle, "Hey, hold your blankety-blank gun up and keep it there— you're fixin' to buy yourself a couple of good dogs." Our notable didn't know straight-up about quail shooting, but he could sure write it.

The other memory—discussing bevy contacts with a nationally accepted gun columnist, I asked him to show me his system of walking in over a pointing dog. Tossing his gun into a high "present arms" and with "eyes front," he all but goose-stepped in a tense advance. A trip would have set off the fireworks, and a scattered bunch of feeding birds would have left him flat-footed at the post. It's useless to attempt reformation because of their great dignity.

At the hunt's start, shooting positions, right or left, should be discussed, assigned and maintained. One man, preferably, should do the dog handling, unless each has one down. Coming up to flush, always try to walk in from the side so that you can keep an eye on your dog; it likes contact, too, so that it can more easily respond to orders. If the dog's pointing a single, go in decisively and put it on its way.

Within wild-flushing distance from a bevy find is time enough to load your gun. But don't push off the safety just yet. Carry the gun with the muzzle no higher than your shoulder; just an easy, natural position with nothing out front to disturb clear vision. Gunstock in between the elbow and ribs, ready to be hitched to the shoulder niche. If you stumble and feel yourself going, don't try to save the gun, just see that it departs muzzle first. And when you pick the weapon up, be sure to see that its muzzles are unclogged. Never put a loaded gun into your horse-scabbard, or into a wagon or car. The quail field is no place for gun guesswork. In loading a double gun, always bring the stock and action up to the tubes and *not* the barrels up in the left palm to join the action. In other words, close the gun just the opposite to the usual way it's done. Should the gun discharge, the tubes are pointed downward into the ground and you're not liable to kill a horse, dog or companion. Remember: in closing a double gun, bring up the right hand—*not* the left, and keep the muzzle *down*.

Shooting singles scattered in sparse woods or among blackjacks, chances mount for wild rises at increased distances. Unless your dogs are slow and under perfect control, such hazard increases. Dry leaves rustle and warn, and, if the weather is warmish, scenting isn't easy there. A bobwhite leaping well out front is almost invariably rising and looking for a place to cut back toward known territory for reassembly. Shooting across or through treetops is largely repression until the opening comes. Snap-shooting is a different proposition. It is instinctive firing. The only thing to do is shoot—not once, but twice; that's why there are so many pellets in a load.

It has been my good fortune to gun with many fine wildfowlers and crack shots at upland game; such men as Captain Harold Money "De Shootinest

Gent'man" and Guy Ward and "Jake" (H. D.) Gibbs of Union City, Tennessee, than whom probably no better all-round trap and game shots ever lived. From the plains and prairies to the lowlands and Gulf coastals I have not only seen such men at work afield and in the blinds, but heard their judgments as to guns and loads. I have also been around field-trial circuits and acted as official gun with some fine shots, and, in so doing often came in contact with many women considered "crack shots" at waterfowl and uplanders. I have been afield with many such. Annie Oakley, of course, built her fame upon her early skill as a game shot. But I consider the late Mrs. Adolph Topperwein, of Winchester fame, the finest all-around woman shot—shotgun, rifle and small-arms—that ever lived. She asked no odds of the men and set them some records at the traps. I never saw her shoot game, but I have an idea that her busy life never gave her the experience afield she might have liked to acquire.

In early February 1958, I judged the Georgia-Florida shooting-dog stake at the Norias Plantation of Walter Teagle, near Thomasville, Georgia; a delightful experience with charming people, a beautifully managed trial and superb shooting dogs. I was a guest and shot quail for three days at the lovely Spring Hill Plantation of Mr. and Mrs. Ralph Perkins of Cleveland, Ohio. And in Mrs. Perkins I saw a quail shot at work who needn't ask odds off any quail shot, man or woman. We averaged forty bevies a day behind top dogs, using the mule-drawn gunning conveyances carrying the driver, three guns and a dog-crate over the courses. Mrs. Perkins, who has been shooting there for many years, not only knows the techniques of quail gunning, but of the bird itself, the dogs, and the shots. In the three days, I never saw her out of position; she was invariably on time at the post, shot quietly and decisively. In short, she is the finished product. I've never watched her shoot plains game, wildfowl or doves—and until I see anyone shoot doves I never consider their reputations safe, as the mourner is the top-bracket ego deflator among all game. But I have an idea Mrs. Perkins will do all right at them, too. In the woods, after singles, I several times saw her wheel and bring down wild-flushing quail. They were the type of shots that many hunters pass up for fear of missing. But she took'em as they came. I have always considered Mrs. Buckingham as the finest woman wildfowl shot I ever saw and she was no slouch at quail. But, having gunned wildfowl with me for years, she, like Mrs. Perkins on quail, was the finished product in any company. But, even so, no man or woman game-gunner has ever lived who doesn't miss'em sometimes. I have a bad habit of usually missing the easiest try I have all day. There are myths, too, in the quail-shooting game. All my life, so far, I've been looking for the quail hunter who goes out with a box of shells and always brings in twenty-four birds; the fellow who shoots from horseback and never misses; the chap who, with his pumpgun, always kills six birds on every rise. And that genius who shoots his quail purposely to one side in order to not put too many pellets in them and spoil 'em as food. But I have heard alibis aplenty, after shooting with several who boasted of such.

Many years of practice have produced consensus that in quail shooting that first bird is dropped at about seventeen paces (or should be) while the second bird of a right and left will be plumped at about twenty-five paces. Gunners somehow get onto singles faster than in a bevy rise; there is less flurry and element of surprise. And yet you hear of many quail killed at forty and even fifty yards. For every bobwhite killed at forty true yards, five thousand are dropped under thirty. The quail, like the dove, has several speeds, is much more canny than the mourner, and, being small, uses his change of pace amazingly to get objects between himself and you. But any well-bored shotgun carrying, in any gauge, a full ounce of $7\frac{1}{2}$'s or 8's will kill at forty and even fifty yards, given a lot of luck. But it's the exception and *not* the rule. The worst enemy of Bob afield is the magazine gun, which, though now curtailed to three shots, sprays a lot of pellets around the scenery and cripples birds that never rise again.

The quail-shooting beginner should satisfy himself first as to where his gun is throwing its charges, rather than *how*. Fit of the weapon's stock largely controls that "where." It will be found that nowadays a stock that fits the user at skeet will come pretty close to being of good service afield. To pattern your quail gun's 26- or 28-inch tubes in 12, 16 or 20 (I do not recommend 28's or .410's for any field use) get several sheets of heavy brown wrapping paper—48 inches square—and spot a 4-inch black bull's eye in the center of each, to aim at, or rather catch the eye. Put up one paper 17 steps away and slightly to the left; the other, at 25 full paces and more to the right. With your gun at shooting position (below the elbow as it should be in quail rise), toss it up and try to hit the closer bull's eye with your cylinder tube, and then, moving swiftly, try to hit the other paper with your improved cylinder or modified tube. Make at least 5 tests with each tube. Center the patterns' heaviest deposit and trace a 30-inch circle about it. Count the "withins" and, knowing how many pellets are in your particular load, the percentage is depicted. Also, you'll find that you've learned something about where your weapon is shooting. You could have missed the paper a time or two?

For instance, I know a gentleman who clings to, and uses effectively, an exquisite, muzzle-loading, flintlocked Manton double. The chaste and crested arm, with nipples and powder chambers silver washed, handles and balances amazingly. Firing from behind shooting glasses (in case of a flare-back), this sportsman uses two and a quarter drams of fine black powder tamped below a single cardboard wad and seven eighths of an ounce of 8's lightly seated beneath a soft, split felt wad. To watch this sportsman at work with such old-fashioned equipment is revealing. And make no mistake—he gets his birds right along with the best of competition.

Individualism can be charmingly expressed in a custom or built-to-order gun; a shade longer or differently tapered fore-end, round or half-oval grip, mealy checking instead of angular treads that scuff one's hands under a heavy recoil, and other refinements in lines and woodworking. A recent announcement by the Winchester Repeating Arms Company that in future its famous Model 21 double-tubed shotguns will be available only in such custom-made models costing from $1000 to $3500 gives impetus to a customer's wish for finish, engraving, and individual measurements. But any gunmaker should be trusted for leeway in mere ounces and pattern percentages. Don't hold the gunbuilder "too-tight." There are too many combinations in powder and shot and too many opportunities for the owner to err in his own tests. Once possessed of a "lifetime" gun, the idea should be to shoot it as often and at as many various species of flying game as possible. The only way to learn to shoot anything is to shoot a lot. So, remember this in your quest for a field gun. Any weapon with which you can consistently break good scores at skeet, will render you efficient service in quail fields, snipe marshes or woodcock coverts. Learn, through shooting a lot, the distances at which you score best—and try to stick to them. And when, in quail shooting, you find yourself shooting with a man who is killing his birds at just about the same distance nearly every time, and one who does not pass up hard tries in the woods, you are in very fast company. And what *is* a good quail percentage of kills?

Nowadays, with bag limits down to from eight to a dozen bobwhites a day, fine shots operating behind well-broken dogs can, or should, sometimes "run straight" or certainly shoot 80 per cent—undisturbed. Back in the days of unlimited bag limits and matches based upon a go-as-you-please basis, it was a different story. But when you go bird shooting; walking or horseback; and, taking them as they come, shoot 60 per cent, you have laid down a satisfactory pattern for your ego.

The day is gone, probably forever in this country, where skill can be acquired through long seasons of practice on wild-game stocks, although the increasing growth of commercial game preserves is aiding materially for public indulgence. We have short open seasons, increasingly expensive state fees for so-called managed shooting on state areas, lower bag limits and fewer birds. The novice, then, had best acquire and whet his skill at skeet fields or hand traps—and carry on from there.

The quail beginner's first thought should be to seek association with a real bird hunter. Far more important than the gun is a soundly tutored knowledge of field manners and tactics as between dog and man. Study killing range and avoid unnecessarily long tries. If you decide on a light 20-bore, shoot its proper load, and never, in any gauge, overcrowd for power. On rises, practice repression, and, as in golf, learn to "groove your swing." And now, one last reference to the "pause" that pays shooting dividends.

When you've fired both tubes at a departing bevy, or single, for that matter, stand still and reload as expeditiously as possible. In reloading fix your eyes on that job alone—and forget the game. Get in shape to shoot and you'll be surprised at how fast the job can be done. How many times have you been caught by additional rises with your gun unloaded? If you have down two birds, don't leave the spot from which you fired. Stick down a stob, or leave your hat. From that you can realign the falls, and give your dog directions, if need be. If it's your dog—handle it quietly and effectively. If it's the other chap's, keep still and let him do the handling. So, now, a good day to you—and good luck.

The Dove

To a grouse and woodcock gunner of the Alleghenies, where dove shooting is indulged in as marginal "recreational shooting," Nash's statement that the mourning dove is "our premier wing target" never ceases to surprise me, though I am conscious that dove shooting is done on a huge scale in the South and Southwest.

Nash's wing-shooting advice in "The Dove," originally published in Field & Stream, *January 1947,* Gun Digest *1959, and in the Nelson edition in 1961, appeals to me particularly because some of it applies to those long open shots all of us get at ringnecks (rarely on ruffed grouse)—shots that don't often respond to a fast swing-through. There is good suggestion as to "gun mounting that coordinates timing, forward allowance and barrel level" (the latter easily overlooked). Nash stresses a fact many of us are not aware of, that for a right-handed shooter, "when you swing a gun left, its muzzle is tending upward—to the right, downward." If you doubt this, try it. And his reminder to think only about that one bird, to the exclusion of all else, is a gunner's Truth. I won't go along with shooting both barrels without determining that the first barrel missed, but it may account for some rapid-fire one-two's I've heard in the grouse woods. And I can't be convinced that Nash had been subjected to everything a grouse can do in the manner of flushing when he rates a grouse below a flushing dove. But then I haven't been treated to the devious ways of doves.*

His recommendation: to locate a fallen bird by looking "for feathers well above the ground, clinging to the lower bushes" has helped me put my dog on a quick retrieve when a winged grouse fell and ran—even pinpointed woodcock still hanging in hawthorn branches. It is such simple products of experience that make Nash Buckingham's pieces what they are.

I have deleted certain portions on dove shooting regulations as they were developed. For readers who care to research the subject, this material can be found in the Nelson version of this article.

What is left here is Nash at some of his conservationist best. The shooting world, like any cross-section of people, is made up of all types, and like most of us, Nash was not spared the sleazier varieties—from the bird butcher to the father raising his son, by example, to be a game thief. But in spite of that aspect of the sport, Nash loved it. The last shooting day of his life was on doves. With "The Dove," Nash almost charms me into trying it.

O UR LIVELIEST MIGRATORY upland game bird, the mourning dove, is our premier wing target but sporting stepchild. Twelve to fifteen years ago, as species and sport, the "mourner" was on its way out. Today it offers more challenges to the finer phases of field gunning than any other sporting species. The dove, at present, is the only nationally resurgent target; made so by antibaiting regulation, half-day shooting, a nationwide tier of northern non-dove-shooting states for replenishing breeding grounds, a tremendous advance in mechanized farming offering ample and diversified foods, and both state and federal study programs affecting the bird's promise as a definitely worthwhile resource. Countless thousands of dove hunters and their families and friends will sing the dove's praises when smothered à la bobwhite or baked within a pie.

For sport at the coo-calling mourners, one needs a well-fitting choke-bored shotgun and a competent load in the gun gauge of your fancy, preferably a twelve-bore, with shot not larger than sixes, nor smaller than eights. Rough-and-tumble dove shooting, pass, high- or low-flightings, and tough cover jump-shooting require fast gunhandling when, as my shooting companion Bob Anderson puts it, "A mob of doves hurtles down on you like a bunch of demoniacal hockey players dodging and skimming down the rink." Swift, comfortable, accurate gun mounting that coordinates timing, forward allowance and barrel level (a trio not easily assembled) is a *must*. Fortunately, American gun manufacturers have vastly improved their gunstock specifications into more competent selectivities at heel and comb.

All too often, however, no matter how well gun-fitted, the bird's naturally versatile and bewildering caper-cuttings bring pinned-back and reddened ears to our dove gunner and his averages—rapidly deflating his ego. From the standpoint of change of pace, aerial gyrations and—especially at high speeds—sheer ability to absorb a lethal punch but keep going, no other American game bird, for its size, can be compared with the dove. The topflight dove shot need not fear to face any internationally gunned species a-wing.

Some years ago, when the dove bag limit was federally overgenerous—stupidly maintained at twenty-five mourners per day for much too long—we took with us into our (baited) field a noted British game shot. He had published his opinion that our doves could not possibly challenge Scotland's driven grouse as difficult targets. Equipped with a hundred shells and his own first-quality British game gun, he was given a choice "stand," an experienced little Negro lad for retriever and left under a cedar tree on a windy knoll. Scads of doves whipped the rolling country. The English expert returned ere long out of cartridges, with eighteen birds. Asked his opinion of the dove as a target, he replied (good sport that he was), grinning broadly, "They are very, very small, dear boy, and fly very, very fahst."

In his recent best-seller-in-its-field, *Game Shooting*, my old friend the late Robert Churchill, eminent British gun manufacturer and internationally famous wildfowl and upland game shot, notes that England's wood pigeon is an all-around, artful dodger and tough customer a-wing. He confirms my opinion that anyone who can score consistently on "woodies" can more than hold his own in almost any shotgun company. And, be it remembered, in addition to the dove's and the wood pigeon's ability to parade dipsey-doodles across the wide blue yonder, as gun yardages increase, these flyers become smaller targets for widening gun patterns—and they're fired on at ranges sometimes far beyond those for many other species of uplanders.

Dove pundits all but ignore the mourner's streamlined chassis and the eccentricities powered by its long, purposeful tail feathers. Manipulating them as rudders to control loops, spins, barrel rolls, flush-wriggles, and other freakish air-braked maneuvers, the dove, at a true forty-yard rise and regardless of cover, requires deft gun handling. Equally important is careful observation of the bird's field behavior. The dove's lengthy caudal appendage wasn't grown thataway for nothing—and the bird knows it. Wriggling slantingly from tall, dense corn-high weeds or cotton, the dove cuts didoes requiring far more astute gun swing than does the closer, more explosive, steadier-rising and course-holding bobwhite, or, for such matter, our canny, noisy foliage-and-tree-obscured Sir Ruffs.

Doves not only have sharp eyes, but seem to pick up footfall vibrations the instant hunters step into a corn field. In feeding flight—unless in a heavily shot community—doves pay little heed to a gunner provided he sits or stands motionless. A minimum of blind is needed, and I have often shot them while crouching in an absolutely coverless field, or from alongside a parked automobile. In a wind-swept corn field well populated by feeding doves there is hardly a more spirited sport than a "walk-up" shoot. Under such conditions, however, go immediately to a fallen bird without removing your eyes from the marked spot. You can sometimes blink and lose it. Forget attempts at the "rights and lefts "almost invariably presented in such flushes, for, all too often, the hunter then loses both falls, unless, of course, you have with you the supreme joy of any field gunning—a competent retriever.

There is no greater thrill in upland game shooting than gunning flighting doves over tall timber or high over plowed ground (with no trees available as yardage markers) and with a stiff breeze on their tails. It's the cream of all wing shooting. With mourners en route to roost and running a bit late, the hunter finds himself on the defensive. Up to forty-five or fifty true yards above the open, the dove is a tiny target for even the tightest chokes, short shot columns and a crafty, evenly swung forward allowance. I repeat, it is absorbed energy that paralyzes game. You've had about all the thrills possible when you blot out an almost overhead fifty-yard dove (the proper angle of shot) and see your bird, well patterned, crumple. Many high, over-head doves are missed by accepting the try too far out front, thereby increasing the angle and causing a deceptive moving slant for both barrel level and eyes. Plain, tough trigonometry in a dove field. This often occurs when the shooter attempts a sensational high right and left.

Don't be greedy. Swing in from behind and think only about that *one dove*. (Or any other flighting fowl for such matter.) Blot it well out, keep swinging—and touch off. And here's a dividend tip. Just for luck—still swinging—let go the second tube. If your initial let-off was a trifle behind, that old chant about "the last shot got 'im" might come true. You'll be pleasantly surprised and never mind which shot did the damage—you've got the quarry. Remember, too, that the high overhead dove (or any other such game) is completely vulnerable to body punctures and widespread wing fractures. In equidistant passing tries, however, the dove is not so completely wide open and unless a head hit occurs, crippling sail-offs often result.

Distance across and over an open field is hard to judge. Eight out of ten clean misses result from insufficient forward allowance. Such swinglead should never be slowed or stopped—the deader the stop, the cleaner the miss. What you should be really trying to hit is a *moving spot* out ahead of the flyer—with the bird target itself carried in your subconscious mind. For its size, the dove has tremendous wing stamina. The shooter should watch with extreme care when—at a bit longer than casual range—he has seen a dove flinch and senses having scored a body hit. If the bird's swerve and sail-off slows and becomes wobbly, watch carefully. A bird thus jarred off pace may crash stone-dead a hundred yards or more downfield. Again, it may flutter to some hedgerow and claw for a hold. Keep your eye on that spot. Later on, you'll probably find it dead under its perch when you pass that way—and make it a point to do so. When followed, if it has a vestige of wing power, will attempt a take-off. I have seen them fly out of game bags. So be ready—with your gun cocked. I've watched many a good retriever thwarted when the cripple it was sent to fetch suddenly got airborne.

The first thing any knowing dove or duck hunter does (novices take careful note along here) when shooting in or at the edge of timber, is to size up tree heights by which to determine gun yardage and subsequent leads. Nowadays it takes quite a tree to tower a hundred feet—roughly thirty-three yards—and with birds flighting five yards above such woods, this can mean a true thirty-eight yards or more. However, if the flight is passing out front, your problem toughens. Several misses will have you sweating, for such dove tries are ego deflators supreme.

On slowish, smooth-flying doves approaching dead trees around ponds or waterholes one scores so well as to invite an enlarged cranium. Suddenly, conditions change. To be shot at, doves must first be seen, and they have a way of easing up on the most alert hunters with incredible stealth. Untoward muzzle-weavings and many misses ensue. At such melancholy moments in a dove field, Dutch doubles accumulate apace and long missing streaks empty shell pockets fast. Discomfiture and near hysteria may indicate a pause for water with two aspirins ahead of it. Truly, the dove makes all gunners equal.

I shoot doves frequently with five friends who are far better than average wildfowl and upland bird shooters. Most of them have top-bracket trap and skeet averages and get their shares of purses around the flyer circuit. They are hard-bitten shotgun veterans who need help acquiring bag limits in any weather or company. They have learned to judge gun yardages more accurately than most, and take the hard with the soft. *But,* when conditions necessitate and game is scarce, they'll reach out and "go to raking and scraping" while trusting their retrievers to recover long cripples and strong runners.

After a spirited and companionable dove shoot we gather at the automobiles, pick and dress our birds, drink Cokes and confess our manifold gun sins of the afternoon. Egos may lie bleeding, but we cling desperately to our senses of humor. We live to miss and laugh another day.

My shooting partner, Bob Anderson, says, "No matter how good a dove shot you think you are, sooner or later the mourners and Ol' Crimp will make a sucker out of you. You may sack several birds in a row when, all of a sudden, up jumps that fickle jade, Lady Luck—and pulls the rug out from under you. After several inexplicable misses you perspire heavily and feel certain that every other guy in the field is enjoying your discomfiture; but, don't worry, chances are that they, too, are mired down in dove troubles. Before long, some of them will be over to borrow some shells."

How many cartridges will the reputed "top shot" require to bag today's federal limit of twelve to fifteen birds—with the proviso that he doesn't "wait 'em out" and literally pick his tries, that he is on a strictly "take 'em as they come" basis, and that he is under constant observation and accompanied by a notary public? Some windy afternoons dove-shooting veterans become first ruffled, then agitated until they finally collapse in admission that they are out of hulls—and with only a few birds sacked. Other afternoons, with the going smooth and off to a heartening straight run, they may be lucky enough to bag a limit with from twenty to a box of shells. Anytime you can kill fifteen doves with a carton of hulls you have just about run competition ragged. With a fifty per cent average you can walk out of any dove field with your head high and stepping briskly. You've done yourself pretty proud, sir.

The most difficult shot at doves? Picture four or five of them with gusty blasts on their tails, very low and heading directly at you across the dun-colored open terrain, with surface dust whorls making matters worse against a dark-skied background. They're hard to spot, infinitely more difficult to separate for the single try. They're sideslipping, corkscrewing and doing their best to stay down under the wind. Somehow, you can't pick a bird or make your gun muzzle do anything but revolve. It jumps from first one to another candidate. So you proceed to miss by a mile with your first tube and then have not the faintest idea where your second charge disappeared. What you should have done was to pick up your first customer away out front and let him have it—twice. Remember that those doves are speeding at you at a clip almost equal that of your shot charge. So try the on-hurtling incomers farther out. It's still the hardest shot in dove shooting.

For another difficult contact—with the breeze still holding—alter the above situation to that of a flight of doves crossing you out yonder—left to right. (Remember now, when you swing a gun left, its muzzle is tending upward—to the right, downward.) If you insist on taking on such a bunch of fast-steppers, try to bring down the leader. If you're lucky, the bird tumbles earthward. Its followers will zip, dart and swoop after it; you've got to be a wizard to pin a second bird. So, if you've been lucky enough to bag the leader, leave well enough alone, and save a shell. If you miss the head dove you are a candidate for a Dutch double.

Entering unfamiliar dove country, pause to size up prospective terrain before selecting a "stand." Look for disturbed, feeding birds and/or steady one-way flight-lane lead-ins of tall hedgeways. When touring a countryside to spot dove concentrations, nothing comes in handier than good binoculars. While doves sitting along telephone wires in any profusion are usually giveaways of a feeding area, the glasses still come in handy at a distance to spot otherwise invisible birds against plowed fields. In shooting doves, geese or big-lake ducks good binocs pay for themselves many times over.

When a dove flight is coming from behind you over tall trees, don't invite disaster by standing at the timber's edge and attempt to snap-shoot the birds. Such tactics will soon have you in a high-voltage swivet. Cut yourself an armful of boughs, pace forty steps out from the woods, build yourself a little hide and face the oncomers. Sit on your campstool (an empty wooden shell case with a shoulder strap makes an excellent seat), keep still, spot 'em coming to you and you've about got the rap beaten. When the doves cross the tree line, you should know how far away they are and get into action— fast. You've got about five yards, give or take, in which to make up your mind. While you're about it, investigate the cover inside those woods—how thick the undergrowth is, in case you drop a long shot flying the timber line. Retrieving can be tough in such cases. If the brambles and weeds are heavy, don't shoot at the crossers. No use killing anything you can't find. You can waste a lot of time and temper tearing through cover and you invariably lose shots by not being out there in the open.

When you are searching for doves that have fallen inside the tree line, first make sure of the wind's drift and look for feathers well above the ground, clinging to the lower bushes. They will have been shot or scraped off the tumbling bird and you will eventually spot your dead or crippled dove well ahead of the feathers. Sometimes the victim will lodge in a bush fork. Last season I found two doves well off the ground; one of them impaled in a thorn tree.

I'll stress again the danger of that pardonable temptation to try for "rights and lefts" in what appears to be reasonably clear cover. This results in re-trieving woes. Even in a clean field dove plumage blends with dry clods and angles of direction have a way of slipping memory's moorings. And you lose tries while searching. The best method after getting down two doves is to immediately drop your hat or handkerchief at the firing point. Place a stick or cornstalk toward the first fall or trace a line in the dirt with your toe. Now go directly to the second fall while you have it firmly in mind. Return and take direction from the marker to your first bird. Always keep your gun with you—and loaded. Don't ever put it down as a marker.

Having lost my gun for a prolonged spell, with much frantic searching—and lost shots—I know whereof I speak.

It was past the turn of the century before state game laws began mentioning seasons on doves. Even then there was but scant observance or competent enforcement. About that time, baiting began as the easiest, fastest way to concentrate doves. A group of congenials would buy a couple of tons of low-grade wheat, borrow some farmer's pasture and pay his helpers to sprinkle the ground with grain, with ice-cream salt here and there. It was deadly allure. About twenty acres of rolling pasture on an ancient family estate (now a municipal golf course in Memphis) was the site of one of our finest dove clubs. By shooting only twice a week, this and other respectable clubs found their sport improved and held pretty well to bag limits of twenty-five birds a day. But the doves, then state property, suffered terrible inroads from wildlife butchers who slaughtered them ad lib. and threw them away to rot.

In 1918 with the Migratory Bird Act, the mourning dove came under federal protection. But gun pressures were mounting and baiting picked up tremendously. Whereas a few seasons back we could hear no guns near our fields, there was now uproar all around us. Hunters were shooting limits (or as many as they pleased) in one field early in the morning and another limit in the afternoon, somewhere else. Such decimation rapidly lowered dove populations. The end became obvious when farmers planted or baited for doves and began charging shooting admissions. But about this same time a group known as "Conservationists" had begun to rally and organize nationally.

The Deep South, rapidly losing its quail stocks through overkills by alleged sportsmen and the depredations of quail bootleggers, began spurring its game departments into some semblance of protection. The waterfowl situation, nationally, had become a saturnalia of slaughterous magazine-gun activities, duck bootlegging rings and loosely run enforcement, state and federal. The situation was such as to stagger incredulity. By 1928 something had to give.

Federal bag limits were lowered, seasons shortened, and, by 1931, the use of live duck decoys was banned. Proponents for better protection of mourning doves moved in to stop baiting. As a civilian member (Executive Secretary of the American Wildfowlers, Washington, D.C.) of the Bureau of Biological Survey's inner sanctum, the writer sat in on the first gathering and discussion on dove baiting held by the then Federal Advisory Board. A bit awed as a newcomer, I listened to fifteen or twenty pro and con debates by summit figures of Conservation. Obviously, the Deep South wanted to continue baiting, and, more obviously, many of the officials and advisers knew nothing of doves or dove shooting. They were simple biologists, theorists and nonhunters, canopied, to some extent, by political clouds.

At this point a judge, representing gunning interests in a southern state noted for its dove shooting, obtained the floor with his panacea—a compromise for the baiting evil. (It occurred to me that of all of the men present probably no one, other than the judge and myself, had ever shot doves in the manner under discussion.) "Why not," he asked urbanely, "regulate so that the bait cannot be placed closer to the guns than one hundred yards?" His listeners, eager for any "out" that might ease or evade the tense situation, stirred under such diplomacy. When my turn came, I said that from long personal experience with the business of baiting, the good judge's compromise was, in effect, the *bunk*. In the first place, I declared, it could, and would, make suckers out of game wardens who would have to carry tape measures, and swear to split inches in court to get, or more probably lose, convictions. And to anyone who knew about baiting you could surround such an area and kill every dove attempting to enter it. But the judge won, and a gracious winner he was, too. Under this senseless regulation dove baiting entered several years of mountebanked administration.

The "distance yardage" baiting farce, replete with petty persecutions, continued until the mourners were again pretty well on Queer Street. Under continued Conservational fire, the baiting supporters offered to increase "guns-to-bait" to two hundred yards. By that time, however, official Washington began to show suspicion and intelligence, resulting eventually in a regulation which read, in effect: "No dove baiting—regardless and period." Of course, violations by wildlife's sneak thieves continued and does to this day—but federal and state game agents at last had a sporting chance though there were not enough of them to stem the violational pace. Clandestine baiting, overkills and especially the "two-limits-a-day" practice mounted. The doves continued to take a beating.

As late as the early 1950s, baiting interests secured a beachhead in Washington. This matured into a U.S. Fish & Wildlife Service regulation permitting wildfowl baiting within "half a mile of the blinds." This stupid and outrageous recession from common sense lasted about one gunning season and was hastily withdrawn. Then the dove baiters eased in another gem by some sly maneuvering in the Department of Interior. The new baiting regulation, while still specifically forbidding the use of salt (for doves), excepted "block salt" for cattle feeding. Any experienced dove hunter knew that doves thronged into cattle "salt licks"; that rains washed off salt deposits, that cudding cattle drooled salinity over pasture—and how could all this be checked? It took a year for Conservation to get that piece of fat-headed business written off the books.

At one time, in three Southern states, it was shown that dove-shooting seasons, since federal law on them went into effect, had been changed twenty-four times. Outdoors Unlimited of the Outdoor Writers Association of America inveighed against the poor sportsmanship of the Deep South, lax enforcement, bureaucratic bungling, and lack of outdoor leadership in Washington. Then Tennessee, taking cognizance of how well half-day pheasant shooting was working in some of the Plains states, said to the Fish and Wildlife Service, "If you do not end the illegal killing of two bags of doves a day in the dove-shooting states, we'll soon have to close dove seasons. Why not try half-day dove shooting?"

To end pressures, Washington paid heed. It was an official face-saver that has salvaged millions of doves for today's breeding stocks. The measure still holds, although, of late, Washington, in a "trading mood" with the states, will swap ten days' shooting for a duck in the bag limit, or what have you. There have been a few takers as to ducks.

Game hogs are still hard at work in all game fields, but, somehow, the doves have continued to better than hold their own. In recent years bag limits—thanks to half-day shooting, an upswing in weather's hatching cycles, tremendous farming operations and resultant foods—have increased from eight birds to ten, twelve, and even fifteen doves a day.

Liberalization of baiting regulations and resumption of all-day shooting with upped dove bag limits in many states at the slightest sign of species increase is not too hopeful a sign for the bird's future resurgence. Present involved baiting regulations—mere invitations to corrupt evasions—are not a credit to the Department of Interior.

There is stirring a strong sentiment against the game hogs who go into dove fields and continue shooting as though limits do not exist, who seek to kill their own and friends' limits, too. Such gun-goons exist around every town in the United States. Some of the worst offenders we have ever seen are men of means and position in the business and civic world. But by far the saddest spectacle in American shooting fields is the father who brings up his son to become a wildlife thief.

The average American sportsman worthy of the title is a pretty fairminded kind of fellow. He will stand just so much, particularly if he has a young son or two coming along with a rightful equity afield.

As the situation stands today (1961), all that is needed to keep the dove in resurgence is for Washington to return to half-day shooting the country over, return to a baiting regulation which says, "No baiting—period" and a daily bag limit of not to exceed a dozen birds anywhere and then give its hard-working game agents and biologists a chance for once in their lives by not involving them in a lot of gobbledygook "can and can't do's" that balk their efforts, imperil decent sportsmen and muddy the waters generally. The dove need no longer be a sporting stepchild. It is just a question of whether Washington has "brains, innards and honesty" in handling this magnificent resource.

Part Four:
DOGS

Point! Judges

The eagerly sought-after National Field Trial Champions 1896-1955 by William F. Brown and Nash Buckingham (Stackpole, 1955), together with Nash's "Memories of the National Championship," which appeared in The American Field, December 1, 1956, and in the Nelson De Shootin'est Gent'man and Other Hunting Tales, 1961, and his "Point! Judges," which was in Tattered Coat, 1944, as well as a series of about twenty pieces in Field & Stream paint a picture of a Nash Buckingham unfamiliar to some of his followers, yet presenting his most significant image to thousands to whom he was "Mr. Field Trial."

As with each person with whom he came in contact, Nash made the people he met at field trials remember meeting him as an intimate experience, from judges at the top stakes to the gruffest handler on the small circuits. All "knew Nash Buckingham" and loved it.

Nash was part of the National Championship. He was a judge there from 1934 to 1951 (the runnings in 1938 and 1944 were called off because of lack of birds; in 1951, a bad spill from his horse prevented Nash from finishing with the other judges). He was a close friend of Hobart and Julia Ames and was a guest at their place, at trials as well as shooting, many times. In "Point! Judges," Nash speaks of Hobart Ames as still living. Mr. Ames died April 22, 1945.

Major J. M. Taylor's book Field Trial Records of Dogs in America covers the trials from the first one run in America in 1874 (won by H. Clark Pritchitt's black setter Knight) through 1907, giving every win, every judge. In "Point! Judges," Nash Buckingham recalls the dogs and the men, not as names but as close friends.

In early competition, separate stakes were run for setters and pointers. Names of those early champions sound like a catalog of Edmund Osthaus paintings—he did portraits of the National Champions into the teens, magnificent paintings that were reproduced and distributed by Du Pont.

Nash always felt close to Gladstone because of his boyhood association with the old fellow. Gladstone's first important all-age win Nash quotes was the Eastern Field Trial Club's trial on Robbins Island, where he was handled by his trainer Caleb B. Whitford, who wrote of him in Training the Bird Dog (Macmillan, 1908).

The 1900 and 1901 National Championships being run "in the Grand Junction, Tennessee, vicinity" should not be construed to mean on the Ames Plantation. Those years the running was on what was known as the "U. S. Grounds." The National was run for the first time on the Ames place in 1902. Nash wrote me:

I began seeing the Nationals at the Ames Plantation in '02. Mrs. Buckingham's great-grandfather John Walker Jones acquired the lands and built "Cedar Grove" in 1847. Hobart Ames told me he had put up earnest money for a preserve near New Albany, Mississippi, when he received a telegram from Jim Avent, at Hickory Valley (almost adjoining the Jones land), inviting him and Mrs. Ames for a week's quail shooting and to see the Jones home and lands, which might be acquired. They accepted, had wonderful shooting and saw wonderful bird lands. Mr. Ames forfeited his earnest money in Mississippi, and took over and settled at Cedar Grove. Thus we see one telegram changing the fate of a nation's field trials.

By an interesting coincidence, Nash mentions the triple National Champion Mary Montrose (1917, 1919, 1920) within the same few lines with John Proctor and Doughboy, the three pointer subjects of a magnificent triple portrait by Edmund Osthaus. This painting is reproduced as end papers in National Field Trial Champions.

Warren Stoner, owner of Eugene's Ghost in the 1922 running, was the father of Robert G. Stoner, Nash's old friend and eventual owner of the Ghost, Nash's favorite field trial setter.

The ideal type of field trial dog demanded in the National Championship, as expressed by Colonel Arthur Merriman and Hobart Ames, is set forth here by a man who judged some of the best of them. Setter men who gloried in the winning in 1939 by Sport's Peerless Pride will be interested to learn, if they consult National Field Trial Champions, *that his sire Sport's Peerless ran in four of the Nationals—1934, 1935, 1936, 1937. 1942 winner Luminary was Nash's ideal pointer, as he confided to me more than once, although his kennel mate and half-brother Ariel was a triple National Champion.*

That all is sweetness and light among field-trialers—even field trial judges— is a myth most men see through. In a letter to a friend upon the death of Dr. T. Benton King, Nash, from the vantage point of eighty-eight, permitted himself the luxury of candor about the long-time judge of the Nationals: "Old Doctor King, who judged field trials for so long, died recently at Brownsville—he was eighty-three. Rated the 'top' field trial judge, he was the poorest Judge I ever rode with and I rode fourteen of my seventeen Nationals with him. In all those years he never covered a 'lay back.' He was self-admittedly a congenital coward when it came to riding out of a trot. . . . What always amused me was how scared he was of Mr. Hobart Ames. But, peace be with him. I sound like the sign in the restaurant: 'Don't kid the butter, you may be old yourself some day.' "

*In "Memories of the National Championship" Nash provides a pleasant look
inside the "Big House" on the 25,000-acre Plantation as he enjoyed his sojourns
there:*

The old-timey clock on the mantel of the northwest bedroom at Ames
Plantation's manor house chimes seven a.m. Daylight has peeped past
lofty window curtains. The door opens and you become dimly conscious
that Albert, the Welsh-born major-domo, places coffee service on the an-
tique bureau, mixes a cup of piping hot black brew, sugared as he knows
your liking, and announces that it promises a lovely "marnin'." He
draws the curtains and light floods the room. While tubbing and getting
into the day's riding togs, you exchange greetings with your compatriot
judge in the adjoining room. Weather makes a deal of difference at the
National. If bitter, there'll be neck mufflers and worsted wrist warmers,
lined jackets and even a greatcoat to repel cutting blasts along exposed
ridge crests; if rain is in prospect there'll be rubber knee boots and
Johnny McNeill will have slickers behind our saddles.

You can set your watch by the arrival of Hobart Ames for breakfast.
We judges, with maybe a house guest or two up for the races, have assembled in the gun room. There'll be a scampering of dogs' feet and several clumber and springer spaniels whisk in among us, followed by the
Chief's towering six-feet-five. After a gruff but smiling "good morning,"
he scrutinizes and taps the barometer, goes out on the west side porch,
reads the thermometer, smokes a cigarette, and returns and notes it all
down on his desk calendar. Albert announces breakfast—and such ones
they are.

After breakfast we go down to the starting point four miles away via
automobile with Secretary Reuben Scott driving. There we find the
horse holders with a mounted gallery of sometimes more than two hundred awaiting. Reporters, celebrities, field-trial addicts the nation over,
even youngsters on mules and ponies. A colorful picture of the American
sporting saga. Then the long, never-dull three-hour ride. If the dogs
prove of championship possibility, excitement mounts and time passes
swiftly. If the caliber is not there, there is always the panorama of the
glorious countryside. I never forget that I have ridden and hunted these
lands before they were Ames lands, but there is little change. Down off
the final high ridge and through the plum-thicketed valley we pelt, and
then comes the hail, "Take 'em up." We hand over our "morning"
mounts to the horse holders and Mr. Scott's car whisks us to the manor
for lunch.

Those National luncheons are happy but businesslike affairs. The invited guests—usually owners of dogs—and we sit down to simple spreads
from the Plantation's vast stores. Cooks have gone to Heaven for less than
those meat pies and salads that stick to the ribs for the long three-hour
ride ahead. Never, during a National, is anything stronger than light ale
served.

A line of grooms files past the box hedges to the brick mounting block
afront the manor. We jog a mile to the starting point beyond the familiar
old pond. The gallery is increased by late arrivals. "Let 'em go!" Settling

into the saddle—three hours to the last split second—we see field trial history made. Hopes rise and fall. After the "take-up" we judges are driven back.

First, there is that cup of fragrant tea with Mrs. Ames seated in her great chair by the library's west window, the spaniels jealously on guard. Later, the invariable hot mustard bath that relaxes stiffened riding muscles, then "forty winks." At seven-thirty our company gathers in the gun room for cocktails. At his desk, Hobart Ames shakes up those dry tongue-looseners with an eye for proportions. Then dinner—of a Saturday night the New Englander's baked beans, brown bread and pickle; on occasion, terrapin Maryland concocted via chafing dish by the Chief himself.

For years, galleryites at the start of the National's first morning would see an old grizzled Negro ride his saddling mule alongside Hobart Ames's mount, doff his cap and reach out a hand for a warm handshake. The two would then chat for a few minutes and then Tom Ewell would ride away to rejoin friends in the gallery. As Hobart Ames told the story, he and the late Cuthbert E. Buckle, the Plantation's first superintendent, were riding some of the western boundaries more than fifty years ago. It was newly acquired and heavily posted land. Hearing a shot, they spotted a distant figure making off and gave chase. After a short ride they rounded up Tom Ewell, who claimed he had shot at a hawk. While they were grilling him, up trotted what Mr. Ames described as the handsomest springer spaniel he had seen, carrying a dead bobwhite in tender jaws. In the face of such overwhelming evidence, Mr. Ames said, "Well, Ewell, if you will sell me that springer, we'll just forget about your poaching. How about it?"

"Well, suh," replied Tom, "I'd sho' lak t' git outa dis misery on account o' my job." He trained dogs for some Eastern people. "But d' truth is dat dog don't b'long t'me—he b'longs to a gen'man in Cincinnati. I'll write an' ast will he sell d' dog and I'll come an' sho' you d' answer."

The owner declined to even consider selling, but Tom Ewell and Mr. Ames became friends through the years. Tom always reported to the Chief to advise that he "hadn't never poached no mo'." In the old days I had many a fine quail shoot with Tom and another good Negro friend, John Watkins, and his famous old blue-ticked setter. "All d' dawgs," John used to connote, "has all d' sickness whut dawgs has, fum mange an' distemper. Ol' Blue, he lays down wid 'em but somehows he manages t' git up an' leaves 'em alayin'. He'll hav' t' be shot down at Judgmint Day ef I wants t' hunt over him in d' Promised Land."

Hobart Ames, even when a bit crippled for rough riding, could climb down off his horse and give a splendid account of himself when dogs stood and bevies whirred from sedge or thickets. He was a grand shot and always did it like the gentleman he was. For all his austerity of mien, he possessed a miraculous sense of humor. In farewell to as fine a setting as the limit of human friendship provides, I remember my last glimpse of Hobart Ames, his gaunt giant's frame on a hospital bed, the clasp of both his great hands over mine as he bade me adieu.

I saw Mrs. Ames at her last trial, standing in the little churchyard near the Plantation's east boundary, where she had come to see the break-away of a second series that did not start. My last view of her was as she stood there, fragile but smiling, in the late winter afternoon's sunshine. William A. Bruette said she possessed "the best pair of hands" of any equestrienne he knew. Julia Colony Ames died in January 1950. It was her request that the 1950 running proceed as planned.

It has been suggested that Nash's florid descriptions could have inspired Hemmingway's bare-boned style. In the above, it must be kept in mind that Hobart and Julia Ames were dearest friends and it seemed important to Nash to delineate each thing they did. Giving snacks to their spaniels was recorded as a ritual, specifying "light or wheat bread." It would be well to re-read that final scene with Hobart Ames: ". . . his gaunt giant's frame on a hospital bed, the clasp of both his great hands over mine . . ." If any writer has done more with seventeen words, I have not read them.

The following story, "Point! Judges," is the first forty-four years of the National Field Trial Championship in capsule. Mr. and Mrs. Ames saw to it, by means of a trust fund, that the National would continue. Nash has assured that the grand old competition and the dogs and the people will live in the memories of those who read what he has written.

F ROM 1874 until 1906, there were four hundred and ten field trials held in the United States. The figures since then must bulk into the thousands.

Major Taylor's record book shows that Gladstone won, as a puppy, at the Nashville, Tennessee, trials (Tennessee State Sportsmen's Association) in 1877. His first important all-age win was at the Eastern Field Trials in 1880: a prize of $200 and a Fox gun for Mr. "Pink" Bryson. Gladstone won four distinctive firsts, fourteen seconds, nineteen thirds, two fourths, and one fifth.

As I was growing up, there was talk of such dogs as Roderigo and Count Noble and Cincinnatus. I recall first rumors of the National Championship stake in 1896. Count Gladstone IV won the first National, and to this day I remember Mr. Wheatley's talking about it in his real estate office over the northwest corner of Main and Madison Streets in Memphis. The stake was canceled in 1897. Mr. and Mrs. Hobart Ames, a young couple from Boston, are mentioned in accounts of that year's National as "riding in the gallery."

College portals cleared, I returned actively to marsh and covert. Those were the days of my setter Jack, along with staunch Kate and keen-nosed

Don. My two greatest shooting dogs of that period were pointer Tom Cotton and setter Jim. I hunted a lot north of La Grange, Tennessee, and heard much of the vast land acquisitions in the same neighborhood by Mr. Hobart Ames from North Easton, Massachusetts. Friends of his also took up land—Messrs. Herman Duryea and Whitney. So rapidly did the Ames holding extend westward that we began having to be careful about lines and posted signs.

In 1900 the National Championship stake was first run in the Grand Junction, Tennessee, vicinity. From then on, in a casual way, I began watching the races. In those times the setter was cock of the walk. Sioux, the great Duryea and Avent longhair, became a sort of legend. She had a black ear; a similar spot on her left hip and tail base. A bird finder from who-laid-the-rail, she bested Geneva in a runoff for her first National in 1901, and triumphed again in 1902. But next year Geneva turned the tables.

I can still see Messrs. Ames, Buckle, Sturges, Avent, Bevan, and many another field trial great. There were lots of birds all over the country in those days, though sometimes bad weather during the trial made them, as now, difficult to locate. I have heard Mr. Ames say they bought quail from Kansas for restocking purposes and that such blood transfusion was of great benefit to the Tennessee bobwhites.

A young handler of 1905, Er Shelley, was just then getting associated with the big-game hunter, Mr. Paul J. Rainey, at his preserve near Cotton Plant, Mississippi. Er Shelley and today's noted outdoor writer and weapons authority, Mr. Charles Askins, handled Pioneer and McKinley respectively in the National. Shelley brought Pioneer back to the National in 1906 and won with him. Not long thereafter Shelley was to purchase the Avent bear dogs that he shipped to Africa and broke there to run nothing but lions. I remember that when he left the Rainey plantation years later, he came to my place of business in Memphis and showed me several chapters of a book he was writing on dog training. This authoritative work has been a best seller in its field ever since. A few seasons ago Er Shelley attended the National Champion stake, and we had the pleasure of talking over old times. He is now living in Illinois and is still a top figure of the out-of-doors.

The last time I saw Paul Rainey was on the eve of his departure for an African safari. His had been an adventurous life since the early days of his Tippah Farm when we used to hold pheasant and duck drives there under the auspices of his game breeder imported from England, Mr. James Craven, who twenty years later assumed charge of a game farm near East Alton, Illinois, for the Western Cartridge Company.

Paul Rainey spent much of his last years at Tippah. When in Memphis, he used to come to my office and sit for hours. The evening he left Memphis for Africa I was shocked by how suddenly his health had seemingly been impaired. He died while crossing the Indian Ocean, of a cerebral rupture, and was buried at sea. I have hunted quail many times since then at the old Rainey place, and every time an airplane went over, his field hands would say: "Dar's Mist' Paul now . . . comin' back t' see ef ev'ything bees all right."

It is worth recalling having seen the first pointer win the National Championship—when, in 1909, Charley Babcock toured the course with a clean, bright, beautifully handling fellow—the great Manitoba Rap. Barely out of his derby time, he satisfied the judges, Messrs. Merriman, Ames and Bevan, that at least one great pointer had arrived. I did not see the fiery Monora win in 1910, but at Rogers Springs that same season I attended the U. S. Field Trials with a party of friends. There I met, for the first time, Al Hochwalt. I can see him, a big powerful fellow, notebook in hand, riding off as Commissioner's leash was slipped for the derby he won.

Among memories of the National Championship, I recall the blazing win of Mr. Fred Stephenson's little setter bitch La Besita, in a second series of 1915. I sat up in that sagging old hotel at the Grand Junction depot half the night, re-running details of her win. I had my first and only glimpse of the immortal Comanche Frank in 1914, with Mr. Jim Avent piloting. Eighteen years before, Mr. Jim had sent the first National winner, Count Gladstone, to victory.

In '16 I saw a lemon and white pointer dog, John Proctor, with that same Mr. Babcock who had handled Manitoba Rap, run a heat that won the title. I saw the great derby Mary Montrose in her first heat in '17, when she went on to win the National and on to realms of the peerless in bird dogdom. Unfortunately, I never saw Doughboy run. On and on go the listings, with Messrs. Ames, Merriman, and that great handler and sturdy gentleman, Mr. C. E. Buckle, doing most of the judging. The setter Joe Muncie licked a sturdy contender, Square Edges; Becky Broomhill, Mr. Louis Haggin's pointer queen of the uplands, is on her way. How well I recall the controversy over Becky's defeat of that roamer, Eugene's Ghost. The decision went hard with Warren Stoner, and harder because charges of "blinking" were lodged against the old Ghost. Meanwhile, outside of judging a small stake here and there, I about parted with field trials.

Along there I could not reconcile a tendency to stress mere bird dog speed and range, while animation, poise, nose, and, above all, handling response were being diverted from that main issue, the gun. After all, shooting forms the basis of bird dog character. When it came to breeding mere coursing whippets in pointer and setter flesh, a new phase of field-trialism came into being . . . but not at Grand Junction. Even now, some of the dogs brought to trials are often only half-broken greyhounds. There is criticism, too, tending to term dogs who really handle, as "machine-like." I might say here that I have seen dogs in the biggest stakes of the nation that apparently didn't know their own names, much less the order "Come here."

Sturdy Susquehanna Tom wins the National in 1932, but loses his life on the Canadian prairies the following summer. In 1933, Mr. A. G. Sage's pointer, Rapid Transit, takes the cup and purse with a sterling performance over such fiery competition as the marvelous bitch Superlette (also the property of Mr. Sage) and that champion of champions, Schoolfield. There was a field trial pointer, my masters! Champion of just about everything called for by the gun and rules of the game covers. The National was the one great prize to elude him, and then only after a bitter fight.

Like that superb setter, Citation, game Schoolfield would put forth a great battle every time he competed. And I keep remembering a three-hour heat I saw Citation and Kremlin run in the National of 1934. The sun was warm, but a terrible freeze was thawing, and the fields lay belly deep in slush and ice rime. I think the score was thirteen bevies for one dog and a dozen for t'other. Had the National ended that night (and there was but one more brace to run the following Monday), there is no telling how the judges would have voted. That last brace produced the stake's winner, Mr. W. C. Teagle's bitch Norias Annie, with Chesley Harris adding to his handling laurels. That was the year I was honored in being asked by Mr. Ames to officiate with himself and Mr. Henry P. Davis in judging the National. Mr. Davis and I also officiated in 1935 and 1936. Since then, I have ridden with Mr. Ames and Dr. T. Benton King, of Brownsville, Tennessee, a long-dominant figure in American field trials.

I look back upon these recent sessions at the National Field Trial Championship with full appreciation for the fine days they have put into my life. I saw much, but not enough, of the late Al Hochwalt. He was with me when he first sickened at Grand Junction during the National and had to be taken to his home in Dayton, Ohio. I recall him at many places I have judged: at the Amateur Championship at Sturgeon, Missouri, in 1934; at Medford's hospitable English Setter Club. I treasure the book Al Hoch-walt wrote and inscribed for me shortly before his passing.

To say that I have learned much about bird dogs and judging from Mr. Ames and many of the fine sportsmen with whom I have ridden is putting it mildly. Fortunately for me, my earlier training by men of the older dog-breaking school made me fully in accord with the test type demanded by the Champion stake.

Here is required the dog who must go to and even beyond extreme course limits and yet maintain between itself and handler that contact which inspires perfect confidence in gun contacts. Here is call, above all else, for a well-broken animal, bold and animated, with running carriage, tail action, pace, and searching directness attractive to the gunner's eye: a dog really and truly out scouring birdy places, the likeliness of which it proves itself in diagnosing. And yet, when found, handling its game with a nose surety and fire amounting almost to abandon.

As with humanity, dogs seem imbued with ambition and a credo of winning, which, at times, challenges credulity. Who recalls the inspired runoff between those two magnificent bitches, Homewood Flirtatious and Sulu, in the National's second series of their year, to reach such heights? Or the fine, upstanding thrust of gallant Sports Peerless Pride in his second series against the threat of streamlined Norias Aeroflow? And again, of stouthearted Norias Annie, keeping always to the fore and fighting her way to the cup against the well-nigh invincible Dr. Blue Willing? Then Sulu's outstanding win, and great Air Pilot's Sam's hairline win over another great second series dog, Highland Bimpkins. "In all my years of judging this stake," remarked Mr. Hobart Ames, while we pondered the verdict, "this is the toughest decision to announce." Another worthwhile memory is the race of a comparatively unknown derby dog from Texas, young Wayside Pat M. His strong and finely handled three hours under Jett Crawford brought him back into a runoff against Lester's Enjoy Wahoo, titlist of that year.

And among many great moments lived in years of field trial judging is this one. It has for setting, the long and rugged course of the Saskatchewan Field Trial Club, out of Moose Jaw. Bill Windsor, of New Philadelphia, Ohio, and I were judging, and who could wish for a finer riding mate under grueling conditions? Uncas Flying Devil, owned by Mr. Howard Eyster, of York, Pennsylvania, running an hour's heat under blazing, near-noon sun, set a terrific pace and—miraculously—found birds.

A tremendous cast took him far beyond the gallery's sight, and even his handler's ken. Finally, with but minutes left to go, the dog's scout wig-wagged the finding signal. Jumping into a Bennett buggy, we drove a mile along a section line, with Dewey English, the animal's handler, galloping pell-mell across the prairie to get his charge. And there, under the fiery sun torment, with head and tail aloft, stood Uncas Flying Devil—with one, lone Hungarian partridge from a departed covey.

It is great in looking back, to remember the man, to my thinking, most responsible for that esprit de corps which dominates American field trials today. The gentleman who, in his seventies, still rides his thirty miles a day and more as each National Championship rolls past, the man who has done more than anyone else to preserve championship caliber at its mightiest: Mr. Hobart Ames. We who have listened to his words of wisdom and partaken of his and Mrs. Ames' hospitality, are in their debt. Behind his austere bearing lurk a gracious geniality and sense of humor matching in their fairness and generosity.

Somewhere back through the years a coolness had arisen between Mr. Ames and Mr. Jim Avent. They spoke, but that was about all. But in all my contacts with Mr. Ames or with Mr. Jim, never did I ever hear either utter a word against the other.

During the running of the 1936 National Field Trial Championship, it was generally known that Mr. Avent had been seriously ill in a Memphis hospital. We were just finishing a morning's three-hour heat and rode up to where a crowd milled about the road and dog trucks. Off to one side, clad in a heavy ulster to shield him from the biting chill, stood a wanly pathetic Mr. Jim Avent. He just had to, somehow, get to the National. The "March of Time" was filming the big races that year and their cameramen were here and there, shooting various scenes. I saw Mr. Ames spot Mr. Avent standing there, all alone. And I saw a smile of genuine liking and friendly sympathy break through his stern features. Instantly he turned his horse, rode well out of his way, leaned from the saddle and stuck out a huge, gloved hand. "Hello, Jim," he said, with a grin, "I'm glad to see you out, and I hope you'll be well enough to ride again before long." If I'm any judge of the light in a man's eyes, I believe that whatever hard feelings existed in Avent's heart died in the quick, impulsive thrust of Mr. Ames' hand and the warmth of his clasp and smile.

Mr. Ames called me to his side and whispered, "Nash, I wish you'd get the moving picture men to film a scene of you and Henry Davis (who was judging with us) shaking hands with Jim Avent—I'm afraid he will not be with us for long, and his likeness at a National should be preserved for posterity." And the shot was filmed. Within three months Mr. Jim passed on. Nor will his superior, or equal, as a woodsman, breaker and handler of hounds or field trial dogs ever appear upon the American outdoor stage.

Years stream on, and the National Champion stake extends its list of winners. That glorious setter, Sports Peerless Pride, turns back a second-series challenge by Norias Aeroflow to become champion. Lester's Enjoy Wahoo, as powerful a striding pointer as ever graced the National's courses, is not to be denied. Ariel, of the Sage-Morton dynasty in field trials, wins the title in 1941. But in 1942, his kinsman, the mighty Luminary, paces off the greatest three-hour heat under adverse conditions that I ever saw or expect to witness. Here, truly, was a dog of destiny. We placed him second in his first derby stake on the Saskatchewan prairies. He was "Nigger" then. But rechristened Luminary, he took the great Quail Futurity not long thereafter. Thence, though not overcampaigned, the fellow went on to win the National Free-for-All and the National. His quick second-series win over Tarhelia Lucky Strike in that competition, with four bevies magnificently handled within eighteen minutes after the start, is something that witnesses will remember. It is 1943, and Ariel, vastly improved over his form of '41 and '42, meets the vaunted Texas Ranger in a second series and disposes of him with almost the suddenness of Luminary's defeat of Tarhelia Lucky Strike the year before. Now it is 1944, and though the National is not run because of conditions beyond control, Ariel has accounted for the Dominion Chicken Championship and annexed the great National Free-for-All at Shuqualak, Mississippi. Years can never efface such memories!

What constitutes the spirit of American field trials? It is an incredible and intangible longing! Something sprung through the ages from savage man's partnership of the cave with his even more savage but loyal dog. This companionship and intuitive common interest in flesh for existence has wielded 'twixt master and beast something utterly unbreakable.

In my mind, it rests somewhere between the spirit hovering over that peaceful animal cemetery on the Ames plantation, and the words of Gaston de Foix. It lies wherever some beloved gun-dog comrade sleeps away eternity in our hearts. . . . "For a hound is the most reasonable and best knowing beast that ever God made . . . of good love . . . and true to his Master."

Give Only To The Honored

This story of a big Chesapeake who shared Nash's sand-bar goose shooting—and a little more—was published in Field & Stream, *November 1945, and the same year in* Game Bag. *Nash's description of Pat in front of "Lakeside's eight-foot fireplace" establishes the period as 1920 or later. A letter from Horace to Nash, written in January 1920, indicates that Nash intended to leave Beaver Dam for Lakeside at about that time. Horace's request that he and Molly be taken to the club "in Arkensaw" was granted, for this situation shows them in charge and carrying on old Beaver Dam traditions in the new setting. Bob Anderson tells me that the old Lakeside Club "is now planted in corn."*

That grand description of pitch-dark predawn and Ole Miss' at flood; Horace's wonderful language—". . . le's be headed f' freedom on d' safe side—jus' in case"; the deep lake being formed by the chute's back-up water, the narrowing main sand bar; goose music across dim "wide-water"; pinwheels of river ducks winking past "against a rim of gray smoulder eastward" is next to being there.

As a non-goose, I am puzzled by honker psychology that prompts geese that have just lifted from other geese in a back bay to feel moved to drop in to a spread of decoys that must look like more of the geese they have left, moments before. But I know it was so, for Nash wrote it. Incidentally, he mentions in this story that Hal was also shooting a Becker magnum.

There is excellent overwriting in the final few paragraphs, and any reader who doesn't experience tingling on the back of his neck has, I suspect, inadequate nerve ends. Or has never loved a dog.

ORMEL'S PAT BECAME our year-old Chesapeake Bay dog as the result of my reading even the ads of an obscure outdoor magazine one bluebird November morning on the upper gravel head of Ship Island sand bar. Settled comfortably in my pit, there was plenty of time for reading. The ad, written from the sand hills of Nebraska, where, as a youth, I'd gunned, rang true. Intrigued, I wrote the man.

His reply, enclosing Pat's picture taken with some youngsters in the family garden, listed a banker and minister as references. He described Pat as already house- and yard-broken, well started on land and water game, and above all, sensible and courageous. In due course, Pat arrived. I loved him from the first moment I saw his trusting and fearless eyes. The dog's superb physical condition, friendliness, and determination to please evidenced the best of previous handling. If all dog deals were as clean-cut and fruitful as mine with the gentleman who sold me Pat, there would be fewer headaches among gun-dog men generally.

I wouldn't give two whoops for any dog I can't convert into a one-man animal, so Pat was immediately installed on a basis of special privilege. Such a statement will wring yelps of scorn from many training purists, but it's my way and has paid handsome dividends. Stick to your own methods if they make your dogs what Pat was to me. Our lovely setter, Lucy, welcomed young Pat graciously to the other ends of her hearth rugs, and all was well.

That summer Pat and Lucy shared my and Irma's out-of-doors completely. Indoors, Pat never learned to walk other than softly on slick, hardwood floors. Innocent romps invariably ended in embarrassing spills. Frozen, slippery duck marshes never gave him half as much trouble even when scurrying after a winged bird. The most difficult part of his finishing, if you could call it that, was to keep him quiet in boat or canoe while bream or bass were being played over the net.

Our greatest fear was that in running around lake and creek banks in summer, Pat might get snake-bit. But luck was with us, and by mid-August when Hal and I began checking on our several dove fields, the growing, sway-backed brown dog sensed doves as part of gunning, which he strongly suspected concerned himself. From the first moment of opening day, when he was put at "sit" out there just off the Williamson grove, Pat became a dove retriever.

Through ensuing years, under difficult and even dangerous conditions, he and I gunned together with affectionate confidence. A practiced stalker, he belly-crawled sand bars, skulking the dips like a fox, or slinking like a wraith through thin cover. Amid corn and wheat patches he left me and circled downwind, actually driving game my way. If nothing flushed, he'd return almost apologetically.

Pat would work only for me, Irma, or Horace, with whom I sometimes left him, although he was devoted to Hal. I've shot mallards in the timber until the load became too heavy for me to pack and shoot too. So I'd hang six or eight across Pat's brawny saddle and lighten the burden. He sleeps beneath a matted rosebush tangle, in a tight casket buried high above floodwater on the old club's knoll. And above him through all eternity will, I hope, sweep flights of the wildfowl that were part of his own fine being.

I'll always remember Pat best by that day he and Hal and Horace and I shot the overflowed lower reaches of Roustabout towhead. Pat was gloriously in his prime. By today's standards every ounce of his eighty pounds was of championship caliber. In those days there were few established retriever trials, and the chances are Pat and I would have been too busy gunning, anyhow. I still judge all retrievers by Pat, with dear old Chub getting a draw on finished style. One day Horace, having trudged two miles to Squire Frank Williamson's plantation telephone, gave me the news. His voice all but trembled with excitement. "Mist' Nash? Lissen, Mist' Nash—this is Ho'ace—yaas, suh—d' ducks done all gone t' d' river—but I done foun' 'em. D' river's floodin' d' whole en' o' Roustabout bar 'bove Norfolk. Ducks an' geese usin' in all dem overflowed corn fiel's an' wild pea patches. Chute water comin' in f'm Hog Pond is pow'ful, but we kin git across t' d' gut. We'll have a fine shoot if you an' Mist' Hall will jes' come. But be sho' an' bring Pat, he'll have t' ac' as d' principal agent in all th' high water. Da's fine, Mist' Nash, I'll be on d' lookout f' y'all 'bout suppertime." Hal and I, with Pat burly as a grizzly, were at the clubhouse before nightfall.

After a supper of Molly's "poke" tenderloins with cream gravy, grits, and deep-dish peach cobbler, with sumptuously fed Pat stretched on the moose-hide rug in front of Lakeside's eight-foot fireplace, Horace revealed his completely mapped invasion plan. We followed every move of the campaign as his ramrod pointer traveled across the blackboard. "We'll leave d' car right heah—clear o' risin' water. I've got John d' fisherman's big skifft an' two pair o' oars right yonder—it'll take some hard pullin'. We'll take plenty o' duck an' goose decoys, an' walk down d' outside bar. Me an' John coulda kilt d' limit easy—yistiddy. D' pits is done dug. Y'all owes John a dollah apiece f' his skifft an' d' labor."

Before bedtime no detail of preparation was overlooked. Having rambled North America's shooting fields together, Hal and I believed in traveling light. Into our packs and Horace's went decoys, shells enough for legal limits of eight geese and twenty-five ducks (if and when); water bottle, camera, lunch, and the usual safety-first-and-pleasure-afterward accessories. An automobile spade and plenty of heavy seine twine completed emergency details of our task force.

At three a.m. Horace eased in with hot shaving water, lit the fire and withdrew behind his customary admonition—"brekfus' ready time y'all is." Soon Molly's elephantine bulk moved noiselessly from stove to table side, proud of her coffee, poached eggs, butter-broiled country ham, and beaten biscuits. Pat, with a long, hard day ahead, had his share of table provender topped off with an extra bait of hamburger and two raw eggs. How I'd like to relive that same morning, with those faithful companions, sitting there in Molly's warm, spotless kitchen.

Our big car soon topped the towering Mississippi river levee. A raw-cold, moonless morning warned that weather-cats might jump any which-away. For several miles a rutty, buckshot road wound through second-growth, old river beds, and matted jungles. Hal braked at the peak of an upgrade. Ahead the road dipped sharply, and into the stillness crept hissing turmoil. The inexorable, tearing ravage of rising floodwater is an ominous sound, all the more in pitch dark. Where we stood had been the river's main bank a hundred years before. Now the gut water, a swirling sheet of bronze, loomed vaguely.

From water's edge Horace called back, "Heah's d' boat—water done riz 'bout a foot las' night, but d' car'll be safe up dere—but turn hit roun', Mist' Hal, an' le's be headed f' freedom on d' safe side—jus' in case." We worked the big skiff through swishing willow tops and out onto furious current. Horace's oars held its head up until I could unship and bend my sweeps. Together we held our own and hit the far bank exactly where the roadway emerged onto the main bar's elevation. Locking the skiff to a cottonwood and hiding the oars, we shouldered packs and hiked down the sand bar's ridge.

Beyond it, to our right, lay a great deep lake being formed by the chute's back-up water. To our left, the ever narrowing main sand bar dwindled toward its spearhead of sloping mud blocks and low switch willows. The farther we walked, the closer licked hungry Ole Miss, sniping and biting at every low spot across which she might gnaw and spew to reunion with the backwater. Abruptly we came to such a place, and Horace slowed uneasily.

"She's goin' thoo heah, an' not be long 'bout hit, neither. When she do we'll be on an islan', but I guess we kin mek it back 'crosst dis afternoon." We stood amid false dawn. Across a dim sea of misty wide-water below us came goose music and thunder mutterings of restless duck myriads. Half a dozen pinwheels of river ducks suddenly winked past us against a rim of gray smoulder eastward. Where the cottonwood ridge bit off sharply, we stepped from clean sand onto rubbery mud blocks.

The pit was so well located and hidden that Horace had a few moments' hunt for it. He and John had made a perfect job of the dig, too. Top-layer mud blocks lifted out whole and used for willow-trimmed sighting shields. Underneath, half clay and sand prevented pit caving. There were comfortable dug-in seats and wall receptacles for supplies. One look and you knew that pit had been fashioned by a master.

Horace lofted a moistened finger. "Wind's fum d' south, Mist' Nash, le's set d' geese d'coys back heah an' d' ducks in d' aidge o' d' water creepin' up down yonder. Dat'll put 'em all to drappin' in 'ginst d' wind." The set was soon completed and spelled bad medicine for visitors. Hal and I jumped into our commodious hide while Horace and Pat retired to the cottonwoods above us and hid among some logs and dwarf bush. They were perfectly hidden, held a commanding view, and there was a downhill start for Pat when needed. Horace was instructed to stop any and all cripples to save Pats having to swim the deadly current on the towhead's far side.

Silvery water pushed uphill toward us and pools united. But our spot looked good for all day against the rise. "I hear geese travelin'," muttered Hal, an ear turned southward—"there they are—swinging off yonder to our right—see?—they're over the shore line—they're straightening—look —get down—they've seen our profiles—they're leveling off—get down—easy does it." Knees bent while his eyes searched through protective willow stems—I saw his thumb push up his twelve-bore magnum's safety catch.

Their excited chatter-gabble meant but one thing: they'd made the wind and were going to join up with us right now. Silence clamped down, and that, too, told its own story. It was now but a matter of heartbeats to zero. Hal and I hadn't doubled on game in twenty years; each knew what the other would do. Hal would let the first incomers rush past and settle before he opened up. Another breathless second and, amid a burst of welcoming gabble, they literally covered us up. Their heavy pinions cracked like sails in a wind, and birds were actually overhead when I scored a right and left at less than thirty yards. Hal had done equally well, and we both reloaded in time to smash down third birds. One of these, however, required Pat's services. Six geese were not bad for a starter.

Hal was lighting himself a cigarette when Horace yelled, "Shoot 'em!" We came up fumbling, just in time to hear wing-whisk overhead and see a tremendous flock of mallards funneling into our ponded stool. Some had lit, others were trying to, while the remnants, wheeling overhead, saw us and lifted with alarm cries. Again it was easy shooting, but even so, Pat had an extended chase clean to the mud bar's point. He returned so highly elated that I decided to let him curl up by the pit. Some bent-down switch willows made him a nest. It was amazing to watch the dog lie there, nose to tail, while ducks and geese swung to the decoys.

The faint, staccato coughing of a motorboat drifted upwind and Hal leveled his binoculars. Ensued five hollow "whooping coughs" of autoloading gunfire over water. "That fellow's shooting from a motorboat and raising thousands of birds—that's against the law—there are two of 'em in the boat—listen." Another volley. A veritable swarm of waterfowl wove toward us, long, darker skeins of geese dragging slowly through the tinier mesh of duck nets. "Let's finish up on geese first," warned Hal, "there's more ducks around than we can use." Countless bunches of mallards, sprig, scaup, widgeon, teal, and gadwall hurtled overhead. But we sat there checking on the honkers. It was a sight such as few wildfowlers see in a lifetime. We heard them lighting in our decoys.

"Great Kingdom Come," whispered Hal, peeping—"two big bunches of geese are heading directly in—not forty yards apart—they're going to light all over us—stand by for a crash—put an extra shell in your mouth—shoot carefully." A tremendous babel of giant gray and black shapes letting down their landing gear. "Okay," sang out Hal.

We waited for their alarm and pandemonium of a hundred clarioned alerts. It jams into one's ear at short range; I can still hear it after all these years. As a gang to my left got airborne, I shot twice just over a mass of writhing black necks. Several wilted. Hal's gun popped twice. Into our guns went the reloads and we all but came heads-on scrambling from the pit for the mop-up. I stopped one cripple legging it through the stems, while Pat rounded up another strong-running fugitive. The big Canada turned and struck at the dog with brave, powerful wings, but Pat dodged, darted in, and the struggle was quickly over. The havoc wrought by Hal's and my twelve-bore Becker magnums with three-inch cases and an ounce and three-eighths of luballoyed fours, had been complete. Six more geese were propped among the decoys.

By ten-thirty of that biting. cloudy forenoon, Hal suggested a count-up. Our bag stood at twelve geese and an even thirty "big" ducks. We had long since ceased firing at anything save mallards, sprig, or gadwall. Horace came down for the conference, and, as usual, talked common sense. "Le's pack d' geese an' ducks on up to d' boat an' save all dat hard work late dis evenin'. I'll warm y'all a snack, an' I know Mist' Hal got t' have his nap. We kin finish up down heah dis afternoon, easy. I'll bet d' decoys'll be full o' ducks an' geese whin we gits back." Horace was right.

By two o'clock when we regained the pit, an enlarged water front and immediate decoys were black with ducks, and a gaggle of geese departed with them. The river had finally cut through the low place, and a ten-foot flowage, gaining momentum every instant, gushed into the lake. By the morrow a boat would be required to cross it.

Half an hour later the motorboat law-violators resumed operations. Through Hal's glasses we watched the fast craft dash upriver, whip above a duck raft, cut the motor, and suddenly sideslip with the current right in on top of the birds. There must have been extensions on their autoloaders, for now every unloading meant nearly twenty shots. Then followed an interlude for raking in the dead, and cripple-shooting. Their daylong depredations brought comment from Hal.

"Buck," said he, "you and I are enjoying probably our last wildfowl shoot under existing bag and possession limits. The violation we are witnessing goes on everywhere, and enforcement is utterly inadequate. Commercialism has muscled in to take the place of old-time market gunning. At the present rate of fire power, plus the collapse of northern breeding areas, waterfowl resources simply cannot withstand the pace."

"And," I continued, "if we went back to town and reported the violation we're watching, we'd be told the government agent was out of town and that he didn't have a motorboat, anyhow." However, the matter would be reported.

I recall something else Hal said, sitting there in the goose pit puffing his cigarette between quick glances aloft or cockings of the ear for the slither of wings. "The day will come when crimes against wildlife will be punished like crimes against human life. What difference is there between game bootlegging of natural resources under the Lacey Act and violating the Mann or Narcotic Acts? Enforcement of the Migratory Bird Treaty Act should no longer be left with some little division of a federal bureau, equipped with a mere handful of wardens to catch thousands of vandals. Enforcement of the Migratory Bird Law should pass to Justice or the F.B.I. Maybe the scum and chiselers would lay off then."

Hal passed on in 1933, but how prophetic were his thoughts. The great drought, from 1929 through 1934, brought waterfowl to the verge of decimation. After a bitter struggle, magazine-gun capacities were curtailed on migratory game birds, and, in some states, on upland birds. Constant pressure by conservation groups improved law enforcement. The Emergency Waterfowl Program did a great job, and the fine work of Ducks Unlimited in Canada has saved the wildfowl for posterity.

It was past three o'clock before the sun fought its way through sky murk and changed the back-bay landscape. With it seemed to come the ducks. Sticking to our policy of big ducks only, Hal and I enjoyed some of the finest shooting of our careers. Pat was kept busy. About four o'clock we had in a magnificent flock of geese that ended our honker limits for the day. But one duck was needed to check out that list, too. "Le's us pack up an' git t' d' boat," advised Horace. "Dark comin' quick befo' long, le's git back 'crosst dat ditch an' d' bad chute."

Loading up, we hit the towhead trail. All at once, as a bunch of mallards swung over the cottonwoods, Hal's magnum leaped to his shoulder. Two quick reports, and a hard-hit drake flared off and crumpled into the terrific current whirlpooling past the ridge. Just as we rushed over the embankment, Pat plunged headlong into the maelstrom, to disappear for dreadful minutes in its suction, and then bob up somewhat bewilderedly fifty yards downstream. Then, high-headed, he began looking for his quarry. Our distracted shouts availed nothing; he'd spotted the mallard and was off, and, borrowing from the current, his powerful stroke bore him from sight through the willow tops. Hal looked at me aghast. "Buck," he muttered, "I shouldn't have shot that duck—I'd rather jump in there myself than have anything happen to Pat."

"Pat'll git back all right, Mist' Hal," comforted Horace. "Ef he don't find d' duck, he'll mek land somewhere an' fin' his way home." With sudden accord we hastened back to the towhead's vantage point. Hal's glasses searched every foot of the mud bar's lower flooded forest. A dying sun bathed the ocean-like expanse in glowing, brassy resurgence.

"Yonder he is!" shouted Hal. "I see him swimming—away down yonder— he's cut back out of the current into the back eddy—he's got the duck, too—Great Kingdom—he's nearly half a mile from here." Dropping the binoculars on their cord he began yelling, "Here we are, Pat, here we are, old fellow, come on—man." By then, Horace and I had picked up the tiny speck, swimming strongly through and around channels studded with obstructions. We just stood there lost in wide-eyed, grateful admiration.

Pat's paws struck wading water and he stalked ashore, the mallard firmly in tender jaws. What a sight he made, shaking his burly form until the sunlit drops of muddy water turned to flecked gold and coppery mist. Hal waved his gun, dropped it, ran to the dog and threw an arm about his neck. Something whispered to me—"What more complete mission in life? His not to reason why, Pat has challenged the treacherous might of one of the most powerful rivers on earth. He's battled its fury, and beaten down every obstacle its restless cunning could devise. Yep, he's licked Ole Miss at her own game, with no odds or quarter asked or given."

So there, fellow wildfowlers, let me leave you Pat and your own memories of gun dogs with brains and courage. Pat, with his powerful chest heaving and sturdy, wide-bowed legs stuck deeply into dripping, chocolate mud. Pat, with kindly eyes staring up into the all but tearful and thankful ones of his comrades, the last of God's sunshine for that rare day pouring warmth and glory upon his gallant soul.

What Really Happens Out Quail Shooting

This was published in Field & Stream, *August 1945, and, like the preceding story, appeared the same year in* Game Bag. *It is excellent advice on certain situations in dog work on quail. Nash's approach to gun-shyness is an understanding one, unlike harsh methods involving starvation.*

It was not uncommon for old-time gunners to send their dog in to flush after the point, but the flush on order and subsequent steadiness to wing and shot is a refinement in bird dog performance few men have seen—one that almost required the dog's dropping at the flush to keep him there.

When Nash speaks of National Champions being first-class gunning companions, it was hunting mounted, not on foot in thick cover. You don't get very companionable with a dog running a half mile ahead of you. Once more, it is well to remember that Nash shot more quail over Don and Kate than over trial winners.

In its form in Game Bag, *"What Really Happens Out Quail Hunting" contained areas on field trial performance deleted here to avoid duplication of material in "Point! Judges."*

WELL MOUNTED, WE follow a brace of rambling, perfectly broken bird dogs across typical bobwhite gunning country of the Deep South. Or, with our guns and a wise setter and pointer of medium range but unerring noses, we walk in search of bevies to which only such dogs can steer us.

Winter terrain affords many adventures. Muffled or breeze-blown, occasional staccato reports drift from brown-belted knolls and lowlands shimmering ocean-like in reflections off sunlit, tawny sedges. "Late of an afternoon," writes a friend, "you can sniff smoke rising from plantation cabins, a mixture of burning oak, pine, and cedar. With a touch of sadness, I see this old life afield slipping away."

At evening, following hunter's hearty repast, we meditate by the fire and mull our day's transpirings. Bevy and singles, hit-by-miss, ours and our dogs' ledgers are audited. What really happened? The whys and wherefores of certain covey finds or unproductives, backs, trailings, and retrieves! Reprimands are administered, citations awarded. Then, parade of our own gunning alibis, until our senses of humor prevail, and, yawning, we yield to the Sandman.

Maybe our dogs were youngsters, "derbies" to the field trial fraternity. Or, "all-age" veterans, canny, bold, and hardened. Steady to wing and shot, or still problem children as to shooting-field behavior. Let's be optimists, however, qualifying them as mannerly in all respects, and tiptop bird-finders.

Recently, Dr. Paul Jensen, of Cornell University, using thirteen field-useless specimens sent by sportsmen-owners, is reported to have studied gun-shyness in bird dogs. He appraised them abnormal, on a basis comparable to "shell shock" and other human neuroses. Competent bird-dog handlers have long known that gun dogs can be "gun-shy," "bird-shy," and "man-shy." Separately, or all at once. From bird-shyness stems one birddog neurosis influencing one of the most misunderstood tribulations of pointing —called "blinking." That phase, however, is a chapter all its own.

It has also long been known that by patient treatment many bird dogs, like afflicted humans, can be rehabilitated for usefulness afield. I have owned and worked with bird dogs and retrievers cringing at the mere sight of a weapon. But by exercise of kindness and infinitely patient individual approach and progressive readjustment of disturbing contacts, I have seen such animals jump for joy at sight of a gun. Shorn of frustrations, they came to associate the fowling piece with pleasures afield, and bounded happily away. Gently supported and talked to like a child nursed through paroxysms of bad dreams, they have come to shake off and surmount such inhibitions.

Riding along, dismounting for bevy rises or snap tries at tricky singles twisting through the blackjacks, let's attempt analysis of incidents ahead of, and even behind, the dogs. Why do dogs sometimes drop on point, or gradually crouch into semiprone positions upon contacting quail scent? What part of such posturing is synthetic or inherited? Is the move wholly precautionary when the dog's nose warns—"Too close to game"? What canine complexes lurk in bird dog make-ups? Is dropping on point a throwback to some ancestor of the studbooks or bar sinister and should it count against a dog under field trial judgment?

My reaction based upon experience and observation while breaking gun dogs is that many factors control or influence the trait. Heredity can easily play a role. Some dogs have a habit of barking furiously when cast for a field trial or hunt. You then ofttimes hear the remark, "That dog's sire (or grandsire) barked like that." Or, when a bird dog running at full speed goes to "yipping," it may be solely from the sheer joy of release—like schoolboys yelling when they rush from classrooms at recess. I therefore dissent that dropping on point should count against a field trial dog, provided the animal's attitude on game is of known loftiness and intensity, and the crouching not too often repeated. Essences of heredity, control, training, scent provocations, and canine metabolisms enter the picture. Some are within our powers of analysis; others are far beyond our present knowledge.

All upland gunners admire and some purists demand "fire" when a bird dog strikes game, but there are times when dogs otherwise vested with great beauty on point—drop! A bird dog may suddenly become allergic to surroundings, ownership, and training habits through causes beyond its control. So why chalk up dropping on point as a generally unfavorable reaction to game? A field trial or shooting dog habitually dropping on point does not fill the competitive picture. The practice becomes tiresome, and such dogs are hard to find in anything like tight cover.

In earlier days some of the best sportsmen broke their dogs to drop on point. My father and his friends used dogs that struck and stood their birds magnificently. Depending upon the terrain, and at caution, they sank into taut crouches, and there they quivered until the handler clucked them into a deliberate flush. At wing and shot they dropped again, and remained prone until ordered to fetch. I frequently gun with John Bailey of Coffeeville, Mississippi. His pointer bitch, Old Miss, known as "Queen," has magnificent range, nose, steadiness, and pointing fire. But she has learned, when striking scent at the edge of some impenetrable thicket or precipitous, thorn-shrubbed gully, to quietly drop and await John's size-up of the situation. Instead of tearing through a thicket or, completely off balance, sliding downhill into the middle of a bevy, John wagers on his own knowledge of the wind and quail habits. He whistles sharply to Queen after he has taken post and she is up and off like a shot. Eight times out of ten, John's guess, plus confidence in his bitch's powers of quick and accurate relocation, gains more open shots and brings to bag bobwhites at which we might otherwise not have had a go. True, the bitch could have stood there beautifully while we tore around trying to move her bevy. It resolves into Queen's having learned to drop and rest, while her boss takes over. If anything goes wrong, she knows that she will not be blamed. I have watched her craftily relocate outside the wind, before coming in closer to herd the bobs our way like a sheep dog moving its charges into a fold.

Is the dropping instinct allied to the cat's when stalking prey? Or an innate impulse that makes any well-broken retriever crouch behind or alongside its master when the latter crawls up on a bunch of ducks? Or are the bird dog's olfactory passages sometimes so suddenly smothered with overpowering bird scent as to compel effort to keep from getting too close to game and avoid fault and correction?

You have undoubtedly watched a bird dog running at full speed strike scent, skid and all but roll over in a desperate effort not to flush? After such a thrilling and beautiful exhibition in your behalf, don't forget to reward your companion with a caress. That is one of quail shooting's most exquisite moments.

Field trial dogs are often described as poor shooting dogs. I cannot remember any really great field trial dog or National Field Trial Champion that was not a first-class gunning companion. But there is a vast difference between hunting mounted and afoot. As at field trials, when just "out hunting," bird dogs are faulted for factors beyond their control. In field trials or the shooting field, wind, weather, cover, and above all, movement of a bevy ahead of the dogs, may combine to put even the craftiest animals wrong for the moment. The gunner should have full knowledge of the habits and probable reactions under dog-pressure of the gamebird species. In other words, under any and all conditions, what the birds themselves are liable to do.

You see dropping on point when dogs intelligent enough to play the wind work Huns and prairie chickens in Canada. Shooting up there has given me opportunities to study such happenings and reactions. It is interesting to observe behaviors among animals broken on such game and those contacting the species for the first time. Edgar Queeny's magnificent setter, Wingmead Billy, handled both species flawlessly the first time he ever scented them. But his bracemate, a rugged pointer named Major, equally wide and fast and as perfectly broken on bobwhites of the South, could never adjust himself to Huns or prairie chickens unless he caught scent where he couldn't see the birds themselves. When that happened we had no trouble, and Major was a picture. But when he saw ground game in low cover, he couldn't take it. First dropping, he then took them out to the horizon. Returning abjectly apologetic, he struggled desperately to make amends.

When you lose your dog and find it dropped on point, think it over before becoming vexed at what some may call a bad habit. You manage to score a double from the ensuing flush, and proceed somewhat mollified after your hunt for old Dell. Suppose, however, old Dell hadn't managed to stop and flop when he hit that bevy scent? You'd have charged him with a flush and certainly not have managed your successful right-and-left. With a split second of nose-warning, however, old Dell dropped—and saved you the shot.

What is the quail odor bird dogs scent? Their "nose power," comparatively, matches "eye power" in hawks. Some authorities describe game-bird scent as carried off particles dropping from feathers to feet and to the ground. Air currents along the ground act as conveyors. The old-timers differentiated between "foot scent" and "body scent." A strong-running bird dog whips into a blazing point! Has it caught foot or body scent? Some dogs run with low heads. Such animals are thought to run, for the most part, on foot scent. Are the odors the same, just "blown" differently?

Surely you have dressed many a bobwhite? Or regretfully picked them up in the field so badly shot-up or dog-mangled as to expose pulped entrails and organs? If so, you must know the cloying, sweetishly acrid, and not overly offensive ordor—a blend of decomposing grains or seeds in the bird's digestive and excretive canals. Observant hunters often detect the near-abouts of a bobwhite bevy by fresh droppings of telltale white pellet-smears.

Does the high-headed dog that "points its game a long way off" strike scent off these comparatively fresh droppings? Is their fume more rank than the "body particles" shed from feathers to feet and ground? Does the dog get the same odor as the one we do in dressing birds? If so, how does the high-headed dog handle foot scent with equal alacrity and facility?

How does it apply to scattered birds? Should the gunner mark them and put the dogs on them at once? Most gunners do, and on moist ground, singles are ofttimes found promptly enough. But many hunters come from the hills declaring, "We just couldn't find any single birds." Aside from unconditioned, tired dogs, with their noses clogged by sinus-affecting seed and grass fuzz, outside factors intervene. Dog reactions vary amazingly. The best of "nose-confident" dogs occasionally flush singles and stop in utter bewilderment. With inexperienced owners along, much cussing ensues. Those singles may, or may not, have moved a foot after they lit. Have you watched a flushed quail sail by and pitch close by? You saw what happened? It either ran or hunkered down to actually pant with fright.

We are still in the dark as to scenting conditions, air currents, and their actions in relaying odors of all sorts. Can we explain why otherwise perfect retrievers pass within a foot of a quail lying flat on its back, dead as a hammer, and never sniff it? Unless it just happened to see the bird, or you pointed it out, the dog finally abandoned the search. Yet five minutes later, under different surroundings, the same dog effected a difficult fetch, with ease.

How often have your dogs struck apparently red-hot scent, tried desperately to locate—but failed? What happened? Did some person or predator flush the feeding or moving bevy? How many times, late of an afternoon, have your dogs trailed or roaded for a quarter mile, only to stand puzzled at no further trace of the bobs? Chances are those fellows simply ran awhile and then flew to a favored roosting ground.

Next time your dog drops on point, put your own powers of dog, bird, and scent analysis to work. You may get badly tricked. Your dog's nose warned it to stop, at all costs, and it did—by dropping.

Beyond a dog's deliberately flushing or chewing up birds, I find no fault when a staunch, hard-working animal drops, trails, roads, low-heads, or even barks on point. When really out hunting I enjoy watching them all work out their immediate problems in their own ways and to the best of their respective abilities. With shells in my tubes, I am neither purist nor carping critic. When a brave and companionable bird dog does the best it knows how, to afford me pleasure, who am I not to accept its offerings other than with sincere appreciation? So try, next time you're afield, to see what *really* happens.

Not Unsung

Like many of Mr. Buck's things, "Not Unsung" came out first in Field & Stream, *this one in the December 1942 issue. It was later included in* Tattered Coat *in 1944. It embraces Labrador and Chesapeake retrievers, a springer spaniel, and English setters.*

That most of the dogs Nash writes about are "perfect" dogs might be explained by his instinct to write only of outstanding individuals. Viewing it realistically as a gun dog fancier of more than normally exacting taste, I'm inclined to doubt the existence of that many perfect dogs. Some of the idiosyncrasies that made certain dogs special, such as rushing promptly to the fallen bird (in some circles called "breaking at shot"), implies that the way to have "perfect" dogs is to accept quirks as qualities. Which actually can often make us closer to our dogs, if not closer to perfection.

Of all his dogs, Chub was probably the most intimate member of Nash's family —one reason for the close rapport between the two.

The Dick Bishop mentioned in the shoot with Edgar Queeny's Labrador, Grouse of Arden, was Richard E. Bishop, the etcher (Bishop's Birds), and a friend of Nash's. Writing me about the 1941 Saskatchewan trip—"We had a grand time up there"—Bob Stoner explained that " 'Nuck" was colonel Enoch Brown of the Memphis Publishing Company.

Nash's story of the Lab at the Arden trial brings back occasions when I've watched my setters, unseen by them, as they handled birds. Dogs seem to work exceptionally well when they think they are entirely on their own, which possibly accounts for a pointing dog's sometimes holding birds best when pointing far ahead of the gun.

Nash's description of the small graveyard in the immense Canadian prairie, where Becky Broom Hill, 1922, 1923 and 1925 National Champion, and McTyre, 1927 National Champion, sleep away the years, was brought to mind when I came across a photograph of the graves. What appears to be a granite border supporting nine sturdy granite uprights connected with a heavy chain encloses a massive marker for each of those grand pointers. Bankers have been buried under less.

DEEP IN EVERY sportsman's heart is the love for some intelligent, intrepid animal. From the experience of fifty years of field and waterfowl gunning, I have worked and judged a great many top champions and competitors among bird dogs and retriever breeds. In the old days I have shot live-pigeon matches with such field trial champions as Powhatan and Ticonderoga retrieving for us. I have watched setters and pointers swim rivers and claw out of dangerously deep ravines, bird in mouth. I particularly recall my great old Chesapeakes, Baltimore and Pat o'Gaul. When I think of ensuing decades, I doff my hunter's headpiece to many another exhibition of dog initiative and accomplishment, such as the heroism of Henry Bartholomew's Fritz and Pat, whose exploits amid the Potomac's waves and razor-edged ice floes are still recalled around Broad and Swan Creeks.

On a rug near my desk lies a sturdy, ten-year-old English springer spaniel, dear to me for his stout heart, faith in me, and an absorbing devotion to the gun. He minds my whistle and "hups" according to the rule book. But he also knows that it is strictly all right with me if he breaks shot when we are hunting in rough country. We lose too much game otherwise. That statement will bring "non-slip" purists about my ears but the perfect gun dog is the animal that understands its master's wishes.

Chub knows what I expect of him under any conditions. If a "sneak and crawl" is necessary, he is a master at it. Ordinarily, out dove shooting or where he figures we have a situation well in hand, he sits quietly beside me. But if we are on the move in high corn or flushing from matted cover, Chub breaks at gun-crack and is there if and when the game hits the ground.

The most memorable of Chub's retrieving performances came when he was a rough, hard-headed puppy of ten months. His initial yard and water work were well advanced; so I took him with me on a goose and duck shooting venture along a Mississippi River sand bar. This was encircled on the land side by a series of shallow ponds amid the willows and cottonwoods. We had a tiny shack hid out in that wilderness, fitted with comfortable bunks and a combination cooking and heating stove.

That morning a skim of ice glazed the long, narrow potholes. Chub and I sat down by one with a sliver of open water down its channel. A light breeze filtered through from left to right, and just after legal shooting hour a bunch of mallards swung past us downwind. Letting them pass unmolested, I sounded a low hail with my duck call and cautioned the quivering Chub. The big birds caught the summons, banked, and beat up wind, looking for what they had heard.

The pair I downed fell well across the hundred-foot water gut and on to dry land near tall, weatherbeaten willows. Chub was off, smashing through slush ice and fighting soft mud. Disappearing in the mutton cane, he emerged with his first find and battled his way back. After handing me the drake, he recast and soon presented me with our second prize.

For more than an hour that puppy worked boldly and untiringly. It would have been a superb job of retrieving for an older dog. During waits he sat beneath my sheep-lined coat, only to be off, eager-eyed, with the crack of my gun. When it was all over, I washed the blue mud from his coat and rubbed him dry. At the shack I cooked him up a bigger bait of ham and eggs than I consumed, with some sugared biscuits thrown in, and put him to snooze on my bed.

That afternoon we walked to the sand bar's end and sat down behind a rooty drift. We needed pre-supper exercise, and river sunsets are always glorious. Suddenly a gaggle of geese swung silently over the bar's rim, and I knocked one of them out of line. It tumbled fifty feet offshore and was swept downstream before I could walk halfway to it. It is easy, under such circumstances, to step off over some deep and hidden reef.

Past me swam little Chub. Outstripping the honker, he got a good hold and shoved his heavy burden ashore down the beach. Was I proud of him? Enough so to stoop down and give the fellow a tight hug.

One of the most interesting afternoons I have ever spent behind a retriever was during November 1939, in a newly flooded pin-oak flat along Bayou Lagrue on the estate of Edgar M. Queeny, north of Stuttgart, Arkansas. Edgar, Dick Bishop, and I, with Grouse of Arden, Edgar's magnificent black Labrador, were exploring new territory for some high timber shooting. Our canoes raised hundreds of mallards as we slipped along the bayou, spilling over its banks in spots.

After finally going ashore, we waded through ankle-deep water to a long, narrow ridge that ended against a canebrake. Jess Wilson and Foy Dinsmore unlimbered their duck calls, and it soon became evident that great sport was in prospect. Grouse had comparatively little to do until, after a particularly lively volley, three cripples sailed through the timber beyond the canebrake and disappeared. They must have hit water in the flat woods down the bayou. Dick and Edgar attempted to wade around the canebrake, but a deep slough threatened their boot tops.

I was using breast-high waders, however, and after some delicate stepping I made it across the "dreen" and into a far-flung fairyland of shallow water stretching away beneath low-hanging, sun-tinted foliage. Grouse swam across the deep chute, waited for me to land, and then, with a look that said "I'll be seeing you again," took off at a run through the backwater. Quartering against the breeze to catch the scent, the big black dog swung a half circle.

I sat down on a chunk to watch the proceedings. After a bit I heard a fluttering down the line of the canebrake, and here came Grouse with a winged greenhead in his jaws. Handing it over, he whirled and struck a left oblique across the woods. I could hear him splashing a long way off, but he was lost to sight. Then he fetched in a dead hen mallard. I had no direction to give him, and he didn't wait for orders. He was gone fully fifteen minutes that last cast, but returned with a badly crippled drake. Handing it to me gently, his eyes seemed to say, "That's gettin' 'em, ain't it?"

We rested a few moments while I gave him a taste of chocolate candy. Then we rejoined Edgar and Dick. It is well to inscribe such feats as that upon the pages of sporting lore.

There's another black Labrador I'll always remember. I was acting as an official gun at the Labrador Club of America's trials at Arden, New York in November, 1939. Narrowed to a small field by the last day, the dogs and judges and guns faced a bitter, low-ceilinged afternoon that drove alternate snow and rain across the mountain lake selected for final water work.

Roland Harriman, on whose estate the trials were held, and I shot from a huge, slanting rock some two hundred yards down the lake from the blind. As each two birds were dropped, some dogs swam to fetch, while others raced around the shoreline for a shortcut before hitting the water. It was getting late, and the fury of the elements increased.

We shot two ducks that fell farther out than usual. The Labrador whose turn it was ran around the land side, plunged in, swam swiftly to the first kill, and returned it to the blind. Then he returned and took up the quest for his second bird. Meanwhile the wind had blown his quarry in under the ledge of the rock beyond which Roland and I stood at the edge of the woods.

The Labrador swam around out in the darkening lake for several minutes, peering vainly for his duck. Then he swam to the rock and crawled ashore. Climbing to the rock's crest, he surveyed what lay beyond and spotted a keeper's boat tied in a lagoon behind us. Pricking up his ears, the dog trotted down to the boat, hopped in, and sniffed from bow to stern. In the stern, under a seat, he came upon a pair of dead mallards which the guide had retrieved and put there an hour or more ago.

Unseen, Roland and I watched the expression of bewilderment that came over the animal's face. Then he picked up one of the ducks and made his way over the rock's crest and down to the water's edge. Just as he was in the act of re-entering the lake, he came upon the duck that floated in against the ledge. He put down the bird he had found and taken from the keeper's boat and stood for an instant, lost in thought. Then, picking up the correct bird, he dashed across the rock, leaped over a fallen log to the shore, and raced to the blind.

The judges could not possibly have seen what transpired. But Roland Harriman and I watched the whole proceeding almost in awe. We could not, of course, mention what we had witnessed until after the awards were made. That dog was, as I recall it, placed third, possibly because he had been slow on his last find. Knowing what I knew, I certainly would have placed him first. That Labrador had a head and he used it.

There was something in that retrieve which was reminiscent of what I saw my greatest Chesapeake Bay retriever, Pat o' Gaul, do once in the high timber around our old Lakeside Club down in Arkansas. Pat and I stood at the edge of the woods along the open water. I took a long shot at a hen pintail that flashed past. I thought she flinched, but she kept on, circling far below us and curving back up lake over the timber. I noticed that Pat kept his keen yellow eyes on the duck for a longer time than usual; in fact, he wheeled around and stood staring after her for quite a while.

We shot there for an hour or more, then picked up and started to wade to our boat. But Pat, without so much as a "by-your-leave," bounced away inland and was lost to sight and sound. I waited at the boat and whistled and called a long time before he showed up. When he did, he had that same hen pintail, dead, in his mouth.

On Saskatchewan's wheat stubble and prairies, Edgar and 'Nuck and I discovered what our dogs, pointer Major and setter Billy, would do on chickens and Huns around the bluffs. Neither animal was experienced on such game, but thoroughly broken on quail. Billy, scion of the best in setter bloodlines, went wide and handsome, handling his birds intelligently and intensively. He caught scent a long way off and gave us opportunities at long rises that would have been longer otherwise. He worked the bluffs to windward first, circled them, and worked game cover entirely new to him as though he had been raised in it.

Major, on the other hand, never quite figured the thing out. If he scented in low cover, where he could sight the Huns or prairie chickens, Major flash-pointed, then crept forward until the birds flushed—and chased. But if he found them in high cover, Major proceeded just as the rule book said. After he had chased a chicken to the horizon, Major returned and offered his apologies.

We were shooting near Gainsborough, Saskatchewan. T. W. Jones of Corinth, Mississippi, who owns and operates his Canadian kennels for shooting and field trial dogs near Pierson, Manitoba, loaned 'Nuck and me a liver and tan-ticked setter named Dan to replace a dog of ours who had sore feet. Dan turned out to be one of the most remarkable animals I have known. The first morning I had him out we worked the meadows along a winding creek, and the way he retrieved ducks from land or water made me open my eyes. But on Huns and prairie chickens the dog became a revelation. He was coming nine years of age, so his range had become somewhat shortened. But he was plenty wide for the country, and his stamina and courage were enormous.

With swinging lope, Dan ate up the open spaces, checkerboarding them with due craft of wind and nose. Striking scent, he whipped into fine, up-standing pointing postures, and, so help me, he had a way of looking around as we approached, as though he wanted to make sure that all was in readiness and our positions satisfactory.

Many times I walked in very close to watch his crafty stalk of birds that had run or fed off ahead of him. There was invariably the catlike stalk, a sort of shoving here and circling snakelike there, that eventually broke the rise from the most favorable vantage point to the guns. When the smoke cleared away, Dan, who had stood there like a hitching post, got down to the finest part of his act—retrieving.

From one bluff 'Nuck Brown and I raised a lot of game, Huns and chickens all mixed up together and flushing from every direction. 'Nuck fired at birds ahead of him, and I took care of flarebacks over the treetops. The ones we downed fell in the clear—out among the wheat stocks. We had seven on the ground, and Dan finally accounted for six of them. Then we moved to another bluff, and after giving it a going-over 'Nuck and I returned by the bluff where the seven birds had fallen. Dan, remembering perfectly, looked around a bit and brought in the seventh bird.

Another afternoon 'Nuck and I were tramping a well-bluffed wheat stubble. Suddenly, from over a rise ahead of me, sailed a prairie chicken, probably flushed some distance away by the incautious Major. Away it flew, under a full head of steam, and about four feet above the prairie. I swung in behind the bird, took six of its own lengths in forward allowance, and cut loose an ounce and a quarter of chilled sevens from my big duck gun. But nothing happened. A bit puzzled, I would have sworn I had landed some lethal pellets in that bird.

All at once that chicken's flight took a swift, and then swifter, upcurve. Higher and higher until, three hundred yards away, it crashed from fifty feet above the dead trees of a bluff. I even heard the crash as the heavy bird plummeted through the interlacing boughs.

About that time Dan hove in sight, and I gave him the direction. I watched him deliberately get the wind on the bluff and start circling it. Then he disappeared. A few moments later he broke from that bluff with my bird, stone-dead and head shot, in his tender jaws. I had never moved from where I had fired.

Dan hadn't seen the chicken, hadn't seen me shoot. He simply took direction perfectly, used his fine brains and experience. He stood there for a few moments while I patted and stroked his grand old head.

We came, Dan and I, one bright forenoon, to a prairie meadow lush with bluegrass through which ran a typical wheatland creek—a mere rill in places, but broadening now and then into pools through which a lagging current rustled tall reeds. Here and there it was overgrown, or ran between high, weedy banks. Hunting parallel to this branch, I thought I saw a teal flutter above the stalks and relight. Without slowing Dan's range out along the edge of some wheat stocks, I walked quickly toward the creek. Thirty yards from it, through a break in the foliage, I saw that my supposed teal was a little blue heron. Another step, and the fellow took off with a croak. The next instant that waterway spouted ducks.

I bowled over two mallards and concentrated sufficiently to shove in a third shell and shoot at a lingering gadwall. All three ducks fell beyond the creek. Dan came on the gallop, took my directional wave at a glance, and swam the pool. Returning me a duck, he repeated the operation twice more, taking direction on each bird with almost human understanding. Never have I seen that retrieving job surpassed. Almost instantly, Dan sensed the fact that the upland quest had been turned into a duck hunt. Coming to heel, he worked the stream bends with an understanding equaling my own.

His crowning feat, however, came on our last day afield. Driving along that afternoon after a grand day's sport, we flushed a magnificent covey of Huns from the roadside. They settled around a clump of sparse buffalo willows in a deeply grassed pasture. 'Nuck and I left Bob Stoner and the dogs in the station wagon and tramped after the birds. They couldn't have risen better for the guns. Two to the left were downed, and another pair, escaping to the right, fell to my gun. I heard 'Nuck shoot twice, and he reported bowling over two with one shot. That made six Huns scattered over a space covering seventy-five yards of deep, dense cover.

We searched for fully five minutes without success. Bob Stoner, sensing our trouble, brought old Dan over on leash, and the fellow went to it. Starting at or near the point where my two birds fell, Dan crisscrossed the nearly waist-high grass with a probing nose. Down the line he went until five birds were sacked. But the sixth gave him a bit of trouble. Finally, he darted off into the meadow, whipped into a classic point and then dived headlong as a crippled Hun attempted to take off. Dan presented that bird to Bob with a look on his face which said as plainly as words, "What do you know about that guy's trying to put one over on the old boy?"

'Nuck and I said good-by to old Dan the last night we were in Saskatchewan. We dined that evening at the summer training camp of Mr. and Mrs. Chesley Harris, with T. W. Jones and his wife along to swell the festivities. Bob Stoner brought old Dan along from our last day's hunt to turn him back to T. W. There was one complex in Dan's make-up that needed explanation: he would positively not enter an automobile of his own volition. Once helped inside, however, he was perfectly happy and well behaved. T. W. said that, when a puppy, Dan had been hit and hurt by an automobile. The memory stuck, and he was as positive in that diagnosis as he was in his sensible way of handling and retrieving game.

The last time I saw Dan was after we fed him a feast of tender beef stew. Then Bob placed him gently in T. W.'s dog truck, and Dan, with a tired smile, sank into his hay bed. I wish him peace and rest for a life's work well done.

Out on the prairie, close to Chesley Harris' camp, is a tiny, beautifully planted graveyard. The chain-enclosed resting place is blanketed with petunias and roses. Up to it grows the wild plant life of those vast Canadian reaches. Beneath the flowers and pure marble grave covers sleep Becky Broom Hill, three times National Field Trial Champion, and McTyre, winner of not only the National title but championships on every species of American upland game.

'Nuck and Ches and I stood there in the chill, deepening twilight, looking down at their graves and thinking of the many times we had watched those champions in action, vibrant with life and courage and at the very peak of their magnificent careers. Turning away, Ches said, "I've told Mrs. Harris that if I die down home in old Alabama, why, bury me there; but if I happen to pass on while I'm up here on the prairies, to just put me here alongside these two. For that matter, I guess there's a part of me already there."

Maybe similar sentiment prompts my writing about Chub and Grouse and Billy and Major and Dan. Let's sit in our dens and clubs with our dogs and spin yarns about them and their deeds. For in every sportsman's heart there should be some gun dog whose deeds are not unsung.

The Great Reprisal

This is my favorite of Nash's four Milton Throcker stories, a select little group that also includes "The Brownie Company Ltd." (Field & Stream, October 1941, and Tattered Coat), "Lady" (Field & Stream, December 1946, and Hallowed Years), "When Time Who Steals Our Years Away" (The American Field, December 6, 1952, and Hallowed Years and the Nelson De Shootin'est Gent'man and Other Hunting Tales).

It is a mistake to assume that any of Nash Buckingham's characters is wholly fictitious, as I had thought Milton Throcker was. It was a pleasant surprise to learn from Berry Brooks that Milton Throcker had, after a fashion, been real.

"Milton Throcker's real name," Berry said, "was Milton Blocker. He was about Nash's age and lived in Byhalia, Mississippi, about thirty miles from Memphis, between Olive Branch and Holly Springs. Milt was mayor there for many years and bought cotton for Ramsay, Austin Cotton Co. He died about 1962. I had lunch with him and Nash many times at the Cotton Exchange Cafe. He was a rapid-fire talker, an excellent quail shot and handler of bird dogs, as well as a trainer. The stories he told were basically true."

If Milton Throcker had been a real person, there was hope that Doug Stamper's "Mermaid Tavern" existed. In answer to my query, Bob Anderson said: "The Cotton Exchange Cafe, Doug Stamper, Prop. was the 'Mermaid Tavern'—an invention of Nash and Paul Flowers." Berry Brooks wrote:

> The "Mermaid Tavern" was really the Cotton Exchange Cafe, located on the ground floor of 84 South Front Street, Memphis, and owned and operated by Doug Stamper, who died January 20, 1970. Several months later it was reopened by Doug's son, Gordon, and is still in operation. Doug's old chef Mingo died about two years before Doug did. For over 40 years Nash and I had breakfast together there during the cotton season. Nash would get up at 5:30 a.m., catch the 6:00 a.m. bus from home, getting off at the Post Office, then walking two blocks to the Cotton Exchange Cafe, where I would be, most of the time, already eating.

I have one further question in my mind: why "Mermaid Tavern"? It is a question I have no intention asking because I do not care to be disillusioned. Instead,

I prefer to imagine that there hangs, above a massive, smoky barlike counter, a lush painting of a reclining mermaid—a warm, rosy mermaid with all those endowments a mermaid has, and with flowing tresses sportingly arranged not to obscure the view (I was never quite certain how far up, or how far down, the scales began)—upon which tired cotton brokers may fasten contemplative wistful eyes and escape, momentarily, the stresses of futures and declining markets—even bird dog deals.

Milton Throcker had, according to Nash's stories, qualities it would pay to keep alert for in a dog trade. It was with interest that I discovered some time after reading "The Great Reprisal" that Nash had, in 1903, bought his "first $50 dog" from Milton Blocker—"a gaunt white-and-lemon setter named Jack." I can't help wondering if he ever changed his lemon spots.

I N DOUG STAMPER's famous Cotton Exchange Restaurant you can tell which way cotton and stock markets are headed. If they are booming, conversation buzzes and there are plenty of laughs. But if they're aboard the toboggan, the boys are hunched silently over their coffees and Cokes like wet chickens huddled out of an all-day rain. It takes upping markets, biting fish or a heavy flight of ducks and geese to make Doug's place sound like a peaceful beehive gone berserk.

Many a Memphis cotton merchant in the dumps forgets his troubles on hearing that bass are hitting popping bugs in Stud Horse Bay. Just as soon as he can lie to his wife, pack some lunch, and grab his tackle box and rod case, he is gone from there right now.

Occasionally, in Doug's chophouse, a stiff cotton deal gets crabbed by some unintentional meddle of shooting or fishing business. It isn't Doug's fault; his customers bring it on themselves. Just when some dealer is fixing to turn over a fat consignment, some fellow barges over to the table and blurts out a wild-eyed story about Tommy Bradley and George Blagden catching two limits of big bass yesterday afternoon in that cove in behind Midway Chute.

Right away the cotton trade blows higher than a cat's back. Next thing the seller knows, his precious buyer is chasing off for his outboard motor and ice jug. His only recourse then is to horn in on the trip himself in order to keep the trade alive.

From Stamper's restaurant to the corner of the Cotton Exchange Building there is a sort of curb market for seasonal piscatorial or shooting dope, called "Fish Information, Please." There has been a lot of talk about employing a full-time executive secretary to analyze and classify the mass of hunting and angling dope accumulating every day. You have to be especially careful about quail- and duck-shooting rumors—to say nothing of bird-dog trades, if you are in the market for a dog. You should always deal with an honest and experienced bird-dog merchant like my old friend, Milton Throcker.

The weather was cool enough to work pointers and setters early of mornings or in the cool of the evening. But the cover was still too green and high to tell anything about the upcoming quail crop, except that, from their size now, many would still be too immature to gun even when the bird season opened.

Well, I was lunching in Doug Stamper's as usual. Imminence of frost-fall called for grub that sticks to one's ribs. There I sat with Leo Carter and Leroy Cooper, and my dough is on Leo to trim and stack his cord of barbecued spareribs before Roy's drive on the corned beef and cabbage gains ground. I was still wondering why guys stall off putting their bird dogs in trim before the hunting season. They come home empty-bagged and bellyaching about how their dogs played out or couldn't smell the birds. They never blame themselves.

That's why I was glad to see old Milton Throcker. Among other celebrities frequenting Stamper's, Milt is the greatest bird-dog salesman of all time. When Milt goes all out on a bird-dog sale, you glow at his oratory and realize the fearlessness of the truths he utters. He puts his merchandise right out on the counter before your very eyes. Milt should have been in the national headlines thirty years ago.

True, he was at his peak, you might say, in the old days when quail were really plentiful and classy bird dogs a dime a dozen. That's what makes his greatness as a modern bird-dog salesman all the more remarkable. Even on a declining market he has kept his art in shape through all these years. The only difference I can detect is a more mellow deftness in his handling of approach and build-up details.

After all, however, you must pay good money to deal with true art or artists, and Milt is no exception. For instance, I'll back him to peddle some snipe-nosed egg-buster with a fat, meaty tail, sight unseen, to any nationally recognized bird-dog authority. Milt would sell him while laced into a straitjacket, and in a nice, easy way, too.

Milton Throcker is the fellow who, some years ago, organized his great shooting dog, Brownie, into a five-man stock company and lived to see his shareholders satisfied with their sport dividends and each unaware he wasn't the sole owner of said Brownie. Why, even Washington heard about that piece of high financing and put out feelers trying to lure Milt down there, but Milt sent F.D.R. word through his Congressman to tell Morgenthau he wasn't interested and to quit writing any more letters to him.

Anyway, Milt knows bird-dog conditioning by heart. In summer his own animals herd the stock to pasture night and morning and follow Milt's horse around the plantation. And he just doesn't believe you can keep a bird dog in fettle on a diet of dishwater and persimmons.

Milt sort of hesitated before putting in his order for lunch. But he finally got himself in hand and ordered a dozen Bayou Cocque oysters. He also sent word to the chef to include three strips of crisp sow-belly. "There ain't no oyster, livin' nur daid," claims Milt, "that ain't improved by a touch o' po'k in some form ur nuther. Not a floatin' aroun' in no grease," explains Milt, "but jes' enough o' the hawg along to tie the bivalve in with a po'k escort and thus complete the gustatory illusion of impeded slipperiness."

All of a sudden Milt turned on me and said, "I finally got even with that fellow."

I hadn't the faintest idea what fellow he was talking about, but I knew it must have something to do with a bird-dog deal: so I asked, "What fellow?"

While Roy and Leo, figuring something was in the wind, ordered dessert and settled down to listen, Milt launched his tale.

"I get acquainted with an elderly gentleman, a doctor named Samples, down in the Randolph Buildin'. He tells me he's got a 2,400-acre farm over in Arkansas and would like to sell it if he could git his price. Sounds like a high-class property to hear him tell it, and, as I buy a lot of cotton all through the same county his place is in, I ease by and take a peep at it. Fine black sandy loam, good home place and fences, and bang-up tenant houses.

"The old doctor says he'll pay full commission on the sale, and that would mean a fat pick-up for me. So do I do some broadcasting! One night I'm out on a party when I meet up with a nice young chap named Pettigrew. We get to talkin' quail huntin' and dawgs. He claims he's got one o' the best young pointers in captivity, and I tell him maybe so, but in such case he is only in a tie with my dawg. You know what I think o' my Tarrant dawg! We arrange a bird hunt down in Mississippi and, sho' nuff, Pettigrew's got a real high-steppin' pottige hound—an upstandin' young pointer—and he give Tarrant a hard race. His dawg is registered, same as Tarrant."

There was no use in asking the Pettigrew dog's breeding—Milt wouldn't know. But if it had been a dog he had for sale and you asked its pedigree, he would have answered right off the bat: "Alpine Lad, or Tribulation stock." All Milt's for-sale dogs stem from those two common ancestors. Milt just doesn't know or use any other sires or forebears. Alpine Lad and Trib are good enough for him.

"Well," he rattled on, "I get to likin' this young Pettigrew, and befo' long he mentions he's picked up a thick batch of coarse bank notes playin' the stock market and would invest it in a plantation if he could find the right place cheap. He also wants to start a field trial string of pointers. So, quick as a flash, I tip him off to the farm ol' Doc Samples owns over in Arkansas. I describe it fully and he smiles and says it sounds jes' like the outfit he has in mind and says he'll go look it over with me.

"I know a feller not far from there who has a lot of quail on his place; so I suggest to Pettigrew that we take his dog and Tarrant along and hunt when we've finished inspectin' the Samples land. He seems mighty pleased with the farm and asks the price. I tell him Doc wants seventy-five bucks an acre on a walkout basis. I suggest stoppin' at the farm commissary to get some crackers and cheese for lunch, but he prefers drivin' on to a small town and eatin' in a restaurant.

"That afternoon we each bagged a limit of quail on my friend's place, and my dawg Tarrant had another hard time barely shadin' Pettigrew's young pointer. I told him his dawg would be hard to beat another season. He says he wouldn't take five hundred dollars for Snap right now. I says I don't blame you, nur me neither."

Milt pinned a sliver of crisp side-meat to half an oyster and munched reflectively. I'd like to see Milt with five hundred bucks laid on the keghead for any dog—Tarrant included.

"I'd taken a likin' to Pettigrew; so in order to hurry up the deal I tell him Doc is payin' me a commission and if it'll help any I'll split it with him. He seems most appreciative; so next week we make another hunt with a friend o' mine in the next county. I ride him around the Samples place agin and buy him a two-dollar sirloin and trimmin's when we git home that night. That dawg o' his improves ev'y time we hunt him, and I'm beginnin' to wonder jus' how big a price he would fetch.

"We made several mo' hunts, and Pettigrew looked over the Samples place right along. Ask me didn't I think it could be bought cheaper. I tol' him there warn't but one way to find that out: to hand the ol' Doc a signed firm offer and see what he'd do.

"One night me and Pettigrew was settin' over a pair of three-buck sirloins in the Four Star Inn when all of a sudden he says: 'Milt, you sho' have been nice tryin' to sell me the Samples place and givin' me all this fine bird shootin'. But,' he says, 'it's such a good one on you that I ain't had the nerve to break the sad news.' 'How is that?' I ask, thinkin', of course, that he was fixin' to kid me 'bout my beatin' him shootin' all the time.''

Roy and Leo sat there stirring their javas and waiting for the blow-off.

" 'Well,' says Pettigrew, sort of drawin' a long breath, 'you see, when you offered me the Samples property, I jes' didn't have the face to tell you that ol' Doc Samples is my stepfather and that he has left me and Mamma the Criss-Cross plantation in his will—or its equivalent if he sells it. You've been tryin' to sell me my own farm, much less the commission you was willin' to split. But I figured you'd appreciate the joke as much as I have and because we've sho' had some fine shootin' over Snap and Tarrant.'

"I damn near choked on the piece of steak in my mouth, and calculated jes' what his joke had cost me in time and gas and oil and all the good dough I'd spent entertainin' him. And worse still, every time we went huntin', I'd give him all the birds, too.'' Milt all but wept at the memory.

"But it warn't no good gittin' mad, because I sort of suspected that if ever the time come when he got unlucky in the stock market, they might have to peddle the farm anyhow. So, I laughed long and loud right on with him. I says to myself, I says: 'Some day, brother, you will pay me off big for such doin's.'

"I seen Pettigrew a lot last summer and always asked him about his dawg Snap and the Samples farm. He said it damn near tickled ol' Doc Samples to death how I'd tried to sell the place to its owner. But deep down it sure rankled with me. I could see Pettigrew settin' there chewin' on them tender three-buck steaks and hollerin' for the waiter to move fast with more cold suds.''

Having finished his grub, but not his tale, Milt put in an order for a cut of sweet-potato pie and black coffee.

"Last fall, when bird season opened, me and Bill Robinson made a hunt down in DeSoto County, Mississippi. My ol' Tarrant dog sho' put on a race that day—they couldn't no dawg of beaten him. Whilst we were drivin' home that evenin' I was sayin' to Billy that I hadn't never seen but one dog in my life I thought could hold a candle to Tarrant excep' the Snap dawg belongin' to young Pettigrew.

"Well, sir, we was comin' along a narrow dirt road this side of a little pea-peck town called Punk Point, and there was another car runnin' 'bout a hundred yards ahead of us. All of a sudden we seen what looked like a bird dawg jump from the weeds 'longside the road and land almost in front of the other car's lights. The driver swerved, but the fender hit the dawg kind o' sideways and throwed it back over the tops o' the bushes.

"It was all done quick as a flash. The driver figgered he'd done killed somebody's dawg; so he stepped on the gas plenty. Billy and me stopped, got out and went down in a shallow ditch. There laid the po' dawg, breathin' heavy, but alive and slowly comin' to. Billy brought his huntin' cap full o' water, and we bathed the dawg's face and a slight cut on his back left leg. There warn't no bones busted, but the dawg's tail was, and that's mighty painful.

"I turned my flashlight on the dawg's collar, and, bless goodness, if the name-plate don't read 'C. T. Pettigrew, Memphis, Tenn.' Then I did look sharp and, by golly ding, if it warn't Snap! I called him by name and petted him, and befo' long he was on his feet. Suddenly I realized that here was my chance to git even with Pettigrew. I never opened my head to Billy, 'cause I know he was expectin' me to go fifty-fifty with him on the dawg if he turned out any good. We put Snap in the car and hustled him to the best veterinary in town. He says Snap's tail is broke so bad he'll have to ampertate. That fitted right into my plans for the future."

Milt stoked a generous paring of sweet-potato pie and smacked his lips.

"After I got the Snap dawg out o' the hospital I'm sure he remembered me and Tarrant from the previous huntin' season. Course, I took Pettigrew's collar off Snap the night me and Billy seen him knocked in the ditch. After thinkin' it all over, I decided to put Bill Robinson wise to the whole business. When Snap's tail healed up and he was ready to run, I took him on down to my plantation and begin huntin' him reg'lar with Tarrant. But I knew I'd have to change him up still mo' than that busted-off tail so Pettigrew wouldn't know him.

"I tried some drug-store dye on his hair in spots, but I couldn't quite match the shade—a deep liver—and when it rained or Snap swum a creek the color sort o' run. Finally I asked our ol' cook, Aunt Sally, if she knowed any yarb-doctor could turn out fast dyes along with his charms and jackballs. She says: 'Dey's an ol' man down in de Pigeon Roost bottoms whut dyes and colors and straightens hair and bleaches skins fum plumb black to gingercake ur almost white.' Aunt Sally said, 'Couldn't Brer Simonson change dat dawg's color, he'd just die hisse'f.'

"So I took Snap to Brer Simonson's cabin, and it took him half a day to put an extra liver spot on each of his sides. You couldn't tell 'em from the natural hair to save yo' life. I asked Brer Simonson what was in his dyes, and he said clays from the earth, stain from the walnut and other vegetables, and frawg oil.' "

Milt stirred his coffee.

"The mo' I hunted Snap all durin' Christmas week and early January, the mo' I realized that I'd done finally got holt of a dawg could pour it on Tarrant. Not over-noticeably, but he whupped Tarrant oftener 'n Tarrant licked him. Looked like ev'y time I hunted him, Snap kept ramblin' wider and wider, puttin' mo' punch into his runnin', handlin' surer, and standin' up to his birds like a stone wall. And was that dawg stylish!

"Billy Robinson and me seen Pettigrew's ads in the papers offerin' a hundred dollars' reward just for information regardin' the dawg's whereabouts. But we laid low. I even met Pettigrew and he told me 'bout how he lost Snap. He says, 'Me and another feller was huntin' afoot and didn't have no business doin' it on account of you cain't keep up with no such big-runnin' dawg lest you're horseback.' Snap got lost in strange country and must o' been huntin' for Pettigrew when he come up out o' that ditch and the car struck 'im.

"Pettigrew said some feller called him up and said he thought he remembered hittin' a bird dawg, but it was done so quick he couldn't rightly remember much about it. Pettigrew says, 'I wouldn't take a thousand bucks for that dawg, even if I knowed he was a cripple for life.' "

Leroy Cooper remarked that such a viewpoint was very sporting on Mr. Pettigrew's part.

"I had done made up my mind to enter Snap in the shootin' dawg stake at the Memphis Field Trial Club's meetin' and see to it that Pettigrew was on hand to watch his own dawg run without knowin' it. So I tol' him 'bout a fine new dawg I'd raised, one of Tarrant's pups out of a King Genius bitch. I said it was without doubt the classiest shooting dawg anybody ever popped a gun over and jes' the type I figgered Pettigrew ought to buy after it won the Hernando stake.

"Pettigrew was right there, too, when the thing started—all dressed up in ridin' britches and shiny boots and a loud coat like one o' these here ads in the magazines. Me and Snap was drawed second brace the openin' mawnin' to run on the birdy second course. I warmed Snap up befo' the start and fed him a little fresh beef and a couple o' eggs. He was sho' fit and rearin' to travel! When Pettigrew seen Snap, his eyes bugged out and he says, 'Gosh, he sho' resembles my ol' Snap dawg, don't he?' He sorter run his hand along Snap's flanks and Snap knowed him, all right. But them two extra spots did the business. They was holdin' color tighter 'n a sinner swingin' onto a baptizin' life line.

" 'Yes, sir,' Pettigrew says, 'excep' for that short tail and them extra spots, he is ol' Snap to the life.'

"Snap was down with Neely Grant's classy bitch Katydidkate, and a darn swell bird finder she was, too. It didn't take but a few minutes to see that a real dawg race was goin' on. They went big and cut up their countries nicely. Pretty soon ol' Snap reached out bigger 'n bigger, and the first thing anybody knowed yonder he was on point. And did he really nail them pottiges! Looked like a million dollars with that stub tail stickin' straight up, and never budged when I shot the gun.

"Then Neely's bitch found, but she was just a bit unsteady to the pistol. And, boy, was Snap handlin' like a glove! Katie run good, but Snap was outside of her mostly. Snap found five bevies in the hour, and Katie four, and they both finished strong. Neely says to me, 'Milt, yo' dawg has shaded mine, but they have both set them others some hard copy to shoot at.'

"The judges placed Snap winner and Katie second when the thing was all over. I had called Snap 'Jim' all durin' the race, but that didn't make no difference. All you had to do with that dawg was to wave yo' hat and give him the beam, and he'd stay on it and use his bird sense.

"Pettigrew was all excited and the first to congratulate me. He wants to know what I'll take for the dog; says Jim reminds him so much of ol' Snap he'd like the best in the world to own him. I took the big lovin' cup on home with me and fed Snap till he quit eatin' of his own accord—which is very unusual for him. But I had discouraged Pettigrew on buyin' the dog.

"A few days later I meet up with Pettigrew downtown, and he comes right after me again, tryin' to buy Jim. I says, 'Aw, man, I ain't had time yet to have that lovin' cup engraved; and besides, yours is 'bout the tenth offer I've done had on the dawg, anyhow.' I says: 'Why, Homer Jones is crazy for him, and so is Johnny Dupre and Ches Harris and Clyde Norton and Dewey English, and all them top handlers have done heard about the dawg and are worryin' me to death wirin' me 'bout breedin' to him. But,' I says, 'I wouldn't sell on no condition unless the purchaser agreed to let me direct the dog's breedin' and general field trial management. I'd want him sent to the prairies this comin' summer. You know,' I says, 'there was a lot of talk at Hernando that I had done slipped in a ringer on the boys and that Jim didn't have no business in any shootin' dawg stake—he belonged up on the big circuit time.' "

Milt actually swelled with righteous indignation at the very memory. He swigged some coffee and took good hold on himself. He was nearing the pay-off.

"Pettigrew says: 'I want that dawg, Throcker, and you can write yo' own ticket on all them counts. I'll give a cool thousand bucks for the dawg jes' like I said I would, down at Hernando.' I says, 'Come on in the Merchants and State Bank, then, and let's see where we stand.' I took a pen and wrote out a bill o' sale on the back of a blank check. It says: 'Received of C. T. Pettigrew one thousand dollars cash in hand and acknowledged for one liver-and-white pointer dog called Jim, but said dog is subject to registration and title believed good. Purchaser agrees that Milton Throcker shall direct future breedings and all handling and field trial contacts of the dog.'

"Pettigrew read it over and says, 'That's okay by me.' He does business with this bank and goes over to the teller's window and comes back with ten one-hundred-dollar bills. I puts 'em in my wallet, and then asks Pettigrew if he wants me to keep the dawg. He says that is satisfactory to him, but he would like to see a piece in the paper that he has bought the recent winner at Hernando, so that everybody'll know he now owns a field trial headliner."

Here Milt's eyes began to glitter.

"Then I says, slow and cool-like, 'Whenever you want to see Snap, why come on by my plantation and play with him.' He says, 'Snap? You mean Jim.' 'Naw,' I says, 'I mean Snap!' Pettigrew's face got white and he whispers, 'What do you mean, Snap?' I says, 'Listen, Pettigrew, you thought you pulled a fast one on me when you let me spend a wad of time and dough on you whilst I was tryin' to sell you yo' own farm, didn't you? You got a great kick out of it, didn't you? Well, maybe you'll git a still bigger kick buyin' yo' own dawg back—how 'bout it?'

"Pettigrew says, 'You're kiddin' me. That dawg ain't Snap.' I pulled Snap's collar out o' my pocket and handed it to him. 'Where do you suppose I got that?' I says. He read his name on the plate and damn near fainted. So then I tol' him jes' how it all happened. I says, 'You can't take it to court, Pettigrew, because you ain't got no case, and besides you got too much sense to open yo' mouth. And besides, my friend Bill Robinson heard you say you'd give a thousand bucks for that dawg Snap jes' to git him back, even if you knowed he was crippled for life.'

"Pettigrew had done got all sobered up, and the tears came to his eyes. He says, 'That's right, Milt, you really saved ol' Snap's life. If I'd got him back, he would still be jes' Snap. But you took him and developed him into a great field trial winner.' I says: 'I ain't had no name engraved on that lovin'-cup. I been waitin' to have C. T. Pettigrew's put there.'

"Pettigrew never said another word. He jes' walked over to the teller's cage again, come back, and handed me another five hundred bucks. He says, 'Here's a bonus for bein' the smoothest son-of-a-sea-cook in seven states, and I'll buy all the thick steaks from here out whenever we hunt behin' Snap and Tarrant.' "

The Family Honor

"The Family Honor," one of the stories in the Derrydale edition of De Shootinest Gent'man, *as well as in the Putnam edition, had appeared in* Field & Stream, *April 1930. Just when it took place—for Pat (not to be confused with Hormel's Pat) was a real Chesapeake Bay retriever belonging to Henry Bartholomew—is not easy to determine. Nash's description of the scene when Henry offered to let him take the puppy Pat to develop places it on a Washington street —one of numerous meetings of the sort. Nash wrote me that he had been located in Washington in the course of conservation work from 1928 until 1936. The story was first published in the spring of 1930, narrowing the time to the late wildfowl season of 1928-29 or 1929-30. Pat was whelped on New Year's Day, and the end of the story took place the last day of the following wildfowl season, a short time after Pat's first birthday. Knowing* Field & Stream's *time schedule— at least three months ahead of publication—I feel safe in saying the action at the end was in January 1929, unless Nash dashed off the story after the event in January 1930 and rushed the manuscript up to Ray Holland in New York by hand.*

I first heard about Henry Bartholomew in that same letter from Nash. It was during World War II and I was stationed at Navy BUAER:

Dear Lieutenant Evans:
   A snare set anywhere in your address area would have caught me, from 1928 till 1936, when I lived in a reasonably sane Washington. When you get to the point where you can't stand it any longer, drop around to the Investment Building (next to the new Statler) and introduce yourself at 216 therein, to Mr. H. A. Bartholomew, President of Continental Life, one of the nation's top sportsmen and gunners. Henry and I have been buddies in game for many years, he has all my books, scads of magnums, two duck and quail marshes, and will drop everything to talk shooting at the slightest provocation. You'll hardly ever find him in his office weekends—first part of the week is his time. The rest is spent at his farm in between Broad and Swan Creeks above Fort Washington, Maryland—across and above Mt. Vernon.

I am truly sorry that the order of things at that time did not embrace my meet-ing and possibly shooting with Mr. Bartholomew.

In this story of the appealing young Chesapeake, Pat, Nash manages, without maudlin anthropomorphizing, to convey the responses of old Beck—thoughts "of canvasbacks . . . slithering into Marse Henry's decoys"; the awfulness of being left behind on a shooting day "when howling hadn't prevailed and restlessness wouldn't slack"; the image of that huge Chesapeake bulging with pup, wiggling up and rolling over, begging to remain.

Only men who have had a part in the shaping of a gun dog youngster will fully appreciate the period when young Pat and Nash grew so close. Pat's reunion with Nash, paws on his shoulders, staring him in the eyes makes me think of a pro-nouncement by an animal researcher to the effect that dogs never look you straight in the eyes. Which leaves me convinced that either my setters are people, or the scientist was working with some shifty dogs.

Nash's sundown at the story's end brings it all to me as I know so well—a season's last day, darkening pink on far shoreline, the end of shooting mixed up with poignancy of day's end, eased by the satisfaction of shots made, birds re-trieved; a wincing pain, above the cold biting into face and gloved fingers, that it is over for another year, yet assuaged by gratitude for such perfection—even a nasty small glee that those distant gunners still firing must relinquish all this with me.

Mine is not the most callous temperament and perhaps my reaction is not a fair one. But I can't read the last two paragraphs of "The Family Honor" with altogether clear eyes. I don't fall for tear-jerking, but I am a pushover for top Buckingham.

P AT, FOR SHORT of the stud book's pompous tally, was one from a litter of six Chesapeake Bay puppies whelped of noble sire and dam. Intelli-gent water dogs, Pat's old folks, Count and Beck, dared conditions that any day could produce. Acknowledged king and queen of their respective terri-tories; he on his side of the Potomac—she on hers. Duck gunners had long since bid high for their progeny. More than once, after some particularly brilliant retrieve, old Beck had heard Marse Henry offered all kinds of money for her. But Beck had quit worrying. Marse Henry's eyes twinkled as he knocked the ashes out of his pipe, just to prolong the suspense of negotiation. Clearing his throat by way of appearing interested, he'd drawl: "Have you got as much as five hundred bucks to lay on the barrel head for a sure enough Chesapeake?" "Yep," more than one wildfowler had shot back at him, "I've got all of that for the like of her!" "Fine," Marse Henry would assent, restuffing his smoke-screener. "In that case you jus' keep on savin' up an' when you've got a thousand or so to go on top of that five hundred—why—why—even then I doubt if it would do any good to take another wallop at me. Why, five grand or a stack of greenbacks high as the Washington monument for this old sister wouldn't interest me in the least." And knowing Henry, they knew he meant just that, sentimental as it seemed or sounded.

But Marse Henry, good friend and neighbor that he is, rarely, if ever, sold a pup. He made a present here and there until, out of Beck's last presentation, only little sister Pat and big brother Fritz remained. Doc had had first pick, but I'm coming to that later. Somehow, first one and then another of her babies "turned up missing." Drifted away mysteriously while Beck was out foraging. Those last two, Fritz and Pat, grew increasingly precious. What a mother! How she petted and loved and licked them. And with what ominous ferocity she guarded them. A grand specimen of the breed, old Beck. A great sway-backed, wavy-withered, lemon-eyed creature; massively compact and rugged. Lying there amid sun patches filtering through Marse Henry's apple orchard, she tenderly dreamed away her youngsters' puppyhood. Hard to tell apart, those two brown, furry balls, rolling, leaping and snarling in rough dispute for possession of the long-suffering house kitten. Beck's misty, blinky eyes wandered from her darlings—along the Maryland heights and far across the lordly Potomac toward Virginia and Mount Vernon. What were her thoughts? Your guess is as good as mine. Of canvasbacks, blackheads, or whistlers slithering into Marse Henry's decoys? Or that terrible day she broke through sharp skim-ice offshore and was trapped in a floe? She had cut her forelegs to ribbons crashing shoreward for her life. A close call, that! But she had delivered the goods, a mere "trash duck," at that. No, Beck and death weren't entire strangers. But stuff like that was all in her day's work. No dog on earth could ever have had as kindly a master, or a happier home. Dog heaven, that farm! Marse Henry to hunt crows with and pitch driftwood for her and the babies to retrieve. And plenty of rabbits to jump and chase through the corn and pasture. If all that was in Beck's mind, she had a great deal to be thankful for, for she gave value received and a golden disposition. Maybe, just about then, she was thinking of how Fritz and Pat happened into this jolly old duck-shooting world.

Last New Year's Day—of all times! For quite a while Beck and the farm-hold had been looking forward to a "blessed canine event." Marse Henry had been overly solicitous of her lately. Beck had noticed him looking at her, counting on his fingers. On several occasions he had quietly latched the kennel and slipped off down to the blind without her. And maybe she hadn't howled! The Colonel had to come and tell her to hush, and ask if she wasn't ashamed of herself making all that fuss. Then he'd grinned and given her a piece of sweet cornpone. Good old girl!

That particular New Year's morning had fetched in a keen, northwest blow, a regular rip-snorter that had been brewing all night. Beck heard it moaning and then roaring around the snug doghouse. She knew there'd be drift ice in the river, and a nasty chop for any dog to buck. When Marse Henry and Doc stalked through the yard snapping their flashlights and adjusting packs, Beck tumbled out, flourished about and made it plain that she expected to punch the clock as a matter of course. But Marse Henry said, "No, old folks, not today—the hay for yours. 'Doc' prescribes rest and quiet!" Then he collared her and patted and joked her back into the shed; thinking, too, he'd snapped down the door catch on his way out. But duck hunters have a way of hurrying, with daylight in the offing. After a bit, when howling hadn't prevailed and restlessness wouldn't slack, Beck suddenly shoved hard against the door—and it swung open. The outer gate was a tight squeeze, but she made it. It was easy, then, to track her men down the river road. She caught up just as they deposited their plunder outside the shack That was Beck's first break.

"Well, I'll jus' be—looka' here, Doc," Marse Henry cussed, trying to frown at her as she waddled up to them; "if here ain't old Beck—why—why—I locked that door—how th' hell, you gotta' go home—this ain't any way to run a duck hunt—you ain't got any business foolin' aroun' this river a day like today." Beck sensed this meant business. Marse Henry was sputtering sore. The situation called for a number of tail wags to get in close enough to roll over and do a "beg." "Hell of a note," chuttered Marse Henry. "It'll take half an hour to lead her back up yonder—darn near daylight—and we can't tie her here on this cold bank." Then Doc made a suggestion, and old Beck got her second break. "Henry," said Doc, "I'll tell you what—let's take her on out to the blind—it's warm and comfortable and she can lie there just as safely as she would in the kennel—anyway—there's a day left—isn't there?" It was coming light with a rush, and Marse Henry weakened. He had bent to rub Beck behind her ears, so she snuggled up closer and gave him a paw-poke. That settled it. "Well," agreed Marse Henry, "all right, but she mustn't do a lick of work!" The blind, that winter, was staked fifty yards offshore. Ira, the handyman, was just skiffing in from anchoring the decoys. A hundred or more black, bobbing specks were swinging with the tide. With much ado as to Beck's comfort, all hands loaded in and Ira effected an easy transfer. Marse Henry lit an oil stove in one end of the hooded blind, and made Beck curl up in some warm straw and sacks at the other end. Ira paddled ashore while Marse Henry and Doc shoved shells into their heavy double guns, tobacco'd their "dudeens" and made ready to operate on any early arrivals. Marse Henry, suddenly remembering something, had just picked up a chain and turned toward Beck's end when Doc hissed, "Henry—Henry—mark left—down—quick!"

Henry ducked, and grabbed for his gun. There was a second or two's quivering ecstasy that is prelude to man's symphony of sport—then—Pop—pop—poppity—pop! A chain rattled on the floor! After all, it was instinct and business pride, with Beck. The family honor must be upheld. She just had to go, and that was all there was to it. Up in a flash; a headlong plunge past Marse Henry's rubber-booted shins—and a leaping dive off the outside splash step. Sheer, teeth-gritting nerve carrying her and a precious burden through an icy surge. More than she had bargained for; she realized it, pretty quick. But, somewhere out there—somewhere out there—puff—puff—cripples might be getting away. That was her business, cripples and dead 'uns. Things would just have to take care of themselves—she'd see them through. She had heard but lost Marse Henry's swearing and bawling —"Come back he'ah, you ole fool." But just then she'd topped a swell, sighted a still struggling canvasback, and flung herself toward it through crest smother. Three such trips she plowed, at each return successfully eluding Marse Henry's frantic efforts to snatch her collar and haul her into the hide. She was about "all in," and glad to climb in with the last duck, panting heavily.

Never had she seen or heard Marse Henry take on so; swearing to himself and wishing to this, that and the other he had herded her back to the kennel in the first place. Half the time she couldn't tell whether he was cussin' or cryin'! He and Doc made all manner of palaver over her after she slunk into the straw. Doc dried her off with an old piece of quilt, and Marse Henry moved the heater closer, and she dropped into a doze. Up on the shooter's bench something was said about "the greatest exhibition of instinct!" Doc was doing most of the talking. Marse Henry was still cussing himself. During a later bombardment, Marse Henry and Doc, in the act of a hurried reload, caught two or three faint whimpers from old Beck's corner and some scuffling about in the hay. Having become familiar with such sounds, they gazed at each other in amazed incredulity. Then Doc dove for a hurried preliminary examination. "Get busy, Doc, this is your first case of the year," grinned Henry, standing around first on one foot and then the other, while cans and blackheads whisked by unheeded. Doc announced, after a while, that mother and children were doing as well as could be expected. Meanwhile Ira had brought the boat, and Marse Henry sent him to the house for a flannel-lined basket and the car. The shoot was abandoned for a while and there was reunion and celebration at the house. Marse Henry chuckled as he and Doc lugged their afternoon's bag up the road at nightfall. "Those sure ought to be great dogs—born right there in the duck blind—what do you know about *that*—if they haven't got every thing a water dog needs, then there's no such thing as prenatal influence." To which Doc made answer, taking cover with small loss of professional dignity, "Not all of us agree, Henry, that there is any such thing—however— I—er—am inclined to believe that this particular case may prove a light-shedding and strengthening factor in affirmative observation!" "Well," came back Marse Henry, "all that you're talking about may be so. In view of medical services rendered, your participation and the happy termination of this salubrious occasion, you get first litter pick—that's fair, ain't it?" And maybe Doc didn't grab while the choosing was good.

Perhaps some such memories flitted through old Beck's mind as she lay under the apple trees that afternoon, watching Patsy and Fritz devil the kitty.

Autumn was in the very air. Hillsides flamed and russet girdle wove in and out among coniferous headlands. Came cool days when Marse Henry, meeting me on the street, cocked an eye aloft and allowed, "Boy, there's that old feelin' in th' vicinity o' my mind sorter like ducks—how 'bout you?" I'd admit it, and find myself hopefully following Marse Henry's slant skyward for a chance glimpse of early migrants. You never can tell about ducks. Then we'd talk ducks awhile longer and branch off onto guns and loads. That particular day, however, Marse Henry had said, "I guess you'll be headin' south, yourself, before long—mos' any day now?" He opened the old pipe's throttle, a sure sign of some truly deep stuff! "How'd you like to take Pat down South where ducks and geese are so plentiful—and—and— sorter start breakin' her for me?"

There is the glimmer of burnished sacrifice in such friendship. But temptation! Take Pat away from Marse Henry and the Colonel, and old Beck? What if something happened to her? It was up to me to hesitate, but I lost. The joys of breaking my own great dogs, gone these several seasons—

and now—opportunity to train a grand ten months' beauty for Marse Henry. It was just too good to be true. Two weeks later, traveling like a queen in state, Pat came to Dixie. Sixty pounds of sleek Chesapeake Bay, and a credit to her blood and raising. A bit timid after the long ride, and naturally homesick for the farm and her folks. But, when she found Miss Irma loved her just as much as she had our own big Pat dog, and that she had the run of the house and could ride alongside her mistress and bark out of the car window as loud as she pleased—why, everything became just right. We took her to our duck club, a comfortable shack alongside a lake full of wildfowl foods and cypress trees. There she came to know Big and Little Jim and Lelia, the colored folks who mind the place, and Buck and Ball, the coon hounds. What a watch dog she became, and what a pet. On hand for a game of "hide me something" the moment we arrived. Some member's slipper to be hunted down, an orange or apple to be pulled off the tall mantel, or a boisterous romp that completely unbedded the dormitory.

At first, Pat was a bit boat-shy. I have seen other Chesapeake pups the same way. But before long she found out what such affairs were all about, and thereafter promptly and possessively manned the front over-deck. Her first "duck" was an old boxing glove, about the size of a bird, and of a texture to make her tender-mouthed. From the boat, I'd toss the glove far into some tall cover, shoot the gun and bid her "bring!" This process was repeated day after day, and then changed, the glove being thrown from a blind across open water. Later, a mud hen, caught in a muskrat trap and badly hurt, became Pat's first blood and feathers. Through all Pat's primer days the flight was coming down. Overnight our lake was reloaded with mallards, sprigs, teal, widgeon, shovelers and gadwall.

Opening day, at last! I was shooting that morning with my cousin. Pat evinced a lively interest in everything en route to the blind. When great bunches of quacking mallards leaped as our boat rounded some narrow trail, she squirmed and whined. She had ducks in her blood, all right, and I knew there was "something shaking." Looking back at me and my gun, she literally licked her chops. There was that noise due, Pat was figuring. While I waded about placing the blocks, Pat solemnly inspected each one. But when I weighted and tossed out the first live caller, there was a hullaballoo. In two leaps that sent water flying, she was on top of the shrieking mallard. But a new tone in my shout of "Let it alone" stopped her instantly. Looking straight at me, as though thinking it all out for a moment, she released the struggling drake and marched meekly to the boat. Never again did she pay the slightest attention to a live decoy.

By six forty-five, all was ready. Seven o'clock is shooting hour at our duck club, so a fifteen-minute interval of delicious agony had to be endured. Hundreds of ducks, routed from our big pond, returned; the air and water were a-twinkle. Pat stationed herself on the boat's prow, just behind the elbow brush, strictly at attention. A handsome mallard, our first customer, was just ahead of three more swinging over adjacent timber. We let him glide straight in and alight. The others circled once and dropped in against a faint breeze. These we bagged, and Ev, with his remaining barrel, accounted for the original incomer. At the report of our guns I was conscious of Pat's taking a header off her station and buck-jumping toward a flapping bird. She hesitated at first, but after a sniff or two, picked up the victim, and with head and tail erect made a perfect retrieve of her first real mallard. Depositing her pick-up, she licked its bedraggled plumage a bit, shook herself furiously, and then smiled up at me. I tossed an empty shell toward a second bird. Instantly she caught the suggestion and was on her way. The sport, from then on, was fast and furious. I let Pat do as she pleased, and she was plenty busy. When time was up she had piled the better part of two limits into the boat. She was a "natural." All that fall, her water and wildfowl and gun lessons continued. I used her for geese on the sand bars and had her follow me wading through overflowed timber. Pat made few failures at spotting shot-down birds under such acid test. Just before Christmas I shipped her to Marse Henry and wrote him I thought she "had everything" and would retrieve anything that was loose at both ends.

In January, with Pat one year old, I returned to the Potomac for some duck shooting with Marse Henry and Doc. He has his own particular hunting system and methods of working out results. He had figured it all out, and reset his blind on the tip of a short point. To its left, the big river "coves," and a right wind swings up-comers in much closer for stooling. Half a mile or so above, the shallow expanse of Broad Creek lets in, a great rafting place for feeders. Behind the blind a belt of heavy woodland thickens down-shore, into a tangle of low shrubs, vines and beach boulders. Off the abrupt bank, a plank walk extends out to the box, perfectly camouflaged, even down around its ankles, with cedar boughs. Four-foot piling allows for tidal variance. Inside are cushioned seats, shell and gun racks, an oil heater for each end, and a heavy tarp cover that can be used as a laprobe to hold in heat during bitter weather. A twelve-inch plank, set at just the right angle, catches the wind and tosses it overhead. "I've found out," said Marse Henry, "that in my own home blind I might just as well be reasonably comfortable—we have to do all our own chores around here anyhow, and there is plenty of grief outside the box." Marse Henry is right about that. When you hunt with him you do a man's work somehow or other. There's plenty of room for six gunners and all three of those big Chesapeakes, Fritz, Pat and old Mamma Beck. "Maybe three brown bears is too much of a crowd," continues Marse Henry, "but they're company for me and the Colonel—I like to fool with 'em and watch Beck teach 'em tricks of her trade." Three retrievers in any other blind than Henry's would be worse than trying to manage three prima donnas in the same opera troupe. But at his place, things are different—even to the actual shooting. When the cans rip off from lines winging up-Potomac half a mile out, and make a dart to look you over—you had better make arrangements to do business. Because, as my observing friend, Horace Miller, would comment: "Dem birds acts so brief." You might just as well begin at a true forty yards and figure outward. I have shot ducks at many a place and under widely varying conditions, but Marse Henry's is where the diplomas are really handed out. Acquire one there, take 'em as they come, and you can slide up to the firing line at any duck blind in these United States and feel reasonably qualified regardless of what you're up against.

That first day there were five of us in the box—Marse Henry, the Colonel, Ira, Doc and I. The Colonel was merely visiting, and Ira was having his gunning helping Doc with the picture machine. I think Pat knew me. She put her paws on my shoulders, stared me straight in the eyes, and grinned. Then she sniffed my jacket carefully, and ended by trying to push me over backward with face lickings. There was a fine flight, that day. At the crack of our guns, out would bounce all three dogs, with Beck invariably first. Fritz held up his end in good shape, but, to my amazement and chagrin, Pat more or less hung back. With three or four birds down amid wind and wave, three dogs have plenty of work cut out for them. "What's the matter with her?" I asked, when several times she held back, or starting rather grudgingly, turned shoreward. "You'd think she'd never seen a duck, much less retrieved one." Marse Henry's brow wrinkled. "I don't know," he parried—"I think she's all right basically, or that she'll develop—maybe after your way of shooting down there, she hasn't 'savvied' this deep water stuff —maybe she's depending too much on the old bitch."

But I couldn't figure it that way. Fritz was out on his own, but all Pat would do was run around in circles. It depressed me terribly after what I'd seen the animal accomplish down home. It was in her, right enough. I had pictures of her retrieving, putting ducks into our boat. I could prove it by Harold, or Irma. Harold could tell 'em about that day, for instance, when

I banged down a timber scraper that Pat chased clean across the pond and into the big cypress. And on her way back she spotted an overlooked drifter and fetched in a double. And that goose she chased to mid-river of the Mississippi and brought in like nobody's business. Something was wrong, somewhere. I grew afraid Marse Henry might think I'd been spoofing him just because Pat was his dog. It wasn't much of a day on Pat's account. Nor did succeeding shoots prove any more satisfactory. Duck season was running out. I waxed almost morose on the subject of Pat's fall-down. She was alert enough, but compared to the animal I'd worked down home, she apparently didn't know what it was all about. Was Pat yellow? Impossible! Brainless? Certainly not! Lazy? Not Pat, of all dogs, with that mother of hers, and the stunts I'd seen her pull off. All I could do was wait, and while nature was taking its course, try to puzzle out the thing.

Last day of the wildfowling calendar! One that shook its fist in our faces and flung a dare to do something about it. Offshore, a quarter mile of milling ice; even the steamer channel was full of heavy floes. Great fields splitting loose from the mouth of Broad Creek and crunching past with a grinding roar that kept us shifting desperately to salvage decoy strings. Inshore the tide-groaning masses piled into towering bergs that fell of their own weight and formed fantastic caves. But our outfit's battle with such elements won and earned its last day's fun. What birds we killed gave Beck a trying time of it. Son Fritz had managed to wire-cut himself and was in sick bay. Pat was on hand, but of little if any help. She was as affectionate as ever, but somehow palpably shy of it all. Her whole attitude was that of a human being trying, beneath some complex, to grope at the past for spiritual urge.

It was coming sundown, with first pink and then a darker gloam mantling Virginia's shoreline. Up- and down-river distant guns were reluctantly booming hunter's fond farewell to governmental regulation. While Marse Henry and Doc loaded a share of the duffle and birds through the woods copse, I set about battening down the blind's tarpaulin. What a gorgeous after-flare from reflecting ice to sky. "Look your last, you gunners," it seemed to say: "today will soon belong to the logbook—say a prayer for the tomorrow that is hope." An edged wind gnawed at my stiffening fingers. My gun leaned against a snag. Suddenly, downriver, across the cove, three shadows blotted a fading patch of ocher east and winked silently our way. Crouching, I snatched my weapon. Black duck! A long way out, but by thunder, I'd have a go at that big center fellow if it was the last shot I ever made.

A dog sprang noiselessly down from the overhead bank and hunkered alongside. I was afraid to take my eyes off the approaching birds. Couldn't be Fritz. A quick, closer scrutiny. Not Beck—her nose and eyebrows were graying. Why—a stabbing blade of hope—it—it—was—Pat. I felt her quiver and heard a faint, eager whine that took me back to sand bars and swamps and boat prows and tall timber. I sensed her lemon eyes ashine, and fixed—with intent to kill. Renewed affection surged through me. This was her game and mine again—together—the kind she'd learned. No more confinement in the blind—the gun—the game—everything in sight. The complex went glimmering.

A swinging lead, and heavy tubes spat a gash across the wind-whistle. The big center duck tumbled. Beating the gun, Pat—the real Pat now—lunged —showering me with muddy gravel as she clawed plungingly out onto the ice field. With a fifty-yard start, her crippled quarry was fluttering toward the distant open channel and safety. Realization of danger swept over me. Bad business out there—for boat or man—much less a dog. Out where the jam ended, a treacherous coating of shaved snow—and off it relentless floes that would drill a yawl. "Come back, Pat," I yelled, rushing after her until I broke through the crust and into boot-deep eddy. "Pat—Pat—here—here —come back." Far out on the ice a racing dot grew smaller and smaller— lost to sight against distant hills. Then I knew. Seeing me crouched there, it had all swept back to her—images from a dream time. In that brief moment, memory flashed of old Beck's bearing Pat's unborn spirit through icy travail. Men are said to "find themselves." Why not a dog?

And then, as night flung suddenly down, out there among waves and the creaking smash of sullen turmoil, Pat disappeared. Marse Henry was alongside by now, listening to the story and calling, with me, out across the gloom. Fifteen, twenty minutes passed. Our voices hoarsened against the tumult, with something dreadfully pathetic tugging at our hearts. A shred of moonlight tipped the crest of Maryland and swathed the river's shroud with pallid paths. And into its widening beneficence, from behind an ice barrier far to our left, crept an almost ghostly, slow-walking Pat. Pat, grizzly with frozen spray, but head and tail erect, with a live, unrumpled black duck between her jaws. Marse Henry's eyes and my own met in unutterable relief—and something much, much more. Into our hearts had surged not alone gratitude for Pat's restoration, or a mere coming into her own. Just the choky tribute of silence, a palm from two hard-bitten duck shooters to a dog's flaming courage and unspeakable devotion.

Part Five:
POSSIBLES BAG

The Neglected Duck Call

"Possibles Bag" is a term Nash borrowed from the mountain men he met on his father's ranch in Colorado—their term for what many of us call a duffle bag, used while riding to hold odd items of accoutrement, almost anything that might be needed. I've used the term as the title for this part because it contains stories and articles that do not seem to fit exactly elsewhere in the book—and because I think Nash would have approved.

"The Neglected Duck Call" was in the famous collection De Shootinest Gent'man, but it was published earlier in Field & Stream, January 1928. It does not take long to realize from Nash's stories that duck shooting was an important matter in the Memphis area, giving significance to thousands of square miles of swamps and flooded backwaters as setting for glorious experience. Probably more than any other shooting, duck shooting spawned specialists in gunsmithing, duck-boat design, and the creation of fine duck calls with variations as personal as decoys carved by individual makers. Beyond the duck call's basic design for tone production and performance, I am impressed with the exquisite ornament, comparable to the checkering on a fine gunstock or fore-end.

Duck calling is to wildfowling what dry-fly casting is to trouting—the refinement that places it above mere taking of game. Bob Anderson was acknowledged a consummate duck caller. Irma Witt, Nash's daughter, says Bob could get more out of a duck call than Toscanini could coax from a full symphony. I asked Bob what his favorite duck call was. He wrote:

> I must explain that on some days ducks would come no matter what you did. On others, nothing would bring them close. I never could figure it out. I know that shooting was always better during the dark of the moon. As to what kind of call I used, it was an "Olt," made of hard rubber. I was never able to find a wooden call to suit me. It is so constructed that you can shorten or lengthen the reed. In those days I blew fairly hard (I couldn't now). Anyway, it was what you blew at the proper time. When ducks were far away, you blew a long "Hail" call. When overhead a soft chuckle. If they started away, four quick quacks as a come-back call, then chuckle again. Nobody could make a bunch of mallards light

if they did not want to. Some people did not seem to understand that. So, Nash started me using Lubaloy 4's. If a duck got within 60 yds. he'd better be careful!

Nash took duck calling seriously, a tribute to the early influence of the expert Perry Hooker. Nash's discussion of technique is worthy of a voice coach, his analysis of the mechanics of the duck call is that of the dedicated student. If he felt humble about his performance with a duck call, it was because he was treated to virtuoso calling by men like Bob Anderson with whom he gunned.

A N EARLY DUCK-SHOOTING memory of mine is of seeing a great many duck calls around but very seldom hearing them blown. Possibly ducks were so plentiful in those days that calls were considered more or less ornamental devices, to be used only in times of abject need, or to furnish sartorial atmosphere.

As I recollect them, the fundamentalist duck hunters of my youth were niftier outdoor dressers than our stereotyped O. D. clan of today. I can visualize some of those old-timers right now. Their duck calls were split-ended affairs, with fancy horn loud speakers. They were worn in a breast pocket or hung from a colored cord knotted about the collars of their London corduroy or velveteen shooting jackets. These latter were cut à la morning affairs of today's semi-formal wardrobe. Hip pocket flasks of today's vintage would have been scorned if lined up beside the leather-bound, capacious receptacles those old sports stowed in the pockets of their tail flaps.

But I can't give their calls much. After a few blows, their reeds either jammed, rattled dejectedly out of tune, or else bit one's tongue. How my dear old dad would swear when he yanked out his call, only to find its slotted throat loaded with tobacco silt or cookie crumbs. It required a world of lung power, unbounded endurance and high optimism to keep them going—much less "tuned up."

Swamp angels and market hunters of that day, however, mothered by a parent necessity, were using handmade calls not much different from today's models. As in most contrivances, our best calls spring from those very models. The most noted of early calls was the "Glodo," made, I think, by a Frenchman famed for his prowess with gun and call on a once well-known southern Illinois marsh. My friend, Guy Ward, of Reelfoot Lake and trap-shooting fame, is the proud possessor of an original Glodo. I have heard that as a reed producer and toner, Glodo's experimental turn for metal manipulation was little short of marvelous.

Naturally, different sections of the country have various models of calls. I have seen them embodying fifty forms of trumpets and more acoustic engineering, inside and out. I have seen them made of cane joint, cocobolo, walnut, maple, pine, hard rubber, and with tongues all the way from German silver or copper to thinned-down clarinet reeds.

Some of them were good, a lot of them bad, and others indifferent. Their operators were, of course, largely to blame, although kinking and corrosion of reeds account for a majority of call casualties.

As my duck-shooting career progressed and the birds became less easy to secure without vocal inducement, I took more interest in duck calls and their possibilities. I bought numerous commercial calls, rebuilt them, cut on, up, down and around them. I made the mistake of trying to perfect the call before I learned how to use it.

I could do fairly well; that is, I didn't make the call sound like "All policemen have big feet." I could tell when I had scared a duck and even had sense enough to realize that ofttimes, my getting in a lot of birds was, for the most part, sheer luck and a good stool of decoys.

I was in the sporting goods business. A friend told me of a pal of his, a great hunter and trapshot, who was transferring to new work in our town. We met, and five minutes after our introduction I knew one thing for sure. That was, so far as duck calling was concerned, "I hadn't seen or heard no calling!"

Holder of mechanical, automotive, electrical and marine engineering licenses, Perry Hooker had applied sound technical training and thought to the production of his call. He threw in a lifetime of wildfowling experience that began in a boyhood of market hunting in Iowa and Oklahoma and progressed through all forms of duck shooting in the South and Southwest. Shooting is still the most important part of his life's work. The instant I saw and heard him manipulate a duck call I knew at once that I was listening to a Master of the Art and became at once a pupil.

Now taking lessons in duck calling isn't a bit different from studying the saxophone or banjo. You must want to learn, and you must work. We worked at it in odd moments back in our shipping department. Off behind tiers of deadening crates, we made the rafters ring. I blew my daily dozen, and he responded in his. Note by note, scale by scale, and beat by beat, I strove to master the clear, high hails; the throaty, chuckling feed roll; the shorter, throatier welcome and numerous other duck idioms, maintaining measures of vocal entertainment and out-loud meditation.

By the time our first duck season was over, I received my diploma in the form of a beautifully engraved duck call. But by comparison it was very much like Caruso's telling some light-opera singer that he could do pretty well. After two seasons, however, I began calling well enough to get out on my own and become a teacher and critic in the absence of the master.

I have traveled around the duck circuit quite a bit and heard a lot of callers. I have never seen or heard one yet that I consider remotely in the same class with Hooker, and there are undoubtedly any number of great duck callers at large.

Then the World War came along, and Perry Hooker went to England as an airplane engine man. A year and a half later—in January it was—he landed and in four days off the boat was home, wanting a hunt the worst way in the world. There were no ducks in our club; so we took a quail hunt across from there, over beyond the levee, among the cornfields and wild lands along the Mississippi. The river was very high, lipping its banks.

I remember that we found one covey of birds in some tall weeds, right at the water's edge, where the river had backed up and flooded a great area of tall willows under the mainland. At the report of our guns, up from the overflowed tree tops went thousands of ducks, mostly mallards and sprigs. We stared at them in amazement. Following our quail singles, we came to where the willow flats petered out.

A fierce wind was blowing from the north, and after garnering our bob-whites, we stopped and watched flock after flock of ducks, disturbed by our firing, milling in the gale out over the vast expanse of willow tops between us and the white-capped river. Many of them swept down toward the narrow gap to our end of the tract, then wheeled and beat up along the shore-line toward the open end of the willow V. Both of us had a duck call, not by luck but by second nature.

We ate a snack, tied up the dogs and told our horse jingler to ride up along the overflow a good piece and shoot every so often at something, just to keep the birds stirred. We had no boat, and there were twenty feet of water off the bank edge. What ducks we could kill would necessarily have to be either called off over the mainland or, if dropped into the backwater, left to be collected next morning with a boat. There was little danger of any driftage, the tree stems being too matted for that.

After a bit, a bunch of greenheads came streaking down the far side of the cut. Hooker opened up. They wheeled across wind and responded beautifully to the absolutely perfect call. Half of them, seeking those un-seen birds back in that pocket, circled inland and beat upwind through the great bare-branched oaks of an Indian mound, amid whose undergrowth of cane and vines we were hiding. He killed four. In fact, we bagged two limits in the next hour and a half; only ten of the fifty fell into the back-water.

Next morning, before daylight, we were again on the scene, but this time we had a boat with us. At dawn thousands of ducks rolled and roared out of the vast flat. In a few torrid moments we bagged twelve or fifteen birds, but the sun came up on a clear, warm, windless day, and few, if any, birds returned.

We retrieved our leftovers of the day before and went ashore, deploring the weather. No cold, heavy wind to load the backwater with mallards, seek-ing feed and quiet in its shelter. But a fire to boil coffee and eat lunch by, a wagon to haul the boat and ducks home, and two good dogs to find plenty of quail 'twixt there and the house.

The next season I made a discovery. Maybe duck callers knew or know it, but neither Perry nor I had ever tumbled. And that is, a good duck call like Hooker's is as effective a goose call as you would want if you can and are not afraid to call geese. An offhand but loud blow with a smothering finger accidentally lifted on the proper note gave us the idea. Ensued some heavy practice. And now, by merely blowing just the right volume into our calls and using the same throat stroking, we can send a long goose note a good way. We can triple-tongue the response and gabble too. However, the best goose imitators I have ever heard are certain gifted individuals, who need no calls.

Duck calls and duck calling vary with duck sectors. I have heard guides on one lake make a noise quite unlike any duck I have heard. And yet the ducks responded. I'll never forget the shock I experienced in a blind at a ten-dollar-a-day, pay-as-you-enter shooting club on the Illinois River. There were five of us in one blind, with a guide who was a cross between a drill sergeant and a musical director.

We "sports" were lined up in a hide overlooking a poultry-wire pen con-taining fifty live mallards, feeding on the little pond and scrambling about amid the open water and floating ice blocks in the enclosure. Happening to look downwind after being assigned by position, I saw a duck beating up toward us. "Yonder comes a duck," I whispered to the sergeant.

He took one look, fell on his knees, closed his nose with thumb and fore-finger, and began to yell, "Eenie, eenie, eenie, eenie!" Frankly, I thought he had gone suddenly crazy, but the duck kept steadily on his course and was killed.

Later I learned that this is a common method of calling ducks on the Illinois and, from what I observe, effective enough too. It seems, however, merely a matter of attracting their attention to the open water pens full of live birds. Then, if the ducks are at all inclined to be sociable, they decoy. But I doubt the success of this method of calling in high timber or obscure slashes, with no decoys to back it up.

Another phase of duck calling which interests me is the struggle between the use of decoys and the use of duck calls. In the last fifteen years I have sold thousands of duck calls and many different kinds of decoys. I have belonged to several duck clubs whose memberships comprised over one hundred duck hunters. In one club particularly are men who have been shooting ducks for forty years.

And yet, looking back on it, I do not recall one man among the whole outfit who knows beans about real duck calling. Yet they all have duck calls, but they usually turn these over to their paddlers and depend upon a large supply of birds and a plentiful stool. Hundreds upon hundreds of hunters, ignorant of beat, note and tone, buy duck and goose calls during the hunting season. This is particularly noticeable to me, as I was in the same situation until I took the trouble required to become proficient in the art.

In an article of mine on the use of decoys this statement was made: "In timber woods and pot-hole shooting I would much prefer to have a call and no decoys than decoys and no call." I also stated that the reverse is true on big water and open shooting where a large stool is the more valuable of the two accessories. I have seen duck hunters—good shots—buy duck calls and produce some of the weirdest squawks imaginable.

A year ago last duck season, a famous sportsman from the East came down to shoot ducks and geese with Perry Hooker and me on the Mississippi. He had used a call some, shooting a great deal out of a blind and sink boxes over big stools, and a good shot he is too. He was at a loss, however, to understand why, in shooting off a big river, we used so few—half a dozen or so—duck decoys. We explained to him that it was because we were shooting in small pot-holes and ponds where decoys would not show until the ducks were close in and that we depended on our calls, adding that in lakes, shallow open ponds and such we used all the stools we could carry.

After listening to Hooker call and actually seeing what such skill could accomplish when pitted single-mouthed, so to speak, against nature, he began to see the light. "Here," he said, "is where I get busy. I've been telling those fellows back home that on big waters a call would help even with big stools, and I have seen what it did with practically no decoys at all. I believe that if I learn to call properly I can get at many a bird up home that would otherwise pass me up."

For the next week, in every spare moment he was to be found sitting opposite Perry down on the river bank, in the tent or blind, patiently quack-quack-quacking away after an even more patient instructor. Last fall I met him in New York. He wore a broad grin and had his duck call along —one that Hooker had given him. He had, he said, proved his point about the value of a call on any kind of water, with or without decoys, and was ready to hang out his shingle as a duck-calling professor.

The most attractive situation I've ever found for a duck call is in a willow or cypress brake, full of sloughs, pot-holes and pond runways—without decoys. Another beautiful location is at the base of some deep cove off a wide shallow lake, with just a few decoys and an overhead pass flight from which to lure a limit of birds by calling. But give me the tall timber spot. Just my gun, my call, and for good measure a fine companionable Chesapeake like old Pat.

There are, of course, some exceptionally good commercial calls, and they deserve a better fate than most of them come to. Naturally, however, mass production, shipping, minor details and misuse by ofttimes ignorant clerks who don't know the first principles of duck calling render them anything but musical instruments. But one can learn to call with any good product on the market today. They can easily be soaked and adjusted to give good tone.

But the pupil must have it in his heart to learn. The average untaught duck hunter simply sticks a call into his mouth, draws in a lungful of wind and emits a loud tooting q-u-u-a-a-c-c-k, or rather an attempt at a quack, that results in a glum quonk. He toots and toots, purpling. If he is in a store, the clerk stops him guardedly. If out hunting, incoming high-fliers mount higher, and lower prospects take advantage of his brazen charity to detour.

Now watch a caller of the Hooker type. With no bird in sight of his blind, he is constantly advertising for customers. One of his calls, with or without a carrying wind, can be heard for a long, long way. You'll hear the resting call, a well-fed, long-drawn-out note—a "Que—Q-U-A-C-K—qua-qua-qua—ack" running across five or more, usually six quacks, with the accent on the second quack. Then a pause. Then three measured quacks given with well-modulated chesty dignity.

Over the cypress may then swing a bunch of four or five mallards who, while yet a long way off, have heard the call and turned. Now a loud welcoming hail, with a rising inflection on the first quack that corresponds to our "W-E-L-L, where th' hell have YOU been?" It runs in three beats, followed immediately by a five beat "Que-quark-quark-quark-quark," repeated rapidly.

Hearing this and, we presume, liking it, our ducks may tumble to a lower circling level. Again the hail; and, if two men are "blinded" together, as Perry and I usually are, one takes up the line or address of welcome where the other leaves off. When our judgment notes sincere interest on the part of the visitors, we begin to offer special inducements, real duck bartering. The loud "Ah-har-har-har—ah-har-har-har" is broken quickly into the muffled chuckling feed roll, sounded by chattering the word "cut" rapidly into the call—"Cut-a-cut-a-cut." By practice you can break it into a "b-u-r-r-ed" vibration by twisting the tongue into an imitation of a quail's buzzing from the grass.

I have read, but strongly dissent, that in blind shooting, once ducks are attracted, it is time to quit calling. That may be all very well on big open water (but I doubt it) over a wide spread of stools where birds can see, hear and come a long way. But Hooker and I have tried it all the ways we know how, and agree that full effectiveness is best obtained by our maintaining the welcome until we drop the calls onto their neck strings and sound off a welcome with our guns.

To most novice duck hunters the call of a duck is a quack. The wood duck may yodel (easily imitated), the sprig may sound his lilting, fluty, two-note quip, the gadwall croak his guttural responses and the teal "tee-hee-tee-ho" its sibilant gyrations—but it is all quack to the novice.

You must study ducks, study tone, and learn to apply their measured tonal characters to individual cases and needs. If possible in your studies, hang around some live decoys at feeding time, early in the morning or about sundown. Try to reproduce with your call their conversational exchanges in quality of tone that blends and sets them off into gladsome refrains. Listen to what they say and how they express it.

But the most delicate adjustment of a call's reed is necessary to successfully maintain tonal reproduction. One kink, and the whole sound changes. If your call jams, don't, if it is an adjustable reed, monkey with it. Blow hard through the other end to loosen possible impedimenta. If there is a kink in the reed, remove it and smooth it evenly, or scrape with a knife blade. But be careful!

Next in importance in learning to call is the use of one's fingers in manipulative muffling or releasing tonal volume. Cup the trumpet end of your call firmly 'twixt thumb and first finger hollow, curving the other fingers out, close together, to complete the megaphonic extension. Shut down or open the megaphone finger by finger and notice the results. Watch the neophyte caller start the operation. I have seen it a thousand times when selling duck calls to supposed duck hunters—some good shots, too.

The beginner sticks the call's whole end into his mouth—that is, if he knows which end is which—puffs out his cheeks into balloonic proportions, and turns loose. The finished caller blows over slightly pursed lips—almost, you might think, through his teeth. A good call requires about a third of the wind necessary to bring volume from the average call. In the expert caller you'll notice, perhaps, a slight vibration of his Adam's apple but that is about all. To throw a far call he elevates the trumpet, but in more intimate passages it is pointed to the water and the finger work carefully choked.

I have seen and tried many first-rate calls—the Harlow, the Beckhart "Big Lake" model, Tom Turpin's new affair, another of cane from Louisiana and others too numerous to recall. To my way of thinking, Hooker's is the most easily blown and best designed I have seen or tried. He constructs his sounding box of walnut or clear maple, scraped very thin, to reproduce quality in the amphitheater, like a cello or violin. Its inset stem is cedar, with the vibration trough very deep and smooth.

His reed, after years of experiment which led him through many alloys and pures, is now a masterpiece of rustless Monel metal. He works these reeds down to a form and thickness all his own. They are hand-scraped, and all his calls are tuned out in the open and across water. This is no advertisement, because any good duck caller with a mechanical turn can do the same thing. Could you get a Hooker call? Possibly so, if he likes you and has the time to make one and present you with it. If he ever should, you're to be congratulated for having come into possession of a "Strad" among duck calls.

Another beautiful call with which Hooker has experimented with considerable degree of success has a sounding rod and box case practically identical with his Monel metal call. The reed of this call, however, is made from smoothed-down hard rubber. In size—that is, width, length and curve—it is a duplicate of the Monel metal reed. The floor, or trap-lines, of the sounding box of the Monel metal call has a curved surface, to accommodate the flippant metal.

His hard rubber reed, however, has to lie on an absolutely straight sounding cover. In other words, the two reeds are not interchangeable. Working down the hard rubber reed is a task, as it has to slope from about $64/1000$ down to practically nothing at the far end. Even then, the work has to be done individually on each reed with a piece of sandpaper, and then each call is blown at intervals as the reed is smoothed down to take the fullest measure of initial energy and tone.

Duck calling has no significance of sex appeal, as has turkey calling during the "gobble" or moose calling in the rut. There is nothing unsportsmanlike about it, far less than in baiting pond holes and blotting out twenty yard masses over pens full of live decoys.

Then give me a good call, my big gun, a sand-bar hole or a tule hide— and you may have the rest. By learning to call you will have gauged an added thrill of accomplishment that will prove an enduring comrade and a pal in need in your blind.

AFTERWORD

Since writing the above (1928) I am glad to say it did its bit and served a purpose in stimulating the national use of duck calls. Within two seasons following publication of "The Neglected Duck Call," I received just short of five hundred letters from men wanting Hooker model calls. Goodness only knows how many poor Perry Hooker had, for finally it became necessary for him to mail a "form letter" to applicants saying he didn't furnish them commercially.

But the art, meanwhile, had taken deeper root elsewhere. Around my old sporting goods store, Tom Turpin was always welcome and instructive company. It was there he met Perry Hooker and became intrigued with the possibilities of duck calls from the gunning, artistic, and commercial standpoint. Tom Turpin never does anything halfway. Months merged into years of experiment. My work took me away from our home town, and for several years I barely sighted Tom. But I knew from an occasional letter and magazine advertising that he had his "calls" on the market and was also putting out phonograph records of them for instruction in the hunter's art.

Last fall (1932) it was my good fortune to find myself in company with Tom Turpin, as quail shooting guests of Mr. Robert M. Carrier at his marvelous bobwhite preserve, "Barnacre Lodge," several miles west of Sardis, Panola County, Mississippi. That night we had a long talk. Tom Turpin has reproduced the celebrated old Reelfoot "Glodo model" duck call, and is experimenting with all sorts of woods, reed metals, and sound passages. Wherever he had heard of a "master" duck caller, he has gone to that individual and put his paces on a phonograph record.

"Buck," said Tom, "I've gone from Iowa to Louisiana; from Reelfoot to the Arkansas ricefields and pin-oaked timber flats and up through the Illinois river regions. Each sector usually has its individual duck-calling champ. And some of them are good. But a thing I've never heard in all my travels is some one fellow who can 'blow' all the different 'duck languages' of the circuit. The Reelfoot guide sounding his 'High-ball' or 'Paducah' call across big water would scare the daylights out of ducks in the timber. And the Louisiana 'Cajan,' twittering away with his throaty little cane instrument and filed rubber reed would draw a smile from the 'feed call and chuckler' of the cypress brakes. But, properly applied to localized needs, they are effective."

"Tom," I queried, "have you ever read what Roark Bradford's Negro character, John Henry, replied in connection with any question as to his spike-driving ability? Well, that's how I feel about your duck calling. John Henry says, in effect: 'I'se John Henry, from th' Black River country whar' th' sun don't never shine—I ain't de bes' spike driver in de worl', but de man whut was, is dead—an dat don't leave nobody but me.' "

Hail and Farewell

Published in August 1934 in National Sportsman Magazine, *edited by William Harnden Foster, and then in* Mark Right!, *"Hail and Farewell" has for its characters Nash and Irma Buckingham's springer spaniel Chub, and Hal Bowen Howard, Nash's friend from boyhood and shooting and fishing companion until both were fifty-three. Hal is part of at least twelve of Nash's stories and is mentioned elsewhere.*

The Howard homeplace near Aberdeen, Mississippi, was the scene .of many pleasant bobwhite shoots when there were almost unlimited coveys and Hal and Nash were "gay young blades," as one of the photographs is inscribed. One picture taken in 1908 near Hal's home shows Nash holding his old Model 1893 Winchester pump gun, his favorite at that time, with "Jimmie," a big raw-boned setter, standing with his paws up on Nash—mentioned with Flash and Ticket in the first paragraph of this story. Nash wears the battered variation-pork-pie felt hat he was wearing in most of his quail-hunting pictures taken the few years before he was married.

Another faded photograph, taken about 1910 on the steps of the Howard home—large white columns, pre-World War I fashions—reveals Hal carrying too much weight even as a young man around thirty. By contrast, his father, Colonel J. Woodie Howard, resembles a fit-looking Teddy Roosevelt. Others in the group are Mary Traylor and Sam P. Walker, mentioned along with Irma and Nash in "Minutes and Years" and "After All These Years."

In "Given Only to the Honored," Nash speaks of "Hal's and my twelve-bore Becker magnums." In this story he describes Hal's "Becker twenty-bore magnum," the first mention of those celebrated guns in twenty-gauge.

At some time, most gunners discover a shooting companion who turns out exactly right. There are usually false starters who, humans being human, don't wear well. But from the outside at least, there are certain shooting companionships that appear more compatible than some marriages—perhaps optimum effort to be agreeable tied in with common interest. As in many ways, Nash was more fortunate than ordinary men in that he had several fine shooting relationships.

Some of these men have survived Nash and each knows how rewarding the friendship was. It isn't fair to say, as an onlooker, that Nash's long years of shooting with Hal Howard were the most gratifying of all—in retrospect he viewed them warmly—but I doubt if anyone was closer to Nash than Hal.

The springer Chub was certainly the most equally Irma's and Nash's of any dog Nash writes about, and he spoke of him long after Chub died. "Hail and Farewell" is a touching tribute to two souls—the young puppy and the close shooting friend, one on his way into Nash's life, the other on the long way out.

TELL ME, IF you can, of anything that's finer than an evening in camp with a rare old friend and a dog after one's own heart. We talked, Hal and I, of fishing and gunning trips we'd made together for all of thirty years. Moose and salmon in New Brunswick, the high Rockies, the old E Bar X range we rode, year in and season out, together. We talked of duck shooting—the camp at Okay, of Horace and Molly at Beaver Dam, and of bird dogs that meant more than a little in our outdoor lives—Flash, and Jimmie, and Ticket. With such talk, with such a friend, comes the spirit that blends naturally with well-steamed beef and beans and corn bread, and imparts a tendency to idle amid smoke wreaths and put off doing the dishes. Of course Chub was with us.

Chub had come to me on Easter Sunday morning, flop-eared little dickens, with a winning way to the potlicker, and the spryness of a cricket, a gift from my friend D. C., who breeds springers. He has slept every night of his life at the foot of my bed. He comes respectfully, if at times boisterously, to family meals. He asks his own way in and out of doors by what amounts to well-sustained canine conversation. On his own in the neighborhood, protecting a private stock of buried bones, Chub wins and loses a normal percentage of fights, all of which are strictly his own affairs because we want no apron-string dog. And how he did grow.

A lake fronts our home, and there Chub had his first lessons in retrieving —before breakfast and in late afternoon, with the swallows and blackbirds kicking up spray and the mallard decoys raising Ned lest their broods be raided. Quick enough at yard breaking, Chub nevertheless was plenty stubborn and hard-headed. Our equipment was a sixty-foot cord, a rolled Kapok boat cushion, and a keen switch, for which Chub developed a keener respect. First dash out of the box, Chub went in over his head, but swam desperately and soon developed a strong stroke. The line drew him ashore when he seized his mock duck. After a series of workouts he developed a first-rate idea of what it was all about.

September first rolled around, dove-shooting season, and we were wondering what Chub would do afield when the guns began to pop. We scattered about the wheat and millet patches that afternoon. Yonder was Hal, with little black Grover packing his camp stool, water jug, and, proudly, the famous Becker twenty-bore magnum double. Percy, gunbearer and bottles, was under the sycamore tree, and Bob at his favorite hangout by the persimmon clump. Irma and Chub and I, with little black Billy, took station up the tall hedgerow a piece, 'twixt late corn and clipped alfalfa. Chub, wild-eyed with excitement, was fully aware that something vitally affecting his career was about to be pulled off. He had pawed and licked our guns like a kid with an all-day sucker.

Just then a dove darted overhead, and by great good luck I snap-pitched it into the mown field. At gun's crack, Chub plowed through the bushes and cast about vigorously in the open. Gun-shy? Not that pup! Irma and I watched—fascinated. A tense half-point—there—he had it—with a quick pounce! Chub, his first bird in mouth! Falling on her knee, Irma clapped her hands and called. Head and stubby tail proudly erect, that sturdy ball of liver and white trotted straight to his beloved mistress and gravely muzzled the softly feathered quarry into her lap.

Of course, by now you've guessed what she did—put both arms around Chub's bull neck and kissed him squarely between the eyes. Dear old Hal, watching the exploit, waved his hat and shouted, " 'Attaboy, Chub!" Such moments mean a lot to folks like Irma and me, hunting and breaking dogs together, going on—oh, no matter how many years. But Chub jerked away and huffily rolled reproachful eyes—much as to say, "Cut out the Little Lord Fauntleroy stuff, will ya—I'm a big dog now—no wimmenfolks business, Missus—us got a job to mind, yonder come some doves—ain't your gun loaded, Boss?"

What an afternoon that was, for sure! What a fagged puppy fell fast asleep during the drive cityward, with his lady almost tearfully unwinding a stray cocklebur or two from his hide. Thereafter, we shot doves twice a week. Hot afternoons Chub had learned to report to Irma for a drink of water from her hat crown. But we had yet to lose a downed or crippled bird that ever hit the ground. When business got slack in our neighborhood, I frequently joined Hal and had Chub fetch for him. You can easily understand the comradeship that sprang up among us.

Came October afternoons when shooting slowed a bit. We spent a lot of time in the open, because now we could work the bird dogs into condition, along with Chub. One afternoon, Chub jumped his first rabbit and went off duty for half an hour. An occasional shrill yelp from the bottoms kept me in touch with him, however. He slunk back dejectedly and lay panting beside me in the shady leaf bed of a thick maple. Then I told him it was all right with me, just so he brought home the bacon, because, frankly, fried rabbit is another one of my many weaknesses.

All the while, however, my thoughts were a long way ahead—to the approaching duck shooting and what a grand time Hal and I would have with Chub.

And here we were, at long last. It is quite a "fur, hard piece," out to that shack of ours in the tall cottonwoods skirting two thousand acres of sand bar. A car doesn't dare it except in dry weather for, if a downpour catches you, chains may or may not drag you back to civilization. Shack describes our hideaway accurately: one room, with a kitchen lean-to, built on stilts fifteen feet above high-water stage of "Ol' Miss"—a mile away. West of the camp—a gut that separates Tennessee from Arkansas, by virtue of a federal decree relocating an original riverbank line of the late fifties. To our east— willow flats, sand-bar sloughs, and, beyond, goose country and river wild-fowling; fields rank with bar grass and cockleburs; habitat of swamp rabbits, occasional bobwhite bevies, and heavily spoored by coon, mink, and possum; forests jackstrawed with freshet litter and viny morass; directly overhead the great Mississippi River wildfowl migrational route.

Taking Nature's cold dare gladly, Hal and Chub and I made camp just before dusk. While Hal and I unloaded the plunder, Chub inspected every foot of the place and enjoyed it all hugely. We were soon shipshape and in behind the suppering.

Before turning in we went for a stroll, sat on a log down the float road a piece, listened to night sounds. A big packet fighting the bend current; blue geese and honkers traveling a Stygian ceiling; staccato motorboating away downriver. Chub sniffed a lot of strange sign. Then he climbed onto the log and sat beside me, a bit awed by the big stillness and cold dark. We expected ice in the morning if the breeze laid. Hal thought he would try for black ducks and geese at the sand bar's edge, with both duck and honker stools out front. I would look in first at a hidden slough down in the back gut territory. Panning nothing there, I'd walk and jump-shoot ponds. That, I figured, would be Chub's best chance.

A knock at the door and Chub yowls. "It's jus' me—ol' Clab!" Big Clab from over the levee, come to help Hal with pit digging and packing the live goose decoys.

"Yaas, suh, how you-all dis frawsty mawnin'?" Hal's voice rumbles from the eiderdown. "Th'ow some wood in that heater, Clab—and—th' coal-oil bottle is over yonder on the shelf."

Lamp wicks go on duty; warmth creeps into the chilly shack. Four-thirty! Two hours and more before firing time, but we've breakfast to eat and a goodly hike ahead. Clab has percolator and skillet well in hand. Long experience has taught Hal and me to eat slowly and make up time on the far end. Clab has done himself proud. "Oughta be er cook," he explains, "whut d' ol' lady ain't learnt me, I got learnt in de levee camp."

I leash Chub, tuck the big gun under my other arm, and hit the trail for Old River bank. Boot-crunchings warn that there'll be skim ice on the ponds. So much the better. I slow down as the path narrows into a pit's mouth of darkness. No use to turn an ankle in the gumbo knifed with mule tracks. I reach the "dreen" leading from the cataway pond I'm hunt- ing, a quarter to the left. Difficult going through here, poles very close, and steering Chub no cinch. We creep finally into a clearing just beginning to gray.

Drawing a chunk to a big willow's base, I sit talking quietly to Chub. I picture Hal and Clab at the sand bar's parapet by now, with Clab shovel- ing furiously and Hal staking out the callers and stool. In the distance, a cotton gin begins to pant. The aviation beacon, far below, ceases to pry the night. The east springs with old rose; high across the pond two specks dart with the wavy speed of hell-bats. Teal! A raucous blue heron sails low overhead, and Chub, spotting it, goes frantic. From Hal's distant sector comes a muted double bark—I can tell his twenty-bore as far as I can hear it.

Ahead, down through the stems, the water is ashake. Only one thing does that—ducks! Step by step, with Chub clucked in at heel, I edge to within spotting distance. Fully a hundred dipping, chuckling, feeding mallards, completely off guard and disporting themselves gleefully! I'll put them up, quietly, maybe get a chance if they sweep back, and then sit and wait for some returns. They'll be drifting in to feed these shallows.

"Go get 'em, Chub!" No second bidding needed. Down through the cover drives my companion, and, with a roar, out pile the mallards. A group of five deserts the main body and swings south. I gamble a tall overhead try and a bird slants from the bunch. Across the gut, in Arkansas, I see it drive full tilt into the burned top of a high tree snag and hurtle from sight.

Chub and I wade the marsh, strike a beeline to the far bank, and emerge into young cane near the big landmark. "Bird," I tell him, "go find it— bird." Into the brush dives Chub—some tall woofing, and out pelts Mister

Greenhead with just enough power left to escape the raging springer and gain altitude. Thirty yards away, I drop it into the water's edge. Chub's first duck. He sniffs the big drake cautiously, takes a slant at me, picks it up gingerly, and then, confidence mounting, fashions a high-headed retrieve. Everything is now all set. Chub has the idea!

Overhead a whisping of wings. They couldn't stay away very long, could they! Two mallard drakes, coming from the river, slide across, wheel, and head for the pond's far end. My call, muted at first, rises to a hail. Right-o! The lead bird topples clean across the slough; the second crashes ice into splintering crystals. Now, Chub, for your rightful baptism. Will he tackle that deep mire and keen ice? Bless his heart, I'll say so—through it in springy surges, splattering mud, half swimming, fighting his way to that feathery drift of green and brilliant blue. A snatch, and he heads shoreward.

Meeting him at water's edge, I take the drake, point, and toss a stick toward the far shore. But Chub has seen that other victim. He recrosses and is back with number two. Forenoon wears away. Nine times more the big gun erupts, and Chub does his act. Mud from tail to eyebrows by now, but what of it! For us the day has ended in a blaze of glory. I pack our limit into the capacious rucksack and hit the trail. At the first water hole along the float road, Chub, rather against his will, gets a needed scrubbing. At the shack I skillet a snack for the two of us; Chub dozes on the veranda, while I tidy.

Then, a few shells in my pocket for chance shots at crows or geese, Chub and I hit away to circle the peninsula, survey its lower reaches, and come by to help Hal and Clab with their load. For a river flight, Hal has been shooting with fair regularity. From a vantage hide in the wood's edge we spot Hal's pit and rig, just in time to see three geese sail past and draw a salvo from the 20-gauge. One topples dead, another, hard hit, slants to the water's edge, bounces from the sand, and regains the eddy. Hal climbs from the pit and attempts what seems futile pursuit.

But he's unaware that Chub and I have cut across the sand ahead of him. Chub's taken in the whole business, and it's right down his alley. Into the shoal he pelts, swimming now toward the faintly struggling black and gray heap. If that goose has life enough left, he may hurt or scare the puppy. But luck holds. Furiously Chub tackles the heavy order, swerves, and with the honker's neck in his teeth makes a brave fight across the current. Two minutes, and Hal grabs an armful of the goose and pup. Clab has made the pickup, and we safari homeward with a fine limit of mixed black and gray mallards and four fine geese. (The other pair were Hal's first that morning.)

At the camp all is snugged, and our car breasts the levee. Clab is dropped at his cabin and minded to be on hand at the ramp, three afternoons later. In an hour Hal and I are unloading Chub at my house. We share a toddy and linger by the smoldery log fire. Chub is lost in dreams on the rug, but comes alive at time for Hal to ramble.

At the car something seems to hold the three of us. Memory, perhaps, of all our years together, and today's added bounty. Hal pats Chub's head affectionately and pulls his tousled ears. "Buddy," he tells him, "you're a grand fellow. We wouldn't take a fortune for you, would we, Buck?" The lake in front of our house is a dying molt of flickering amber. "Good night," he calls. "We'll try 'em a couple more barrels—good night, Chub."

Still held by that vague shadow, Chub and I stand looking into the purpling dusk, after Hal, wheeling away into the gloaming; stanch, golden heart into a golden west, fading around life's bend. For Clab will wait in vain at the levee's ramp, three days from now.

Chub and I go slowly into the house, for Hal has gone—away and away and away, to that far shore already so close upon him then—where, God willing, all hunters will some day meet again.

The Ropes and Tools
of Goose Shooting

This article, which constitutes a manual on goose shooting by an expert, first appeared in Field & Stream, *November 1924, and later in the collection* Ole Miss'. *Nash advises about the care of a gun in the sandy conditions of a goose pit, warns of the dangers of soft mucky mud ("loblolly" along the Mississippi doesn't mean "pine") and speaks with experience of the treachery of the big river.*

His comment about swans, "that once a species lowers beyond a certain danger line, it vanishes with startling rapidity," should be warning to those concerned about parallel situations, such as the persistently low ruffed grouse populations over the past ten years in the eastern grouse ranges. Too many persons involved with both wildfowl and grouse have sucked knowingly on their pipes and blown smoke rings at the suggestion that gun pressure has an effect.

Re Nash's experience while reading in the goose pit, I would have had to spare that honker if he had peered over at me from the brink of the pit, but I forgive Nash almost anything when I read a passage like: " . . . the glory of dawns with wavy lines of early voyaging Canadas." At such times he draws with the incisiveness of a drypoint.

Mention of the "automobile" shovel—a short tool furnished to dig a car out of sandy ditches—pins this action to a period long before this piece was published, or perhaps Nash was unaware that Detroit did not still provide them. (Berry Brooks and some of Nash's friends say that Nash, to the best of their knowledge, never drove a car.) The last "automobile" shovel I can recall came as accessory to my father's 1912 Hudson. If today's gunners could have done their goose shooting in that era, few would have complained.

M Y EXPERIENCE IN wild goose gunning extends from prairie holes and fence corners to Currituck's brush blinds and the natural hides of Louisiana and Texas coastals. For better than forty years I've enjoyed sport at the big migrants from sand bar pits, cornstalk hutches and switch-willow patches along the middle Mississippi's bewildering territory. To me, goose shooting's greatest charm has lain in its environment. Many goose hunts develop into first-rate ducking adventures, and I have flushed and taken toll of deer, wild turkey and many another species while out after *Anser canadensis*. Goose shooting along the Mississippi presents situations on land or water which may change for the worse and more deadly, any moment. For instance, pottering around the big river after nightfall, you may be exposed to fog, wind, whirlpools, a jab at your craft from snags or driftwood, or worse, being buried under a caving bank. When you have listened to the rumble of acres at a time going into the undermining current, or crept along in pitchy darkness while a stuttering gas engine carried the tune to your prayers, you may get some faint impression of what I mean. I have come to have great respect for the Mississippi River.

After yanking a skiff around the Mississippi's currents and bars a season or two, you begin to learn about labor saving. If a good sand bar is across from your camp, you learn how to take advantage of the heavy current and "borrow" off it in order to hit your landing mark going and coming. I've seen fellows in skiffs run aground away out on a gently sloping sand bar and work for hours trying to haul their boat closer. When, had they known the river, they'd have spotted a reef and swung in through that to where they wanted. Another fear of river shooting is jelly mud and quicksand. The former causes considerable grief, and the latter is dangerous to humans and animals. Several times, with one foot on apparently hard beach sand, I've bogged down to my thigh on the other leg. All I could do was unload quickly, and roll to safety. The wet spot would close with a gulp·and await the next victim.

In a goose-hunting range of twelve to fifteen miles around a river bend, you'll find such territory well equipped with mud traps. But good goose range one season may be gone the next. A level stretch of sand bar this fall will be ankle deep in silty paste next season, with switch willows sprouting. When the river is falling, know your mud. Don't attempt to retrieve geese or ducks dropped into innocent-looking loblollies. Throw down litter and build a shaky causeway across such a jelly, or lose the bird. Such muck may look solid, at times, but use caution.

Floods rip whole bars from one place and land them another. Mighty current cuts through a low point and a huge "old river bend" is formed. Where your decoys once stood may be solid farm land or mid-river. Mud flats and switch-willow patches tapering off lower ends of newly building bars are splendid hiding and feeding grounds for ducks and geese. Muddy approach makes them inaccessible. Willows hide the sun and keep the blue mud soft. In such places the novice bogs down and serious results may accrue. I have had my Chesapeake Bay dogs fight desperate battles with jelly mud.

On an open, exposed bar, mud blocks are reasonably safe. But even then, when not keeping alert for "corruptious" spots, you may come a cropper. If a wet spot with a white fringe catches your eye—step lightly. On such a bar, however, fine pits can be fashioned by lifting out five or six mud cakes and placing them in a circle. Underneath, in fine, hard sand, dig your pit. Tuck switch willows into the mud blocks, and you may have to hunt for your own hide.

When the Mississippi is rising rapidly and cutting across a low place to "connect up" with the main stream, you had better be very careful. A ten-foot, dribbling trickle at daylight often becomes a deep, hundred-foot channel by going-home-time. Unless you have a boat handy, crossing such places afoot is extremely perilous. And above all, never potter around over-flowed sectors of innocent-looking beach. Lower water discloses innumerable reefs, over which a careless gunner may be wading along ankle-deep and suddenly plunge to oblivion. Make haste slowly, and shuffle the bottom with your feet. Eternal vigilance should be the goose-shooting watchword along "Ole Miss'." Yet despite precautions, each season takes its toll.

When goose shooting, you may have help around to do it for you, but when I start digging a pit I take off my jacket or windbreaker and lay my gun on it—loaded. Before going on a sand bar, clean your weapon with gasoline—leave it dry as a bone—totally minus oil. And aways have along a screw driver and a clean rag. Much sand bar gun trouble results from carelessness. I've tried full-length canvas gun covers, but experience has taught me to take my gun on a sand bar just "as is." In the pit, I put a stick across the walls and lean my gun clear of the sand. If the wind blows I shroud it with a coat. I found that in the excitement of a decoy, I often trampled the gun cover into the sand, which later put more of it into the action, or breech.

Having selected a bar or mud flat for its general adaptability as a goose flyaway, the most important factor governing pit location is the wind. No matter from which direction the flight happens to be working, geese will decoy against the wind. In so doing, they rarely make more than one "close in" circle. Once the "set" is okayed, they generally head straight in. And ofttimes I have seen them, lowering rapidly, come in without a vestige of caution. Sometimes, traveling with or against the wind, geese in direct flight will ignore live and inanimate stool. Experience teaches you to judge such intent. I have often dropped a goose or two from such silent passers-by, risking the shot because I realized their intent to mind nothing.

Some days geese seem to all work from the same general direction. So, let's say the wind is in the north. While you dig, your companion puts out the decoys. With two guns along, dig two pits; they are safer, more convenient, and may be placed with benefit to the bag. The pits are dug with their "backs" to the north wind. They should be small, breast-deep, and the sand shoveled from them should be scattered far and wide. It dries quickly, and is unnoticed. Two-thirds of the way down your pit's inside wall, dig a comfortable seat that can also be used as a "step up." At the pit's bottom, clear foot space. You can stand awhile, or sit down and read, comfortably. When geese are sighted, seat yourself, lower your head and listen. No matter from which direction their approach, you should know that the birds will eventually come in against the wind. If you are giving the signals, do so; otherwise be ready for your companion's zero call. I remember being seated in my goose pit one morning, reading a copy of *Redbook* magazine. All at once I became conscious of something's looking at me. I was using only profile decoys. But a goose had decoyed silently, fed about awhile and then, wandering along, came abruptly upon my pit. A mad scramble ensued in which I lost my place in the book, but the big honker lost his life.

I have been in double goose pits with chaps who became, once game was sighted, human corkscrews. When the shooting moment breaks, novices invariably jump too soon and open fire with the flock just out of range. When decoying, geese loom large and look much closer than they are. In goose pit or duck blind there is one infallible rule: shoot the first shot from whichever position you are in—sitting or standing. Adopt a policy and stick to it. Wildfowl detect movement with uncanny rapidity. The shooter's rising unsteadies him and flares the goose, a miss ensues, followed by others in anger and frustration.

When two pits are dug, they should be placed about thirty yards apart, with the decoys in a "V" between and behind them. The latter should be headed upwind, and so arranged that a circling flock will always have the side view of some birds standing on the sand. Flocks generally sit about with the wind in their favor for an emergency takeoff. Three or four profile decoys should be set about each pit so that the gunner can peep beneath one in case the approach becomes confused. Geese generally light a bit away from another flock and walk up to it. Thus, with the decoys set in behind the pits, the decoying birds will be pulled in closer. If they are nearer your companion his fire will flare them over you, and, in beating up against the wind, the ones escaping are coming nearer.

Once you have birds down, remember that the only certain goose is a dead one. Attend to foot-loose cripples, they can pack away a lot of shot. And in the hullabaloo of chasing, be careful of your step and your gun. Take your time. I've seen a novice cave in a pit and fill his gun with sand that put it completely out of commission. I've watched fellows throw down their gun and chase off after a winged honker unarmed.

The hours geese keep is guesswork, although their feeding time in certain localities ofttimes holds to a close schedule. But on a sand bar, all that is different. My rule is to let daylight find me in my hide, with decoys set. Fifteen or twenty minutes can make a difference in several shots. Wildfowl begin to move at daylight. With the present federal regulations establishing seven a.m. as "shooting hour," necessity for old-time goose shooting's early activities is removed. While this is perhaps conservationally sound, many a sandbar hunter will miss the thrill of before-daylight questings, and the glory of dawns dotted with wavy lines of early voyaging Canadas. In sand-bar goose shooting, the first two or three hours after sunup are usually the most productive. Hunters, boats and inland field croppers send the flocks on their ways. On the other hand, I have sat all day without seeing or hearing a goose, and then, with an hour or so left of daylight, witnessed a tremendous movement of the birds.

Years ago, on opening day of the season, Eugene Palmer and I explored a mud bar and switch-willow patch that had "made in" during the summer, leaving Hal Howard at the houseboat to put things shipshape. The tender young willows formed cover better than half a mile long and perhaps three hundred yards wide. We dug three pits at their upper end, and three at the lower. In these last we took a long snooze after our hard work. During early afternoon Eugene, becoming discouraged, went to the houseboat and sent Hal up for whatever the afternoon might bring. Hal had with him a lone live goose decoy, as we had taken no stool of any sort with us on our working expedition. We staked the bird on some open sand outside the willows and prepared to sit out the hoodoo. Within an hour of sunset, I happened to look over my shoulder toward the land side of the bar. Some geese rose from what I knew was a hidden slough between the bar's crown and mainland, and winged toward the switch willows. Not a sound did they utter. Our pits were beautifully camouflaged. There was a faint breeze from the northeast. The geese, circling, spotted that lone decoy and sailed straight in from the southwest, giving us good shots at all of them.

Hardly had the excitement of such luck cleared away, when four more birds sailed down the same air lane. Behind them, other flocks rose from the slough. We downed the four, but our shooting failed to disturb their followers. Seemingly, every goose on the bar had selected the lower end of that mud bar for roosting space. It required but a few more salvos to get down all the birds we wanted. And then we witnessed a strange sight. At dusk there were probably three or four hundred geese, fussing, gabbling and strutting about within almost touching distance. A bunch of cattle fed down off the mainland, and a flock of incoming geese stampeded them. We became the center of a milling, bucking, bellowing, honking neighborhood. When order finally restored itself, we got out of the pits, gathered our slain, and walked off down the bar. A few geese nearest us rose and flew off a bit to one side, but their main body remained undisturbed. Next day our early-morning shooting was again rewarded from that hidden pond. And you may be sure we never bothered the refuge, either.

One morning I was shooting from a pit in those same switch willows but I noticed that the flight, working from the south, was passing me up to alight on the main sand-bar plateau several hundred yards above me. Grabbing an armful of profile decoys, I ran to a pit I had already dug out there, and stuck them in position. As I mounted the slope on my second trip, a bunch of geese sailed overhead and pitched directly at the stools I had set up. Crawling to the parapet of the plateau, I watched proceedings through my binoculars. The new arrivals lit outside the decoys, did some gabbling, and proceeded to give the shams a rigid once-over. Then their leader, with pontifical, if somewhat pigeon-toed tread, waddled over to the nearest profile, and, with neck extended, glared it straight in the eye. Apparently infuriated by the dead pan and unblinking hospitality extended, Mr. Goose flew on that decoy, wings, beak and toenails. Under the assault, the dummy flopped to the sand with a dull thump. Mr. Goose, in turn, bellowed like a bull calf and scuttled back to his companions. Then, waddling up and down the company front, he delivered a stirring lecture. Suddenly all chatter ceased and without a sound the whole outfit took wing.

Goose hunting requires no special type of clothing, other than well-blended color and warmth without weight. There is work to goose shooting, and long waits should not be endured while still perspiring. Dress as lightly as possible, but have along a woolly and mackinaw, or good windbreaker to take care of such a situation. I prefer an old hat to a cap; one whose brim can be adjusted by a mere touch to offset sun angles. Lightweight rubber boots, worn turned down and strapped below the knees, are preferable to leather boots. The latter are only as waterproof as the care given them, and sand will soon cut seams. Besides, situations are constantly being encountered which call for wading better than knee-deep. Only rubber boots answer such an emergency. I have long since learned to carry my entire goose-hunting outfit in a commodious canvas shoulder pack. Into it go two dozen lightweight, hand-painted goose profiles, extra shells, binoculars, camera, featherweight slicker and iron rations. Atop the outfit is the inevitable automobile shovel. There have been, and still are, various goose-calling devices, all the way from a metal "tooter" to a slate-scraping contraption that produces an ingenious simulation of the goose's tonal inflections. The only real goose call lies in the human throat and will beat all the mechanized effects ever produced.

Times have changed along the Mississippi, the Missouri and the Platte. Good roads and automobiles bring hordes of goose hunters from hundreds of miles inland. If water stages are low, they reach the sand bars afoot. If high, the outboard motor puts them there. It takes high water, bitter weather and rough going as to roads, to give the geese a break. Nowadays "bar-walkers" trouble what is left of the knowing goose hunters. It is discouraging, with a fine bunch of birds headed for one's pit and no disturbance in sight, to see them suddenly lift in haste and wheel away. Your binoculars will reveal a white-shirted "bar-walker" somewhere in the picture. But by far the most disastrous blow at goose shooting has been its commercialization. Federal bans on baiting and the use of live stools have slowed such destruction somewhat. But so devious are America's methods of law evasion, and so thoroughly steeped its human predators of wildlife masquerading as sportsmen, that it will require sterner federal and state measures to separate wildlife resources from the taint of the dollar. Only those who have studied the atrocities perpetrated in commercial shooting resorts realize this.

Preference for goose guns and loads will continue a pleasant field for discussion and argument, until the last bird falls. Unquestionably, as in duck shooting, a majority of today's wildfowlers use magazine guns, federally curtailed to a three-shot loading capacity. The knowing goose hunter will do well to go no lower than the twelve-bore realm. I have killed geese with every gauge gun from a .410 to a four-bore single tube. But to "bring home the goose" there are two answers to the gun argument. Never send a boy on a man's errand. And—"the good big one beats the good little one—every time."

Thou and Thy Gun Bearer

While I was thumbing through Nash's own copy of the Derrydale De Shootinest Gent'man, *it fell open at page 171, the beginning of "Thou and Thy Gun Bearer," where a folded letter was attached with a paper clip that had worn a small round hole in the laid paper. Addressed to Nash in Memphis, the letter was dated Huntington, West Virginia, June 8, 1964.*

Dear Nash:

I am just out of the hospital after an operation. What I am writing about is to tell you that when I went into the hospital I took two books —the Bible, which I read often, and a copy of your *De Shootinest Gent'-man.* I enjoyed reading every chapter again. But my favorite chapter is, I believe, "Thou and Thy Gun Bearer." This is indeed a choice morsel which helped me much in my recovery and I just wanted you to know about it.

Best wishes and God's blessings, always,

Herman P. Dean

"Thou and Thy Gun Bearer," also one of my favorites, was written during the peak of Nash's creativity. It appeared first in Field & Stream, *March 1922. Like "The Harp That Once—" and "De Shootinest Gent'man," it shows the relation between Negro and white in the South, a relation that existed, whether you like it or not. Lack of comprehension of the devotion of the Southern black man to his white folks is found most frequently in those persons unable to grasp why the Negro was affectionately called "Uncle" or "Aunt." If you don't know, you will never learn. Berry Brooks expresses it this way:*

"I had the pleasure and privilege of knowing Nash for over fifty years. We had much in common although I was about twenty years younger. I have lived in the same area and hunted and fished nearly all the forests and streams he did. We were both lovers of the out-of-doors with a common feeling for the Negroes. We had both been brought up with them, felt like we were obligated to take care of them, understood and appreciated them. We also had their admiration and respect. Some of our happiest recollections were of hunting with them."

Nowhere does a closer bond exist between the two races than in the shooting field. A famous such friendship was the lifelong one between Archibald Rutledge and Prince Alston. It is not, as Nash explains, a simple arrangement between a shooting man and a servant, though the Negro unquestionably was not the one waited upon. The Negro has a feel for the woods, for game, and for dogs. Often he had the most to offer in terms of knowledge of local coverts and resourcefulness, repaid beyond actual wages by opportunity the white man could provide— hunting and fishing in restricted areas or in far places, especially in the old days when such trips were the prerogative of the wealthy. And the Negro loved it.

It was difficult to find a greater snob than the Negro servant of one of the old families. They knew "quality" and jealously guarded it in their white folks; no one responded more appreciatively to style and flair, no one could more acutely spot a fraud. There have always been those in the North and South who spoke of the Negro's "knowing his place." I'm suspicious of the person who is disturbed about another's "place," for it is a fair sign he may be out of his own.

Nash's portrait of Uncle Phil Gwynne could not have been painted from an imaginary person. His background as chef on river boats, in New Orleans, in the duck club; his goatee; above everything, his yarns of the War Between the States with his participation in several battles simultaneously, make him the genuine article. The delineation of Uncle Phil's kitchen at Wapanoca is a beauty, coming from the memories of a youngster who cut his teeth on duck club fare. However, I suspect the Buckingham touch and wonder at the old man's recitation of each of those dishes. But I accept it, knowing how Nash enjoyed every one he set down.

Nash tells of sluicing ducks on the water in his first sorties—bloodthirsty little savage that he was—and tells it without a trace of remorse. Instead, he enjoys the memory of the affair shared with Uncle Phil.

In Nash's papers I found a fragile yellowed newspaper clipping from The Evening Scimitar, *dated April 6, 1901. The name Bun Price is inscribed in ink beside the title "Tribute to a Negro from a White Friend" set in steamboat type-face. There is a halftone of a photograph with the caption: "Phil Gwynne Holding a Canvas-Back Duck at the Wapanoca Clubhouse Landing." The piece is written with sincerity and ends: "No colored man has died for many years past who was more beloved or respected than 'Uncle Phil Gwynne' and the sportsmen of this city will never look upon his like again." The date of this clipping suggests that Phil Gwynne died in 1901 when Nash was twenty-one, but Nash speaks of himself in "Thou and Thy Gun Bearer" as "child that I was," indicating the period as before that.*

"Thou and Thy Gun Bearer" is steeped in the mood of Strauss's Death and Transfiguration—*the gradual extinction of a human flame. Nash expresses in a paragraph what men will feel for as long as one of them stands under the stars and listens to the wind on the night a friend dies.*

I HAVE NEVER HUNTED in Africa, where gun bearers of the safari type do service; Negroes upon whose nerve and coolness in time of. acute danger depends life. But being Southern-born and practically raised afield, it has been my happy lot to come in contact with full many a Negro hunter. Over a period of well-nigh forty years, I call to mind several specimens of the Afro-woodsman offshoot whose stanch help and teachings have had much to do with my later successful traverse of the outdoorsman's domain. The kind I knew has pretty nearly passed, but on my native heath there are many men who realize the fiber of the breed I mean. He was the Negro who loved the hunt with all the innate understanding of his jungle fore-bears. He played a humble second fiddle in all save toil and glad acclaim in the spoils of the chase. He knew the silent paths and stillest corners of the big timber; the swamp crossings and bayou tracings were open books. "Varmint" haunts and the lore of graveyard rabbits came as second nature, and the cult of "yarbs" and influence of the moon upon planting and biting fish required but a turning of nature's pages. Winds whispered to him certain mysterious meanings; he foretold the fates by virtue of cloud linings and prophecy of the rainbow. He lived in the very lap of season! Who knew the covey grounds as well as he; who skulked a squirrel woods with as flitter-ing and shadowy patience; who took more certain toll from turkey roosts that yielded victims with the mingling of moon flight and dawn? Flight lines and goose-tracked sand bars knew no more adept hound, while his traps and deadfalls outmatched the denizens of a region where footprints told no tales! And he knew all these things in his own particular way; which means that his understanding was past our own and subject only to his own pleasure and friendship for the imparting thereof. This was the man who served because he knew faith and honor. To him no road was too long if duty called. He fetched and carried and bore heavy burdens willingly, read his Bible diligently and frowned upon the tendencies of an encroaching generation. When he accompanied his "white folks" afield there was com-panionship without intimacy, comradeship in common purpose and full realization of appreciation on both sides. But alas! with the coming of civilization we find them now retreating from the trenches of service into more peaceful billets of reminiscence. An old hewn-log cabin far beyond the "new ground," a comfortable rocking chair outside in the shade of summer and a warm fireside in winter—and a pipe always! The incidents I recall here I mean simply enough as a tribute to a faithful friend who taught me much and did for me that which was best in his conception of the theory of life and unselfish service!

Such was "Uncle" Phil Gwynne, clubhouse keeper, cook, paddler-in-chief and general all-around generalissimo of our duck club Wapanoca. Way back in the early eighties, when the club was organized from a shelter tent into a log cabin and thence into a small white cottage, Uncle Phil was unanimously put in charge. He knew intimately and personally all the gentlemen who comprised the limited membership of that day, by virtue of having waited on poker games, served at banquets, cooked on deer hunts, and played around generally with most of them for many years. Uncle Phil had been born a slave, was proud of it, cast in his lot with the Confederacy and lived and died an ardent and argumentative Democrat. Given three toddies of any of his gentlemen friends' good liquor, Uncle Phil could produce the most enthralling rhapsody concerning the benefits of democracy that any political organ ever breathed o'er Eden as accompaniment. He had personally danced attendance upon practically every Confederate general of any note, and been present at every "who's who" battle of the late unpleasantness, to hear him tell it, and although at times a variance of dates claimed his presence at two battles at the same time, he was never at a loss and supplied details of so colorful a nature in the interim that his audience overlooked mere trifles of a few years.

But at heart and soul Uncle Phil was a thoroughgoing sportsman and an admirer of every gentleman who knew and owned a good gun or dog. No pot-metal guns or low-blooded bird dogs for Uncle Phil! He owned an old ten-gauge Westley Richards himself, and called all the fine dogs of his patrons his own. Yet with it all no humbler soul ever saw sunrise; no kindlier spirit ever sought firm ground for its circle of friends. When I first knew Uncle Phil I was a mere lisping shaver just graduating from "kilties" to "pants." Even then he had given up hard paddling and exposure and taken over the clubhouse and cooking end of the game. Occasionally, if a shortage of pushers occurred or he wished to convey an especial privilege, Uncle Phil went on the lake—and when he did it was always a memorable day for the lucky one. He was a natural-born hunter, a keen shot, and quite the best marker-down of cripples I have ever seen. I have seen him out with Daddy and Mister Arthur and Baltimore, his huge Chesapeake Bay dog, when the flight was intense, the mud and rushes deep and thick, and excitement at its height. Sometimes there would be three or four ducks down or falling. Yet Uncle Phil was never at a loss. He went overboard to one side and Baltimore another, and before long the pair would come slushing and mushing back, and Baltimore was hardly ever more than "one up" on the old chief.

Uncle Phil's education, gleaned from the contact of a lifetime with quality "white folks," was far beyond the average of his race at that time, and he put it to good use. By religion he was a devout Methodist and in a log church which his "flock" had erected on a nearby Indian mound his faith and goodness shone forth in service that involved preaching, ministering to the sick and teaching Sunday school. When Christmas time rolled around Uncle Phil visited the city and carried back with him enough good cheer to make a real Yuletide for his colored folks. But it was, after all, Uncle Phil's kitchen that held for me a magnetic attractiveness. His culinary domain was housed in a commodious quarter aft, connected with the club-house by a covered gangway off which was set the game and paddlers' plunder room. It was my custom, upon return from shooting, to ease quietly into Uncle Phil's place of business and, from the vantage point of a seat upon an empty shell box, set well aside from channels of traffic, amid pots and barrels and crocks, listen to the old fellow's discourse upon hunting, cooking, the theory of the universe or a tolerant discourse upon the rise and fall of the Roman, black, yellow, or Caucasian empire.

There was a wide, open fireplace and chimney corner, a region pendant with soot-covered rods and hooks, and gratings turning brick red in the heat of glowing coals, while from a big range came bubblings and rumblings as covered pots and stewpans gave vent to pent-up emotions of cookery. Hams hung from the rafters and there was invariably at the evening hour a comforting odor of hot, browning biscuits and coffee that at times brought one to a condition bordering upon mutiny against patience. And all the while Uncle Phil pottered in and out, his two sprigs of gray twisted forelock and aristocratic "goatee" giving him a weird shadow upon the curtains. He peeked into a pot here, poked a sinister but ministering fork there, opened the oven and prodded a pie or scanned a batch of biscuits or corn muffins— and talked all the time. At such periods the old man's fancy naturally enough ran to food. In slave days and after, for he was an old man even then, he had been a steamboat cook on the palatial liners that ran from Memphis to New Orleans. He had cooked in private kitchens of Louisiana aristocrats. And many of our club members had taken him with them to the Dakota prairies and sloughs when they went for chicken shooting. He knew each member's fads and fancies in the way of food and service. While I sat on my shell box and elicited talk by an occasional inquiry, Uncle Phil would run riot on his cooking prowess.

At such times Uncle Phil harked back to brave steamboat and New Orleans days. He babbled of eggs "Coquelin" and oysters "Rockefeller," of snipe broiled whole as M'sieu Gaston himself had taught him amid frightful admonitions in event of failure in the matter of a certain daring and piquant sauce.

There was catfish court bouillon, with crab omelet and mushroom dressing; demi-lyonnaise potatoes and smoking drip coffee. Thence flights of gastronomic revery winged toward gumbo and red snappers, the latter baked in fine herbs, with panfish or sheepshead done in versatile measures of excellence. There were roasted fat mallards from some rice marsh; teals, garlanded with oysters tucked up with bacon strips and broiled into a buttery state of utter deliciousness. He conjured gnawing pictures of game stew, a lowly *poule d'eau,* for instance, shriven into a marvel of appetite by a mere turn of curry, tomato and rice, garlic and a potpourri of secret ingredients. Thence Uncle Phil trailed off into courses of upland yield, while I, knees drawn to chin and mouth adrool, listened while he prated of smothered quail and roast prairie chicken, with spring lamb on the side, when available for a feast—a mere babe of, say, thirty pounds, roasted as only such a morsel offering should be, with delicate baste and mint extract timed to the second.

Followed crappies and bass, fried de luxe out of doors, in a delirium of sputtering fats and fancies, with corn pone and coffee on the side and potato chunks browned to taste and served with drawn butter over all. Entered tender young squirrels, with a rich tang from mulberry feasting, hips padded with pork slivers, with just a dash of tabasco and done rare over hickory coals. There were tales of venison, stalked and slain by one Maspero and roasted in the ground as to ribs and chops and balanced into sausage with "shoat" shavings, pepper, "yarbs" and a faint soupçon of rare old wine. Flanking these came roasting ears, butter-oiled and fumed under oak shavings; new potatoes and bales of limp, succulent asparagus. Or, if Uncle Phil's fancy fell upon a course dinner, his musings ran the gamut of anchovies and oyster cocktails on down to orange brulé. But when he reached barbecue and stuffed beef heart and a pan dish of sweet potato and tomato bread balls and squirrel dumpling all mixed up and browned over the top, the voice of appetite crashed into a crescendo of demand, and I usually fell from my shell box and ran beyond the lure of his voice; or else, taking advantage of Uncle Phil's turned back, yielded to temptation and robbed the nearest pan. I can taste those stolen tidbits yet, they still set my mouth a-watering.

A memorable occasion brought us to the club one time just after I had strained at the bonds of youth until given a gun of my own, and Daddy, not wishing to be bothered with me or bother the others, left me in charge of Uncle Phil. There was considerable bantering and betting in the crowd as to who'd be high gun that evening. During the forenoon I hunted the cypress brakes around the clubhouse and amassed a bag total of four squirrels and a "flicker," and after lunch cast about for a try at some more worthy quarry. About midafternoon Uncle Phil whistled up Baltimore, told me to get my gun and shells, and we piled into his private bateau. My delight knew no bounds. We paddled silently up the mile or more of narrow creek that drained from the lakes. It was a glorious late November afternoon, when the warmth of midday had just begun to tingle with the crisp approach of impending frost, and the sun filtered comfortably down through the interlacing cypress giants that overhung the bayou. From Little Lake we heard two or three guns at work, and as we approached its entrance we heard from up on Big Lake the deep roaring "b-o-o-m" of the black powder of that day.

Uncle Phil ran the bateau ashore just before we reached the spread of water, and led me across a waste of spongy willow flat to a mud slough cast away from sight behind a wall of cypress timber. At the water's edge a gigantic stump offered a wonderful hide, and I could tell by its warm, sawdusty interior that this was a much-used and favorite haunt of Uncle Phil's. We made ourselves comfortable, Baltimore curled up at Uncle Phil's feet, and that worthy, after lighting his pipe, lapsed into quiet drowsing. Not a duck in sight! But the roar of guns on the lakes continued and I grew restless and denounced my guide's choice of a blind. The old man awoke, listened to my say, smiled knowingly—"Jus' you wait, l'il Boss; dey'll be he'ah!" Then, in the midst of a soothing yarn as to what he did when the Yankees were on the point of blowing up the *Queen-of-the-West,* there came from overhead the whistling banter of many wings, and into that mud puddle sifted a great swarm of clustering mallards. Down we crouched, and I can see the eager strain in Baltimore's yellow eyes as he realized that his afternoon's fun, too, had begun. To check my movement of preparedness, Uncle Phil seized me by the shoulder and pressed me down. "Hol' still, l'il Boss, hol' still—mo' comin'!" And how they did circle and chuckle and flutter down into that loblolly hole! The very air seethed with applicants for space.

As though it were yesterday, I can still hear my black mentor's word to fire—he with his ten-gauge and I with my twelve-gauge. How those ducks did pile out of there when that dose of shot raked them on the water and again as they rose! It was unsportsmanlike, but it was business to Uncle Phil and me, for the old rascal had a purpose in taking me out that afternoon. I dashed from the blind and all but dove into soupy pond, with Baltimore ahead of me and surging to business among the slain! Uncle Phil cut a long pole and with this as a rake and much adventure in the mud and Baltimore's aid we at length retrieved the kill. Twenty-nine magnificent mallards—I blush now, but I swelled with pride at the time! Piling them into bunches of five and hiding them out, we renewed our policy of watchful waiting. I was now a thorough convert to Uncle Phil's method of acquiring game and joyfully proclaimed our joint prowess. After a little while another swarm of birds dropped in, and again we made a red afternoon with them. Then, as the afternoon waned, they came in pairs and smaller gangs, and I banged away to my heart's content, while Uncle Phil alternately bowled over a greenhead and instructed me as to distance and lead. At length, when the sun had left us but a cold rim through the cypress, Uncle Phil eyed his huge silver watch and began transporting our bag to the bateau. "Time t'git home and start gittin' supper!"

The limit was fifty ducks and by count we had fifty-nine, so Uncle Phil appropriated the extra nine for table use, and hung my bunch of fifty handsome birds in the game room. When the grown-ups arrived there I was, apparently unconcerned and trying to appear at ease at their wondering queries; but I fear there was no small amount of unconscious swank—and I know that I asked odds of no monarch—that night.

My first wild turkey! The New Year's Day when Daddy and I and a pusher—old Fred—tipped over an ice-coated bateau up in Little Lake and sank ingloriously into two feet of water so cold it fairly burnt. But we paddled like mad down the creek to the clubhouse, and what with having kept circulation going and a warm fireside and a rub-down with dry clothing, we emerged none the worse. Daddy said that insofar as he was personally concerned he was willing to call it a day—and did. But none o' that for Youth! Uncle Phil donned his gum boots, took down the ten-gauge and 'lowed that he and l'il Boss would go down the creek a ways and see what they could "scar' up!" Save for a narrow strip of channel, the bayou was frozen and a four-inch snow had us well put to it to thread the jungle. We were standing just outside the wall of a giant canebrake, debating a shot at some mallards flying the open water, when some distance below us a drove of great, clumsy-looking birds rose from the timber opposite and sailed across to our side.

"Dar, now!" muttered Uncle Phil, turning hurriedly into the cane. "Come on, l'il Boss, les' head 'em off!"

"What are they, Uncle Phil—buzzards?"

"Turkey!" he threw back over his shoulder and split the bush. We ran until I fairly gasped for breath. Suddenly at the foot of a huge oak just off a clearing in the underbrush, Uncle Phil sank to his knees and drew forth a bit of whitened bone. He was going to "call," and an instant later the quaint yelp sounded through the snow-clad woods. "Dey most likely won't, but dey may," he muttered. But in just a moment, it seemed, with a great flapping of wings a giant bird rose some distance off and came sailing directly over us. I saw him coming and it seemed to me that with cold fingers the drawing of my hammers seemed hopeless. But somehow I got them back and with a prayer in my boy's heart I swung the tubes out past that mottled head until I lost it and pulled off both barrels. As in a dream I saw the turkey waver and come swirling down. But when he hit the snow he lit running and then ensued a race that laid Uncle Phil, shouting with laughter, against a tree root. A winged racehorse of a wild turkey hot-footing it for life, with a frenzied boy in hot pursuit. Uncle Phil told Daddy afterward that the turkey and I tore a right-of-way through the woods big enough for a steamboat; but, be that as it may, I know that at that moment when I was about played out Mister Gobbler became entangled in a vine. And there, between puffs and pants, I stood at ease until my wind came back, and then with malice and aforethought I shot that bird soundly dead—and bore him back in triumph. A fine gobbler he was, too, with a beard that was worth keeping and wattles that set off the bronze of him to perfection. What a day that was! We lost all sense of time and direction for a while, for Uncle Phil's blood was up and he set to work with a will. Three more fat birds fell into his vocal snare and we took turns laying them low. It was nigh sundown when we circled out of the timber and made it across the fields to the clubhouse. We had four turkeys, had seen deer tracks, and I am sure that a trade of jobs with the Czar of all the Russias would have been a paltry offer to me that night.

Years later—years that multiplied with adventures as the trail led on and on—Uncle Phil began to fade. He pottered cheerfully about and never complained—but he knew! One of his grandchildren came to aid him in the kitchen and he still talked to me evenings. But his old ten-gauge hung idle from its antler'd rack, and his hunting days were always to be—tomorrow. Good old soul! He still crawled painfully to church meetings occasionally and Christmas was always made an event to be remembered for him. But finally there came a day when the best thing Uncle Phil could do was to smile a wan smile from his bed—and rest there. We all sensed that now he was slipping fast. How well I remember his last night, for I was over there with Daddy and Mister Arthur and several other members who cherished the old slave. For hadn't they been together when storms beat upon them; when suns rose o'er the stubble of the Northlands and set for them in the dark undergrowth of Southern canebrakes? Hadn't they known together all the joys of the chase and found therein for one another boon comradeship and respect? We sat around the yawning fire-place that bitter-cold night, each one for the most part busy with thoughts of sadness for the quaint old soul so near the verge. At length, Mister Arthur and Daddy, unable to stand it longer, slipped quietly away and went across the pasture lot to Uncle Phil's cabin. And I, unnoticed, trudged along behind them—I wanted to see Uncle Phil, too.

A dim light burned in the room where the old man lay, and, as in most Negro homes when the final hour impends, a group of friends and relatives had gathered, standing and sitting about in various postures of dejected waiting. We tiptoed to the bedside and stood looking down at the pathetic figure, lying there so frail and still. Child that I was, his likeness in the fullness of manhood came sweeping across the years. I saw him tall and vigorous, scarce bending under the weight of a deer, or outlined a black statue as he stood to pole the buck boat into the very teeth of a wintry gale. I saw him again as he peeked and pried into the pots and pans and cast his shadow upon the kitchen curtains! Mister Arthur bent down and spoke very gently—"Uncle Phil—this is Mister Arthur—how do you feel—do you know me?" The drooping eyelids fluttered and for a moment the old man's eyes searched Mister Arthur's face without understanding, and then just the drift of a smile repaid the understanding that his treasured friend had come to him in this hour! And then he whispered—"Th' mud is deep, suh, I'se holdin' onto de willers but I'se sinkin' fas'!" Mister Arthur placed his hand upon Uncle Phil's and I believe that as the white hand clasped the black one there passed between those two old friends a message that they alone understood—and perhaps from that hour looked forward to! Silently Daddy and I stepped forward and patted Uncle Phil's hand, and each time the eyelids fluttered feebly. He had seen us—and understood—I know. Then we went quietly again, out into the night. Ah! Surely it was an evening—a noble evening for the soul of a tired but true old hunter to fare forth alone upon the long mystery trail. For a wind had risen, a near gale from the south that sent clouds scurrying northward and yet somehow beat upon us with a touch of warmth in its breath. It meant, that breath, that ere daybreak the ice would boom and crack and show great lanes of black open water and that upon the heels of the blow a rain would scour the glazed remnant and send the first challenge of spring into the sloughs. And with it the premier voyageurs of a winged host would spiral from the broad bosom of the lake and send their flight lanes toward northern climes. Sunrise would flash upon the brilliant plumage of transient sprigtails and bands of fickle teal would dart about the favorite blinds that Uncle Phil had built and loved so well.

From the cabin behind us—where a light still gleamed faintly—came a low, minor wail that mounted as a chorus of blending voices wound their chords into a death chant. We halted and Mister Arthur and Daddy stood with bowed heads.

"We were just in time, Arthur," said Daddy. "Uncle Phil has gone!"

"Yes, Miles," replied Mister Arthur, and his voice trembled just a bit. "Uncle Phil is with Bun and George and Robert and all the old boys of ours in the Happy Hunting Grounds—Heaven grant him a good flight and God rest his good old soul!"

Wax and Wane

Reading these notations, selected from those published in Blood Lines, *is as close as most men will come to seeing a gun diary of Nash Buckingham's. John Bailey says he knew of no gun diary that Nash kept, but that he made notes in duck club logbooks as well as wrote from memory. Dr. William Andrews spoke of "Mr. Buck's remarkable memory, especially for a man in his eighties." These excerpts, dated in the manner of a journal, while not dealing altogether with shots and points and game, were obviously from some sort of record kept almost daily during the latter part of 1937, and reveal how valuable his diaries would have been.*

Early shotgun training for a boy is always interesting, though for many of us our experience happened so long ago. "Young Jim" in the first section was the son of Nash's sister, Mrs. Arthur Ware. Nash's advice to Jim in the January 21 entry is excellent advice for any shooter: to hold the gun well down until he picks out the bird to focus on.

"Bayard" in the November 25 entry was Bayard Snowden, whom John Bailey describes: "They were pals as boys, young men and old men; they ranched to-gether in Colorado." Nash's talk of himself and "white-haired Bayard" getting on in years as shooting men, was premature in 1937. (Bayard Snowden died in October 1968.) This hunt was on Huntley May's place, which adjoined the famous Ames Plantation at Grand Junction. Nash's axiom "Never, if you can help it, start a shooting season with a miss" is excellent advice in open quail terrain and in a duck blind but it can make a basket case out of a ruffed-grouse gunner.

Nash's love for people—almost any people—comes through in his description of the carnival mood of the crowd in De Witt the night before duck season opens. The excitement of opening day is one I believe Nash never lost, and he captures it beautifully in the November 27 portion—the young nephew's wonderment, Nash checking his watch by flashlight several times before time to arise. I think in that enthusiasm lies the secret of his vitality that lasted nearly to the end of his more than ninety years, eighty of them centered about shooting.

Bob Anderson describes the type of duck shooting in the De Witt area:

I should explain that most of our shooting was done in flooded woods in eastern Arkansas. Much of the country from Forrest City to Little Rock is suitable for cultivation of rice. For rice you need water. Some rice growers pumped, others built reservoirs along stream beds, flooding trees. Sometimes the trees died, leaving dead snags in ponds. On Club 16, which I built and where Nash and I went many times for 20 years, we tried to get the water off at season's end and put it on in September or October. We cleared out small places so the ducks could see decoys, and built blinds, though both of us would as soon lean against a tree. If you stayed still against a tree a duck could not see you. Trees in that country were not over 90 feet tall, so we shot ducks over the tree tops and enjoyed it. All mallards in that rice country.

In these episodes of shooting at De Witt, Nash describes numbers of ducks that seem to negate his concern for dwindling wildfowl populations, but speaks of them being relatively more heavily gunned than in the market hunting era. In an entry I have omitted, there is a passage describing mallard shooting I feel is one of Nash's finest:

One unforgettable sight made my day. We were walking along when overhead whisked a bunch of at least a hundred mallards. I blew just one loud hail and that great mass of birds put on the brakes, cocked sideways and poured down through the sun-shot oak tops. It was simply dazzling as the mass of gorgeously plumaged birds sifted through a funnel of brown and lemon leaves. I could have discharged "Bo-Whoop" up through that surge and bagged a one-shot limit. In five seconds they were sitting all about us with Foy and me hugging our trees.

The Christmas Eve and January 31 entries are experiences all of us share—the final cleaning and laying away of a gun for the season, and none of us knows for how long. If the thought tugs at the heart, take courage. Nash enjoyed shooting for more than thirty seasons after that.

November 20, 1937

WELL, DOVE-SHOOTING SEASON is long past and so is frost on the pumpkins. Fifteen, twenty years ago we had been after ducks and quail for weeks. Bag limits of that day seem like a dream. But age mellows all that. Nephew Arthur James Valentine Ware, a husky of fourteen, has been helping me run the dogs. We generally manage to work around the farm and come home via the Wolf River bottoms. The river has been crystal-clear for a month, and the dogs take to the gravel bars and cool shallows like a bunch of porpoise.

Young Jim is going into his third intensive season of scatter-gun training that began with a .410-gauge. But before being taken afield, he was patiently taught the structural nomenclature of a shotgun, from its locks and butt plate to the front sight. Then loading, handling, and head-up, binocular firing at a swinging target. Twenty-five paces from the limb of a giant oak, Jim shot away many a box of shells at tin cans suspended on wires and set swinging from side to side and forward and backward. You have no idea what splendid practice this is for both angles and tries at incomers and climbing birds. Then Jimmy sat under a persimmon tree in the Goodman pasture and popped away to his heart's content at hurtling, twisting doves. At the beginning of his second season he was handed his first twelve-bore— the first Winchester pump gun ever to reach the state of Tennessee.

The late Irby Bennett, grand sportsman and for many years district manager of the old Winchester Repeating Arms Company, offered it as a prize for schoolwork between my older brother and me. Miles won it, of course, but after a few trials turned it over to me and went back to his own long, heavy, hammer double gun. The new-fangled, trombone-action Winchester was a thirty-two inch, heavy-metal, solid-frame affair, 1893 model, with its open-top action.

But the long tube looked sway-backed to me, so I took it to an old German gunsmith and had a solid steel rib laid along the barrel, thus making it unquestionably the first Winchester shotgun with a raised rib. The half pistol grip didn't suit me either, so I whittled it off with my jackknife. My first wild turkey was bowled over with that corn-sheller, too. But one fatal day at Wapanoca, Dad took it out with him and never shot his ten-pound Greener duck gun any more. I struggled with that for a while, but it was no go. I traded it to big Owen Pittman at the gun store for a lighter Bone-hill double with rabbit-ear hammers. Owen still has that big Greener.

For the next twenty-five years the old Winchester made Wapanoca its home, and, in off seasons, when Aaron wasn't using it, Osborn Neely had it after bear, deer, turkey, and the general run of varmints. There is no way to estimate the enormous amount of wild game this old gun has killed. Two seasons before Dad's passing I had the 1893 model action removed and the modern 1897 type inserted. After Father passed on, just as the newer powders began their vogue, I sawed six inches off the barrel and got Perry Hooker, the master draw-borer, to tool in a splendid all-around game choke. Young Jim soon developed into a first-rate shot at doves and quail, and is he looking forward to his first real try at ducks!

November 23

Was out this afternoon with Kota, Gracie, Lad, and a Joe Willing young-ster Guy wants me to start. Kota seemed off his feed a bit, but Gracie was her usual self. Lad behaved fairly well, but is headstrong as a grained mule. The Willing pup went so big Jim said the only thing to do is put him down in one county and then hop in your car and advertise in the adjoining county newspaper. Anyhow, we've got a prospect. Now to open the season.

November 25

Bayard, Johnny, and I drove out to Huntley's farm last evening and shot quail today. We were only after a jolly day and to see how our dog string looks and acts under fire. An enjoyable evening by the big fire in our bache-lor host's cozy home on a bench of sedge and conifers above "persimmon seeds and sandy bottoms." Hard for me to realize, looking at him, that white-haired Bayard and I are still toeing the shooting scratch.

The night was overcast and today threatened rain. Hot, gusty winds played havoc with scenting conditions, dry as it was. We worked Gracie and Lad this forenoon. The bitch did great work, but Lad was a disappointment. He bungled practically every chance, and if Gracie hadn't been bombproof we'd have had little sport. She picked up several bevies around a heavily wooded and eroded area—full of brushy islands and deep ditches. Getting at the singles was a cross between mountain climbing and a slippery slide. But highly exciting snap shooting. By noon we had eighteen birds, not bad when three men take turn and turn about, practically over one dog. We always draw lots when gunning threes. The odd man stays up at the first find. The other two have rematched and the loser gets only the bevy shot. He then remounts and the up-man has a go—and so on.

Virginia's Thanksgiving lunch took up a deal of slack and Huntley's spiced toddies did the rest. We turned loose the Willing pup after lunch, but let Gracie amble out a bit of overtime. Just as she found her third bevy it came on to rain hard and the Willing dog was A.W.O.L. We galloped to the house in order to get safely over the backwoods dirt road. Happy (the Willing product) checked in from some outlying sector just as we were fixing to leave him. Well, I downed my first shot of the season. If I can duplicate on ducks, day after tomorrow, all will be well. Never, if you can help it, start a shooting season with a miss.

November 27

Wick the Scotchman, Jim, and I are home after two days of glorious sport at mallards in Elmer La Cott's pin-oak bottoms. Bully quarters awaited us at Mrs. Burnett's hospitable residence. Strange to say, we were the only three club members present the first day. We drove over Friday afternoon, arriving at De Witt about dusk. Between Stuttgart and De Witt we saw thousands of ducks coming in on the rice fields. Always this country is reminiscent of days long before rice came to the great stretches of prairie marsh, when Hal and Charley Cleaver and I shot snipe day after day during their great swing northward in spring. You never knew what species of game would leap from a "slash," and among the timber islands and bottoms any fallen treetop might hold a buck. In those days the quail bevies were found around the wooded patches, and when flushed, fanned out into the sedgy vastnesses. What single-bird shooting—with, like as not, a woodcock or snipe taking off along with bobwhite.

Baggage stowed at Mrs. Burnett's, we walked downtown for dinner and contact with De Witt's night life. Every hamlet or city has its big moment, and the evening before duck-shooting season opens is by long odds De Witt's—and a truly delicious experience. The town square, centered by a mammoth modern courthouse, is ablaze with lights. Wildfowl gunners from all over the United States mingle with professional guides, and the populace is out to see the show. Hotel office counters are piled high with shotgun shells, and clerks are busy dispensing hunting licenses. Hardware stores are thronged with last-minute purchasers of rubber boots, warm socks, and other paraphernalia and impedimenta of the blinds. Khaki figures in rolled-down hip boots knot street corners.

The night air, sharpened by frost on the rice paddies, is raucous with duck calls being tested. Pretty much every youngster, field hand, and outdoor businessman-hunter in that whole region can do pretty well on a duck whistle. Why not? The rice region boy babies—and some of the girls—cut their teeth, not on rattles, but on wooden or hard-rubber duck calls. Celebrities are pointed out 'most everywhere; their disguises don't save them. World Series baseball players, movie stars, and run-of-the-mine industrial spotlighters. United States senators and big-shot bankers jostle for the limelight in reflected glory off some well-known commercial shooting proprietor. Parking space is at a premium and side tracks are full of private cars. Railway magnates with shooting parties from all points of the sport globe cram the throngs. Some of the town won't go to bed for long tonight—and some not at all. In the jammed restaurants strident pianolas and the influence of

Bacchus lend ear to the music and foot to the dance. And that women like duck shooting is evident by gay presences here everywhere. It is all 99 per cent good, clean fun.

We turn in toward midnight, having long since sent young Jeems beddy-bye. Somehow, in the stout lad sleeping there on the eve of his long-awaited baptism at wildfowling, I see again my own first night at old Wapanoca and the sugar plums of sport that danced through my head. If I say a prayer it is that he may know the joys of gun days as I have lived them.

A bedside flashlight and my watch tell me several times that the rising hour neareth. Elmer's reminder that his pin-oak bottoms are crowded with mallards is the best alarm clock, however. Jim bounces out of the blankets at first call, but the Scotchman, replete with an evening's late bibbing, lags. Finally accoutered, we drive to the New Way Restaurant for standard break-fastings—barring Wick's "tay." Elmer and Foy are already on hand and going around stacks of wheatcakes like coopers round a barrel.

Then five miles north on a black-top highway with just a faint suspicion of impending dawn. Crossing the familiar and increasingly tricky bridge turn we bump along that same damnable stretch of road to the camp. Jeff, the resident guide, is finishing his coffee afront the big tent. We start for the first pools with twenty minutes to spare before official gunning hour of seven a.m. Gosh! it is fine to be alive and back at the grand old game! Jim fairly quivers with eagerness. We reach the water's edge and wade ahead through flooded timber. Jim and the Scot are warned to make haste slowly, for there's many a slip and catch in tangled undersurface limbs and slippery log butts. Two hundred yards of this and Elmer unlimbers his call for a trio with Foy and Jeff's instruments. Overhead lugs a great bunch of clucking mallards. Off ahead just a bit, hundreds of roosting birds leap skyward. Wick and Jim stand openmouthed.

"Take trees," laughs Elmer. "We don't need to go any farther." By now the heavens are literally alive with mallards. "Look out," warns Foy. "They'll knock your hats off in a minute." I want my companions to see this sight. And seemingly in a trice ducks begin lighting all about us, completely filling the open pools for an acre. There are still ten minutes to go and each fellow hugs his oak tree. Hens and drakes glide here and there, loud calls burst from the mob. Then, down below us, beyond Elmer's fence line, guns roar. With thunderous clamor our ducks take the air, but fully half of them settle down again. "You all had just as well load up and begin to get busy," opines Jeff. We do.

I sit quietly watching Wick and Jim. Foy shoos away our resident birds

because the treetops are aweave with incoming customers. A bunch plum-
mets from the treetops and Wick tears into them with his three-shotter.
Jim takes toll with his first crack of the old pump; misses a second try, but
is cool enough to land a plump young drake with his third. Four decoys
are thus rigged out. A pair of fine drakes crosses out above the treetops and
I can't resist. Down comes one of them. And so goes the battle. Long before
eight o'clock we have our three limits of ten birds each and are headed for
camp. Jim and Wick have "done noble," and the youngster bemoans having
to await the morrow. Elmer and I leave Wick and Jim at Mrs. Burnett's and
drive on to Stuttgart to pack, record, and ship our birds home. Also to meet
Ed Queeny and a Mr. Russell, from St. Louis.

They arrive with considerable baggage, including a Labrador dog. But
what care good sports for a bit of crowding? Barring one puncture, we make
De Witt in time for Ed and Mr. Russell to make a lightning change and
light out for the afternoon shoot. They return wilder than March hares.
That evening not less than a million yarns of the day's opening adventures
are swapped around the square. There is apparently no law against Sunday
hunting in Arkansas's rulebook. There are thirty days in which to do all
that they can do to the ducks, and full advantage is taken of the "sittyation."

Next morning we are in the pin oaks betimes. The Scotchman stops at
one place with Jeff to call for him, Ed and Russell take another station with
Elmer broadcasting, while Jimmy and I and Foy push on out into the brake
for a catty-cornered stand. What an uproar! It doesn't take Jim and me long
to acquire two quotas and we wade over to visit with Wick. Shouts are heard
from the direction of camp and soon Bill Kent and young Bob Carrier come
bungling up to us. As we are through, they are put to work—with witnesses.
Foy laughs. "They sure begin putting a heavy fog over the property." Then
here comes Elmer. Ed Queeny and Mr. Russell are through and want us all
over to help complete some Technicolor movies. "I never dreamed such
duck shooting as this existed," says Ed. It is fine, I reflect; but somehow
I'm wondering what any of these younger moderns would say to wildfowl
flights I've seen. Oh, there are still lots of ducks about in highly concentrated
areas, but the birds are being, comparatively speaking, more heavily gunned
than in old market-hunting days. It is a good thing restoration programs
have been under way in northern breeding habitats, along with the estab-
lishment of flyway sanctuaries. But vastly improved law enforcement must
come about, and also supervision and proper taxation of commercial shooting. Certain federal shooting regulations need some common sense injected
into them; notably those of possession and transportation limits.

P.S. That Labrador dog of Ed Queeny's—Grouse—is a grand fellow!

November 28

Ira Richards wired he would land at the airport next Friday evening for our annual quail and duck safari. Last season we put in two fast mallardings at Elmer's, one at Mr. Brown's wildfowl spa, and two perfectly glorious bobwhite days at Barnacre with Bob Carrier. Bob Stoner is working Kota and Jim while I'm gone. My daughter and her husband, Roy, will arrive Wednesday afternoon with Hugh Vandeventer and Ted Hazen for a hunt at Elmer's. They've really come to see the Universities of Tennessee and Mississippi clash at the stadium Saturday afternoon. Makes you feel kind of old. Thirty-five years ago, almost to the day, my own Tennessee varsity licked Ole Miss' right here in Memphis, and now my son-in-law, who captained his Volunteer eleven in '28, is a duck-shooting onlooker.

December 10

Quite a bit to record, for I've been on the move. The "children" arrived about three p.m. Wednesday a week ago, and after a brief time out for a spot of tea, we lads climbed into the station wagon and lit out for Arkansas. Lovely afternoon, and Roy, driving, hung the needle on seventy and let her drift. It was the fastest run to De Witt I've ever made: two hours and forty-five minutes to the door of Mrs. Burnett's home. We had a great session in the pin oaks both days. The boys had never seen any such shooting and we strung it out so as to enjoy life in the open. Roy stepped in over his boots twice, but that is all in the day's work. It was pretty cold, both days—enough ice to make us break out open holes until the thaw set in. How the mallards did pour in that afternoon! The boys shipped out their first day's kill and went home with legal quotas. Roy got me to the airport just in time to meet Ira as the big plane rolled up to its chocks.

Next morning Arthur and Jim Ware drove Ira and me out to Huntley's for a quail shoot. The weather looked none too good and the roads, once off slushy gravel, got "turribler." By the time we saddled up, a cold mist was falling and Arthur, Jim's father, decided to do his gunning with a fireside book. Jim and Ira and I, with Pete along to hold horses, turned loose Kota and Gracie. Birds hole up in approaching bad weather with considerably more vision than humans. Kota stood one bevy in a deep ravine under a blown-down treetop. Ira and Jim got down a bird each, but the singles went across almost impenetrable country. Half an hour later, with two finds behind us, I noticed Ira looking pretty stiff. "What time," he asked, "does that football game start?" We beat it for the house as rain fell heavily. It was touch and go getting the car up that long muddy road from Huntley's to the gravel, but we made it. Arthur dropped us at the stadium ten minutes before the kickoff, and, to my great joy, Tennessee gave Mississippi a swell lacing.

December 20

Our children have been home with us for the holidays since Sunday. Roy and I have had two glorious days at Huntley May's farm. We were asked to Hugh Buckingham's preserve, but had promised Huntley to collect him some Christmas "pottiges." This morning Roy and I penetrated as far as the boundary line between the May and Ames places. There is a magnificent twenty-acre patch of pines on that hilltop, and around them we raised four bevies. Kota did a magnificent bit of roading on one of them, and Gracie achieved a thrilling retrieve of one crippled bird that ran a hundred yards down a dry ditch and hid in a hole under a tree root. But the bitch dug it out and smilingly handed me the victim. It was barely wing-tipped, a slobbery bit of shooting on my part. So I tossed the fat little hen bird into the air and watched her sail away down through the timber and side-slip into a sedge patch. She'll get along safely. Roy was out of shells by now, so after lunch he picked up Huntley's twenty-bore in place of his own sixteen-gauge, and we idled along on the eastern bottoms rim, picking up what we needed over Jim and the bitch. She had lots of fire and style and I'm going to keep an eye peeled for her next winter.

December 24—Christmas Eve

Roy and I decided to have a last try at the mallards and give Jim Ware a holiday shoot as well. Roy and Irma Jones went to a ball and Roy had only about an hour's sleep. It was raining when I called him at three a.m. We went by for Jimmy Ware. After he got in the car I asked if he had his Arkansas license. He said yes rather dubiously, I thought. We livened up with black coffee and doughnuts at a one-arm lunch. It was after we'd got across the bridge over Ole Miss' that Jim voluntarily admitted he'd forgotten his license, after all. I said, "Well, there's a bus leaving Stuttgart that'll get you home by noon and you can get it and come back tonight. It'll only cost you today's shooting." He wasn't sure I didn't mean it until I got to Stuttgart, either. There I was fortunate enough to establish identification with an old warden friend, and get a receipt. We got into the pin-oak flat by seven-thirty. Elmer and Jeff were already there and young Bobby, Elmer's kid brother, went with us to have a shooting match with Jim Ware. Had a great day. Jim Ware is going to make a crackerjack shot. He isn't fast, but is listening to advice and learning to judge distance. Shooting's fundamentals are just as important as those of any other sport. Next morning, a mild "bluebirdy" affair, shooting was slow. We bagged enough, however, by noon, to decide to hit it for home and help dress the Christmas tree.

I'm calling it a season—and a grand one, too. I'm giving my big gun, "Bo-Whoop," a thorough going-over from locks to front sight. Then, carefully but lightly oiled, old "sweepstakes" will be laid away until next dove season. And now, to the ducks, if I never see you again, "*Ya vash durovia!*"

January 21

Jim Ware and I slipped off and made a Lakeside hunt today—only this trip we rode around the south end. Much of the country being plowed and birds driven into weed patches and heavy thickets. But Kota and Gracie all but managed us two limits. Jim is going to make a hard guy to beat with a few seasons behind him. I'm making him hold the gun well down until he masters picking out the bird he's going to focus on. This is especially valuable when working on bevy rises. In afteryears the "waiting hitch" becomes instinct. The briers along that big dredge ditch back of the Negro church all but tore the breeches off Jim and he stepped in over his rubbers retrieving a bird from the slough. What a pleasure it is to gun with a youngster who really loves the game and, above all, is willing to listen, take his time, and honestly try to learn! They're like bird dogs, though. Some need but little "breaking."

January 31

Well, even the bird-shooting season expires tonight, and here is the last entry permitted by the red gods in the record. For which I thank them devoutly.

Johnny and Frank and I drove over to the Miller place, got three dandy mounts, and made a long hunt around the Decker bayou and Lakeside sector. We covered the ground where Johnny and I found all those birds, and then swung down around the club, across the levee, and into those big cornfields where the geese used to feed. There was a lot of water in the country, and the birds take full advantage. The fields are full of plowing farm hands, and when put up, the bobwhites whisk out over backwaters, or into sloughs too deep for knee-boot wading. I rode up one luscious bunch in a weed patch and they pitched in a viny tangle right at the water's edge. Just managed to catch one single as it towered the willows, and it dropped in four feet of water, quite a piece out in the lake. But Gracie swam out and got it. What a bitch—tops as a plantation dog, for my money.

Coming home, we had a grand rise from a cornfield bunch that Gracie pointed. I watched two singles down and managed to land one of them. We crossed the levee at the old Martin place and started across darkening fields on a short cut to the Miller place.

From a cabin came tin-panny piano music. I rode by to ask if my horse could wade across the slough. Who came to the door but the widow-woman. I said, "Widow-woman, what in the name o' time are you doin' away over here?"

She said, "Cap'n, dese folks is th'owin' a party heah dis night, I boun' yu."

"What are you doin' so early, Widow-woman—warmin' up?"

"Yaas, suh, Cap'n, I'se allus pretty warm, but ef yu-all got som' mo' o' dat burnin' fluid yu gimme las' time, I kin do lots better."

"Go git you a tumbler," I told her, and in a jiffy she was back for the bait of rum I began pouring.

"Cap'n," she said, "yu is sho po'in' sweet joy an' glad tidin's inta d' po' widder-'ooman's heart, but f' Gawd's sake, Cap'n, don' spill none of it."

Gracie pointed in an almost bare sedge field not three minutes after we rode away. Johnny jumped off just as a giant bevy zoomed off the bare ground ahead and winged up the slough. We started in pursuit, but it was too dark. More young to that outfit for next season. And more power to them.

So now the new hammer-gun Greener double that Ira gave me has had its first season, and to shoot it at upland game is a joy. It, too, will now have a stem-to-stern going-over and careful putting-away until maybe a try at skeet brings it forth. The hammer gun. Somehow, it brings memories of my other one—long years agone. Memories of Dakota and Saskatchewan stubbles, and of a youngster who followed a noble race of sportsmen from marsh to mountain. Smoke drifts low over swampy waters. And so, with a sigh and a grin, I write "finis."

The Prodigal Years

This piece was published in the winter 1969 American Sportsman, *the deluxe quarterly, and followed "Birdy Dogs" in the fall 1968 volume. It was not the last work by Nash to be published but it was the most nearly his final expression. Of those magazine articles that came out after "The Prodigal Years," one was a short one on dogs, the others were largely compilations of excerpts from former works, with the old drive to kill essentially unaltered. "The Prodigal Years" re counts a few experiences told earlier but with a significant change in attitude. In his old age, Edward Ringwood Hewitt, dean of trout fishermen, remarked to the effect that we all begin as little hogs—taking every piece of game available— growing out of it, sometimes all too slowly, when we educate ourselves to under-stand that it is the sport, the manner in which the kill is made and not the killing. Nash Buckingham was orthodox in his beginnings, and it might seem that he reached the age of discernment a bit late. I noticed the change in his later cor-respondence. On September 28, 1970, he wrote:*

> As to shooting, I've about racked up on the doves and quail barring immediate devouring. Dove shooting is getting to be a horror of too-soon opening, poorly grown birds, guerrilla warfare by hordes of ground-shooting invaders, and a constant raising of limits by alleged "biologists" whose bounden duty is to obey the wants of said guerrillas.

In a letter to his literary agent, Lurton Blassingame, in August 1968, Nash discusses "The Prodigal Years." At that time he called it "The Greedy Years"— perhaps a bit more abrasive but I'm not sure it wasn't the more telling title.

Dear Lurton:

I share your feelings re the enclosed A. B. Frost art for "The Greedy Years." I've always admired Frost's work extravagantly. It occurs to me that a bit of search would reveal pix reflecting a more national spread of resources depletion. My assignment was from 1889 through 1909 and covers from the Pas in Saskatchewan on down what's today the Miss. Valley flyway, west to Colorado and south to the Louisiana and Texas coastals. There was also some offshore duck shooting on an island—

Wood's Hole country—we lived with fishermen and fed off oatmeal, fish, mergansers and coffee. I never cared for the sink-box shooting off Havre d'Grace; too stormy and expensive. The last time I shot Currituck was either '29 or '30, from small boat blinds with the big boat downwind— cans and honkers.

About two or three years ago, Remington celebrated some anniversary with a series of about seven lovely paintings and sent me a set. They were corkers; the one showing prairie chicken shooting being exception- ally lovely. The last chickens I shot were north of Bismarck, N.D., in '44 and '45 making movies for Grant Rice's *Sportlight*.

I wonder who the *American Sportsman* got to handle their snipe story? Snipe have Gone With the Wind, but what a "go" we had with them. Today's hunters don't even know the snipe when they see 'em; they're too lazy to mush after 'em and can't hit 'em when they flush. And what plush eating in the old Louisiana days when cooked properly. Recipe on application. Good luck and regards,

NASH BUCKINGHAM

Nash's talk about early guns and loads is enlightening, his description of the dawn flights of herons like a Harold von Schmidt painting, his recounting of duck club menus so typically Nash.

"The Prodigal Years," written in 1968 when Nash was eighty-eight, shows how great his change of attitude had been. The 1,100-duck one-day kill at Wapa- noca in 1898—something to brag about in an early story—and the one hundred pintails (ninety-two pintails, eight mallards as described in "Comin' Twenty- One") with Judge George Gilham, are recounted here, perhaps not with outspoken compunction, but there is a distinct implication that it had begun to sicken him. Large bags are viewed in this piece for what they were—overindulgence, not glory —and market hunting is seen as the blight it placed on game. When fifty ducks per day was the quota, even if self-imposed at Beaver Dam, it was a goal to strive for and the effort set off a frenzy of killing. This holds true today where bag limits are in some cases too high. Nash's being content with a ten-duck limit, or less, proves how men respond.

"The Prodigal Years" is a looking back at a long journey through lands stiff with game, a journey on which it was impossible not to leave behind the small boy eagerly shooting anything in any way presented. This is a man for whom a coming of age took place in his eighties. I consider it to be Nash Buckingham's last statement of principle on game shooting.

BY 1889, when I was nine years old, I was afield with my own gun in an atmosphere of bird dogs and retrievers, quail, squirrels, and rabbits. I had not yet been taken duck hunting, but I had seen many a sack of geese, swans, and ducks brought home for neighborhood distribution by my Dad, and this way I got to know the species. We kids made Indian war bonnets from the feathers.

Somehow, my hunting memories seem to stem from Christmas morning in 1888 in the huge, high-ceilinged living room of our old home. Folks got up early to celebrate in those days. I recall my father standing near the grand piano that my mother played so beautifully and presenting my older brother and myself with a 16-gauge Parker hammer gun and a set of boxing gloves.

Shortly after the first of the year, I had lowered my first bobwhite, and was taken to Arkansas where I got my first glance at prairie chicken, a species even then being pushed to the brink of extermination by promotional greed. This was at the shooting lodge of one of my father's friends on the Grand Prairie, where deer, wild turkey, prairie chickens, quail, ducks, geese, snipe, and other birds were abundant. Rice had not yet become God's gift to Arkansas.

The lodge was near a hamlet called Goodwin, and we traveled there by the new railroad. I recall afternoons on the prairie when, over the distant woodlands, myriads of waterfowl kept the skies atwinkle until dark. In those days, two-horse buckboards carried the hunters afield, along with hard-driving bird dogs questing the vast, unfenced land. The pointers and setters made thrilling points, and it was anyone's guess what species would flush.

But I sensed the decline of the prairie chicken in the early 1890's, as my elders talked of the market hunting and the increased number of hunters. A two-year closure of hunting prairie chickens was brought about, but when the season was reopened, the railroads ran excursions for the grand slaughter. By the turn of the century, prairie chickens had pretty much passed into history in Arkansas.

In 1904, I went with my father and a party of friends on a prairie chicken hunt to Brown County, South Dakota. We traveled by private railroad car, sidetracking at a village and hunting for a week, with the routine much the same as in Arkansas years before. There were no pheasants or Hungarian partridge as there are today, just clouds of prairie chickens and ducks. On the railway platform I saw barrels of prairie chickens en route to eastern markets.

At that time, almost anywhere, you could buy all the prairie chickens you wanted from produce dealers, and find them on the menu at hotels and restaurants. Market hunting was legal, but it was draining the vitals of wildlife resources, and the damage would be irreparable.

Definitely the public ate more game. Merchants bought wildfowl and game for a song and resold to hotels and restaurants at a profit that would be laughable today, but was then considered satisfactory. Individual hunters shared their game with neighbors, and also sent much of it to church homes, and charitable institutions. Families were larger then, servants easily available, and little game fetched home was wasted.

In the period of which I write, people appreciated being sent game; few do today unless it arrives picked, dressed, and preferably frozen. The arts of yesterday are forgotten; few of today's cooks know how to roast, bake, fry, smother, broil, or stew game. I've eaten game prepared by some of the nation's finest chefs, and I'm taking nothing from them, but I'll still take a corn-fed mallard or plump teal prepared with the succulence bestowed by Molly Merritt, our old cook of long ago at Beaver Dam. Nor have I ever partaken of barbecued mallard comparable to that prepared by Nollie Pennington and her mother, Mrs. Kerr, at their home in Clarendon, Arkansas. Food fit for the gods!

Game came into the cities by many routes and conveyances. Trains, steamboats, and wagons all were used. As to quail, the "pot-hunters" brought their bobwhites in with their chickens and eggs and butter, and had what were known as "bird routes." Pot-hunters shot birds on the ground, or trapped them. Some customers preferred trapped birds because there were no pellets in the flesh.

An old-time meat and grocery house in Memphis used to do an enormous business in game. I have seen as many as twenty-five deer hanging in one cold-storage room, along with more than fifty wild turkeys and all the prairie chickens, quail, waterfowl, and assorted other birds imaginable. Ammunition was unbelievably cheap, and market hunters had little overhead.

At the turn of the century I was friendly with the Wards, a famous family operating a hotel and market-hunting business at Walnut Log, Kentucky, on the upper end of Reelfoot Lake. "Pap," the father, and his two sons Guy and Monk were also trap shooters of note; Guy in fact became one of the best professional trap shots of the time. I once asked him the biggest bag of ducks he recalled his family making in one day. (They all shot magazine guns.)

Guy replied, in his quiet and thoughtfully considered way: "I remember one day when we caught everything just right in a small cove. There were scads of ducks and we worked 'em over all day long. It took a two-horse team to wagon 'em out that evening. There were well over four hundred birds." Do you wonder that even the prodigious migrations were beginning to feel the effects of such enterprise?

To observe today's remnant waterfowl populations in contrast to what I saw in 1890 is but to mourn. Land drainage was in the distant future.

Lumbering of the South's great hardwood and cypress stands was in its infancy. Lakes and marshes of the lower Mississippi River states all the way to the Gulf lay in pristine condition for wildlife.

I gunned most of the famous duck clubs and public shooting grounds of the time: Reelfoot Lake; Big Lake; on down the Mississippi along which Menasha, Lakeside, Mud Lake, Beaver Dam, Wapanoca, and a hundred others were located; and all the way to the famed Delta Duck Club in Louisiana. I shot geese, mostly Canadas but a few blues and snows too, from practically every worthwhile sand bar between Cairo, Illinois, and the Texas coastals. Memories of shooting canvasback and redheads from the flats off Rockport, Texas, and San Jacinto Bay (before oil) are priceless. You really saw ducks and geese then! But even so, after 1890 the swans disappeared. Like the prairie chickens in Arkansas, I saw them vanish suddenly from a favorite hangout, the Wapanoca Outing Club, as if they had evaporated. And Wapanoca, for its size, held the finest concentration of waterfowl in what is now known as the Mississippi flyway.

Consider that at the turn of the century I could sit in a goose pit on the Mississippi River all day and watch enormous rafts of waterfowl float down with the current, steadily. Around three o'clock in the afternoon they would come up on the rims of the sand bars and preen. Then, as if by signal, they would resume their downstream drift. In the evenings, huge flocks of waterfowl would arch the skies, wave after wave, until darkness obscured the panorama.

I have in an old diary a record of a Christmas-week hunt at Wapanoca in 1898. The daily bag limit imposed by the club was fifty ducks and as many geese as one could lower. That day at Wapanoca there were twenty-two guns: sixteen members and six sons home from college. Everyone bagged his limit of ducks, and thirty-eight Canada geese were killed. Today on Wapanoca—now a federal wildlife refuge—you would be lucky to bag a federal limit of four ducks.

I have another record of Wapanoca, on Washington's Birthday in 1901. Judge Gilham and I bagged an even hundred pintail, mostly drakes, before ten a.m. Not like the ducks in today's skies.

It didn't take long for wildfowl marketeers and sportsmen to realize that they could sack more ducks, geese, and birds per day—and faster—with the comparatively light-weight, six-shot repeaters than with the ponderous, heavy-recoiling, near-cannons they had been using. Muzzleloaders gave way to 8- and 10-gauge doubles, hammerless weapons, pump guns, and autoloaders.

As early as 1906 the Boone and Crockett Club passed resolutions calling for action against the autoloaders. The first of the repeaters I saw and used were the 12- and 10-gauge lever-action weapons by Winchester. My 12-bore cost about $15, but at eleven years of age I found that I couldn't work the levering very well with my short arms, so I sold the piece for $10. You can still see these guns around today in repair shops and in collectors' cabinets.

My earliest recollection of a pump gun was a Spencer patented in the 1880s. It threw its discharged shells almost straight up. I saw one recently in a collection; it was in excellent condition, with a Damascus tube, and worked smoothly. My first contact with the Spencer was in 1892 at Wapanoca, and it was used by a Mr. Bonnie, a great wildfowler from Louisville, Kentucky. He had a son about my age and our fathers used to shoot together. We would watch in wonderment as Mr. Bonnie downed five or six mallards from a decoying flock. He let many of the fowl begin lighting and then shot into the upper tiers, sometimes taking three or four ducks in the air and with time to pick off rising birds. In later years that system became regular practice with the users of magazine guns. My father shot a ten-pound English-made hammerless double by W. W. Greener, which had 32-inch tubes bored for 3¼-inch cases. Yet sometimes while acquiring their limits of fifty ducks, Mr. Bonnie would have to slow down and wait for Dad to catch up.

There was also a pump gun called Burgess on the market in those years. It differed from the other pumps in that the repeating action was in the pistol grip. Instead of pumping back and forth with the left hand, you shoved the right hand and pistol grip forward and pulled it back to reload. It was a beautifully finished and balanced weapon, but it somehow never caught on with the trade. There also appeared a two-shot pump gun by the Young Arms Company of Springfield, Ohio, an invention of Charles "Sparrow" Young, destined to become a renowned hunter and trap-shooting champion. The last time I saw "Sparrow" was when he won the Grand American Handicap at Vandalia, Ohio, with one hundred straight from a twenty-three-yard handicap in 1926.

Ammunition, from 1889 to the mid-1890s, was largely hand-loaded, although some factory loads—UMC and Winchester—were available. Sporting goods dealers supplied these, and also did a flourishing business with hand loads from their own establishments. My first shotgun loads came from J. G. Schmidt & Son of Memphis, still a high-grade firm today. Most lads were taught by their fathers to load their own. In our neighborhood, dining-room tables were cleared after Friday night supper and the kids loaded ammunition on an assembly-line basis. Our parents furnished the loading kits—capped empty hulls, wads, shot and powder with measures, and the crimpers. Then they rode herd on the proceedings.

It was a day and time when powders were changing from black to semi-smokeless, and then to smokeless—dense or bulk. The bulk powders were measured in "drachmas," or drams, and the dense in grains. Our parents kept their canisters of powder out of the house and in iron containers. Our field load measures were carefully set for three drams of bulk, with one ounce of No. 8 shot. The wildfowl loads were $3\frac{1}{4}$ drams of bulk, with $1\frac{1}{8}$ ounce of No. 6 shot. We were told to keep hands off the dense stuff.

We went wood duck hunting in those long-gone days from late summer until early fall, being on our stands well before daylight. With dawn came one of the most beautiful flights and sights ever witnessed by outdoorsmen. First came slowly drifting thousands of little white herons, followed by a myriad of blue herons. Immediately following came the great white herons —or cranes, as we knew them. Their flocks were separate and distinct. They were going somewhere, and would do the same tomorrow. Then came the wood ducks. Leaving their roosting area in a portion of ponded cypress, they flew in small family groups and larger bunches, and decoyed nicely to wooden teal decoys. Bag limits were, as I mentioned, fifty birds per day.

The famous Hatchie Coon Club above Marked Tree, Arkansas, on the once-beautiful and unpolluted St. Francis River, is an example of what real sport could be in those days. No automobiles, no outboard motors, no deep-freezers, and no market hunting on wood ducks. There was a rule at Hatchie Coon Club that not more than fifty largemouth and smallmouth bass could be taken in a day. We would pole upstream to the saw-grassed spreads, shoot a limit of fifty woodies, then catch a limit of bass en route to the clubhouse. After lunch there would be time for a snooze before the afternoon train back to Memphis, unless a two-day jaunt was planned. Sometimes, under such circumstances, we deliberately laid off catching our limits in order to fish late. Now, remember, these scenes were being enacted all over the South in the period 1889-1909.

Life at such a shooting and fishing club as old Hatchie Coon (three or four clubhouses have burned, but each has been replaced along the same plan) was tranquillity itself. The great bottomlands of the St. Francis and Little River basins lay all but inviolate. From the high embankment of the pioneering Frisco Railroad, a tramway hand-car dared narrow-gauge de-railment out through the forests to the gorgeous St. Francis. The clubhouse, built high on stilts above the crest line of the inevitable floods, provided a huge living room, cavernous fireplace, dining room, and kitchen. Sleeping quarters and baths accommodated goodly parties. In early times, mosquito bars hung over each bed. A wide boardwalk, high above the surroundings, led several hundred yards to the boat house.

Clubhouse keepers at Hatchie Coon offered wonderful seasonal cuisines. Pre-breakfast coffee was slashed with choice brandy and a lump of butter; quite an eye-opening beverage if you've a mind to try it. Country hams, bacon, sausage, melons, berries, and scuppernongs—a cultivated muscadine grape—were "home folks." Maybe you'd sup on the haunch of a great turtle or a venison roast. Among fish offerings, "fiddler" cats were the choice of many. Vegetables were in profusion, for the earth of those gardens would grow gold dollars. And it was much the same story at all of the clubs in those days. I'd still like to meet up with a big pan of Bryant Cole's shredded coot, potatoes, and tomatoes sugared and baked with a top dressing of crumbs and parmesan cheese.

However, by 1900, when I was twenty, I knew that change was on the way. The outdoor magazines wrote chilling reports on dwindling wildfowl resources and the abuses of upland game. I realized, too, that some of the clubs in the immediate tri-state area of Tennessee, Mississippi, and Arkansas were cutting their daily bag limits from fifty to forty ducks. Yet market hunting continued, and commercial interests mocked the early voices that were protesting the decimation of the flocks and calling attention to the destructive droughts and drainage on the breeding grounds in Canada. By 1910, with no federal or state intervention, the pressure of shooting was making visible gaps in the migrations.

It was not until 1916, however, that President Wilson signed the Treaty between the United States and Great Britain for the Protection of Migratory Birds in the United States and Canada. Opponents of conservation fought on until 1918, when by decision of the United States Supreme Court the treaty and statute were upheld. For the majority, Justice Oliver Wendell Holmes declared: "But for the Treaty and the Statute, there might soon be no birds for any powers to deal with. We see nothing in the Constitution that compels the government to sit by while a food supply is being cut off and the protectors of our forests and our crops are destroyed. It is not sufficient to rely upon our States. The reliance is in vain, and, were it otherwise, the question is whether the United States is forbidden to act. We are of the opinion that the Treaty and Statute must be upheld."

Thus the beginning—some fifty years ago—of the endless struggle to keep game birds in the sky. Today, violations of the migratory bird law carry no social stigma and are about on the same level as raids on watermelon patches; the illegal theft of waterfowl probably exceeds the legal take.

An aged gunning friend wrote me recently: "All I can say is that I am thankful our generation really flourished when things were as they were supposed to be."

It is easy to agree. It was exhilarating on those careless, greedy days so long ago to feel that the mysterious and generous North would continue to send us wildfowl in profusion, if not in perpetuity, so that we could "shoot faster, and kill more," as the prevailing fashion decreed. Certainly our heedless outings were more pleasant than the warfare of conservation, in which many of us eventually were engaged. Little did I ever think it would be my fight.

Yet there were too many of us, all too accurate with our efficient guns, and so the prodigal days have passed and a leaner time is upon us, and perhaps for now that's as it is "supposed to be."

Part Six:
STAR AT EVENING

A La Belle Etoile

I have selected this to be Nash Buckingham's swan song. Through all my long association with him and his writing I have known him as a shooting man. That he fished—spoke of it often—did not change my image of him. Written solely for Blood Lines, "A la Belle Etoile" is most tellingly Nash with rod in hand, from the Little Miramichi to sluggish bream water.

Henry Davis asked Nash to name the one day's fishing he would like to experience again, and it is typical of Nash's uncurbed enthusiasm that in answer he should name six fish that he considered great. The day he describes on Colorado's White River fishing with his Irma—just one year after they were married—is the true episode of this piece, not alone as angling but as a moment of intimacy. Writing the last paragraph in 1938 on their twenty-eighth anniversary, Nash speaks of ordeals they had shared since that first anniversary, not knowing what they would go through in their eighties. That they did face those last ordeals—he almost alone at times—and face them gallantly, gives this passage special luster.

In June 1970, Nash wrote me: "Few men equal my luck in celebrating their 90th birthday May 31, and next day their 60th wedding anniversary with 'the glorious and unquenchable star at evening.'"

Memphis, June 1938

My dear Henry:

YOU HAVE ASKED a question delightful in retrospect, yet requiring deliberation. Not necessarily a poser, however. "Had you your life to live over," you write, "which episode in your entire fishing career would you prefer repeating—and do you see any prospect of beating the sport you've enjoyed?" Well, Henry, I can answer that latter part, right off. I could never better the kind of fishing I've enjoyed through life. Because association and fellowship make true sport, I would rather fish a day with a friend along some quiet stream than stalk the waters of the earth in frenzied search of mere records. There's a thrill to publicity and being a titleholder and all that, but I'm talking now about plain fishing. I deplore these fishing rodeos which amount to little more than mass destruction of wildlife; rivers and bays and lakes churned by thousands of humming propellers, and gang hooks trolled in every direction.

When I was a kid my father used to take us fishing in Big Creek, a wide alluvial bayou shaded by lacy cypress and lined with virgin timber such as once blessed our vast Southern lowlands. Big Creek flowed out of Wapanoca Lake and joined with Tyronza and St. Francis in a voyage to Ole Miss' and the sea. Negro paddlers eased our bateaux into patches of shade where voracious bream sank our bait at the first toss, or up against log jams from beneath which crappie, calico bass, and bigmouths seized our live minnows and fought like bulldogs. There were spreads at lunchtime, with cots along on which our elders took siesta while we youngsters helped Uncle Phil Gwynne and Columbus with the camp chores.

One morning I asked to be put ashore to fish from the bank of a small run spilling into Big Creek from what was known as the Otter Hole. Exploring it a piece until I discovered a deep, overhung pool, I baited with an active potbelly and let it sink alongside a jutting cypress bole. Almost instantly my bobber dove from sight and the pole was all but yanked after it. Then began a battle fierce and fell. In the excitement I recalled Colonel Butts Steadman's retort to my daddy's shouted admonitions when the Colonel one day hooked a gigantic bass on his newly acquired and delicate fly rod.

"Play him, Butts," Dad had yelled, "play him!" To which, with a mighty heave that all but wrecked his expensive outfit, Colonel Butts had bellowed sputteringly, "P-p-p-l-l-a-y—'im—h-e-l-l—I'll—p-p-p-p-l-a-y—'im—on—th'—b-b-b-a-a-n-n-k!" So, with feet braced, I put the strain solidly up that pole and line—and heaved! There was an awful roar and smother of foam from that water hole. Fortunately, I had a stout, seasoned cane and a short-shank heavy hook of the sort Uncle Phil used on his trotline and swore by as unbreakable. "Son," he used to say, "d' feesh mout' com' big ernuff t' brek dat hook, but I doubts hit. Ef yu gits holt o' one big ernuff t' even bend d' hook—why, jes' go on an' giv' 'im d' pole, too."

Suppressing a desire to shout for help, I suddenly remembered my new

hunting knife—the one with deer-foot handle and long spring blade—that
Mother had given me for my birthday. Gradually working my way around
to the head of the pool, I dropped off the bank into ankle-deep mud and
put everything I had into beaching the quarry. The pole snapped, but I
wound the line about a forearm and engaged the monster in a tug of war.
And out onto the mud squirmed a giant catfish. Two desperate stabs of my
knife blade behind the fish's head and the battle was over, and I couldn't
have stood more proudly had I slain a panther in single combat. Covered
with mud and blood, I dragged my victim down to Big Creek and hailed
Father's bateau. The catfish weighed eighteen pounds, so the ruination of
everything I wore was forgiven. A right considerable day, Henry, and something to live over again, if you're asking me.

Since then, Henry, I've rounded out years, from Gulf and Atlantic sea-
boards up around the provinces and down the Great Lakes. From muskies
to lake trout and smallmouth—and back again. But of all such times I recall that gay day just before deer and moose season opened the fall Hal and
Jim and I were in the big woods with Arthur and Claire and Eddie Mc-
Aloon. Forests were donning more somber hues and log fires felt good of
an evening. Arthur had suggested our bringing fly rods along to dally with
a few grilse in the headwater pools of the Little Miramichi away down in
the gulch below Shedd camp. So that morning we came around the mountain and scrambled down through the conifers and tamaracks until the
gurgle of bright water filtered through the alders. All I had was a light bass
rod and forty yards of level line with a salmon leader and a Black Dose on
the far end of it. Just a makeshift outfit to keep us in fish perhaps, until
one of us hung up a buck. I waded out into the side shallows of a long
glassy pool and sent my fly down and across. Halfway home something boiled
at the fly trace and I struck into substance that felt like a baby grand piano.
If I were writing a story, Henry, perhaps I'd put some flourishes into a description of the fight that ensued; just me and some good but very light
tackle entertaining a twenty-four-pound salmon—that's all. Somehow I'd
managed to get him upstream and start a foot race with Salmo in order to
get a bit of slack coming back down. Twenty minutes later and two hundred yards downstream I "drug" that fellow into a cove and Eddie meshed
him in a home-made landing net just about big enough to get over Salmo's
head. But we had him. I've taken bigger fish since, but I wouldn't trade
that battle for the biggest tarpon I ever pumped off the jetties. I could go
on from there into the moose season, Henry, but this is about fishing.

I once took a seven-and-a-half-pound bigmouth bass from a pond near my home in Tennessee. But the most exciting part of that struggle was having my sister's two children in a mighty "corruptious" tin skiff paddled by a little black boy who was scared of the fish. How on earth I ever boated the lunker, I don't yet know, what with no net and two yowling youngsters. Jimmy and Mary Ware weren't at all frightened, all they wanted to do was jump in and tackle Mr. Bass. So, what with one thing and another, a pleasant afternoon was had by all. Looking back over some of the days I've fished Wapanoca and that long "Blue Hole" below the Sterling Withers plantation brings some goose pimples, too. As do those magnificent reaches along the old St. Francis River, these thirty years agone when Oak Donnic and Hatchie Coon were in their prime and glory of undrained wilderness resources. You could bend on a lead and dropper and be fighting two big 'uns most anywhere from Stud Horse to the dock or "Spreads." And there were some top-hole smallmouths down the river, too, above and below the St. Francis Club. In those days you could camp and fish a week and maybe not see two people.

But along such lines I guess I'd like best a return engagement with that seven-pound smallmouth (yep, Henry, I said *smallmouth*) I took late that September day—or rather night—in the lower end of Long Pond at Lakeside. What such a specimen was doing in that overly typical bigmouth slough is more than I can explain, unless he came in with an overflow and got stranded. "Little Jim" was Enoch's boatman and I had that lazy, good-for-nothing Mose. Enoch and I had agreed to keep only the four-pounders or better, so that meant we threw back a lot of nice bass. Just the same, I had three whoppers in the live box when I told Mose to head on home before the mosquitoes opened up on us—it was almost dusk dark and they were beginning to sing. Out in the middle of Long Pond we passed a round piece of floating moss—probably five feet in diameter—and just for luck I made a pass at it with my squirrel tail and a little gold spinner. And I hit it center, too, trickling the bug gently off and twitching it along the water for a retrieve. That was to have been my last toss. But some giant thing broke from beneath that patch of scum and followed my lure—its back fin fairly sliced the water. I gave plenty of time and then struck to hang it in him plenty. His first dash and bulldogging salute made Mose and me yell. We had no landing net that time, either, so I warned Mose to be careful and start running if anything went wrong at his end. From my own? Suicide! Well, Henry, "me and him had it," as the old saying goes. Out there on the broad lagoon with stars beginning to pop out, perspiration trickling, and

Enoch, at a safe distance, doing some tall sidelines coaching. Gradually I wore down old Cream Belly, and as I eased him alongside, Mose got a second warning. But that worthy managed to lock a long black finger and thumb through mouth and gills and the mossback had run his course. And if you doubt it's being a smallmouth, Henry, yonder he hangs on the wall. Count the scales and spines and apply all the other piscatorial metabolisms you've a mind to, and the answer will check out correct.

Aye, lad, that was a braw moment and called for a Tom Collins doubled and redoubled while Enoch and I donned pajamas and prepared to sup off Lelia's platter of fried crappie, corn pone, and spuds. But what about that pair of matched five-pounders I nailed off the cypress point above the club-house that afternoon you and I and Mac were at Lakeside? A nifty twain, my brave fellow! That was the time I had Lelia cook the fifteen-pound buffalo "Big Jim" speared—and made you believe it was a gigantic bass! You gave me the devil for not mounting a record fish—and I took your stinging rebuke so meekly! And remember John, who used to push your boat and holler, "Aw, Gawd, Mist' Hinry, don' let 'em loose!" when you'd hooked a garfish or grindle? It was John who said his shotgun had no fore-end, but he shot "them High-Volley" (Peters' Hi-Velocity) shells just the same. When you registered awe that he and his ancient fowling piece hadn't been blown to smithereens ere then, John just guffawed and said, "Naw, suh, Mist' Hinry, dem big loads don' bother my gun none. Hit do sorter blow open at times, but I jes' hol's down on hit an' slams her back t'gether." I could use a few of those afternoons again, old top!

But, Henry, I'd have to think a long time before deciding against a May day at old Beaver Dam, when Irma and I first took our baby girl bream fishing! I can repicture that chubby little bundle of sweetness right now, in her overalls and sunbonnet, coming up the path through the sunflowers and holding tight to Horace's big black hand! She was a bit scary of the cockroach bait, but determined to see it through. While Horace was loading the boats I walked out on the dock and saw a big bream floating idly in the shade. Pointing it out to "Bunksey," I stuck a roach on a hook and whispered to her to lower it right in front of Mr. Fish's nose. He struck and frightened her so she dropped the cane and ran. But I saved the day, and once she had a taste of landing a fish she and Horace became champion "breamers" of the club. Yep! That day will get into the second series—maybe!

But now, I'm thinking about a real day's fishing. It was Irma's and my job at Big Beaver Ranch to provide the trout whenever tourists were expected—and that was before the gold strike in dude ranching, too. With us, they just happened! But such folks did like fresh mountain trout and could eat a sight of them when "Grandma" Cole sent in baked spuds and sweet corn bread along with her big tin platters. That particular day I'm thinking about, we saddled up Prince and Balzac after lunch and took the shortcut up across the mesa to where Oak Ridge breaks out above the White. The river was still booming high so we decided to picket the seldom-feds in a tiny park under the hill and walk half a mile downstream to fish back. Just above old man John Dunlap's hayfield we came to the ford. I figured I could make it across, but whether the new missus could or not was something else. So I put her to my left against the boil of the current and we started. She put her hand against my shoulder and I held her, arm's length out as a sort of breakwater. Of course we took a soaking, but who minded?

Walking across a rocky bar and false-whipping line to get a flying start at the river, I hung my fly in a tree behind us—wretched carelessness that nettled me. I yanked savagely—more dunderheadedness—and the next split second I took a wallop on the back of my head that all but rabbit-punched me to my knees. That released taut line had sprung back and buried the No. 8 Heather Moth past its barb, right where my hair was shortest. A fine sucker I'd hooked! Irma diagnosed the bloody situation and was calmly resourceful. We sat down at water's edge and prepared to operate. I whetted her sharp little penknife to a fine edge. She always packed along a Zozodont bottle full of Old Patterson liquor—just about two snifters each for when we came out of the cold river at nightfall. A smear of Old Patterson did for asepsis. Then she burned the knife blade, dipped it in the bourbon, told me to hold on tight, and with a deft slit lifted out the hook. More Old Patterson dribbled into the nick and the afternoon's fishing business had undergone complete reorganization. We separated and got down to the brass-tacks end of trying to throw our flies where "trouts used."

Below Old Man Guilley's west-eighty hayfield we met again. Irma had, among others, three trout good for all of that much poundage each—better than I could show. Wading out to a submerged flat-topped rock, I shot my Heather Moth in behind and into the spumy backwater of a log jam. The whole diggings erupted. It was well along toward dusk and after that first ripsnorting leap I knew I had a whale of a trout aboard. We never used landing nets; just thin white cotton gloves, which when wet would grip and hold an eel. There was no sense trying to fight that trout from where I was perched, so I slid off the boulder and gave ground while looking for better territory on which to slug it out. Finally, downriver a piece, I got my fish ashore on a strip of caved-in meadow bank and beached a six-and-a-half-pound rainbow.

Irma had quit the stream up above and met me in the pony park. Prince set up a lusty nickering because the sight of Irma meant just two things to him—affection and sugar lumps. It was plumb dark by then and the bright blaze I kindled felt good while we dried out before climbing into our saddles. We half emptied the Zozodont bottle of Old Patterson while we stood around the fireside—and did finish it just as Balzac and Prince climbed out of the gulch. We had a fat catch in our creels and tourist grub was now the least of our worries. On the mesa our horses got their heads.

You see, Henry, my reason for wanting that particular day's fishing over again is because—but wait a minute! It wouldn't make any difference whether we two—Irma and I—were young again—in fact, I believe I'd rather spend those happy hours together again just as we are now! Because, too, while we might not be as spry, I believe we're better fisherfolk for having breasted many of life's rivers—together always—since then. And some of them have been as tough as the old White could be in early June—and tougher, too! But my particular reason for wanting to fish that day over again, Henry, is that I'm writing this on the selfsame date as that long-ago first anniversary of our wedding day—the day "knee deep in muslin-minded June" when a lovely, brave, and generous gentlewoman did me the very great honor of that forbearance and true comradeship which passeth all understanding. And, boy, men like you and me who land such catches have indeed walked at evening with the glorious and unquenchable star!

Good luck to you and Mack and Sue,

BUCK

On January 22, 1971, Nash wrote his last letter to Kay and me, with Irma hopelessly ill in a nursing home. She was then, as she had always been, his "glorious and unquenchable star." If typography permitted, I would have it printed in gold:

Dear Friends:

Recuperation from a series of congestive chills prevented me from telling you how much we appreciated your lovely Christmas card. My first serious illness in 91 years. But at least I have managed to beat the rap. My beloved mate of 61 years is holding her own in the nursing home, and I am trying to put together a last book of rather unusual mixed contents. But getting a publisher in these times of national tobogganing is not going to be easy.

We do so hope you've had and are still enjoying good sport over that grand dog. Do you intend visiting the National Championship at Ames Plantation, Grand Junction? I wish I could attend the drawing evening of Sunday, Feb. 15. But I just can't leave my lovely mate. She has filled my whole life.

Good luck and God bless you both thru the years.

IRMA & NASH BUCKINGHAM

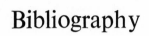

Bibliography

Bibliography

BOOKS by Nash Buckingham

De Shootinest Gent'man. 1934, The Derrydale Press, New York, 950 copies; 1943, G. P. Putnam's Sons, New York.
De Shootinest Gent'man, The Harp That Once—, Lost Voices, Bob White Blue! Bob White Gray!, All Over Gawd's Heaven, What Rarer Day?, Play House, The Neglected Duck Call, Thou and Thy Gun Bearer, The Family Honor, A Shootin' Po' Soul, The XIVth of John, and five poems

De Shootinest Gent'man. 1941, Charles Scribner's Sons, New York. 24 pages of the one story.

Mark Right! 1936, The Derrydale Press, New York, 1250 copies; 1944, G. P. Putnam's Sons, New York.
Ol' Sol, Episode Without Blemish, Opportunity Flies But Once, Armistice, Bobs of the Bayou Bank, Heart's-Ease, Hail and Farewell, Buried Treasure Hill, Barrier of the Years, The Closed Creel, A Ranch Day's Trouting, Amid Whirring Wings, Here's How in Quail Shooting, Witch Watah!, A Candle to Her

Ole Miss'. 1937, The Derrydale Press, New York, 1250 copies; 1946, G. P. Putnam's Sons, New York.
Burnin' Daylight, Paths and Mousetraps, Surrender to Youth, Dominus Regit, How Come?, "Two-Cats" Benny, The Ropes and Tools of Goose Shooting, Question of Judgment, "—Over the Brook Cedron," Lay of That First Goose, Down by the Riverside, Broccoli, Old Crab, and two poems

Blood Lines. 1938, The Derrydale Press, New York, 1250 copies; 1947, G. P. Putnam's Sons, New York.
Blood Lines, Lest We Forget, The Battle of Saratogas, À la Belle Étoile, The Ruination of John Haley, Minutes and Years, The Comedy Drama of Long Range Duck Shooting, Decorations, Wax and Wane, and one poem

Tattered Coat. 1944, G. P. Putnam's Sons, New York, 995 copies; also a regular edition.

Tattered Coat, Leaf Among Leaves, Not Unsung, The Sally Hole, Brimstone, Figment of Destiny, He That Kindled the Fire, The Brownie Company, Ltd., P-o-i-n-t Judges, Pin-Up Dogs, Castle Tomorrow, First and Last Days, Great Day in the Morning!, After All These Years

Game Bag. 1945, G. P. Putnam's Sons, New York, 1250 copies; also a regular edition.

Given Only to the Honored, The Gallows Bear, Ghost Trout, Bird Dog "Blinkers"!, Like Old Times, Wild or Tame Game Birds, The Great Reprisal, A Certain Rich Man, What Really Happens Out Quail Shooting?, Januaries Afield, Jail Break, A Pretty Place for Pheasants, Backward—Turn Backward, and one poem

Hallowed Years, 1953, The Stackpole Company, Harrisburg, Pennsylvania.

Comin' Twenty-One, Death Stalked the Spring-Stand!, The Cricket Field, The High Sign, Carry Me Back, Lady, Tight Place, Remember, Snake-Eyes!!, Odd Happenings at Field Trials, The Bigger They Come!, Hallowed Years, "When Time Who Steals Our Years Away"

National Field Trial Champions (1896–1955), by William F. Brown & Nash Buckingham. 1955, The Stackpole Company, Harrisburg, Pennsylvania.

De Shootin'est Gent'man and Other Hunting Tales. 1961, Thomas Nelson & Sons, New York, 260 copies; also a regular edition.

De Shootin'est Gent'man, Play House, The Best All-Round Dog I Ever Saw!, Firsts and Lasts For Everything!, Goodbye and Good Luck!, The Dove, Voices of Orphans and Old Folks, Memories of the National Championship, Uncrowned, "When Time Who Steals Our Years Away," Pipeline "Pottiges," Jump Shooting's Joys, Blow, Blow—and Blow the

Ducks Down!, Recall to Eden!, Duke, Are We
Shooting 8-Gauge Guns?, Amid Whirring Wings,
Here's How in Quail Shooting, The XIVth of John,
Brawl at Big Fish, and one poem

CONTRIBUTIONS TO BOOKS

Classics of the American Shooting Field, edited by
John C. Phillips and Lewis W. Hill. 1930, Hough-
ton Mifflin, Boston and New York, 150 copies; also
a regular edition.
De Shootinest Gent'man

The Sportsman's Anthology, edited by Robert E.
Kelley. 1944, New York.
Salute to Youth

The Great Outdoors, edited by Joe Godfrey, Jr., and
Frank DuFresne. 1947, St. Paul; 1949, Whittlesey
House, New York.
Quail Shooting

Hunting Trails, edited by Raymond R. Camp. 1961,
Appleton-Century-Crofts, New York.
Broccoli

MAGAZINE CONTRIBUTIONS

The American Field
Figment of Destiny (Dec. 7, 1940), Permanent
Truce (Dec. 6, 1941), Brimstone (Dec. 4, 1943),
Beatae Memoriae (Dec. 2, 1944), The Hallowed
Years (Dec. 2, 1950), Death Stalked the Spring-
Stand (Dec. 1, 1951), "When Time Who Steals Our
Years Away" (Dec. 6, 1952), Voices of Orphans
and Old Folks (Dec. 3, 1955), Memories of the
National Championship (Dec. 1, 1956), Old Min-
strels Harp Their Lays! (Dec. 7, 1957), Uncrowned
(Dec. 6, 1958), Pipeline "Pottiges" (Dec. 5, 1959),
Blow, Blow—and Blow the Ducks Down (Dec. 3,
1960), Recall to Eden (Dec. 1, 1962), Goodbye
and Good Luck! (Dec. 5, 1964), Yankee—Don't
Go Home!! (Dec. 3, 1966)

The American Rifleman

Jump Shooting's Joys (Jan. 1948), Let Your Subconscious Alone (June 1948), "All Purpose" Shotgun Myth (Oct. 1949), Get Thee Behind Me, Satan!
(Nov. 1952), Bird Shooting on the Prairies (Oct.
1953)

The American Sportsman

Birdy Dogs (Fall 1968), The Prodigal Years
(Winter 1969)

Field & Stream

My Daddy's Gun, poem (Aug. 1920), My Dog Jim,
poem (Oct. 1920), Quail Story (Sept. 1921), Rich
Man—Poor Man, poem (Oct. 1921), Moose Story
(Nov. 1921), Bark Horn, poem (Jan. 1922), Thou
and Thy Gun Bearer (March 1922), All Over
Gawd's Heaven (Nov. 1922), Bob-White, poem
(Jan. 1923), I Wish, poem (Feb. 1923), Anti-
Automatic (May 1923), The Closed Creel (June
1923), Lost Voices (March 1924), The Ropes of
Goose Shooting (Nov. 1924), Sell Ole Dan?, poem
(March 1926), Decoys on Fresh Water (Jan.
1927), Me and Capri, poem (Sept. 1927), All in
the Day's Work (Dec. 1927), The Neglected Duck
Call (Jan. 1928), Thar She Putts! (July 1928),
Play House (Jan. 1929), The Family Honor (April
1930), Golden Sedge and Whirring Wings (Oct.
1930), Eye-See, Not Hear-Say (Sept. 1931), What
Rarer Day? (Nov. 1931), The XIVth of John (Dec.
1931), Norias Annie Wins (May 1934), Home-
wood Flirtatious Wins (May 1935), Beauty in the
Sedge (May 1936), Calling All Champions (May
1937), Setter in the Sun (May 1939), Write Your
Own Ticket (Oct. 1939), P-u-l-l-! (Nov. 1939),
Lester's Enjoy Wahoo Enjoys (May 1940), Leaf
Among Leaves (March 1941), Great Day in the
Morning! (April 1941), Ariel—Prince of Prairie
and Sedgelands (May 1941), The Brownie Com-
pany, Ltd. (Oct. 1941), The Sally Hole (Dec.

1941), Dog of Destiny (May 1942), Not Unsung (Dec. 1942), They Do Come Back—Ariel Wins Again (May 1943), The Great Reprisal (Sept. 1943), Valley of Contentment (Dec. 1943), And Still Champion Ariel! (April 1944), Bird Dog for the Ages (May 1945), What Really Happens Out Quail Shooting? (Aug. 1945), Bird Dog Blinkers (Oct. 1945), The Gallows Bear (Feb. 1946), In Memoriam, poem (Feb. 1946), Mississippi Zev Wins National (May 1946), A Dog's Life (June 1946), Lady (Dec. 1946), The Dove (Jan. 1947), Tri-State Duck Survey (March 1947), Remember? (April 1947), Bird Dog of Destiny (May 1947), Duck Shooting's Two Ultra "Musts" (Oct. 1947), They Do Come Back (Feb. 1948), Golden Jubilee Dog (May 1948), So You Want to Be a Wing Shot (Sept. 1948), The Champagne Pointer (March 1949), Sierra Joan Wins National Field Trial (May 1949), The Cricket Field (June 1949), Heads or Tails It's Doves! (Sept. 1949), Brownie Doone Sees It Through (May 1950), Drake's Debut (July 1950), Tight Place (Sept. 1950), Calling All Ducks (Oct. 1950), The High Sign (March 1951), National Field Trial (May 1951), Great Day in the Morning!, second use (Nov. 1955)

Gun Digest
The Dove (1959), Are We Shooting 8-Gauge Guns? (1960)

Harvard Monthly
Uncle Willis, Skimpy, and the Cotton Bale (Feb. 1900)

Hunting Dog
Hunting Dogs Think—and Remember (Feb. 1969)

National Sportsman Magazine
The Palm of Victory (Oct. 1924), Hail and Farewell (Aug. 1934)

Outdoor Life

It Reminded Him (June 1918), In the Southlands
Open Season, poem (Oct. 1920), How!, poem
(Jan. 1921), To the Spirit of the Covered Wagon,
poem (Jan. 1924), Consolation, poem (July 1925),
Duck Scarcity—and Its Remedy (Sept. 1927),
Some Bird Dog Deals (Oct. 1927), De Shootinest
Gent'man (Nov. 1927), A Shootin' Po' Soul (Feb.
1928), To an Ol' Cullud Fren', poem (March
1929), The Coaster (part one, March 1929; part
two, April 1929), Duke (Aug. 1952), A Remembering Fellow (Dec. 1953), Magnum Opus (Sept.
1955), Big Shots (June 1968), Gone Are the
Honkers (June 1969), Feeling Like a Goose (Sept.
1971)

Recreation

First outdoor stories (beginning 1909), De Shootinest Gent'man (Sept. 1916)

Southern Outdoors

The Best All-Round Gun Dog I Ever Saw (part
one, July-Aug. 1955; part two, Sept.-Oct. 1955)

Sporting Goods Buyer

Articles on conservation (circa 1924)

Sports Afield

First and Last Days (Jan. 1943), Januaries Afield
(Jan. 1944), Ghost Trout (April 1945)